Theorising Social Change in Post-Soviet Countries

Balihar Sanghera
Sarah Amsler
Tatiana Yarkova
(eds)

Theorising Social Change in Post-Soviet Countries

Critical Approaches

PETER LANG
Oxford · Bern · Berlin · Bruxelles · Frankfurt am Main · New York · Wien

Bibliographic information published by Die Deutsche Bibliothek
Die Deutsche Bibliothek lists this publication in the Deutsche Nationalbibliografie; detailed bibliographic data is available on the Internet at ‹http://dnb.ddb.de›.

British Library and Library of Congress Cataloguing-in-Publication Data:
A catalogue record for this book is available from *The British Library*, Great Britain, and from *The Library of Congress*, USA

ISBN 978-3-03910-329-4

Hochfeldstrasse 32, Postfach 746, CH-3000 Bern 9, Switzerland
info@peterlang.com, www.peterlang.com, www.peterlang.net

Contents

Culture

Economy

Acknowledgments

This book, perhaps more than many, is a collaborative product. It was initially born out of papers presented at a sociology conference held in Bishkek, Kyrgyzstan in June 2003, organised by Balihar Sanghera, Tatiana Yarkova and Mehrigiul Ablezova. The organisers and the participants shared a common experience of working in what some called an 'intellectual vacuum', an alienation not only from social scientific research disseminated in the 'west', but also from theorising itself. While locally hosted international conferences have been one way of redressing these imbalances, knowledge produced in and about former Soviet societies continues to be marginalised in mainstream social science. This collection of essays is a response to this problem on two fronts. First, it integrates research about former Soviet societies with that written from within them, and second, it highlights new work which aims to critically theorise social change in these societies.

Along the way, we have been inspired by many people working to reform, transform or revolutionise education in the region, particularly within the Central Asian republics where our work has been primarily based. Among them are Gulnara Aitpaeva, William Hansen and Yasmin Lodi. While no longer in their original positions, each has left his or her progressive footprints on the post-Soviet history of education. There are many others whom we also consider to be unsung heroes of the 'transition', individuals who have worked tirelessly together and alone to articulate and construct the sort of education they feel will best contribute to human development. In particular, Mehrigiul Ablezova, Gulzat Botoeva, Gulnara Ibraeva and Madeleine Reeves have been instrumental in sustaining the critical promise of sociology, and the promise of a critical sociology, in Central Asia.

So too we are indebted, and remain committed, to the innumerable lecturers and students who have personally inspired and humbled us in their courage to pursue intellectual work under extremely difficult material and spiritual conditions. The image of students from Ulan-Ude University in Siberian Russia sitting huddled together in a freezing lecture room to discuss ethnicity functions not only as evidence of commitment to learning, but also as an impetus for expanding the opportunities afforded to intellectuals throughout the former Soviet republics.

Finally, we thank the institutions which have made this work possible – the Open Society Institute, Critical Sociology Network, and the former Civic Education Project (now renamed Academic Fellowship Program). Ayman Salem, a good friend, critical colleague and founder of the CSN, deserves special mention. His advice regarding both the intellectual content and logistical preparation of this book has been invaluable.

SARAH AMSLER AND BALIHAR SANGHERA

Introduction
Post-Soviet Social Science: Reaching Beyond Neoliberalism and Neoconservatism

As the historical distance between the collapse of soviet communism and the present expands, everyday practices and lived experiences throughout the former Soviet Union increasingly challenge the theoretical expectations of social scientists, and we are compelled to be more reflexive about how we theorise one of the major social processes in our lifetime. As with any moving object of study, scholarly attempts to identify and explain the nature of post-Soviet society require imagination, speculation and uncertainty as well as rigorous research. Whilst we enjoy moments of clarity, we are also humbled by our fallibility and inability to fully grasp the pace of change in diverse societies that until twenty years ago were largely isolated from external cultural influence. This collection of essays by social scientists writing from and about former Soviet societies critically interrogates the usefulness of existing theories to understand and explain social transformation in post-Soviet space.

Despite, or perhaps because of the daunting intellectual challenges facing scholars of post-Soviet transitions, a plethora of social scientific work on post-Soviet societies has emerged. The book reflects the rise of three main approaches to the sociology of post-Soviet societies, which transect epistemological and political projects: studies guided by or oriented towards neoliberal theory and/or practice, work which may be termed neoconservative in orientation, and which is often a response to the first, and a third type of work that we may consider both critical and reflexive, and which seeks to transcend the limitations of the other approaches.

Post-Soviet Social Science beyond Neoliberalism and Neoconservatism

In neoliberal approaches, western and post-Soviet scholars draw upon classical liberal theories of economic modernisation and progress to analyse post-Soviet societies. Concepts such as liberalism, the market economy and the enlightenment are applied either to demonstrate how post-socialist countries are moving towards a convergence with industrial capitalist ones, or to identify the obstacles to realising this western model, and to define what measures might be required to ensure the 'transition'.[1] The central problematic in this approach is the degree to which post-Soviet societies are successful in imitating and implementing capitalist models of economic and liberal political organisation (such as privatisation schemes and parliamentary democracy), as well as the implementation of reforms in the areas of liberal education and, to some extent, human rights.

However, these travelling ideas are challenged on two fronts. In the former soviet region, individuals, policy-makers and local organisations have also interpreted neoliberal models of development as being neocolonial, or contributing to a new world order of Western imperialist domination. They therefore resist the advance of neoliberalism in social, economic and political practices, or seek ways to adapt it into their local contexts.[2] In the West, too, many social scientists are critical of the neoliberal orthodoxy and have pointed out that it is both inaccurate and inappropriate to extend universal laws to socially specific spaces where history and culture matter.[3]

There have been two broad reactions to this realisation. One is a reactive neoconservative approach to social research which can be irredentist, hostile and reluctant to countenance radical changes.

1 Graham Smith, *The Post-Soviet States: Mapping the Politics of Transition* (London: Arnold, 1999).

2 Caroline Humphrey, *The Unmaking of the Soviet Life: Everyday Economies after Socialism* (Ithaca: Cornell University Press, 2002).

3 William Outhwaite and Larry Ray, *Social Theory and Postcommunism* (Oxford: Blackwell Publishing, 2005).

Instead, social scientists adopt tribal-like positions, defending traditionalism and drawing on history to define the nature of contemporary post-Soviet space. These conservative thinkers are against not social transformations *per se*, but rather against their orientation.[4] Within the western academy, this approach is also bolstered by a postmodern fetishism of difference, in which critical concern about resisting Western hegemony can at times be reified to the extent that questions about moral principles are bracketed or even rejected. Practices such as shamanism in Siberia, bride kidnapping in Kyrgyzstan, nepotism and clan politics in Kazakhstan, and 'strong' leadership in Russia may even sometimes be legitimatised and escape criticism. More positively, postmodern understandings of difference have been increasingly integrated into analyses of post-socialism, which have in turn shifted from positing a singular experience of social transformation to asserting the existence of multiple and diverse post-socialisms.[5]

However, this too has been unacceptable to many social scientists[6] that are immersed in both Western thought and post-socialist experience. Unhappy to accept neoliberal maxims and universal theories of modernisation, and equally unsatisfied to labour under conservative or particularistic ideas, these scholars attempt to craft critical and reflexive approaches to the moving object of inquiry.[7] They seek to integrate broad theoretical ideas with particular human narratives, the universal with the particular, theory with research, and scientific

4 Michael Burawoy and Katherine Verdery, 'Introduction' *in Uncertain Transition: Ethnographies of Change in the Postsocialist World*, ed. by Michael Burawoy and Katherine Verdery (Lanham: Rowman and Littlefield, 1999), pp. 12–14; Katherine Verdery, *What was Socialism, and What Comes Next?* (Princeton: Princeton University Press, 1996)

5 Valerie Bunce, 'Postsocialisms', in *Between Past and Future: the Revolutions of 1989 and their Aftermath*, ed. by Sorin Antohi and Valdimir Tismaneanu (Budapest: Central European University Press, 2000), pp. 122–152.

6 For example, the members of the Critical Sociology Network (CSN), founded in Tbilisi, Georgia in June 2002.

7 For example, Joma Nazpary, *Post-Soviet Chaos: Violence and Dispossession in Kazakhstan* (London: Pluto Press, 2002); Ruth Mandel and Caroline Humphrey (eds.), *Market and Moralities: Ethnographies of Postsocialism* (Oxford: Berg, 2002).

rigour with political and moral normativity. While they are embedded in the social and historical specificities of post-Soviet societies and are cautious of over-extending ideas, their theories shed light on phenomena beyond the specific issues or regions under investigation. Indeed, this dialectical element in their research brings it to bear on the study of post-socialist societies as a whole.

Critical Approaches to Post-Socialist Change

We can identify five characteristics of work within this critical approach, noting that this serves not only as a description of our position, but also our aspiration. Given the nature of their specific enquiries, the chapters in this book may include some, though not all, of these elements in their accounts.

First, *critical post-socialist narratives argue that post-Soviet societies are socially and historically situated.* As several of the authors note, economies are relatively path-dependent: they can neither escape the strictures of the past, nor be fully bound by them. Consequently, ideas may not travel well across temporal boundaries without some modification; abstract mechanisms must be concretised in past and present lived experience. Vanessa Ruget's 'communitarian perspective' on citizenship in Kyrgyzstan, for example, offers a discussion of how theories produced in one society may (and may not) be usefully employed to analyse another. Olga Boiko and Elena Chernyshkova adopt a similar perspective, exploring how far theories of discourse analysis may be used to understand the relationship between the media and social policy in contemporary Russian society.

Critical social scientists also resist both universalism and particularism, and recognise commonalities and differences across post-socialist societies.[8] Post-socialist societies do not lend themselves to the totalising discourses of either modernism or post-modernism, and

8 See William Outhwaite and Larry Ray, *Social Theory and Postcommunism* (Oxford: Blackwell Publishing, 2005).

critical social scientists recognise the dangers of grand narratives on society. To this end both Lukasz Hardt and Maks Kobonbaev critique the 'institutional disequilibrium' which emerged after the transplantation of structural adjustment policies to Poland and Kyrgyzstan, and which they separately argue has stymied organic developmental processes in these countries. While Kobonbaev points to a number of practical reforms that might follow from this analysis, Hardt introduces a new theoretical paradigm for understanding institutional development in post-Soviet space, which combines elements of New Institutional Economics with the sociology of institutional change.

Second, these accounts are culturally and identity sensitive. As several authors argue, identities matter in both intimate and political spheres. We are purposeful agents, mediating structural constraints and opportunities to realise goals, projects and concerns such as political identity, academic standards or personal commitments.[9] Critical post-socialist narratives thus also seek to avoid determinism and voluntarism, and recognise the unpredictability and contingency of the post-socialist project. Balihar Sanghera and Aibek Ilyasov, for example, illustrate the value of this perspective in their chapter on moral sentiments and professions in Kyrgyzstan, which argues that social behaviour is neither neoliberal nor neoconservative, but moral and enacted by reflexive agents.

Third, critical accounts are normatively inflected. The value-free/normative dichotomy breaks down in analyses of issues such as economic poverty, political corruption, symbolic domination, social respect, civil rights and human needs. In rendering human suffering and flourishing, we are simultaneously making empirical observations and normative judgements; theoretical problematics of need, respect and domination have both descriptive and evaluative imperatives.[10] The critical approach recognises that lay and scientific normativity inform practical understandings and explanations of post-Soviet societies. Social research therefore cannot be considered private; it de-

9 Margaret Archer, *Structure, Agency and the Internal Conversation* (Cambridge: Cambridge University Press, 2003).

10 Ruth Groenhout, *Connected Lives: Human Nature and an Ethics of Care* (Lanham: Rowman and Littlefield, 2004).

mands ethical engagement. This concern is particularly prominent in Boris Kapustin's chapter on 'Violence and Post-communism', Sarah Amsler's chapter on post-Soviet academic imperialism, and Sebastian Eckhardt and Andreas Goldthau's critique of the 'post-Washington consensus' on post-Soviet development.

Fourth, critical studies of post-Soviet societies assume that discursive elements of experience reciprocate with non-discursive or material ones. Language embeds social life in three ways:[11] language is part of social action employed in particular ways (such as official documents, reports, speeches, conversations and debates); language represents social action in specific ideological ways (e.g., the neoliberal discourse of economic exchange); and language is part of the performance, projecting particular styles of identities and values (such as an open, friendly and relax style of political action). Although analytically separate, they always operate simultaneously on social action. Several authors in this book – George Welton and Adrian Brisku, and Anna Horolets – contribute to a better understanding of the post-Soviet language by exploring the significance of discourses on 'Europe' in post-Soviet space, revealing together that interpretations of the concept are socio-historically embedded. Several authors also highlight how political and familial relationships are ideologically represented and reflexively experienced. In this vein Ivan Chorvat dismisses western discourse of feminism, arguing that it fails to grasp the history of soviet motherhood and family structures of Slovenian women. In a slightly different variation on this theme, both Zoltán Berényi and Stephan Nikolov explore how neoliberal reforms in Hungary and Bulgaria, respectively, have had deleterious consequences for basic human relationships of trust and community.

Fifth, critical accounts are grounded in both theory and empirical enquiry.[12] Causal relationships generate actual outcomes which can be understood through both qualitative and quantitative social research. For example, Julie Droeber's chapter, based on primary ethnographic

11 Norman Fairclough, *New Labour, New Language?* (London: Routledge, 2000), pp. 144–145.

12 Andrew Sayer, *Method in Social Science: A Realist Approach* (London: Routledge, 1992).

fieldwork with a Dungan community in Kyrgyzstan, offers a rare insight into how economic strategies are embedded in everyday culture, and how this embededness conditions agents' relationships with foreign aid agencies. Her study demonstrates how practitioners can develop appropriate sensibilities for constructing accounts that are both descriptive and evaluative. Critical post-socialist narratives recognise that a grounded understanding of lived experience in the post-Soviet region must accompany its abstract conceptualisation. Donnacha Ó Beacháin uses existing research about the status and movement of ethnic Russians in Kazakhstan to reflect on the 'hidden agendas of Kazakhisation', and provocatively considers the possibility of a 're-colonisation' of Russian-dominated areas by an ethnically Kazakh majority. Given the immense scale of social transformation in post-Soviet societies, as well as its unpredictability and emergent properties, ethnographic fieldwork and grounded investigation has also become increasingly important.

Across the Divide

As a second, but by no means secondary concern, the editors have sought to redress the existing division of labour in post-Soviet social science, which segregates 'western' and 'post-Soviet' scholars into different languages and spheres of communication. The chapters thus offer a broad spectrum of approaches towards social scientific research, authored by scholars both from former Soviet countries and from the west. It is our hope that this diversity of voices and perspectives will contribute to the ongoing debate on globalising intellectual work, give recognition to marginalised scholars as well as renowned ones, and introduce western readers to regional developments in post-Soviet social science.

Outline of the Book

The book is divided into three parts, addressing polity, culture and economy. In each section, authors endeavour to transcend both neoliberalism and neoconservatism. Critical social science is a broad church, and authors vary in their own approach. However, all try to move towards carving out frameworks that will enable them to overcome the weaknesses of extremism in the social analysis of post-Soviet societies and to develop a more rigorous and at the same time more comprehensive and critical understanding of social change.

Bibliography

Archer, Margaret, *Structure, Agency and the Internal Conversation* (Cambridge: Cambridge University Press, 2003).

Bunce, Valerie 'Postsocialisms', in Sorin Antohi and Valdimir Tismaneanu (eds.), *Between Past and Future: the Revolutions of 1989 and their Aftermath* (Budapest: Central European University Press, 2000), pp. 122–152.

Burawoy, Michael and Verdery, Katherine, 'Introduction', in Michael Burawoy and Katherine Verdery (eds.), *Uncertain Transition: Ethnographies of Change in the Postsocialist World* (Lanham: Rowman and Littlefield, 1999), pp. 1–17.

Fairclough, Norman, *New Labour, New Language?* (London: Routledge, 2000).

Groenhout, Ruth, *Connected Lives: Human Nature and an Ethics of Care* (Lanham: Rowman and Littlefield, 2004).

Humphrey, Caroline, *The Unmaking of the Soviet Life: Everyday Economies after Socialism* (Ithaca: Cornell University Press, 2002).

Mandel, Ruth and Humphrey, Caroline (eds.), *Market and Moralities: Ethnographies of Postsocialism* (Oxford: Berg, 2002).

Nazpary, Joma, *Post-Soviet Chaos: Violence and Dispossession in Kazakhstan* (London: Pluto Press, 2002).
Outhwaite, William and Larry Ray, *Social Theory and Post-communism* (Oxford: Blackwell Publishing, 2005).
Sayer, Andrew, *Method in Social Science: A Realist Approach* (London: Routledge, 1992).
Smith, Graham, *The Post-Soviet States: Mapping the Politics of Transition* (London: Arnold, 1999).
Verdery, Katherine, *What was Socialism, and What Comes Next?* (Princeton: Princeton University Press, 1996).

Polity

BORIS KAPUSTIN

Violence and Post-Communism

> [T]he real political task… is to criticize the working of institutions, which appear to be both neutral and independent; to criticize and attack them in such a manner that the political violence which has always exercised itself obscurely through them will be unmasked, so that one can fight against them. (Michel Foucault)[1]

Introduction

A theme of political violence is present in the theoretical discourse on post-communism only as a reference either to the ethnic violence that broke out in some parts of the former communist world after its disintegration, or to the repressive measures taken by certain post-communist regimes that failed to democratise. In both cases, violence is seen as something unrelated to the nature of post-communism, moreover, it is seen as a phenomenon that curbs and distorts the process of societal growth and maturation which is basically perceived as an evolution towards democratic capitalism.

I think there are two basic explanations for this benevolent vision of the relation between violence and post-communism, more precisely, a perception of the absence of any intrinsic relation between them. First, post-communism is understood in the mainstream literature as a *negation of the violence* inherent in communism, literally, as '*a revolt against violence* and oppression at the individual, societal, and nation-

1 Michel Foucault, *Reflexive Waters: The Basic Concerns of Humankind*, ed. by F. Elders (London: Souvenir Press, 1974), p. 171

al levels'.[2] Moreover, this revolt occurred in a nearly perfectly non-violent manner, that is, without any bloodshed worthy of talking about, except for Romania. Second, Western political theory has been devaluing, if not neglecting, a category of 'violence' since the mid-seventies until very recently,[3] although some neo-Marxist and post-structuralist conceptions of violence stand out as remarkable exceptions. Basically, however, it has become reduced to 'physical violence', which has hampered the tracking and pinpointing of more subtle and less manifest, although no less important, forms of violence.

A benevolent rejection of any substantial relation between violence and post-communism however, looks implausible. First, the 'exit from communism' involved too much suffering of too many people to make us presume that some forms of violence over them did take place during this 'exit', and that they were not accidental and therefore cannot be morally and politically written off as 'concomitant circumstances' of an otherwise unequivocally liberating and non-violent process. Second, political theory, at least since Machiavelli, has been familiar with an observation that all 'founding moments' are necessarily violent, albeit in different ways.[4] If the 'exit from commu-

2 Aleksander Smolar, 'History and Memory: The Revolutions of 1989–91', in Larry Diamond and Marc Plattner (eds.), *Democracy after Communism* (Baltimore: The Johns Hopkins University Press, 2002), p. 164 (my emphasis).

3 Some writers even believed that the theories of violence could not be salvaged from 'losing their raison d'être' in the post-bipolar world–so much were they impressed by the global effects of the 'nonviolent' revolutions in East–Central Europe. On this, see John Keane, *Reflections on Violence* (New York: Verso, 1996), p. 9.

4 See Michael Walzer, 'Regicide and Revolution', in Michael Walzer (ed.), *Regicide and Revolution: Speeches on the Trial of Louis XVI* (Cambridge: Cambridge University Press, 1974), p. 5. Relatively recently, Jacques Derrida illuminatingly reexamined this subject and concluded, 'the foundation of all states occurs in a situation that we can thus call revolutionary. It inaugurates a new law, it always does so in violence. Always, which is to say even when there haven't been those spectacular genocides, expulsions and deportations that so often accompany the foundation of states, great or small, old or new, right near us or far away'. Jacques Derrida, 'Force of Law: The Mystical Foundation of

nism' brought about new political regimes, systems of law, structures of economy and, in many cases, new states then it must certainly be viewed as a 'founding moment' or a series of such 'moments', which justifies giving it an appellation of the 'revolutions of 1989–91'. But if so, how can this 'exit' be perfectly or even essentially nonviolent?

In this paper, I seek to discern the forms of violence that were operative in and indispensable for 'exiting from communism' as a series of actual events that occurred in the late 1980s to early 1990s. It is in the 'nature' of the originating violence to make itself 'forgotten' or 'taken away' from the political-legal system established by it, on the one hand, and on the other hand, to reproduce itself in the functioning of such a system and, in particular, to 'jut manifestly and fearsomely into existence' when a smooth working of this system is threatened.[5] Therefore, I intend to disclose the presence of the forms of the originating violence whereby post-communism was begotten in the structures of domination it embraces. This, I believe, is a kind of critique of post-communism that, without dismissing what it has accomplished in terms of the removal of the characteristically communist forms of violence, strives to figure out new objectives of and possibilities for emancipatory struggles that can never arrive at a happy end.

I will proceed in the following way. First, I will overview the existing theories of the 'revolutions of 1989–91', breaking them into four categories in accordance with what they see as the major accomplishments of these events and what they mean in terms of liberty and oppression. Then I will consecutively examine and critique each of these groups of theories with an eye on which elements and aspects of the post-communism-violence nexus they reveal or conceal. My purpose is not to subvert or 'deconstruct' these theories. Rather, it is to attain as thorough an understanding as possible of this nexus.

Authority', in Drucilla Cornell, Michel Rosenfeld and David Carlson (eds.) *Deconstruction and the Possibility of Justice* (London: Routledge, 1992), p. 35.

5 See Walter Benjamin, 'Critique of Violence', in Peter Demetz (ed.), *Reflections: Essays, Aphorisms, Autobiographical Writings* (New York: Schoken Books, 1986), p. 286; Jacques Derrida, 'The Laws of Reflection: Nelson Mandela', in Jacques Derrida and Mustapha Tlili (eds.), *For Nelson Mandela* (New York: Seaver Books, 1986), pp. 18, 22.

My vision of this nexus is not meant to serve as a 'general theory', applicable across the former communist world. It is true that the post-communist nations are growing more and more dissimilar – to the extent that they seem to diverge in terms of their historical trajectories, rather than just in terms of their different locations along the same overall path of transformation towards the democratic-capitalistic 'normalcy'.[6] The starting points of their post-communist evolutions were not identical either. Much of what I write is inspired by my observations of Russia and, however extensively I use materials produced by those who researched post-communism elsewhere, I would be happy if this essay is treated as another study of the 'Russian case'. Yet I hope it can contribute to demystifying what Timothy Garton Ash called 'a great mystery' of the extraordinarily successful transitions from communism.[7] This is not to say that they were unsuccessful. This is just to reiterate that if we avoid asking questions like 'for whom?', 'from whose viewpoint?' and 'at whose expense?' we would never get in our approaches to politics anything better than mysteries.

Four Approaches to the 'Revolutions of 1989–91'

Principally, there are four basic approaches to determining the nature of the 'revolutions of 1989–91'.

1. The first approach qualifies these events as revolutions without any reservations. Moreover, they are seen as the 'late-modern' replicas of the classical revolutions of early modernity. This is meant to explain, among other things, their otherwise puzzling intellectual banality, i.e. their inability to put forth any novel ideas that was so

6 See Valerie Bunce, 'Postsocialisms', in Sorin Antiohi and Vladimir Tismaneanu (eds.), *Between Past and Future: The Revolutions of 1989 and Their Aftermath* (Budapest: Central European University Press, 2000), p. 145.

7 Timothy Ash, 'Conclusions', in Antiohi and Tismaneanu, *Between Past and Future*, p. 399.

uncharacteristic of earlier revolutions of comparable scope and historical significance.[8]

A unique feature of these revolutions is seen, however, in their self-limiting and strictly nonviolent character, which makes them nearly perfect embodiments of morality. Some writers are prepared to go as far as to assert that rational dialogue reminiscent of the Habermasian concept of a 'communicative ethics', rather than any kind of coercion usually associated with a revolutionary *coup de force*, makes up the moral-political 'core' of these revolutions.[9] But even more cautious accounts belonging to this group of theories insist that they 'represented the triumph of civic dignity and political morality over ideological monism, bureaucratic cynicism, and police dictatorship'. No tragic, bloody or morally reprehensible events and phenomena that followed these revolutions can ever compromise their ethical perfection.[10]

2. For the second approach, these revolutions are not remarkable for moral loftiness. They are seen as well-crafted 'revolutions from

8 Jurgen Habermas, 'What Does Socialism Mean Today? The Rectifying Revolution and the Need for the New Thinking on the Left', *New Left Review*, 183 (1990), p. 5; Ralph Dahrendorf, *Reflections on the Revolution in Europe* (London: Chatto and Windus, 1990), pp. 23, 37; Bruce Ackerman, *The Future of Liberal Revolution* (New Haven: Yale University Press, 1992), p. 1. Some writers of this group maintain that the 'revolutions of 1989–91' were not unequivocally liberal. They highlight a more democratic 'republican' component of them and claim that it was no less important than a liberal one. See Jeffrey C. Isaac, 'The Meaning of 1989', in *Democracy in Dark Times* (Ithaca: Cornell University Press, 1998), p. 152 ff. For the contradistinction of the 'republican' and 'liberal' interpretations of the 'revolutions of 1989–91', see Gideon Baker, 'The Taming of the Idea of Civil Society', *Democratization*, 6, no. 3 (1999), pp. 2–11. Whatever the role of the 'republican' component was, it could hardly make these 'revolutions' less intellectually banal since 'republicanism' was no more an 'invention' of theirs than 'human rights' or 'free market'.

9 See how the Czech philosopher Jiri Suk makes such a conclusion as cited in Stefan Auer, 'The Paradoxes of the Revolutions of 1989 in Central Europe', *Critical Horizons*, 5 (2005), p. 377.

10 See Vladimir Tismaneanu, 'Reassessing the Revolutions of 1989', in Diamond and Plattner, *Democracy after Communism*, pp. 115–116 ff.

above'.[11] Regardless of what triggered them, they were made possible and feasible by a gradual conversion of considerable and influential segments of the communist officialdom into 'political entrepreneurs' eager to barter their political capital for an economic one. Their strategies and choices were grounded in a concrete situation shaped by factors such as the economic stagnation of the Eastern bloc, mounting difficulties in meeting the welfare obligations before the population, the advent of global capitalism that offered them new opportunities they could seize in their 'capitalist' capacity, Gorbachev's abandonment of 'Brezhnev's doctrine' in regard to the Soviet satellites, etc.[12] Nothing, however, was preordained by these factors and the 'revolutions of 1989–91' emerged as 'man-made' events wherein 'political entrepreneurs' played a decisive role.

An interesting variation of this theme is Mancur Olson's theory of the destruction of 'bureaucratic competition' that used to be a *modus operandi* of the Soviet system throughout its 'classical stage' by the collusions of increasingly cohesive bureaucratic coteries that managed to *de facto* privatise political and economic resources in accordance with the 'logic of collective action'. This, finally, undermined centralised planning, as well as any kind of efficient centralised control over society, and inaugurated the kind of economically underproductive and dangerous market characteristic of post-communism.[13]

The 'founding moment' of post-communism is largely shaped by overt and covert bargaining between the communist and anti-communist elites and, according to this approach, it does not look an 'absolute rupture' with the past. In fact, continuity is emphasised to the

11 Jadwiga Staniszkis, *Post-Communism: The Emerging Enigma* (Warsaw: Institute of Political Studies, Polish Academy of Sciences, 1999), p. 11.

12 See Kazimierz Z. Poznanski, 'The Morals of Transition: Decline of Public Interest and Runaway Reforms in Eastern Europe', in Antiohi and Tismaneanu, *Between Past and Future*; David Lovell, 'Introduction: Making Sense of the Transition from Communism', in David Lovell (ed.), *The Transition: Evaluating the Postcommunist Experience* (Aldershot: Ashgate, 2002), p. 3 ff; Krishna Kumar, 'The Revolutions of 1989: Socialism, Capitalism, and Democracy', *Theory and Practice*, 21, no. 3 (1992), p. 322 ff.

13 See Mancur Olson, *Power and Prosperity: Outgrowing Communist and Capitalist Dictatorships* (New York: Basic Books, 2000), pp. 138 ff, 174 ff).

extent that some authors characterise their conceptions as nondeterministic 'evolutionary theory of step-wise changes'.[14] However, neither *some* role played by the grassroots 'collective subjects of politics'[15] nor discontinuities that marked the 'exit from communism' are disregarded.[16] This is why these events are still viewed as 'revolutions'.

3. The third approach does not consider the 'revolutions of 1989 to 1991' to be revolutions. Ironically, the authors of this group build on one of the most essential components of the first approach, but assign to it a much greater weight and therefore arrive at different overall conclusions.

Let us recall: according to the first approach, the 'revolutions of 1989–91' were *just* 'rectifying revolutions', to borrow Habermas's term. They were *non-creative*, destined to remove the (criminal) errors committed in the course of the communist 'experiment', thereby *returning* East-Central Europe to the well-trodden path of the liberal and capitalistic 'normalcy', apparently to its *outset* because the institutions, procedures, habits, etc. that make up this 'normalcy' were yet to be produced in this region. Moreover, since the 'revolutions of 1989–91' are believed to be nonviolent through and through, such a production must be *the opposite of revolutionary constructivism* (in Hayek's sense of the term), that is, it must be non-revolutionary, if not anti-revolutionary, by nature. A question arises: is not a 'rectifying revolution' a *contradiction in terms*? Why should we consider a *return*

14 Staniszkis, *Post-Communism: The Emerging Enigma*, p. 13.

15 What this approach denies is that the collapse of communism was an overthrow of the 'ancien regime' by the (nonviolent) uprising of the masses, that it was a victory of 'civil society' over the party/state Leviathan. Even the 'Polish case' singled out by the unique role of Solidarity is described as unfitting for a model of the victory of civil society over the state. See Poznanski, 'The Morals of Transition', p. 224 ff.

16 Jadwiga Staniszkis, for example, specifies 'three patterns of noncontinuity' in the processes of transition: 'implosion' (a sudden or prolonged de-institutionalisation of the regime), change in the content of institutions coupled with their formal preservation, and 'revolution from above' in a narrow sense of the term, that is, actions taken by reconfiguring elites aimed at establishing new foundations of their domination. See Staniszkis, *Post-Communism: The Emerging Enigma*, p. 30 ff.

to the past accomplished through *non-revolutionary methods* a 'revolution'?

The gist of the third approach is handsomely captured by Richard Sakwa: 'the anti-communist revolutions of 1989–91 transcended the logic of modern vanguardist revolutions by espousing specific rather than universal goals, by transcending sectarian agendas with national ones and by rejecting rather than innovating…[T]hese were "anti-revolutions", repudiating the dynamic of revolution and counter-revolution in their entirety. In short, post-communism is post-revolutionism'.[17] Two problems, however, arise regarding Sakwa's 'post-revolutionism'.

First, it is not clear why 'anti-revolution' is believed to transcend the dynamic of counter-revolution rather than *embody* it. From Joseph de Maistre onwards, counter-revolution has been perceived not as 'contrary revolution, but the contrary of revolution',[18] that is, precisely, as 'anti-revolution' rather than the reversal of the revolution in an opposite direction. The German historian Ernst Nolte seemed to be more consistent when he asserted that 1989 appeared to be a fulfillment of the *counter-revolutionary* programme of de Maistre, a negation of the revolutionary logic of the twentieth century as a whole and a substitution of the logic of *restoration* for it.[19] Do we have to invent new terms when we can use the well-elaborated and respectable concept of *counter-revolution*?

Second, how are we to understand Sakwa's 'transcendence' of the revolutionary-counter-revolutionary dynamic of the 'high modernity' of the twentieth century? Does it imply a departure from modernity to post- or pre-modernity, if not to John Stuart Mill's 'stationary state'?

Relapse into pre-modernity (or early modernity) seems to be a more popular option among the commentators on post-communism.

17 Richard Sakwa, *Postcommunism* (Buckingham: Open University Press, 1999), pp. 90–91.

18 Joseph de Maistre, *Considerations on France*, translated by R.A. Lebrun (Cambridge: Cambridge University Press, 1994), p. 105.

19 Ernst Nolte, 'Die unvollstandige Revolution: Die Rehabilitierung des Burgertums und der defensive Nationalismus', *Frankfurter Allgemeine Zeitung*, 24 January, 1991, p. 27.

Gyorgy Konrad, for example, conceives of 1989 as 'an homage, at a remove of two hundred years, to the revolution that first proclaimed the civil rights of the individual'.[20] Here, a relatively modest counter-revolutionary programme of de Maistre's type seems to have been surpassed: the idea to remove two centuries of history belongs to a very different strand of thought, namely, *fundamentalism*, although in the ideological context of the 'global war on terror' this term is normally associated with the 'anti-Western' rather than 'pro-Western' political orientations.

As for post-modernity (understood as modernity's self-deconstruction, rather than its supersedence), Jean Baudrillard convincingly explained that post-revolutionism or post-communism would amount to nothing else but the 'undoing of history'. This would mean the proliferation of remakes of the elements of the original version of modernity. Since the latter consisted exactly in 'doing history' (with all its crimes and humanitarian achievements) the post-communist remakes of it, as the products of 'undoing', would appear to be signs detached from their (original) signifieds, i.e. they would be simulacra. They won't be able to manifest themselves in *actions*, but only 'as a virtual and consensual form of interaction, not as drama, but as a universal psychodrama of liberalism'.[21]

In a nutshell, the post-modern transcendence of the revolutionary-counter-revolutionary dynamic of modernity boils down to such a 'revisionism of history itself' (Baudrillard) that deprives it of any vector and of the political dimension (of 'doing history') as such. This reduction of history to a 'psychodrama' is a counterpart of the pre-modern transcendence of the dynamic of modernity that reveals itself as fundamentalism.

20 Gyorgy Konrad, *The Melancholy of Rebirth: Essays from Post-Communist Central Europe*, 1989–1994 (San Diego: Harcourt Brace, 1995), p. 22. Francois Furet explicitly describes 1989 as an 'extraordinary reversal, unpredictable and unforeseen' that returns us to the dilemmas of democracy as they existed at the end of the eighteenth century. Francois Furet, 'From 1789 to 1917 and 1989: Looking Back at Revolutionary Traditions', *Encounter* (September 1990), p. 5 (emphasis mine).

21 Jean Baudrillard, *The Illusion of the End*, translated by C. Turner (Stanford: Stanford University Press, 1994), p. 30.

4. The fourth approach to the 'revolutions of 1989–91' is espoused by their left-radical critics, primarily Trotskyites and neo-Trotskyites. They also describe these events as counter-revolutions, but for them, contrary to the writers of the third group, counter-revolution means disaster rather than a blessing.

On the one hand, the 'revolutions of 1989–91' are seen as a continuation of the counter-revolution launched by Stalin's overturn of the 'proletarian State' in the late 1920s. Stalin's regime was a combination of public ownership of the means of production with the dictatorship of the bureaucratic caste, whose particular interests were increasingly diverging from those of the working class. This gave rise to ruthless economic exploitation of the proletariat, cynical ideological manipulation and political repressions orchestrated by the bureaucracy. Yet the USSR was recognised as a 'degenerate workers' state' as long as public ownership of the means of production prevailed.

This is what the 'revolutions of 1989–91' changed. Thus, they signaled a break with the 'workers' state', however perverted.[22] Hence, we have a two-sided phenomenon: continuity on the level of the structures of domination that, in conformity with their 'immanent logic of evolution' led to the transformation of the exploitative and oppressive bureaucratic caste into a capitalist class, and discontinuity on the level of the political-economic infrastructure; a conversion of a public ownership into a private one. This transformation was made possible by another defeat of the proletariat in the course of *perestroika* and the first round of the liberal 'reforms' that ensued from it.[23] A new version of *Bonapartism*, however 'democratically' disguised, is the only kind of political regime that matches this condition, according to the fourth approach to the 'revolutions of 1989–91'.

22 This is seen, by Trotsky's followers, as a fulfillment of the prophesy he pronounced in The Revolution Betrayed regarding the restoration of the capitalist order in the USSR if the bureaucratic dictatorship was not timely replaced by the socialist power of the workers. See Vadim Volkov, 'Introduction', in Ted Grant, *From Revolution to Counter-Revolution* (1997), at: http://www.luxadmin.org/~bhentges/misc/articles/en/from_revo_to_counter-revo.html

23 See Grant, 'The Meaning of Perestroika', in *From Revolution to Counter-Revolution.*

Now, let us look at the post-communism-violence nexus through the lenses of the conceptions we have overviewed. Which elements or aspects of this relation do they reveal and conceal?

A Critique of the First Approach

The first approach is focused on those aspects of post-communism in which it appears as a removal of and liberation from violence produced by communism. Violence, in this case, is associated with (although never conceptually defined as) what some writers call 'physical violence' – harm caused by the victimizer to the body and/or property of the victim that shows moral disrespect towards the victim's autonomy.[24] The communist state and its agencies are identified as perpetrators of such violence on the level of politics, so their replacement by the (gradually consolidating) liberal political-legal institutions bound to secure civil and political rights of the individual is viewed as liberation from violence. This is, to be sure, a very important development conducive to the reduction in or containment of the *political physical violence* that acquired terrible proportions under communism, particularly during its Stalinist phase.

A problem, however, is whether political theory can ignore other forms and manifestations of violence. Even if we stick to the notion of *physical* violence, we can wonder if a staggering upsurge of crime in many post-communist nations has made the 'average citizen' more rather than less exposed to violence, in its entirety, than he/she used to be under the late phase of communism.[25] Is this a political problem or

24 See a recent elaboration of this approach to violence by John Keane: John Keane, *Violence and Democracy* (Cambridge: Cambridge University Press, 2004), chapter 2; p. 36.

25 In Russia, a 'coefficient of criminality' (a number of annually perpetrated crimes per 100,000 people) soared from 700 in 1985 to 968 in 1990 to 1756 in 2000. See Vladimir N. Kudryavtsev, *Contemporary Problems of Fighting Crime in Russia*, at: http://www.rusetsky.com/art.htm (in Russian). These statistics, however, can well be reflecting just the tip of the iceberg; according to

something that is just a matter of what Foucault called disciplines of 'normalization'? More importantly, we cannot analytically and politically reduce violence as such to physical violence. Minimally, we must take into account its structural and symbolic forms that, on the one hand, can produce results no less pernicious than physical violence and, on the other hand, usually exist in (one or another type of) symbiosis with each other and with physical violence.[26]

This is not the place to enter into huge debates over structural and symbolic violence and their subcategories (or what some writers believe to be other 'independent' forms of violence).[27] Suffice it to say that I basically accept Pierre Bourdieu's interpretation of symbolic violence.[28] As for structural violence, I agree with a 'standard' Marxist or quasi-Marxist reading of it as a feature of structures of inequality (rather than a product of intentions of individual actors) wherein and whereby one side accumulates advantages denied to the other side.[29]

I think, however, that this formulation should be qualified in an important way to avoid violence being lumped together with such concepts as domination, exploitation, alienation, etc. since they do not necessarily implicate violence – as long as they are perceived by the

data provided by the Russian Attorney General Vladimir Ustinov, the law-enforcing agencies normally register less than one third of the total number of crimes (Crimes in Russia Cannot Be Counted, at: http://www.gazeta.ru/print/2005/03/09oa_150643.shtml (in Russian). Corruption and inefficiency of the Russian law-enforcing agencies that explain the statistical oddities Mr. Ustinov mentioned are part of a larger problem of the 'decay of the State'.

26 This is why Niklas Luhmann concluded that 'there is ... no pure physical coercion' and rejected 'an opposition or a one-dimensional polarity, existing between legitimacy and violence, or between consensus and compulsion'. Niklas Luhmann, *Trust and Power* (Chichester: John Wiley and Sons, 1979), pp. 148, 152.

27 I presented an overview of these debates, a more detailed classification of the forms of violence as well as an expanded discussion of their interdependence, elsewhere. See Boris Kapustin, *Moral Choices in Politics* (Moscow: The Moscow State University Press, 2004), part III (in Russian).

28 See Pierre Bourdieu, *Pascalian Meditations*, translated by R. Nice (Cambridge: Polity Press, 2000), chapter 5.

29 See Terence Ball, 'Two Conceptions of Coercion', *Theory and Society*, 5, no. 1 (1978), pp. 104–108.

underprivileged as 'natural', and their will does not resist them and therefore is not oppressed by the persistence of these structures. This means that a category of violence loses its critical bite and its *differenttia specifica* if it is not structured from the perspective of the victim and does not incorporate the dynamic of his/her will that is capable of 'denaturalizing', mentally and practically, the structures of inequality, thus turning them into structures of violence *par excellence.* At the same time, such a 'denaturalization' reveals for both the victim and victimizer what constitutes truly nonnegotiable props of a given status-quo, whose other definition is a sort of injustice for which there can be no recourse in (existing) law, as opposed to negotiable arrangements remediable under such a law.[30]

This is why it would be inaccurate to say that the magnitude of structural violence in post-communist nations should be determined by the statistics of absolute and relative poverty, unemployment, numbers of waifs, deterioration of health conditions, falling life expectancy at birth (in some countries, including Russia), soaring rates of self-destructive behavior (including homicides), the re-emergence of forgotten diseases that rarely appear in developed countries, etc.[31] These can be viewed as indicators of the levels of exploitation, marginalisation, social destructiveness of the existing orders, *anomie* and so on. They can characterise violence only to the extent that these phenomena are *actually* perceived by the population as unnatural and unjust. This perception is, in fact, quite widespread, so that in Russia, about 50% of those polled in nation-wide representative surveys hold social injustice as the major problem that worries them[32] and 61% do not

30 See Bernard Harrison, 'Violence and the Rule of Law', in Jerome Shaffer (ed.) *Violence* (New York: David McKay, 1971), pp. 159–160.

31 All the relevant figures describing the situation in Russia can be found in a comprehensive and eloquent report presented by the Organization for Economic Co-Operation and Development (OECD) in 2001. See *The Social Crisis in the Russian Federation* (Paris: OECD Publications, 2001).

32 See Vladimir Shlapentokh, *Equality and Justice in Russia and USA* at: http://www.nir.ru/socio/old/scipubl/sj/34–shliap.htm (in Russian).

believe that it is possible to restore justice by legal means secured by the (post-communist) state.[33]

If so, why is Russia so politically tranquil, apart from the occasional acts of terror and assassinations that have origins other than structural violence, that it amazes most perceptive Western observers?[34] Certainly this cannot be explained in terms of some alleged 'national traditions' of endless forbearance and servitude, since Russia erupted more than once in the course of the twentieth century when it believed, rightly or wrongly, that an alternative to the status-quo became feasible. This happened most recently when communist rule disintegrated. But since 1997, we have observed an unstoppable and dramatic decline even in such peaceful measures of resistance as strikes, although they have never been quelled by the post-communist authorities and almost never managed to solve the problems that brought them about.[35]

But presently, are any alternatives to the fundamentally unjust post-communist status-quo perceived as feasible? According to some estimation, from 50 to 57% of those who are dissatisfied with what is going on in Russia believe that it is totally useless to take *any* action to change the situation.[36] An insightful analysis of public opinion surveys regarding attitudes to the market-oriented reforms that were conducted in Russia in the 1990s arrives at the following conclusion that deserves to be quoted at length.

> Evidently there was a genuine social consensus for market reforms at that time, with around seven in ten supporting some kind of change and just 6.4 percent

33 See Levada-Center: *More Than Half of the Russians Are Sure That Justice Cannot Be Restored by Legal Means*, at: http://www.apn-nn.ru/print.php?typ=event&id=561 (in Russian).

34 Steven Fish, 'Postcommunist Subversion: Social Science and Democratization in East Europe and Eurasia', *Slavic Review*, 58, no. 4 (1999), p. 812.

35 See a very illuminating analysis of the dynamic of strikes in the post-communist Russia, supported by a wealth of statistical information provided in Galina Anisimova, 'Wages and Strikers' Activity, from 1990 to 2000', in D.O. Tchurikov (ed.), *Workers in Russia: Historical Experience and the Present Condition* (Moscow: URSS Press, 2004, in Russian).

36 Vadim Damje, 'Social Atomisation and Social Self-Organisation in the Russian Context', in Tchurikov, *Workers in Russia*.

> opposed...It seems that the severe consequences of marketisation – rapid inflation, increasing inequality and poverty, the threat of unemployment – did not lead to rising opposition to marketisation....What can be ruled out immediately is support based on expectations of immediate material gain, notwithstanding extravagant promises of rapid improvement given by the political leadership...Personal material expectations for the immediate future were gloomy. Twice as many people supported transition as expected their family personally to benefit from it....The conclusion must be that *such support is of the 'there is no alternative' variety.*[37]

As Bourdieu explained, 'symbolic violence is the coercion which is set up through the consent that dominated cannot fail to give to the dominator (and therefore the domination) when their understanding of the situation and relation can only use instruments of knowledge that they have in common with the dominator, which, being merely the incorporated form of the structure of the relation of domination, make this relation appear as natural...'.[38] That alternatives are unthinkable by those who suffer most, however strongly their sense of justice is offended by what they are subjected to, is the surest sign of power and even (for the time being) of the invincibility of a given structure of symbolic violence. This means that the fullness of the appropriation by the dominators of the universal, i.e. of what is reasonable, thinkable and lawful, remains uncontested on the part of the dominated or, in other words, that there is practically no struggle for the universal.

Such a fullness of the appropriation of the universal by the dominators is, to be sure, a rare occurrence in history. A specific explanation is due of how and why it happened in the post-communist condition, which is usually associated with institutional flux or instability, fluidity or protracted consolidation of political forces, profound economic rearrangements and so on that seem to be defying the very idea of a solid 'structure of the relation of domination' incorporated by the dominated as a symbolic schemata of the world they share with their dominators. We will try to find this explanation when we look at the second approach to the 'revolutions of 1989–91'. Meanwhile, we have to address an (imaginary) objection to how we

37 Matthew Wyman, *Public Opinion in Postcommunist Russia* (Houndmills: Macmillan, 1997), pp. 176, 183 (my emphasis).

38 Pierre Bourdieu, *Pascalian Meditations*, p. 170

juxtaposed post-communism and violence that can be produced by those who identify these 'revolutions' with a 'revolt against violence and oppression'.

'Even if we concede, for a moment', they would say, 'that structural and symbolic forms of violence exist in the post-communist condition, what do they have to do with the political emancipation we are focusing on, brought about by the substitution of the communist state with liberal-democratic institutions? How does their existence diminish the importance or tarnish the reality of liberty achieved through these political-legal changes?'

The existence of these forms of violence neither diminishes the importance nor tarnishes the reality of the achieved measure of political liberty. Their existence just shows the limits of this measure as well as the causal determination that sets them. Moreover, it shows a functionality of *this* measure of liberty for the reproduction of the existing structures of the two forms of violence I mentioned. Let me explain.

It is well-known that the formation of political democracy in the West, that is, in the first place, a gradual extension of franchise and conversion of legislatures into more representative and publicly accountable institutions, was driven by the redistributive demands of the underprivileged classes and forced concessions of the ruling classes, partly necessitated by their internal rivalries, intended to preserve the essentials of the status-quo through sacrificing what was believed to be less important elements of the structure of domination. In this sense, democratisation as a transformative process of changing political equilibria represented a commitment to the redistribution of wealth and, in fact, served to decrease inequalities and material disparities between classes.[39] It can be said, contrary to what Hannah

39 See Daron Agemoglu and James A. Robinson, 'Why Did the West Extend the Franchise? Democracy, Inequality, and Growth in Historical Perspective', *The Quarterly Journal of Economics* (November 2000), p. 1167 ff. Some other scholars are more reserved about this correlation. 'Although there have been redistributive eras in capitalist democracies since the advent of a universal franchise,' writes Ian Shapiro, 'there is no systematic relationship between democracy and downward redistribution'. Ian Shapiro, 'Why the Poor Don't Soak the Rich: Notes on Democracy and Distribution', in *Democracy and Dis-*

Arendt maintained, that political freedom in the West, as inseparable from democracy, was made possible by the entry of the 'social question' into the realm of politics that hitherto, as 'pure politics' had remained an aristocratic-oligarchic structure of oppression of the many.[40]

The most striking feature of the post-communist democratisation consists, precisely, in its Arendt-esque expulsion of the 'social question'.[41] Furthermore, this democratisation has been coupled with the dismantling of a welfare state, as it existed under communism, with no adequate substitutes for it forthcoming – something that even some articulate proponents of the transition to capitalism and democracy like Janos Kornai deplore as an obstacle to modernisation (as distinguished from marketisation).[42] How could this happen when a universal franchise is a given fact of political life? How could democratic politicians, supposedly accountable to the public, take measures so immensely politically costly and negligent of the short-term negative feedback on the part of the voters?[43]

Politically, the limits of the measure of liberty introduced by the 'revolutions of 1989–91' were set by the very devices that are credited for an allegedly nonviolent 'exit from communism', i.e. round table-type agreements between the communist and anti-communist elites (in many cases anticipated and prepared by the covert dealings between their representatives thoroughly documented, among others, by Kumar.[44] The backbone of these agreements, theoretically reflected by

tribution, Conference Papers, November 12–14, 1999 (New Haven: Yale University, 1999), p. 1

40 See Hannah Arendt, *On Revolution* (New York: The Viking Press, 1965), chapter 2.

41 No wonder some commentators on the 'revolutions of 1989–91' believe that Arendt's thought is 'particularly relevant to a better understanding of 1989'. See Stefan Auer, 'The Paradoxes of the Revolutions of 1989 in Central Europe', p. 362; Jeffrey C. Isaac, 'The Meaning of 1989', p. 163, etc.

42 See Janos Kornai, 'Ten Years after the "Road to a Free Economy"', Annual World Bank Conference on Development Economics (Washington, D.C.: The World Bank, 2000), p. 100.

43 Valerie Bunce, 'Postsocialisms', p. 133.

44 Krishna Kumar, 'The Revolutions of 1989: Socialism, Capitalism, and Democracy', pp. 344–348.

a 'transitological' concept of 'pacted democracy', was exactly the expulsion of the 'social question', as well as of all other *substantial* questions, like those of property relations, ethnic settlements, national boundaries and identities, etc. upon which the life of a given society truly depends. 'Transitological' wisdom aptly calls this a 'limitation of the agenda of policy choice'.[45] Such a 'limitation' relegates the substantial questions to the realm of a quasi-naturalistic rule of the 'invisible hand' (of the market, ethnic strife, national rivalries and what not) that, in fact, always turns out be the hand of the politically powerful. The kind of democracy that emerges from such a 'limitation' is what one can call a 'socially emasculated democracy'[46] whose very irrelevance to the substantial questions of life makes it *functional* for the reproduction and proliferation of the relations of structural and symbolic violence.

To limit an 'agenda of policy choice' by expelling from it the most burning substantial issues is, undeniably, a manifestation of great power. Who possessed it? For an explanation, let us turn to the second approach to the 'revolutions of 1989–91'.

A Critique of the Second Approach

It is quite often assumed that one of the major problems of the post-communist transitions consists in the absence of politically important agencies motivated by 'transformative interests', that is, real interests

45 Guillermo O'Donnell and Philippe C. Schmitter, *Transitions from Authoritarian Rule: Tentative Conclusions about Uncertain Democracies* (Baltimore: The Johns Hopkins University Press, 1986), pp. 41, 69.

46 Russell Hardin, apparently confusing such an 'emasculated democracy' with modern democracy per se, writes: 'in general, democracy works only on the margins of great issues. Indeed, it is inherently a device for regulating marginal political conflicts'. Russell Hardin, *Liberalism, Constitutionalism, and Democracy* (Oxford: Oxford University Press, 1999), p. 22. One is left to wonder why citizens of those countries wherein 'great issues' are really pressing hard should care about such a democracy immaterial for their problems and exigencies.

in substituting capitalism for communism.[47] This implies, in our case, that there must be capitalists (and their allies) to make capitalism accomplishable. Since they are not there in East-Central Europe *before* the transition occurs and, moreover, brings about some structurally tangible results, the construction of capitalism is explained idealistically, by what Max Weber called 'ideal interests', as opposed to 'material interests',[48] ascribed to the most 'advanced' groups of the population and/or by a widespread rejection of socialism that is believed to make people 'automatically' opt for capitalism.[49]

This explanation is flawed and a problem of the absence of agencies with 'transformative interests' should be considered a pseudo-problem for several empirical and theoretical reasons.

a) As evidenced by the documents of the most powerful and democratic anti-communist movements in East-Central Europe, the rejection of 'actually existing socialism' did not automatically lead to the acceptance of capitalism, furthermore, it coincided with the rejection of capitalism normally expressed in the 'ideologies of the third way'.[50] It is an interesting problem how these democratic aspirations

47 See Jon Elster, Claus Offe, and Ulrich Preuss, *Institutional Design in Post-Communist Societies* (Cambridge: Cambridge University Press, 1998), pp. 273–274; Janos Kornai, 'The Affinity between Ownership and Coordination Mechanisms: The Common Experience of Reform in Socialist Countries', in Kasi mierz Poznanski (ed.), *Constructing Capitalism: The Reemergence of Civil Society and Liberal Economy in the Post-Communist World* (Boulder: Westview Press, 1992), p. 107; Edmund Mokrzycki, 'Eastern Europe after Communism', *Telos* (Winter 1991–92), p. 135.

48 Max Weber, *From Max Weber: Essays in Sociology*, ed. by H.H. Gerth and C. Wright Mills (New York: Oxford University Press, 1981), p. 280.

49 Bunce, 'Postsocialisms', p. 132 ff.

50 Suffice it to cite the programme of the Polish Solidarity that emphasised the 'Christian ethics' and the values inherent in the 'workers' and democratic traditions of the labour world' and which envisioned a kind of future society considerably different from what is normally understood by 'capitalistic society'. See 'Programme Adopted by the First National Congress', in Peter Raina (ed.), *Poland 1981: Towards Social Renewal* (London: Allen and Unwin, 1985), pp. 327–330. See also Maurice Glasman, 'The Great Deformation: Polanyi, Poland and the Terrors of Planned Spontaneity', in Christopher Bryant and Edmund Mokrzycki (eds.), *The Great Transformation? Change and Continuity in East–Central Europe* (London: Routledge, 1994). One can also consult the Czech

were frustrated and suppressed shortly after the collapse of communism.

b) Many public opinion surveys conducted in the latest phase of communism show that, although a general attitude to 'socialism' *as a concept* (or ideological sign) was negative, the majority of respondents accepted and even praised certain specific features of it *as an actually existing formation*, like welfare provisions, type of ownership, redistributive role of the state, etc. Moreover, the very critique of socialism was largely couched in its own idioms: it was blamed for its failures to conform to the norms of egalitarianism, public morality, social justice, and so on.[51] In this light, 'the rejection of socialism *en bloc*' looks an ideological fetish of the post-communist discourse of the dominators which must be deconstructed by an inquiry into which elements of the social constellation called 'the actually existing socialism' were really rejected by the democratic aspirations of the dominated and which, in fact, were congruent with them.

c) The 'acceptance of capitalism as such' seems to be another ideological fetish of the same origin. To begin with, as we know, at least since Max Weber, there is no such a thing as 'capitalism as such', other than an ideal type useful for an examination of a huge variety of capitalisms. Furthermore, since an indispensable condition of the emergence of a minimally 'rational capitalism' consists in *restraint* of the impulse of acquisition and gain[52] and since we, in our 'post-metaphysical' world, can hardly rely on personal ethical beliefs to achieve this, restraint becomes a political problem *par excellence*–a problem of who can restrain, and how they can restrain, the acquisitive impulses of those who otherwise can and would satisfy them with impunity. In other words, a concrete form of capitalism, acceptable or not, that would emerge in a given country directly depends on the restraining power of democratic resistance to the capitalistic drive of the

'Charter 77' and Vaclav Havel's description of the 'post-democratic' and 'self-organising' society of the post-communist future. See Vaclav Havel, *The Power of the Powerless*, ed. by John Keane (New York: M.E. Sharpe, 1985), pp. 92–94.

51 Jadwiga Staniszkis, *Post-Communism: The Emerging Enigma*, pp. 49–50, 67.

52 Max Weber, *The Protestant Ethic and the Spirit of Capitalism* (New York: Charles Scribner's Sons, 1958), p. 17.

dominators. This resistance can, if successful, turn contemporary versions of 'imperialist', 'booty', 'fiscal', 'rent-based' and 'speculative' capitalism into a (tolerably) 'rational' version of it.[53]

d) That all important social formations, capitalism and democracy included, do not come into being as the result of the implementation of somebody's designs was a great discovery of the Scottish Enlightenment. This is so not just because human reason, a producer of such designs, can never be an outsider to particular historical contexts whose immanent and specific tensions and possibilities it cannot help reflecting in the most utopian and daring ideas. This is so as well because the best calculated human actions produce unintended results and, after all, they are most important for the course of history since they oppose purposive humans as 'objective reality' that shapes their further designs and actions.[54] For our immediate purposes, this means that capitalists are not needed to produce capitalism and democrats to produce democracy. Both appear as the 'unintended results' of the contestation of forces, each of them 'naturally' craving for domination, whose conflicts make them opt for 'rational capitalism' and procedural democracy as, so to say, second-best choices.[55] The cap-

53 It is possible, as Valerie Bunce does, to establish a correlation between the intensity and scope of mass mobilisation at the closing stage of communism and the 'successfulness' of post-communist transitions. I think, however, contrary to Bunce, that the major importance of such a mass mobilisation lies in pressuring new ruling elites rather than in allowing them to ignore what she calls 'authoritarian interests', that is, conservative opposition to the chosen course of reforms. See Valerie Bunce, 'Rethinking Recent Democratization: Lessons from the Postcommunist Experience', *World Politics* (January 2003), pp. 172–174.

54 These two points are combined and articulated by de Tocqueville in his account of the French Revolution as a 'radical break with the past' that was decisively determined by its unintentional borrowings from the past as well as by its outcomes that inadvertently reproduced some crucial features of the ancien regime. See Alexis deTocqueville, *The Old Regime and the French Revolution*, translated by S. Gilbert (Garden City: Doubleday, 1955), pp. VII–IX. For a general explanation of the historicity of reason, see Hans-Georg Gadamer, *Truth and Method* (New York: Crossroad, 1986), p. 245 ff.

55 For the view on Western democracies as 'byproducts' of the basically undemocratic cravings of competing elites, see Valerie Bunce, 'Comparative Democratization: Big and Bound Generalizations', *Comparative Studies*, 33, no. 6/7 (2000), p. 726. For a broader account of the Western transitions to liberal

italist identity of capitalists and the democratic identity of democrats do not precede the production of capitalism and democracy but are formed in its course.

Humans, however, have to pursue their designs so that the unintended results of their activities can coalesce into 'history'. The greatest merit of the second approach to the 'revolutions of 1989–91' consists in showing the role(s) played by the most powerful agency in the post-communist transitions, i.e. that section of the communist *nomenklatura* that turned itself into a class of 'political capitalists' (Staniszkis), managed to outmaneuver its orthodox opponents, co-opt (offering certain concessions) a substantial part of the leadership of the democratic movement[56] and tie to its interests and power positions a fledgling class of 'independent' entrepreneurs. It is beyond the scope of the present essay to discuss the political-economic mechanisms whereby this was accomplished.[57] Let me jump straight to the conclusion: transition to capitalism, including 'spontaneous privatisation', is 'a process whereby political capital is converted into economic

democracy, see Frederick Watkins, *The Political Tradition of the West: A Study in the Development of Liberalism* (Westport: Greenwood Press, 1982), esp. chapters 5 and 6.

56 'Co-option' manifests itself in the fact, rightly emphasised by Adam Przeworski, that there is no substantial difference in post-communist politics between how those on the right and on the left approach reforms in general and economic reforms in particular. See Adam Przeworski, 'Comments on "Political Determinants of the Success of Economic Transitions"', in D.L. Weiner (ed.), *The Political Economy of Property Rights* (Cambridge: Cambridge University Press, 1997), pp. 82–83. 'Co-option' largely explains another interesting phenomenon of post-communism: a general low degree of elite turnover coursed by the 'revolutions of 1989–91', although certain differences in this respect between post-communist countries should not be overlooked. On this, see Jacek Wasilewski, 'Hungary, Poland, and Russia: The Fate of Nomenklatura Elites', in Mattei Dogan and John Higley (eds.), *Elites, Crises, and the Origins of Regimes* (Lanham: Rowman and Littlefield, 1998), pp. 147–167.

57 One of the most sophisticated accounts of those mechanisms I basically agree with is offered by Jadwiga Staniszkis in her conception of 'political capitalism' and that of the control over 'meta-exchange' (exchange on super-ordinate markets, trading upon the terms of exchange themselves), in particular. See Staniszkis, *Post-Communism: the Emerging Enigma*, p. 54 ff.

capital... It is a way for the old oligarchy – the apparatus and its managerial functionaries – to salvage its power'.[58]

A concept of the 'political capitalist class' may well give us an answer to the question we posed at the end of the previous paragraph – who was powerful enough to limit the agenda of political choice at the roundtable discussions (or their equivalents) that ushered in the post-communist transformations? The power bases of this class, including the mechanisms of private capital formation, had been established long before the 'revolutions of 1989–91' broke out, so that, referring to Russia, Archie Brown was right to conclude: '[t]he most significant and, in many respects, most successful part of Russia's political transformation – namely, the transition from communism – took place while the Soviet Union was still in existence. Far too often, the break-up of the Soviet Union and the transformation of the communist system are conflated'.[59] At the same time, although Brown hardly meant this, this explains that the solidity of the relations of structural and symbolic violence under post-communism, far from having emerged with its advent, had been established and incorporated by the dominated when their countries still had been 'socialist'.

However powerful the 'political capitalist class' was and still is in carrying out its designs, post-communism turned out to be another example of the 'sedimentation of unintended results' in and even *as* history. This is what the second approach to the 'revolutions of 1989–91' underestimates.

This class, in cases like Russia, could have been prepared to go to the extremes implementing the most radical neo-liberal policies. But they appeared to be so dangerous for the very viability and governability of societies it sought to control and exploit that it had to recoil, leaving many post-communist economies in a condition of pastiche, made up of different modes of production and survival strategies.[60]

58 David Stark and Laszlo Bruszt, *Postsocialist Pathways: Transforming Politics and Property in East Central Europe* (Cambridge: Cambridge University Press, 1998), p. 60.

59 Archie Brown, 'From Democratization to "Guided Democracy"', in *Democracy after Communism*, p. 209.

60 For more on this, see Boris Kapustin, 'Modernity's Failure/Post-modernity's Predicament: the Case of Russia', in *Critical Horizons*, 4, no. 1 (2003).

The overall result turned out to be a unique kind of capitalism, if capitalism at all, that has little in common with its Western varieties and that seems to be to nobody's liking, including capitalists themselves.[61]

This class could be purposefully weakening the state and plunging it into a condition bordering on incapacity to maintain law and justice, to say nothing about its ability to fulfill the functions of the safety net. This was perfectly congruent with the policies of 'spontaneous privatisation' through which this class acquired and/or 'legalised' its riches and abandonment of social responsibility for the population. These developments, however, at a certain point started to endanger the ability of the dominators to secure a 'regime of stability' for their privileges and possessions that is inseparable from the 'authoritative state'.[62] As a result, an awkward regime of 'guided democracy' or 'impotent authoritarianism' appeared, incapable of accomplishing the main goals of the state but socially paternalistic, economically *dirigiste* and politically obtrusive. Its apparatuses swelled, their efficiency plummeted.[63]

Especially in Eurasia, this class pursued policies of the fastest insertion of the countries it was ruling into the global economy through boosting financial and natural resource sectors at the expense of all other industries and the high-tech sector in particular. This has

61 See David Lane, 'What Kind of Capitalism for Russia? A Comparative Analysis', *Communist and Post-Communist Studies*, 33, no. 4 (2000), pp. 493, pp. 496–497.

62 Stephen Holmes aptly remarked that the fate of liberalism (identified, in the first place, with the Humean 'stability of possessions') hinges in East-Central Europe on 'a problem of authority – not a problem of how to limit the state'. See Stephen Holmes, 'Can Weak-State Liberalism Survive?', in Zdeněk Suda and Jiří Musil (eds.), *The Meaning of Liberalism: East and West* (Budapest: Central European University Press 2000), p. 210.

63 See Lilia Shevtsova, 'Russia's Hybrid Regime', in Diamond and Plattner, *Democracy after Communism*. 'The Russian Federation is estimated to have 1.7 times more bureaucrats than the Soviet Union had in 1989, despite there being 130 million fewer people to administer'. Financial Times, London, 27 June 1995. Since then, the bureaucratic class has only increased. See Novaya Gazeta, Moscow, 2–4 July 2001, p. 2 (in Russian).

led to such an *involution* of the economy at large[64] that it has become a threat to the integrity of the countries in question through the feudal-like separatism of the richer regions and deep resentment of poorer ones. This is not to mention profound distortions of 'pillars' of the capitalist economy such as labor markets, price mechanisms, money (largely replaced by barter)[65], etc. which, in the Western 'classical' examples, served as integrators of the nations and instruments of their governability. This made the ruling class revise, partly and inconsistently, the one-sided privileging of the financial and natural resources sectors and introduce some rudiments of 'industrial policies' that certainly fall short of reversing the tendencies of the 'third-worldisation' of the post-communist nations of Eurasia.

If we take into account this combination of the designs of the post-communist ruling classes and the 'unintended results' of their implementation, we would be in a better position to understand the counter-revolutionary nature of post-communism emphasised by the third and fourth approaches to the 'revolutions of 1989–91'.

A Critique of the Third and Fourth Approaches

Two elements of the third approach look unacceptable at the outset:

a) That the alleged nonviolence of post-communism stems from its rejection of the idea of large-scale social experiments, so typical of revolutions, and from its commitment to incremental improvements, characteristic of counter-revolutions.[66] Doubtlessly, all the 'big bangs' many post-communist nations went through, all the reforms that

64 See Michael Burawoy, 'Transition without Transformation: Russia's Involutionary Road to Capitalism', in *East European Politics and Society*, 15, no. 2 (2001), pp. 269–290.

65 David Woodruff, *Money Unmade: Barter and the Fate of Russian Capitalism* (Ithaca: Cornell University Press, 1999).

66 See Karol Soltan, '1989 as Rebirth', in Antohi and Tismaneanu, *Between Past and Future*, p. 29 ff.

Leszek Balcerowicz justly described as 'moments of extraordinary politics'[67] *were* social experiments of the most large-scale and daring kind, although they did not mire down in massive physical political violence.

b) That counter-revolutions are healing and reuniting, whereas revolutions are harmful and divisive. History certainly cannot prove this. E. P. Thompson, to give just one relatively 'innocent' example, tellingly described the English counter-revolution from 1792–1832: 'the revolution which did *not* happen in England was fully as devastating, and in some features more divisive, than that which did happen in France'.[68]

Yet, there is an important grain of truth in considering the 'revolutions of 1989–91' to be 'counter-revolutions'. To understand this, we have to expand our interpretation of de Maistre's classical definition of 'counter-revolution' as being 'the contrary of revolution': we must look at the substance of this 'contrary', not just at its form, i.e. methods whereby counter-revolutions are accomplished.

One the central currents of the struggle for emancipation in the nineteenth and twentieth centuries was focused on the problems of the 'non-owning class', its elevation from the condition of the 'rabble' (Hegel) the bourgeois civil society reduced it to, and the overcoming of the dependencies it suffered from as a result of its lack of property. After the Industrial Revolution, it gradually became clear that private property could never be restored as a *universal* foundation of human well-being and moral dignity (i.e. autonomy, as opposed to the heteronomy of dependencies stemming from the absence of property) and that, contrariwise, wage labour became a (nearly) universal human condition.[69] This meant that private property ceased to be a (universal) right and was turned into a (particular) privilege, however disguised

67 Leszek Balcerowicz, *Capitalism, Socialism, Transformation* (Budapest: Central European University Press, 1995), pp. 160–163.

68 Edward P. Thompson, *The Making of the English Working Class* (New York: Vintage Books, 1966), p. 197.

69 However, even some philosophers of T. H. Green's calibre and moral stature entertained illusions to the contrary. See Thomas Hill Green, 'The Principles of Political Obligation', in John Rodman (ed.), *The Political Theory of T.H. Green* (New York: Meredith Publishing, 1964), p. 164.

by a liberal rhetoric that it continued to be a right as a universal 'permission' to own property.[70]

In this situation, the only way to secure the well-being of the underprivileged and restore their moral dignity (in the Lockean sense of 'Property in his own Person') was widely seen in establishing a kind of *collective property* in which they could efficiently participate. This implied a partial or complete de-commodification of the labour force, since it being a (pure) commodity represented an ultimate form of subjugation and deprivation of autonomy, a full meaning of which the early capitalism demonstrated very conclusively.[71] The stakes in this struggle were truly great: it was what Lukács called 'the decisive feature of capitalist society'. 'The most decisive feature of capitalist society...is that economic life ceased to be a means to social life: it placed itself at the center, became an end in itself, the goal of all social activity.... Everything ceases to be valuable for itself and by virtue of its inner (e.g. artistic, ethical) value; a thing has value only as a ware bought and sold on the market'.[72] Should the labour force be treated as just one of these things?

However, the understandings of such collective property, as well as a degree of the desirable de-commodification of the labour force, differed considerably. The so called 'revolutionary Marxism' chose a complete de-commodification and elimination of private property as a way to constitute the proletariat as a 'total subject' through belonging to which every individual proletarian was expected to regain his/her

70 See J. Ronald Pennock, 'Thoughts on the Right to Private Property', In J. Roland Pennock and John Chapman (eds.), *Property*. NOMOS XXII (New York: New York University Press, 1980), p. 173.

71 This meaning was grasped not only by Marx in his famous notion of 'hired slavery', but also by Kant, who in full conformity with the principles of his moral philosophy, banished the categories of hired labour from his 'civil commonwealth' as lacking 'civil independence' (a correlate of 'moral autonomy') and therefore 'civil personality' and thus deserving, in a very Aristotelian fashion, to be parts of the commonwealth but not its members. See Immanuel Kant, *The Metaphysics of Morals*, edited by M. Gregor (Cambridge: Cambridge University Press, 1996), pp. 91–92.

72 Georg Lukács, 'The Old Culture and the New Culture', in Epifanio San Juan, Jr. (ed.), *Marxism and Human Liberation* (New York: A Delta Book, 1973), p. 6.

free subjectivity and social well-being. Social-democracy and its allies opted for what, in the French political tradition, is known as 'social property', allowing for a) social appropriation of certain services and collective goods (health, education, etc.) and b) personal appropriation of protections guaranteed by social legislation on the basis of work. Both make up a kind of social wealth conducive to the social rehabilitation of non-property-owners.[73]

This is not the place to discuss how and why the project of 'revolutionary Marxism' failed. Etienne Balibar may be correct that subjectivation probably cannot be accomplished through the appropriation of property at the level of labour time – this possibility can arise only at the level of leisure time, provided it is emancipated from the dictates of capital.[74] It seems that the greatest demerit of the fourth ('Trotskyite') approach to the 'revolutions of 1989–91', despite its many sharp observations, consists in its inability to grasp the roots of the failure of the 'revolutionary Marxism' which was attributed to Stalin's 'betrayal' and further aggravated by the counter-revolution of the capitalistically degenerate *nomenklatura* in the late twentieth century. Such a streamlined account of the events obliterates their historical specificity and novelty, and this renders them as uninteresting for political theory as their representations qua 'rectifying revolutions' offered by the first approach.

'Social property' is compatible with private property and envisages only a partial de-commodification of the labor force – this to the extent that some portion of the wage eludes the market and a mode of access to certain social goods is constructed that does not fall into the system of market exchange. Nonetheless, 'social property' exerted a profound and far-reaching impact on the 'decisive feature of capitalist society'. All its flaws and shortcomings notwithstanding,[75] 'social

73 Robert Castel, 'Emergence and Transformation of Social Property', *Constellations*, 9, no. 3 (2002), p. 328.

74 Etienne Balibar, ''Possessive Individualism' Reversed: From Locke to Derrida', *Constellations*, 9, no. 3 (2002), pp. 309–310.

75 Foucault offered one of the most succinct and penetrating examinations of the shortcomings and ambiguities of 'social property' viewed from the angle of the problematic of subjectivation. See Michel Foucault, 'Social Security', in *Polit-*

property' enunciated a shift from 'the problematic of private property' as assimilating, according to Locke's formula, 'Lives, Liberties, and Estates'[76] to 'the problematic of collective security' that, to a large extent, uncouples 'Lives and Liberties' from 'Estates'. Such an uncoupling signified a kind of escape from the brutal 'dictates of the need' that the power of private property over non-owners was built on: the latter acquired *some* ability to master the present and plan for the future, according to their personal strategies.[77] This is the farthest the worldly autonomy of non-owners can extend to in the real society of inequalities and domination.

It may well be that, since the 1970s, neo-liberalism has been undermining 'social property' across the Western world and has achieved something approaching a partial revenge of private property on 'social property'.[78] This can be said to be a creeping counter-revolution seeking to undo the emancipatory achievements of modernity related to the social and moral well-being of the non-owners. It is an interesting subject how this counter-revolution was facilitated by the decay and later disintegration of communism in East-Central Europe. Eric Hobsbawm's observation that many of the democratic gains in capitalist democracies can be looked at as a consequence of the ruling elites' fear of the appeal of the alternative presented in East-Central Europe does not seem to be off the mark. 'Whatever Stalin did for the Russians', Hobsbawm concluded, 'he was good for the common people of the West'.[79]

ics, Philosophy, Culture: Interviews and Other Writings, 1977–1984, edited by L.D. Kritzman (New York: Routledge, 1988).

76 John Locke, *Two Treatises of Government*, edited by P. Lasslett (New York: A Mentor Book, 1965), p. 395.

77 See Castel, 'Emergence and Transformation of Social Property', pp. 325–326.

78 See Robert Castel, op. cit., pp. 328–31. Thus, referring to the US experience, Ian Shapiro concludes that 'the past thirty years have indeed been a period of regressive redistribution in the US, out of step with the distributive politics of the hundred years before that'. Shapiro, 'Why the Poor Don't Soak the Rich', p. 33.

79 Eric Hobsbawm, 'Good-Bye to All That', *Marxism Today* (October 1990), p. 21.

At the moment, however, we are more immediately concerned with the reverse effect of the Western counter-revolution on what happened in East-Central Europe. In this region, a creeping Western counter-revolution was transformed into a full-blown and unbridled one. Private property's triumph over 'social property' and the recommodification of the labour force, coupled with the dismissal of the unfit to serve as commodities, turned out to be complete and remorseless. In fact, this amounted to what one commentator aptly called, paraphrasing the title of E. P. Thompson's epic, 'the unmaking of the East-Central European working class'.[80] Peasantry, as many anthropological studies demonstrate, hardly fared any better.[81] This involution in terms of 'human' and 'social capital', destruction of institutions that raised humans beyond commodities, and subversion of the degree of autonomy of the non-owners won in the course of century-long struggles make up the real counter-revolutionary aspect of the 'revolutions of 1989–91'.

Conclusion

Without recapitulating what has already been said, I would express in several sentences what the link between post-communism and violence basically consists in.

In one of his books, Claus Offe wrote that 'the core substance of democratic politics… is the question to what extent market outcomes must be accepted (in the name of efficiency) or corrected (in the name

80 David A. Kideckel, 'The Unmaking of the East-European Working Class', in Chris Hann (ed.), *Postsocialism: Ideas, Ideologies, and Practices in Eurasia* (Florence: Routledge, 2002).

81 See Chris Hann, 'Land Tenure and Citizenship in Tazlar', in Ray Abrahams (ed.), *After Socialism: Land Reform and Social Change in Eastern Europe* (Oxford: Berghahn, 1996); Myriam Hiron, 'Local Resistance to Privatization in Rural Russia', *Cambridge Anthropology*, 18, no. 2 (1995); Deema Kaneff, 'Responses to a 'Democratic' Land Reform in a Bulgarian Village', in Abrahams, *After Socialism: Land Reform and Social Change in Eastern Europe*.

of equity and justice)'.[82] A somewhat more radical version of this question would enquire, 'when and why is the market out of place? What harm, or rather harms, does market exchange do and to which goods and services and spheres of life is it therefore inappropriate?'[83]

The violence of post-communism manifests itself, in the first place, in an impossibility of posing these questions, democratically and in a politically significant way. This means that 'the core substance of democracy' has been removed from it and it has been transformed into a mere source of political legitimation of the existing order.[84] The tendencies of the like transformation are visible in the West as well (better known as 'democracy deficit'), but this is of little comfort for the population of East-Central Europe. Workable democracy is more urgently needed in the East since its counter-revolutionary regress has been much more radical and harmful. In its turn, the failure to satisfy this need can be explained only by those relations of structural and symbolic violence that post-communism inherited from socialism, refined or created anew.

It is yet to be seen how a new round of struggles for democracy in East-Central Europe and Eurasia, one grounded in the liberating effects of the 'exit from communism' and, at the same time, resisting its counter-revolutionary aspects, can be launched.

82 Claus Offe, *Modernity and the State: East, West* (Cambridge: The MIT Press, 1996), p. X.

83 Steven Lukes, 'Invasions of the Market', in Ronald Dworkin (ed.), *From Liberal Values to Democratic Transition* (Budapest: Central European University Press, 2004), p. 57.

84 This is why Joseph Schumpeter called democracy, under capitalism and socialism, 'a sham', albeit for the former this was true to a lesser degree than for the latter. See Joseph Schumpeter, *Capitalism, Socialism, and Democracy* (New York: HarperPerennial, 1975), p. 302.

Bibliography

Ackerman, Bruce, *The Future of Liberal Revolution* (New Haven: Yale University Press, 1992).

Agemoglu, Daron and Robinson, James, 'Why Did the West Extend the Franchise? Democracy, Inequality, and Growth in Historical Perspective', *The Quarterly Journal of Economics*, 115, no. 4 (2000), pp. 1167–1199

Anisimova, Galina, 2004, 'Wages and Strikers' Activity, from 1990 to 2000', in D.O. Tchurikov (ed.) *Workers in Russia: Historical Experience and the Present Condition* (Moscow: URSS Press, 2004, in Russian).

Arendt, Hannah, *On Revolution* (New York: The Viking Press, 1965).

Ash, Timothy, 'Conclusions', in Sorin Antiohi and Vladimir Tismaneanu (eds.), *Between Past and Future: The Revolutions of 1989 and Their Aftermath* (Budapest: Central European University Press, 2000).

Auer, Stefan, 'The Paradoxes of the Revolutions of 1989 in Central Europe', *Critical Horizons*, 5 (2004), pp. 361–390.

Baker, Gideon, 'The Taming of the Idea of Civil Society', *Democratization*, 6, no. 3 (1999), pp. 1–29.

Balcerowicz, Leszek, *Capitalism, Socialism, Transformation* (Budapest: Central European University Press, 1995).

Balibar, Etienne, ''Possessive Individualism' Reversed: From Locke to Derrida', in *Constellations*, 9, no. 3 (2002), pp. 299–317.

Ball, Terence, 'Two Conceptions of Coercion', *Theory and Society*, 5, no. 1 (1978), pp. 97–112.

Baudrillard, Jean. 1994, *The Illusion of the End*, translated by C. Turner (Stanford, CA: Stanford University Press, 1994).

Benjamin, Walter, 'Critique of Violence', in *Reflections: Essays, Aphorisms, Autobiographical Writings*, ed. Peter Demetz (New York: Schocken Books, 1986).

Bourdieu, Pierre, *Pascalian Meditations*, translated by R. Nice (Cambridge: Polity Press, 2000).

Brown, Archie, 'From Democratization to "Guided Democracy"', in Larry Diamond and Marc Plattner (eds.), *Democracy after Communism* (Baltimore: The Johns Hopkins University Press, 2002).

Bunce, Valerie, 'Postsocialisms', in Sorin Antiohi and Vladimir Tismaneanu (eds.), *Between Past and Future: The Revolutions of 1989 and Their Aftermath* (Budapest: Central European University Press, 2000).

—— 'Comparative Democratization: Big and Bound Generalization', in *Comparative Political Studies*, 33, no. 6/7 (2000), pp. 703–734.

—— 'Rethinking Recent Democratization: Lessons from the Postcommunist Experience', *World Politics*, 55 (January 2003), pp. 167–192.

Burawoy, Michael, 'Transition without Transformation: Russia's Involutionary Road to Capitalism', *East European Politics and Society*, 15, no. 2 (2001), pp. 269–290.

Castel, Robert, 'Emergence and Transformation of Social Property', *Constellations*, 9, no. 3 (2002), pp. 318–334.

Crimes in Russia Cannot Be Counted, at: http://www.gazeta.ru/print/2005/03/09oa_150643.shtml (2005) (in Russian).

Dahrendorf, Ralph, *Reflections on the Revolution in Europe* (London: Chatto and Windus, 1990).

Damje, Vadim, 'Social Atomization and Social Self-Organization in the Russian Context', in D.O. Tchurikov (ed.), *Workers in Russia: Historical Experience and the Present Condition* (Moscow: URSS Press, 2004, in Russian).

Derrida, Jacques, 'The Laws of Reflection: Nelson Mandela, in Admiration', in Jacques Derrida and Mustapha Tlili (eds.), *For Nelson Mandela* (New York: Seaver Books, 1986), pp. 18, 22

—— 'Force of Law: 'The Mystical Foundation of Authority', in Drucilla Cornell, Michel Rosenfeld and David Carlson (eds.) *Deconstruction and the Possibility of Justice* (London: Routledge, 1992)

Elster, Jon, Offe, Claus, and Preuss, Ulrich., *Institutional Design in Post-Communist Societies* (Cambridge: Cambridge University Press, 1998).

Fish, Steven, 'Postcommunist Subversion: Social Science and Democratization in East Europe and Eurasia', *Slavic Review*, 58, no. 4 (1999), pp. 794–823.

Foucault, Michel, 'Social Security', in *Politics, Philosophy, Culture: Interviews and Other Writings, 1977–1984*, edited by L.D. Kritzman (New York: Routledge, 1988).

Furet, Francois, 'From 1789 to 1917 and 1989: Looking Back at Revolutionary Traditions', *Encounter* (September 1990), pp. 3–7.

Gadamer, Hans-Georg, *Truth and Method*. (New York: Crossroad, 1986).

Glasman, Maurice, 'The Great Deformation: Polanyi, Poland and the Terrors of Planned Spontaneity', in Christopher Bryant and Edmund Mokrzycki (eds.), *The Great Transformation? Change and Continuity in East-Central Europe* (London: Routledge, 1994).

Grant, Ted, *From Revolution to Counter-Revolution*, at: http://www.luxadmin.org/~bhentges/misc/articles/en/from_revo_to_counter-revo.html (1997).

Green, Thomas Hill, 'The Principles of Political Obligation', in John Rodman (ed.), *The Political Theory of T.H. Green* (New York Meredith Publishing, 1964).

Habermas, Jurgen, 'What Does Socialism Mean Today? The Rectifying Revolution and the Need for the New Thinking on the Left', *New Left Review*, 183 (1990), pp. 3–21.

Hann, Chris, 'Land Tenure and Citizenship in Tazlar', in Ray Abrahams *After Socialism: Land Reform and Social Change in Eastern Europe* (Oxford: Berghahn, 1996).

Hardin, Russell, *Liberalism, Constitutionalism, and Democracy* (Oxford: Oxford University Press, 1999).

Harrison, Bernard, 'Violence and the Rule of Law', in Jerome Shaffer (ed), *Violence* (New York: David McKay Co, 1971).

Havel, Vaclav, *et al.*, *The Power of the Powerless*, edited by J. Keane. (New York: M.E. Sharpe, 1985).

Hivon, Myriam, 'Local Resistance to Privatization in Rural Russia', in *Cambridge Anthropology*, 18, no. 2 (1995), pp 13–22.

Hobsbawm, Eric, 'Good-Bye to All That', *Marxism Today* (October, 1990).

Holmes, Stephen, 'Can Weak-State Liberalism Survive?' in Zdeněk Suda and Jiří Musil (eds.), *The Meaning of Liberalism: East and West* (Budapest: Central European University Press, 2000).

Isaac, Jeffrey C., 'The Meaning of 1989', in *Democracy in Dark Times* (Ithaca: Cornell University Press, 1998).

Kaneff, Deema, 'Responses to a 'Democratic' Land Reform in a Bulgarian Village', in Ray Abrahams (ed.), *After Socialism: Land Reform and Social Change in Eastern Europe* (Oxford: Oxford University Press, 1996).

Kant, Immanuel, *The Metaphysics of Morals*, edited by M. Gregor (Cambridge: Cambridge University Press, 1996).

Kapustin, Boris, 'Modernity's Failure/Post-modernity's Predicament: the Case of Russia', *Critical Horizons*, 4, no. 1 (2003), pp. 99–145.

—— *Moral Choices in Politics* (Moscow: The Moscow State University Press, 2004, in Russian).

Keane, John, *Reflections on Violence* (London: Verso, 1996).

—— *Violence and Democracy* (Cambridge: Cambridge University Press, 2004).

Kideckel, David A., 'The Unmaking of the East-European Working Class', in Chris Hann (ed.), *Postsocialism: Ideas, Ideologies, and Practices in Eurasia* (Florence: Routledge, 2002).

Konrad, Gyorgy, *The Melancholy of Rebirth: Essays from Post-Communist Central Europe, 1989–1994* (San Diego: Harcourt Brace, 1995).

Kornai, Janos, 'The Affinity between Ownership and Coordination Mechanisms: The Common Experience of Reform in Socialist Countries', in Kasimierz Poznanski (ed.), *Constructing Capitalism: The Reemergence of Civil Society and Liberal Economy in the Post-Communist World* (Boulder: Westview Press, 1992).

—— 'Ten Years after the "Road to a Free Economy"', *Annual World Bank Conference on Development Economics* (Washington, D.C.: The World Bank, 2000).

Kudryavtsev, Vladimir N., *Contemporary Problems of Fighting Crime in Russia*, at: http://www.rusetsky.com/art.htm, in Russian.

Kumar, Krishan, 'The Revolutions of 1989: Socialism, Capitalism, and Democracy', *Theory and Society*, 21, no. 3 (1992), pp. 309–356.

Lane, David, 'What Kind of Capitalism for Russia? A Comparative Analysis', *Communist and Post-Communist Studies*, 33, no. 4 (2000), pp. 485–504.

Levada-Center: More Than Half of the Russians Are Sure That Justice Cannot Be Restored by Legal Means, at http://www.apn-nn.ru/print.php?typ=event&id=561 (in Russian).

Locke, John, *Two Treatises of Government*, edited by P. Laslett (New York: A Mentor Book, 1965).

Lovell, David, 'Introduction: Making Sense of the Transition from Communism', in David Lovell (ed.), *The Transition: Evaluating the Postcommunist Experience* (Aldershot: Ashgate, 2002).

Luhmann, Niklas, *Trust and Power* (Chichester: John Wiley and Sons, 1979).

Lukács, Georg, 'The Old Culture and the New Culture', in Epifanio San Juan, Jr. (ed.), *Marxism and Human Liberation* (New York: Delta Book, 1973).

Lukes, Steven, 'Invasions of the Market', in Ronald Dworkin (ed.), *From Liberal Values to Democratic Transition* (Budapest – NY: Central European University Press, 2004).

Maistre, Joseph de, *Considerations on France*, translated by R.A. Lebrun (Cambridge: Cambridge University Press, 1994).

Mokrzycki, Edmund, 'Eastern Europe after Communism', *Telos* (Winter 1991–92), pp 129–136.

Nolte, Ernst, 'Die unvollstandige Revolution: Die Rehabilitierung des Burgertums und der defensive Nationalismus', in *Frankfurter Allgemeine Zeitung* (24 January 1991).

O'Donnell, Guillermo and Schmitter, Philippe, *Transitions from Authoritarian Rule: Tentative Conclusions about Uncertain Democracies* (Baltimore: The Johns Hopkins University Press, 1986).

Offe, Claus, *Modernity and the State: East, West* (Cambridge, MA: MIT Press, 1996).

Olson, Mancur, *Power and Prosperity: Outgrowing Communist and Capitalist Dictatorships* (New York: Basic Books, 2000).

Pennock, J. Ronald, 'Thoughts on the Right to Private Property', in *Property. NOMOS XXII*, ed. J. Ronald. Pennock and John Chapman (New York: New York University Press, 1980).

Poznanski, Kazimierz, 'The Morals of Transition: Decline of Public Interest and Runaway Reforms in Eastern Europe', in Sorin Antiohi and Vladimir Tismaneanu (eds.), *Between Past and Future: TheRevolutions of 1989 and Their Aftermath* (Budapest: Central European University Press, 2000).

'Programme Adopted by the First National Congress', in Peter Raina (ed.), *Poland 1981: Towards Social Renewal* (London: Allen and Unwin, 1985).

Przeworski, Adam, 'Comments on "Political Determinants of the Success of Economic Transitions"', in D.L. Weiner (ed.), *The Political Economy of Property Rights* (Cambridge: Cambridge University Press, 1997).

Sakwa, Richard, *Postcommunism* (Buckingham: Open University Press, 1999).

Schumpeter, Joseph, *Capitalism, Socialism, and Democracy*. (New York: HarperPerennial, 1975).

Shapiro, Ian, 'Why the Poor Don't Soak the Rich: Notes on Democracy and Distribution', in *Democracy and Distribution Conference Papers. 12–14 November 1999* (New Haven: Yale University, 1999).

Shevtsova, Lilia, 'Russia's Hybrid Regime', in Larry Diamond and Marc Plattner (eds.), *Democracy after Communism* (Baltimore: The Johns Hopkins University Press, 2002).

Shlapentokh, Vladimir, *Equality and Justice in Russia and USA*, at http://www.nir.ru/socio/old/scipubl/sj/34–shliap.htm (in Russian).

Smolar, Aleksander, 'History and Memory: The Revolutions of 1989–91', in Larry Diamond and Marc Plattner (eds.), *Democracy after Communism* (Baltimore: The Johns Hopkins University Press, 2002).

Soltan, Karol, '1989 as Rebirth' in Sorin Antiohi and Vladimir Tismaneanu (eds.), *Between Past and Future: The Revolutions of 1989 and Their Aftermath* (Budapest: Central European University Press, 2000).

Staniszkis, Jadwiga, *Post-Communism: The Emerging Enigma* (Warsaw: Institute of Political Studies, Polish Academy of Sciences, 1999).

Stark, David and Bruszt, Laszlo, *Postsocialist Pathways: Transforming Politics and Property in East Central Europe* (Cambridge: Cambridge University Press, 1998).

The Social Crisis in the Russian Federation (Paris: OECD Publications, 2001).

Thompson, Edward P., *The Making of the English Working Class* (New York: Vintage Books, 1966).

Tismaneanu, Vladimir, 'Reassessing the Revolutions of 1989', in Larry Diamond and Marc Plattner (eds.), *Democracy after Communism* (Baltimore: The Johns Hopkins University Press, 2002).

Tocqueville, Alexis de, *The Old Regime and the French Revolution*, translated by S. Gilbert (Garden City: Doubleday, 1955).

Volkov, Vadim, 'Introduction', in Grant, Ted, *From Revolution to Counter-Revolution*, at: http://www.luxadmin.org/~bhentges/misc/articles/en/from_revo_to_counter-revo.html (1997).

Walzer, Michael, 'Regicide and Revolution', in Michael Walzer (ed.) *Regicide and Revolution: Speeches on the Trial of Louis XVI* (Cambridge: Cambridge University Press, 1974).

Wasilewski, Jacek, 'Hungary, Poland, and Russia: The Fate of *Nomenklatura* Elites', in Mattei Dogan and John Higley (eds.), *Elites, Crises, and the Origins of Regimes* (Lanham: Rowman and Littlefield, 1998).

Watkins, Frederick, *The Political Tradition of the West: A Study in the Development of Liberalism* (Westport: Greenwood Press, 1982).

Weber, Max, *The Protestant Ethic and the Spirit of Capitalism* (New York: Charles Scribner's Sons, 1958).

—— *From Max Weber: Essays in Sociology*, edited by H.H. Gerth and C. Wright Mills (New York: Oxford University Press, 1981).

Woodruff, David, *Money Unmade: Barter and the Fate of Russian Capitalism* (Ithaca: Cornell University Press, 1999).

Wyman, Matthew, *Public Opinion in Postcommunist Russia* (Houndmills: Macmillan, 1997).

VANESSA RUGET

Social Rights and Citizenship in Kyrgyzstan: A Communitarian Perspective

Social rights, which T. H. Marshall[1] defines as encompassing a 'wide range from right to modicum of economic welfare and security to right to share full in social heritage and to live the life of a civilized being according to the standards prevailing in the society,'[2] have particular significance in Kyrgyzstan. The country has undergone a transition from a communist system and its planned economy, which provided (in theory) equal resources to its citizens, to a free-market economy, which has not yet produced enough wealth to compensate for increased poverty. Under the Soviet Union, Central Asian societies depended totally on the state and expected it to provide what they needed.[3] In contemporary Kyrgyzstan, governmental social spending has been reduced and many social services have been privatised. As a result of this and of the economic difficulties, and despite the support of the international community and some ambitious poverty reduction plans, the poverty level is very high (in 2003 it was evaluated at 41%). In March 2005, poverty and corruption spurred a rather unexpected and spectacular popular uprising that deposed President Akayev,[4]

1 Thomas H. Marshall, *Class, Citizenship and Social Development* (New York: Anchor Books Edition, 1965).

2 For Marshall, rights of the citizens can be classified as threefold: civil (e.g., freedom of speech, thought and faith, and private property), political (e.g., right to vote, to be elected) and social rights.

3 Pauline Jones Luong, 'Central Asia's Contribution to Theories of the State', in Pauline Jones Luong (ed.), *The Transformation of Central Asia, States and Societies from Soviet Rule to Independence* (New York: Cornell University Press, 2004).

4 On March 24 2005, protesting the partiality of the February 27 and March 13 parliamentary elections (which were riddled with violations of the electoral code) and following several weeks of unrest in the south of the country, protests

proving how dramatic the situation had become for many Kyrgyzstani citizens.

Following Beiner,[5] it is possible to distinguish between three theoretical perspectives on the question of membership and inclusion: liberalism (the individual transcends the group), communitarianism (emphasizing the cultural, ethnic ties of individuals) and republicanism (emphasizing civic bonds).[6] In the case of Kyrgyzstan, no approach captures in a satisfactory fashion the complexity resulting from a mix of traditions and practices (the traditional society, the legacies of the communist period, and the political and social context since independence). Republicanism does not constitute a relevant framework for analysing Kyrgyzstan given the transitional nature of the society and the low levels of political trust and efficacy under Akayev.[7] Liberalism offers more perspective, mostly through Marshall

in Bishkek led to the departure of the president and the installation of a temporary government. On July 10, a former political opponent from the south, K. Bakiev, was elected president with 89% of the vote after having served as interim president. It is worth noting the important differences between the Kyrgyz event and the Georgian 'rose' and Ukrainian 'orange' revolutions. In Kyrgyzstan, the mobilisation was much shorter and yet less peaceful than in these two countries, with looting and destruction of public and private assets happening in the days immediately after the departure of the president. The opposition was divided during the Kyrgyz uprising and only in the following weeks did a consensus emerge around Bakiev. The results of the contested election were not cancelled, as they had been in Georgia and Ukraine. Finally, the Kyrgyz popular movement did not have an anti-Russian component and, if Western funded NGO's and media played a role, it remained quite limited compared to that of the two other post-soviet revolutions.

5 Ronald Beiner, *Theorizing Citizenship* (Albany: State University of New York, 1995).

6 This last perspective is particularly associated with the work of German philosopher Jürgen Habermas and his notion of a public sphere.

7 Citizens of the former Soviet Union who were used to paternalistic states, constrained political participation (Holmes 1997) and who had no understanding of the rule of law (Carley 1995, Gyarfasova in Liebich and Warner 1995) tend to have low level of political efficacy. According to Roger Kangas (1995), the democratic transition in the Central Asian republics is even more challenging than in other parts of the former Soviet Union largely because Central Asian political culture is characterised by values and attitudes less conducive to pluralism.

(described by Faulks as a 'social-liberal' thinker)[8] and his emphasis on social rights. Marshall argued that citizenship rights, which provide 'the right to live the life of a socialized human being,' balance the inequalities brought by market forces.[9] He therefore stressed the significance of such rights in a transitional and fragile economy. But this approach remains limited. Most aspects of post-independence Kyrgyzstan do not exemplify a liberal society, in either social, political or economic spheres (despite the reforms engaged in the early 1990s by the Akayev administration).[10]

On the other hand, I argue that although communitarianism has been developed to address Western societies, and whilst it has lost some of its initial appeal, it offers key concepts and hypotheses to grasp the relationship between social rights and feeling of belonging in Kyrgyzstan.[11] The purpose of the article is therefore to highlight some of the basic propositions of communitarianism regarding social citizenship and to discuss them in light of the 'Kyrgyz situation.' I specifically examine three key communitarian precepts: the embedded self, communal loyalty and responsiveness, and the politics of the common good. I argue that these contribute to formulating hypotheses about types of communal solidarities existing in Kyrgyzstan for the last fifteen years, and about citizens' social expectations towards the regime. Although fascinating, purely ethnic, cultural, linguistic, and religious aspects of citizenship will not be considered in this article.)

This research was conducted during the two years that preceded the March 2005 uprising. Politically, the country belonged to the 'gray area' category that Carothers[12] calls 'dominant-power poltics,' i.e. a system characterised by limited but still real political space and the

8 Keith Faulks, *Citizenship* (London: Routledge, 2000), p. 62.

9 Marshall, p. 92.

10 For more details, see for example, Askat Dukenbaev and William Hansen, *Understanding Politics in Kyrgyzstan*, American University in Central Asia, DEMSTAR – Bishkek, 2003.

11 Interestingly, according to Kymlicka (2002, p. 228), citizenship is a concept reconciling liberalism and communitarianism since its components are both membership, and rights and responsibilities.

12 Thomas Carothers, 'The End of the Transition Paradigm', *Journal of Democracy*, 8, no. 4 (October 1997).

domination of one political grouping (movement, party, extended family or a single leader). The regime has been defined as mild authoritarianism or as a 'quasi-liberal system,'[13] an intermediate category that makes forming hypotheses difficult. Culturally and socially, Kyrgyzstan exhibits a complex mix of ethnic, linguistic cultural and regional diversities, which Russian and Soviet influences did not completely erase.

The hypothesis developed in this article is unique. Communitarian thinkers have primarily written about Western liberal democracies, with occasional references to other societies (such as India with Walzer or Singapore with Bell). For instance, they distinguish between liberal and non-liberal societies, where communities are too 'thick' and oppress individuals. It is therefore partly artificial to apply their concepts and hypotheses to other contexts, especially a complex one like Central Asian societies.

Lastly, communitarianism is not a unified, or necessarily coherent, body of thought. As argued by Miller,[14] it exists in a left-oriented version (then close to socialism), a right-oriented one (its extreme version is to be found in benevolent authoritarian regimes) and even in a liberal version. In addition, communitarianism is both a philosophical approach (what Miller calls a 'philosophical anthropology') and a political agenda (for example with the Communitarian Network). Community, its central concept, can take various forms: the family, the neighbourhood, a cultural/religious group, or the whole nation. Consequently, at times communitarianism means the pre-eminence of the larger unit to the detriment of the smaller communities, but at other times, for example in French intellectual discourse, it refers to smaller groups and indicates fragmentation. In the first section of the article, I look at small-scale communities in Kyrgyzstan, especially families, clans, and neighborhoods, while in the second part, I study the nature of the social pact between the government and citizens; community here refers to the nation itself. I do not undertake

13 John Anderson, *Kyrgyzstan, Central Asia: Island of Democracy?* (Amsterdam: Overseas Publishers Association, 1999).

14 David Miller, *Citizenship and National Identity* (Cambridge: Polity Press, 2000).

an exhaustive literature review of communitarianism but discuss its most famous assertions as they are articulated by renowned philosophers and socials scientists such as Etzioni, Sandel, and Walzer.

A final foreword concerns some aspects of the Kyrgyz society which would qualify as 'communitarian' but are mostly omitted in this article because they do not pertain to the social components of citizenship. This is particularly the case with ethnicity, undoubtedly a strong form of identification in the country. Kyrgyzstan, like other Central Asian countries, possesses a multi-ethnic population; more than eighty ethnicities can be distinguished with the major groups being Kyrgyz (about 65.7%), Uzbeks (13.9), and Russians (11.7).[15] Ethnicities were supposedly silenced during the Soviet Union,[16] yet were also in some ways reinforced (for example, passports did, and still do, bear mention of a person's ethnicity). Interestingly, to the question 'Which of the following best describes you' (above all I am (1) Kyrgyz (2) Uzbek (3) Russian (4) I belong to some other ethnic group (5) I am a 'Kyrgyzstani' first and a member of some ethnic group second), only 12% of respondents to the World Values Survey chose the last option.[17] Hence, Kyrgyzstani citizens seem to identify themselves first with an ethnic group rather than with a larger citizenry. (it is also possible that this is the way people are used to thinking after decades of reporting their ethnicity on all administrative documents).[18] Ethnicity is nonetheless only considered in this paper in its socio-economic (and not political and cultural) dimensions.

My argument relies on two sets of survey data used to investigate citizens' perceptions and expectations of citizenship: semi-structured interviews conducted in 2004 with twenty Kyrgyzstani citizens, and the results of the World Values Survey carried out in Kyrgyzstan in the summer of 2003. The second must of course be interpreted with

15 According to the United Nations Population Fund in Kyrgyzstan (www.unfpa.org.kg).

16 Since nationality and citizenship were separated (see Akiner, 1997, Lowe, 2003).

17 The World Values Survey was conducted in Kyrgyzstan in 2003.

18 It is also worth mentioning that more 'Europeans' (i.e. mainly Russian and Ukrainian ethnics) than Asian (mainly Kyrgyz and Uzbek ethnics) see themselves as Kyrgyzstani first (25.5% compared to 12.1% Asian).

caution. The World Values Survey was initially designed and implemented in the United States and its relevance might be lost in translation or simply in cultural and political diversity. For example, when people were asked to situate themselves on the right/left spectrum, this arguably made little sense to them. One also has to take into account the fact that people in the former Soviet Union are not accustomed to being asked for their political opinions and might feel uneasy expressing them (although this is now progressively changing). It is also difficult to objectively study political perceptions and expectations. In particular, nostalgia about the past often contains a great deal of idealisation of how things used to be. Nevertheless, the results present original quantitative information that partly supports (or invalidates) some of the hypotheses presented below.

The article is divided into two sections, each discussing a particular hypothesis. The first hypothesis is that Kyrgyzstani citizens are embedded in communities towards which they have a sense of loyalty and which today offer vital alternatives to inadequate governmental support. The second hypothesis is that under the Akayev regime, there was no 'Walzerian' social contract between the government and citizens, and that there were unmet expectations from the citizens. The results were a lack of trust in the government, a weak feeling of membership and nostalgia for the communist regime.

The Embedded Self

The most famous assertion of communitarian thinkers is that citizens are 'embedded' or 'situated' in communities and in the social and cultural practices they entail. As suggested by a well known communitarian philosopher, we consider ourselves 'as the particular persons we are – as members of this family or community or nation or people, as bearers of this history, as sons or daughters of that revolution, as citizens of this republic.'[19] Communitarian thinkers also reckon that it is difficult for most individuals to leave these communities and practices, hence opposing liberal's core belief in individualism and the idea that human beings are able to freely join or leave groups.

Communities take different forms and rely on different mechanisms; according to Bell they can be psychological, geographical and memory oriented. Etzioni[20] provides three dimensions to define the community. First, a community 'entails a web of affect-laden relations among a group of individuals, relations that often crisscross and reinforce one another.' Second, a community supposes a 'commitment to a set of shared values, norms and meanings and a shared history and identity.' Finally, he argues that communities are characterised by a relatively high level of responsiveness and loyalty, and that they are usually '*layered*', i.e. arising from membership in more than one community.[21]

This internal solidarity is often held to be robust in more traditional or religious societies such as East Asian countries influenced by Confucianism.[22] Regarding citizenship, while liberals tend to place the emphasis on citizen's rights (mainly civil and political), communitarians, along with republicans, stress obligations. Citizens' responsibilities are mainly of a civic and political nature (as emphasised by civic republicanism), but the distinctiveness of communitarianism is to emphasise loyalty inside constitutive groups such as the family, the neighbourhood, a cultural or religious group and so forth. Responsiveness happens within communities that are 'solid but not overbearing,' particularistic rather than universalistic.[23] This is also what distinguishes communitarianism from communism. Whereas 'Marxist perfectionism ranks ways of life according to a trans-historical account

19 Michael Sandel, *Liberalism and the Limits of Justice* (Cambridge: Cambridge University Press, 1982), p. 179.

20 Amitai Etzioni, 'The Responsive Community: A Communitarian Perspective', *American Sociological Review*, 61, no. 1 (February 1996).

21 Etzioni, 'The Responsive Community', p. 10

22 Daniel Bell, 'A Communitarian Critique of Authoritarianism: The Case of Singapore', *Political Theory*, 25, no. 1 (February 1997).

23 Amitai Etzioni, 'Particularistic Obligations: A Communitarian Examination', *The Responsive Community* (Winter 2003/04).

of the human good' says Kymlicka, 'communitarianism ranks them according to their conformity to existing practices.'[24] For Etzioni, for example, the type of bonds promoted in totalitarian or authoritarian regimes lead to alienation: 'particularistic bonds, and hence obligations, protect us from the inhumanity that has often arisen in the past from strong commitments to abstract and general ideas, leading those who believed in these ideas to fight for the betterment of humanity but to care little about their fellow human beings.'[25]

Regarding community responsiveness, Kyrgyzstan stands out as a complex case. As I show below, traditional solidarities are still alive. Families, clans in particular, are expected to offer support. On the other hand, the imposition for seven decades of a communist regime has arguably added other expectations, this time towards the state. In fact, as indicated by the survey results, a majority of Kyrgyzstani citizens support a return to a more egalitarian society and are nostalgic about the Soviet Union. I believe that these expectations towards the government can also be comprehended by a communitarian outlook, through the principle of the common good, a hypothesis I discuss in the next section.

Poverty and the Decline of Government-Provided Social Rights

Kyrgyzstani citizens exercise, to some degree, the type of responsive behaviours highlighted by communitarians. These constitute crucial coping strategies, given the paucity of government-delivered social rights and the high level of poverty. According to a World Bank survey and the Kyrgyz National Statistical Committee, more than half of citizens fall below the poverty level (RFE/RL, December 22 2002, quoted by Hansen and Dukenbaev). A weak economy, shortage of resources and undermining corruption are forcing large numbers of citizens out of employment or to seek positions abroad; in fact, these factors appear to be one of the leading causes of the March 2005

24 Kymlicka, 'Citizenship Theory', in *Contemporary Political Philosophy: An Introduction*, second edition (Oxford: Oxford University Press, 2002), p. 220.

25 Etzioni, 'Particularistic Obligations: A Communitarian Examination', p. 45.

events. For example, among the 1,043 persons interviewed in the framework of the World Values Survey, only 26% were working full-time. 16% were unemployed, 10% were part-timers, 10% were self-employed (11% were retired, 15% house wives and 6% students). Average monthly wages in US dollars have decreased from $38 in 1996 to $25 in 2000.[26] Reflecting upon their financial situation over the past year, a majority of Kyrgyzstani citizens (51%) stated they had just 'gotten by', while 25% had spent savings and borrowed money and 21% had saved some money (World Values Survey, 2003). In 1999, Mikhalev and Heinrich[27] concluded pessimistically that there were 'few winners from the market reforms.'

While poverty and unemployment mean that social rights are crucial for large parts of the population, these rights have in fact been declining in many sectors. Under the Soviet Union almost half of the citizens (mainly pensioners and children) were entitled to some state benefits,. But at the beginning of the 1990s, economic reforms cut these expenses by half, leaving a growing number of citizens in poverty. In particular, the government of Kyrgyzstan decided in 1995 to target its assistance on the neediest citizens, reducing many categorical subsidies. Also, a notionally defined contribution pension system is likely to be adopted and replace the Soviet inherited pay-as-you-go. Pensions would then become personalised and probably more unequal. In addition, pension payments for people still working will progressively be suppressed and the pension age increased by three years.[28]

Besides, beneficiaries do not always receive or care to collect what they are entitled to. Benefits are sometimes paid in kind, for

26 Country Profile, The Economist Intelligence Unit, Kyrgyzstan, Tajikistan, 2001, at: www.carleton.ca/cifp/docs/Kyrgyzstan.pdf.

27 Vladimir Mikhalev and Georges Heinrich 'Kyrgyzstan, A Case Study of Social Stratification', *World Institute for Development Economics Research* (United Nations University, September 1999).

28 Kathryn Anderson and Charles Becker, 'Post-Soviet Pension System, Retirement, and Elderly Poverty: Findings from the Kyrgyz Republic,' 1999, at: http://econ.cudenver.edu/cbecker/Papers/MOST_final.pdf.

example in flour, or even in bras![29] Some beneficiaries do not collect government checks because they estimate the process to be too difficult or time-consuming. Finally, and more dramatic in the short run, is what can be called a 'de facto privatisation' of the social services. Education, public health, and housing services have been quasi-commercialised with evident practices of bribe-taking and favouritism. As expressed by a Kyrgyzstani citizen,

> Everyone thinks that education is a paid service. So is health care. Now, if we go on like this, we will be paying for being born since life itself is a service. If we charge money for everything, life will become absurd.[30]

The Role of Informal Networks in Kyrgyzstan

In Kyrgyzstan, ethnographic evidence points to the existence of various 'Etzionian-type' communities which have played an important role since the pre-socialist period. As argued by Morgan Y. Liu,[31] research on Eurasia has in fact neglected the small-scale level of the community and individuals, where one witnesses 'the most innovative and unexpected practices for coping under conditions of dramatic, disruptive state transformation.' In terms of offering economic and social support, the most significant communities are families and relatives, clans, and networks of neighbours and friends. There is no substantial evidence that ethnic and religious groups currently constitute a strong channel for economic and social support.

First, citizens of Kyrgyzstan, as in most traditional societies, express responsibility towards their *family*. It is, for example, expected that older and/or successful children should provide for their siblings while the youngest son will stay with his parents to take care of them

29 Jane Falkingham, 'Measuring Household Welfare: Problems and Pitfalls with Household Surveys in Central Asia,' MOCT-MOST: *Economic Policy in Transitional Economies*, 9, no. 4 (1999): 379–93.

30 Balihar Sanghera and Elmira Satybaldieva, 'Roll Back the Market: Moral judgments and market limits in a post-socialist society – a case study of Kyrgyzstan', unpublished research paper, October 2004.

31 Liu, p. 1.

in their old age. Quantitative data confirm this high level of familial cohesion: 87% of the respondents to the World Values Survey agree or strongly agree with the idea that 'one of their main goals in life has been to make their parents proud'. Also, 94% agree that 'regardless of what the qualities and faults of one's parents are, one must always love and respect them' (comparatively, this is the case for 78% of respondents in the 81 countries, both developing and developed, covered by the first three waves of the World Values Survey). 'Taking care of one's family' was also acknowledged by the respondents of the semi-structured interviews as one of the four major responsibilities of any citizen.[32] Familial responsibility is recognised as being part of Kyrgyzstani national culture and is engraved in the constitution in articles 26.1 ('able-bodied, adult children must take care of their parents') and 26.3 ('respect for old people and support for relatives is a sacred tradition of the people of Kyrgyzstan'). It is much stronger in the countryside than in the cities (notably Bishkek) where the traditional family is evolving and the above-mentioned behaviours are not as systematic. Familial solidarity is of crucial importance when resources and jobs are scarce and when salaries and states subsidies are falling. In the mid-1990s, Jude Howell observed that among those she interviewed, 'there was a general perception that people who did not have any relatives were more likely to be poor.'[33]

An extended version of the family, *clans* also offer opportunities for resources and support. Kathleen Collins defines clan as 'an informal social institution in which actual or notional kinship based on blood or marriage forms the central bond among members.'[34] According to myths, the Kyrgyz nation is composed of forty tribes[35] but today clans (also sometimes referred to as tribes) are smaller and tend to comprise from 2,000 to 20,000 members. They function within an

32 The three other responsibilities most frequently chosen were to respect the law, vote and respect others.

33 Jude Howell, 'Coping with the Transition. Household coping strategies in Kyrgyzstan,' Working Paper no. 15, Save the Children (1996), p. 19.

34 Kathleen Collins, 'Clans, Pacts, and Politics in Central Asia', *Journal of Democracy*, 13, no. 4 (October 2002), p. 142.

35 Juraev Shairbek, 'The role of sub-national identities in political competition in Kyrgyzstan', Senior Thesis, American University – Central Asia (May 2004).

'extensive web of horizontal and vertical kin-based relations'[36] and are grouped by so-called 'wings' (right, left and center). Despite the Soviet efforts to eliminate this 'pre-modern' feature of Central Asian societies, clans have survived – kolkhozes and sovkhozes were in fact all clan based. Clans also played an important role in public life under Akayev,[37] providing access to resources. Clan divisions partly correlate with regional ones, in particular the north/south divide which was salient during the March uprising.[38]

Friends, neighbours and colleagues offer a third major source of communal support. Several researchers have highlighted the importance of financial or material loans between friends and neighbours,[39] which increased after independence. 'Reciprocal borrowing between neighbors and friends has emerged as an important survival strategy', writes J. Falkingham.[40] In 1997, 23% of households received a significant amount of private transfers, compared to 14% in 1993. According to Kuehnast and Dudwick, in isolated parts of the country neighbors are in fact as, if not more, vital to the poor than are family members.[41] The cost of traveling to where relatives live can be prohibitive for individuals who are barely surviving. For example, in two

36 Collins, p. 141.

37 See the Internet site of the Eurasia foundation at http://iicas.org/english/enlibrary/libr_10_06_02kg.htm.

38 Dukenbaev and Hansen, 'Understanding Politics in Kyrgyzstan'. This divide is reinforced by ethnic majorities (Uzbek and Tajik in the south;, Russian and Kazak in the north). While the north (mostly Bishkek city and the Talas and Chui regions or 'oblasts') is more 'Russified' and partly wealthier, the southern population living in Batken, Jalal-Abad, and Osh oblasts are on average more traditional and family oriented and tend to feel forgotten by the 'Bishkek elite.' Although not constituting communities per say, regional differences create different expectations towards the state. See Shairbek Juraev, 'The role of subnational identities in political competition in Kyrgyzstan'.

39 Howell, ibid., 1996; Falkingham, 1999; Kathleen Kuehnast and Nora Dudwick, 'Better a Hundred Friends than a Hundred Rubles? Social networks in transition – the Kyrgyz Republic,' *World Bank Economists' Forum*, vol. 2 (2002).

40 Falkingham, p. 5.

41 Kuehnast and Dudwick, 'Better a Hundred Friends than a Hundred Rubles? Social networks in transition–the Kyrgyz Republic,' *World Bank Economists' Forum*, 2 (2002).

villages surveyed in 1995, 55% of the households acknowledged having borrowed money and food from relatives and only slightly less (40%) from neighbours.[42]

A Decline of Traditional Solidarity?

Increased poverty and lack of opportunities have nevertheless taken a toll on these communitarian practices. According to Gulnara Aitpaeva, professor of anthropology at the American University – Central Asia, there is a growing gap between traditional thinking and actual practices. In her words, 'the main peculiarity brought by the changes of the last decades is the necessity to survive. The situation of survival influences all social structures, including the family.'[43] It is also her impression that 'many Kyrgyz people come to old people's homes (retirement houses) now.' Indeed, as argued by Kuehnast and Dudwick[44] and based on the results of the focus groups they undertook in 1999, 'the poor are being excluded or are withdrawing from those social networks that once offered important support'. Informal social networks are still solid and more diverse for the better off, but they have weakened for the poorest, in particular because the latter are unable to return favours, are forced to remove themselves from gift exchanges, and are unable to attend or organise costly ceremonies. Hence, while government-provided benefits are declining, traditional solidarity for the worse off has also deteriorated, damaging communities' ties. Also weakening the family is work emigration to Russia, with parents forced to leave their children with relatives in the village.[45] This corrosion of traditional support groups is an interesting lesson from the 'Kyrgyz case.' Communitarian thinkers writing about the West rarely consider a situation in which family or communal

42 Howell, p. 18.
43 Personal email communication with Gulnara Atpaeva, January 2005.
44 Kuehnast and Dudwick, p. 54.
45 Roza Zhalimbetova and Gregory Gleason, 'Migrant Labor, Labor Rights, and the Eurasian Economic Community', *Central Eurasian Studies Review*, 1, no. 1 (Winter 2002).

obligations become such a financial burden that the most impoverished citizens cannot sustain them.

Favoritism and Corruption

In addition, in some cases (or rather viewed from a different angle), these privileged relationships take the form of favouritism and corruption. While communitarians argue that in modern, liberal societies corruption thrives when communal bonds are too loose, in a country where resources are scarce, institutions are failing and public accountability is not guaranteed, helping members of one's group, family, or clan also means giving preference to individuals from one's group, extorting money from others to secure the well-being of one's own relatives, and entertaining networks of friends and clients. The view that privileged relationships between members of the same clans or groups often entail corruption is common among Kyrgyzstani citizens, who often lament the 'clan system' (including the new president of the country, who recently declared 'a merciless war on corruption').[46] 'I cherish our culture', says a Kyrgyzstani citizen, 'but I also respected the Soviet Union, the party effort about our welfare. Education and healthcare were free and stable. We were protected. Now it is the clan system. The authorities are corrupt, they forgot about their obligations.'[47] Also, 81% of the respondents to the World Values Survey believed that under Akayev the country was run by a few big interests and not in the interest of all (while this was the case of only 64% of citizens in the other countries studied in the first three waves of the World Values Survey). Finally, respondents to the semi-structured interviews argued that clans were a great obstacle to the constitution of a strong citizenship (chosen by eleven out of twenty persons). This sentiment was expressed by a 38-year-old Kyrgyzstani woman who

46 'Kyrgyz president declares war on corruption,' BBC Monitoring Service, United Kingdom, 17 August 2005.

47 Interview by the author, April 2004.

notes, 'I associate Kyrgyz citizenship with the privileges of those who have money.'[48]

Hence, while 'exported' to the Kyrgyz case, a communitarian outlook helps emphasise the importance of micro-level coping strategies. Nevertheless, it does not provide an appropriate prism for comprehending the weakness of these strategies in times of extreme poverty. A communitarian outlook also inadequately explains social and political practices in a democratising regime where the state is unable to provide sufficient resources for its citizens and where community bonds lead to corruption and favouritism.

Nature of the Social Contract

Another essential argument among most communitarian thinkers concerns the nature of politics in general and the state in particular. Put simply, they posit that liberalism, with its emphasis on individual rights, self-determination and the 'neutral state,' fails to recognize that human beings are dependent on society. According to Charles Taylor, for example, a state that remains 'neutral' weakens the sense of common good that he believes is necessary for citizens to accept the sacrifices demanded by the welfare state. This 'substantive conception of the good life,' which provides a standard for society and which communitarians advocate, is commonly referred to as the 'politics of the common good.'[49] Taken to its extreme, this idea of the 'social common good' captures the nature of Central Asian benevolent authoritarian regimes in Turkmenistan or, to a lesser degree, in Uzbekistan. In these countries, authoritarian leaders maintain an artificial and closed economy supported by propagandist messages. The situation in Kyrgyzstan in the 1990s and early 2000s was much more complex. The government was committed to carrying out market reforms which prevented an authoritative distribution of resources and an artificially maintained

48 Interview by the author, April 2004.
49 Will Kymlicka, p. 220.

economy. As a result, while a majority of Kyrgyzstani citizens would have liked the state to intervene more in the economy, the government did not have the resources to provide the benefits needed by most, and was finally forced out of office.

More importantly, communitarianism offers an interesting insight into the social contract and the relationship between membership and social provision. While liberals tend to give priority to liberties and rights over social welfare,[50] many communitarians, especially on the left, argue that it is the government's responsibility to provide its citizens with the resources they need to lead a decent life. They also refute Rawls' 'veil of ignorance' for its abstraction.[51] This is, for example, the case with Michael Walzer. Reflecting upon membership and needs such as welfare, Walzer argues that the social contract cannot be grounded on a hypothetical situation. 'In a world of particular cultures, competing conceptions of the good, scarce resources, elusive and expansive needs, there isn't going to be a single formula, universally applicable.'[52] 'Only its [community] culture, its character, its common understandings can define the 'wants' that are to be provided for.'[53] The social contract is therefore an 'agreement' based on 'shared understanding of citizens' needs.' Crucially, this contract is 'subject to ongoing political determination in detail.'

50 Faulks, p. 62. As expressed by John Rawls in *A Theory of Justice*: 'it has seemed to many philosophers, and it appears to be supported by the convictions of common sense, that we distinguish as a matter of principle between the claims of liberty and right on the one hand, and the desirability of increasing aggregate social welfare of the other, and that we give a certain priority, if not absolute weight, to the former' (*A Theory of Justice*, Cambridge, Harvard University Press, 1971).

51 According to the American philosopher John Rawls, principles of moral equality can be derived from imagining an 'original position' in which people are placed behind a veil of ignorance. According to Rawls, individuals, not knowing their place in society, their social status, skills and intelligence, or even their own conception of the good, would chose principles that would be fair to all.

52 Michael Walzer, 'Welfare, Membership and Needs', in *Spheres of Justice* (New York: Basic Books, 1983), p. 205.

53 Walzer, *Spheres of Justice* p. 204.

In Kyrgyzstan, no such contract between the citizens and the government was in place under the Akayev presidency (and it is still too early to tell whether President Bakiev and his new team will be able to secure one). First, independence from the Soviet Union was imposed on the citizens who expressed by referendum their desire to maintain part of the federation.[54] Also, given the low level of accountability of the Akayev government, no real negotiation of the contract was at stake.[55] Finally, the legacy of the Soviet Union still weighs heavily on citizens' conceptions of the 'wants' that Walzer refers to.

Concretely, a majority of citizens regret the disappearance of the welfare state and yearn for a larger role of government in the economy; feelings that are congruent with a communist past. As stresssed by Liu[56] 'the subsequent disintegration of 'social protections' is widely regarded throughout Central Asia as a breach, even a betrayal, of the state's duty.' For example, both the World Values Survey and the semi-structured interviews showed that Kyrgyzstani citizens believe there is a gap between what they should be entitled to and what they actually receive. Indeed, asked which factors (out of ten) most hindered the constitution of a strong Kyrgyzstani citizenship, the twenty persons interviewed chose three in almost equal proportion: 'people are more concerned with their economic well being,' 'the Kyrgyz government is not securing people's well being and security' and 'the law is not the same for all.' In 2003, as indicated by a World Values Survey question asking respondents to reflect on what the country should aim to become in the future, 52% favoured strongly or somewhat strongly 'an egalitarian society where the gap between rich and

54 In March 1991, 88.7% of Kyrgyzstani citizens approved a proposal to maintain the U.S.S.R. and create a 'renewed federation' (for more details on the historical context of independence, see for example the US Department of State fact sheet on Kyrgyzstan at http://www.state.gov/r/pa/ei/bgn/5755.htm).

55 See Emil Juraev and Vanessa Ruget, 'Political Culture in Post-Communist Polities. The Soviet legacy in Kyrgyzstan,' paper presented at the Eurasian Political Studies Network, 2nd International Conference, Yekaterinburg, Russia, 2004.

56 Morgan Liu, 'Detours from Utopia on the Silk Road: Ethical Dilemmas of Neoliberal Triumphalism', *Central Eurasian Studies Review*, 2, no. 2 (Spring 2003), p. 7.

poor is small, regardless of achievements', while only 37% favoured strongly or somewhat strongly 'a competitive society where wealth is distributed according to ones' achievement'. Finally, when consulted about whether 'the government should be taking more responsibility to ensure that everyone is provided for,' Kyrgyzstani citizens were strongly in favour: 31% chose 'one' on a 'one-to-ten' scale and 64% chose from one to five.

Dissatisfaction with the Akayev government was confirmed by the narratives of individuals who declared in the non-directive interviews, for example, that 'the system is not effective', that 'everyone has to work at the bazaar' (this from a 50-year-old Kyrgyz man living in Osh), that 'I am not able to live well in my own country' (a 33-year-old Kyrgyz man now living in Almaty), or that 'the present government cares little about its citizens' (30-year-old Kyrgyz woman). Reflecting upon the new language requirements in government, a Russian woman said, 'the government ought to think first about the social conditions of people, poverty, economics. Language is very secondary. We can not go to the theatre, everyone has to work at the bazaar.'[57] A young Kyrgyz woman had similar views: 'I feel at home only in Kyrgyzstan' she said, 'but the government does not care much about us. I am disappointed.'[58]

Surveys show that a majority of Kyrgyzstani citizens favoured alternatives to the Akayev government, although interestingly not the one they finally demanded by force in March 2005. In 2003, 60% believed that having a strong leader would be a very or fairly good way of governing the country and 33% that having the army rule would be very or fairly good.[59] Interestingly, this high level of enthusiasm for authoritative rule runs counter to Etzioni's hypothesis that

57 Interview by the author, April 2004.

58 Interview by the author, April 2004.

59 Compared to 35% and 14%, respectively, in other countries covered by the World Values Survey. Differences between north and south were striking: 68% of southerners compared to 45% of northerners believed a strong leader might be good for the country and 40% of southerners compared to 26% of northerners considered that the army would be a good way of governing the country.

strong communities help minimise state coercion,[60] a phenomenon easily explainable by the socio-economic and political disparities between Western and Central Asian countries.

Resentment and unmet expectations about social benefits have regularly expressed themselves through nostalgia for the Soviet regime. As underlined by the authors of a recent report, 'a return to a planned economy which is still widely perceived as having guaranteed good welfare services and benefits would probably command widespread support among the population, especially the elderly and poor.'[61] Indeed, when asked their opinion about how things were going under the Soviet Union, citizens of Kyrgyzstan overwhelmingly ranked the communist regime favourably.[62] On a scale from one to ten ('one' meaning that 'under the communist regime things were going badly,' 'ten' that they were going very well), the median position was eight; with up to 33% choosing the highest score. These results are consistent with the results of the 'New Democracies Barometer', which show that in eight post-Soviet countries, the Soviet political and economic system was preferred to the existing one (particularly in Armenia, Georgia, Kyrgyzstan and Moldova).[63] Uzbeks were from far the most praiseworthy for the communist regime, with 56% giving a score of ten.

Semi-structured interviews confirm that longing for the Soviet Union is grounded mostly on the loss of social rights and benefits. 'I feel less a citizen today' said a 40-year-old Russian woman. 'There was equality during the Soviet Union, and belief in tomorrow. I had job security. Today the situation is more uncertain.' Similarly, a 38-

60 Amitai Etzioni, 'Particularistic Obligations: A Communitarian Examination,' p. 44.

61 'Country Profile, Kyrgyzstan, Tajikistan,' p. 15.

62 Positive opinions of the communist system are higher among lower-salaried people (61% considering that things were going well under the Soviet Union), while this is the case for only 42.5% of those with the highest salaries, and among individuals who during the past year had just gotten by financially (68%, compared to 40% of those who had saved money).

63 Stuart White, 'Introduction: The politics of economic citizenship', in *The Civic Minimum: On the Rights and Organization of Economic Citizenship* (Oxford: Oxford University Press, 2003).

year-old Kyrgyz housewife from the south explained: 'life is difficult today; everyone was provided with jobs and therefore money. During the Soviet Union, we could get education. Now we have to beg.' In Kyrgyzstan, the communist party has enjoyed great popularity since independence, almost certainly because it is seen as the party associated with generous social rights.[64]

How citizens regard the social contract also depends on their ethnicity. Russian ethnics have been significantly less satisfied with the contract, probably because they have had more fragile safety nets (they do not belong to clans and have fewer relatives and friends, especially since many left after independence). Indicative of Russian ethnics' weak feeling of membership under the Akayev regime is their massive emigration, especially at the beginning of the 1990s, and the fact that they still gather in large numbers each at the Russian consulate hoping to obtain a Russian passport or exit visa. Russians are significantly less proud of their country (the World Values Survey shows that only 12% of ethnic Kyrgyz citizens surveyed were not very proud or not proud at all of their country, compared to 17% of Uzbeks and 44% of Russians).[65] Being a Kyrgyztani citizen, for a 56-year-old Russian, is 'sailing in a small boat instead of a big ship' (semi-structured interviews). Another Russian, a 40-year-old woman, thinks that 'many Kyrgyz are humiliated abroad because our government is weak and unable to protect us.'

Thus, several indicators suggest that the social contract between the government and citizens under Akayev was weak. In other words, and to borrow Walzer's terminology, a 'simple' system of (in)equality prevailed under Akayev. Money (and familial affiliation) were dominant goods ('possess one and all the other come in train,')[66] as they

64 When asked 'which party they would vote for if there was an election tomorrow' and choosing among 27 parties, 17% of the respondents chose the Communist Party of Kyrgyzstan. Although a low percentage, it was the highest achieved by any party. The Women's Democratic Party of Kyrgyzstan was second choice with 12% and third the Ar-Namys or Dignity party with 8%.

65 This is only a rough evaluation as another group of people defined themselves as 'Kyrgyzstani first'. The results are quite similar when with language spoken (Kyrgyz, Russian, Uzbek) is accounted for.

66 Michael Walzer, *Spheres of Justice*, p. 11.

gave access to social, medical and educational goods. Citizens had the sentiment that the contract offered by democracy was not respected and asked for radical change when the opportunity arose.

Conclusion

This short exploration of Kyrgyztani communal practices and social expectations under the former regime calls for two distinct concluding remarks. First, it is evident that the major challenge for the new government will be to re-establish legitimacy, in particular, through a re-foundation of the contract. Although there is no doubt that ethnic, regional and clan cleavages are a potential source of instability, I argue that the lack of social rights and of economic opportunities for citizens is a higher obstacle to the creation of national unity and membership.

From a theoretical point of view, I believe that the 'Kyrgyz situation' puts forward interesting questions for a theory of citizenship, in particular the impact of severe economic and social changes on types of loyalty and identification. While it is not surprising that theories devised for the West are limited when applied to other contexts, the paper also shows the complexity of post-communist societies, especially regarding time frames. In Kyrgyzstan, the March 2005 uprising clearly constitutes a fundamental and immediate rupture. But longer-term political practices and social and economic hardships under the Akayev regime have also strongly impacted the society by weakening family ties and traditional solidarities. Finally, the communist system has left an enduring legacy and is still considered to be a political alternative.

Bibliography

Anderson John, *Kyrgyzstan, Central Asia: Island of Democracy?* (Amsterdam: Overseas Publishers Association, 1999).

Anderson, Kathryn and Becker, Charles M., 'Post-Soviet Pension System, Retirement, and Elderly Poverty: Findings from the Kyrgyz Republic,' (1999), at: http://econ.cudenver.edu/cbecker/Papers/MOST_final.pdf.

Barbalet, J.M., *Citizenship* (Minneapolis: The University of Minnesota, 1988).

—— 'Citizenship, Class Inequality and Resentment', in Bryan Turner (ed.), *Citizenship and Social Theory* (London: Sage Publications, 1993).

Beiner, Ronald, *Theorizing Citizenship* (Albany: State University of New York, 1995).

Bekbolotov, Kumar, 'The Ethnic Minority Factor and Democratization in Kyrgyzstan: The Uzbek Case,' unpublished senior thesis, American University–Central Asia (May 2003).

Bell, Daniel, 'A Communitarian Critique of Authoritarianism: The Case of Singapore', *Political Theory*, 25, no. 1 (February 1997), pp. 6–32.

—— 'Communitarianism,', in Edward Zalta (ed.), *The Stanford Encyclopedia of Philosophy* (Spring 2005 Edition, forthcoming), at: http://plato.stanford.edu/archives/spr2005/entries/communitarianism/

Bulmer, Martin, and Rees, Anthony (eds.), *Citizenship Today: The Contemporary Relevance of T.H. Marshall* (London: UCL Press, 1996).

Carley. P., 'The Legacy of the Soviet Political System and the Prospects for Developing Civil Society in Central Asia', in Vladimir Tismaneanu (ed.), *Political Culture and Civil Society in Russia and the New States of Eurasia* (London: M. E. Sharpe, 1995).

Carothers, Thomas, 'The End of the Transition Paradigm', *Journal of Democracy*, 13, no. 1 (2002), pp. 5–21.

Collins, Kathleen, 'Clans, Pacts, and Politics in Central Asia', *Journal of Democracy*, 13, no. 3 (2002), pp. 137–152.

Dukenbaev, Askat, and Hansen, William, 'Understanding Politics in Kyrgyzstan,' Unpublished research paper, American University–Central Asia, DEMSTAR (Bishkek, 2003).
Etzioni, Amitai, 'The Responsive Community: A Communitarian Perspective', *American Sociological Review*, 61, no. 1 (1996), pp. 1–11
—— 'Particularistic Obligations: A Communitarian Examination', *The Responsive Community*, 14, no. 1 (Winter 2003/04).
Falkingham, Jane, 'Measuring Household Welfare: Problems and Pitfalls with Household Surveys in Central Asia,' *MOCT-MOST: Economic Policy in Transitional Economies*, 9, no. 4 (1999): 379–93.
Faulks, Keith, *Political Sociology: A Critical Introduction* (Edinburgh: Edinburgh University Press, 1999).
—— *Citizenship* (London: Routledge, 2000).
Holmes, Leslie, *Post-Communism, An Introduction* (London: Polity Press, 1997).
Howell, Jude, 'Coping with the Transition. Household coping strategies in Kyrgyzstan,' Working Paper no. 15, Save the Children (1996.)
Inglehart, Ronald and Welzel, Christian, 'Political Culture and Democracy: Analyzing Cross-Level Linkages' (2002), at: http://www.worldvaluessurvey.org/library/index.html
Kangas, Roger, 'State Building and Civil Society in Central Asia', in Vladimir Tismaneanu (ed.), *Political Culture and Civil Society in Russia and the New States of Eurasia* (London: M. E. Sharpe, 1995).
Kuehnast, Kathleen and Nora Dudwick, 'Better a Hundred Friends than a Hundred Rubles? Social networks in transition – the Kyrgyz Republic,' *World Bank Economists' Forum*, 2 (2002), pp. 51–88.
Kymlicka, Will, 'Citizenship Theory', in *Contemporary Political Philosophy: An Introduction*, second edition (Oxford: Oxford University Press, 2002).
'Kyrgyzstan: Social Protection in a Reforming Economy,' World Bank Country Study (1993).

La Torre, Massimo, 'Citizenship and Social Rights: A European Perspective,' European University Institute Working Papers (March 1998).

Liebich André, Warner, Daniel and Jasna Dragovic, Jasna (eds.), *Citizenship, East and West* (London: Kegan Paul International, 1995).

Liu, Morgan 'Detours from Utopia on the Silk Road: Ethical Dilemmas of Neoliberal Triumphalism', *Central Eurasian Studies Review*, 2, no. 2 (Spring 2003), pp. 2–10.

Lovell, David 'Trust and the Politics of Postcommunism', *Communist and Post-communist Studies*, 34 (2001), pp. 27–38.

Lowe, Robert, 'Nation Building and Identity in the Kyrgyz Republic', in Tom Everett-Heath (ed.), *Central Asia: Aspects of Transition* (London: Routledge, 2003).

Luong, Pauline Jones, 'Central Asia's Contribution to Theories of the State', in Pauline Jones Luong (ed.), *The Transformation of Central Asia, States and Societies from Soviet Rule to Independence* (New York: Cornell University Press, 2004).

Marshall, T. H., *Class, Citizenship and Social Development* (New York: Anchor Books Edition, 1965).

Mikhalev, Vladimir and Heinrich, Georges, 'Kyrgyzstan, A Case Study of Social Stratification', *World Institute for Development Economics Research* (United Nations University, September 1999).

Miller, David, *Citizenship and National Identity* (Cambridge: Polity Press, 2000).

Muller, Katherine, 'Towards Contributory Approaches: Pension Reforms in the Transition Countries,' draft version of a paper presented at the DSA Annual Conference, Glasgow, 2003.

Namazie, Ceema, 'Early Evidence of Welfare Changes in the Kyrgyz Republic: Have Things Got Worse with Reforms?' Discussion Paper, no. DARP 63 (November 2002).

Pilon, Juliana 'Democratic Transition in Central Asia: An Assessment,' *SAIS Review*, 18, no. 2 (Summer/Fall 1998).

Pinker, Robert, 'Introduction', in *The Right to Welfare and Other Essays by T. H. Marsall* (New York: The Free Press, 1981).

Pototskii, Vladimir and Sharma, Rakesh, '2001 IFES Survey in Kyrgyzstan,' (USAID, May 2002).

Rose, Richard, 'Where are Postcommunist Countries Going?' *Journal of Democracy*, 8, no. 3 (July 1997), pp. 92–108

—— 'How Muslims View Democracy: Evidence from Central Asia', *Journal of Democracy*, 13, no. 4 (October 2002), pp. 102–111.

Rutkowski, Michael, 'The Quest for Modern Solutions: Pension Reforms in Transition Economies,' paper presented at 'Ten Years After: Transition and Growth in Post-Communist Countries' Conference, Warsaw, 1999,

Sandel, Michael, *Liberalism and the Limits of Justice* (Cambridge: Cambridge University Press, 1982).

Shafir, Gershon (ed.), *The Citizenship Debates: A Reader* (Minneapolis: University of Minnesota Press, 1998).

Stewart, Angus, 'Two Conceptions of Citizenship', *British Journal of Sociology*, 46, no. 1 (March 1995), pp. 63–78.

Walzer, Michael, *Spheres of Justice* (New York: Basic Books, 1983).

—— 'Citizenship', in T. Ball and J. Farr (eds.), *Political Innovation and Conceptual Changes* (Cambridge: Cambridge University Press, 1989).

—— 'The Communitarian Critique of Liberalism', *Political Theory*, 18, no. 1 (February 1990), pp. 6–23.

White, Stuart, 'Introduction: The politics of economic citizenship', in *The Civic Minimum: On the Rights and Organization of Economic Citizenship* (Oxford: Oxford University Press, 2003).

GEORGE WELTON AND ADRIAN BRISKU

Contradictory Inclinations? The Role of 'Europe' in Albanian Nationalist Discourse

Introduction

In recent times the 'European' nature of the Albanian nation has become an uncontested part of the intellectual, political and popular discourse within Albania. Albanians consider themselves to be Europeans, not only in terms of their geography but by historically and culturally subscribing to European values they believe that they clearly form part of the European family. Simultaneously, the aspiration to join the European Union is almost universally accepted. According to the President of Albania, Alfred Moisiu, such aspiration 'has no opposition in Albania and enjoys a full consensus in the whole political spectrum as well as in public opinion'.[1] Certainly the approval of EU membership amongst elite groups seems hard to question. As summarized in the study conducted by the Albanian Institute for International Studies (AIIS), 'The figures [supporting EU membership] speak for themselves; 96.43% in the Media Category, 96.91% in Businesses and 99.38% and 100% in Public Administration and Local NGOs respectively'.[2]

1 Official Website of the Albanian President, "President Moisiu's Speech in the Session Entitled 'European Enlargement: The Dimensions and Architecture of This Enlargement'" (25 June 2004), at: http://www.president.al/shqip/info.asp?id=1216

2 Albert Rakipi and Aldo Bumci (eds.), *Albania and the European Union: Perceptions and Realities* (Tirana: Albanian Institute for International Studies, 2003), p. 5.

How seriously should we take the expression of identity, and the repercussions of it, remains unclear? The majority of the academic literature on nationalism and political identity will accept that to some extent all national identity is 'imagined'. However, this does not help us understand the extent to which characteristics of national identity constrain or direct the decisions of political elites.

Traditional analysis of national identity exists along a continuum reply to mail between the two extremes of rationalism and discursive accounts. This continuum reflects the extent to which identity is seen as a constraint on action. In the rationalist analysis, explanations are made in terms of the material cost and benefits that motivate political action, and national identity is merely seen as a justifying rhetoric offering no real constraint on action. In discursive accounts, the national identity itself is often seen to drive social actions because it defines the parameters of politically permissible behaviour.

A rationalist analysis of Albania's European discourse, for example, would see EU membership as an economically motivated objective that manipulated national identity to serve this goal. A discursively inclined explanation would explain the same discourse as a constraining political reality that, at least partially, depends on Albania's historical self-understanding.

Neither of these explanations is entirely convincing and this chapter will seek to investigate the strengths and weaknesses of both. The extreme rationalist position does not explain the unanimity of support for EU membership. The benefits created by membership are likely to be unequally distributed but this is not reflected in its breadth of support. In addition, the rationalist account fails to explain the apparent need to discursively project this current aspiration into Albania's historical self-understanding.

The account that focuses upon discourses, however, is also deeply problematic because national identity seems to be open to so many different political appropriations. Before it is possible to understand the impact of nationalism on political decision-making, it is necessary to investigate the limitations inherent in a particular nationalist discourse. This chapter will investigate this issue by adopting a historical approach, reviewing the way in which Europeanness and Nationalism have been connected since the birth of the Albanian nationalist movement.

In doing this we see that while there have been dominant strands in the discourse, there have always been contradictions which have, at certain points, provided the resources for those opposed to Europe. On the whole, Europe has been seen as a benchmark of modernism and an aspirational model for development. In this way identifying themselves as 'European' has been part of an attempt by Albanians to claim European economic and political development as their birthright. However, two opposing trends have also continually threatened to undermine this positive association. First, even where Europe is seen as an aspirational political and economic model, its power is also understood to be a continuing threat to the autonomy of the Albanian state. Second, though Europe is unquestionably seen as the birthplace of modernist and enlightenment values, contemporary Europe has, at various times, been seen as a poor expression of those values.

Both of these trends have parallels in the current discourses on Europe and can therefore be useful in both highlighting the contested nature of identity construction, and suggesting ways in which the current discourse might change in the future.

To do this the chapter will start by reviewing the way in which discussions of nationalism have evolved in the theoretical literature of International Relations and nationalism studies. The second section will then review the analytical basis of rationalist arguments for attitudes to Europe. The bulk of the chapter will, however, consider the way in which the Albanian perception of Europe and nation have emerged and been connected before finally attempting to draw some connections between these historical discussions and contemporary trends in the discourse on Europe.

Constructivism in International Relations and Nationalism Studies

Over the last 20 years or so the study of International Relations and of nationalism have been moving towards each other from opposing ends of the theoretical spectrum. In International Relations constructivism emerged with its focus on the concept of 'identity' as a response to the ontological and theoretical limitations of rationalism. Where rationalism tried to explain political action in terms of the costs and benefits related with particular decisions, constructivism highlighted the conceptual and ethical constraints which both produce interests in the first place and influence our choice between political options. This re-emergence of an interest in identity took many forms, focusing on key characteristics of individual national leaders or national elites,[3] the co-constitution of security identities,[4] or the role of national identities in shaping, directing and constraining foreign policy options.[5]

In the study of nationalism, a tendency to focus on the 'constructed' or 'imagined' nature of national identity has arisen not in response to any rational choice inclination but rather as a corrective to the essentialist accounts offered by nationalists themselves. Etienne Balibar summarises the essence of the myth:

3 For example as in the papers presented in Steve Smith, 'Belief Systems and the Study of International Politics', in Richard Little and Steve Smith (eds.), *Belief Systems and International Relations* (Oxford: Blackwell, 1988).

4 See for example, Peter Katzenstein (ed.), *The Culture of National Security* (New York: Columbia University Press, 1996); Alexander Wendt, 'Anarchy is What States Make of it: The Social Construction of Power Politics', *International Organization*, 46 no. 2 (1992), pp. 391–425; Alexander Wendt, *Social Theory of International Politics* (Cambridge: Cambridge University Press, 1999).

5 This literature is immense but just two examples would be David Campbell, *National Deconstruction: Violence, Identity and Justice in Bosnia* (Minneapolis: University of Minnesota Press, 1998); Jeffrey Checkel, 'Norms, Institutions and National Identity in Contemporary Europe', *International Studies Quarterly*, vol. 43 (1999), pp. 83–114.

> The illusion is twofold. It consists in believing that the generations which succeed one another over centuries on a reasonably stable territory, under a reasonably univocal designation, have handed down to each other an invariant substance [their national identity]. And it consists in believing that the process of development from which we select aspects retrospectively, so as to see ourselves as the culmination of that process, was the only one possible.[6]

This has worked its way into studies of European politics where there has been a theoretical movement back to discussions of identity. These discussions have included the possible emergence of a post-national European identity across the existing EU member states[7] and the role of Eastern Europe as a cultural 'other' against which the European Union has historically defined itself.[8] In addition there has been an increasing discussion over the way in which the nationalist discourse is structured generally.[9]

However, if the debate has been decided against essentialism and rationalism and in favour of constructivism, this has not decided the questions concerning the nature of the processes driving social construction. Benedict Anderson's belief that nationalist ideology is not only 'imagined' but exists in a state of 'philosophical poverty and

6 Etienne Balibar, 'The Nation Form: History and Ideology', in Geoff Eley and Ronald Suny (eds.), *Becoming National: A Reader* (Oxford: Oxford University Press, 1996), p. 132.

7 Thomas Diez, 'Europe's Other and the Return of Geopolitics', *Cambridge Review of International Affairs*, 17, no. 2 (2004), pp. 319–335; Mathieu Deflem, 'The Myth of Postnational Identity', *Social Forces*, 75, no. 1 (1996), pp. 119–143 ; Gerard Delanty, 'The Limits and Possibilities of a European Identity: A Critique of Cultural Essentialism', *Philosophy and Social Criticism*, 21 (1995), pp. 15–36 ; Lars-Erik Cederman, 'Nationalism and Bounded Integration: What It Would Take to Construct a European Demos.' *European Journal of International Relations*, 7, no. 2 (2001), pp. 139–174; Sean Carey, 'Undivided Loyalties: Is National Identity an Obstacle to European Integration?' *European Union Politics*, 3, no. 4 (2002), pp. 387–413.

8 Bahar Rumelili, 'Constructing Identity and Relating to Difference: Understanding the EU's Mode of Differentiation', *Review of International Studies*, vol. 30 (2004), pp. 27–47.

9 Matthew Levinger and Paula Franklin Lytle, 'Myth and of Mobilisation: The Triadic Structure of Nationalist Rhetoric', *Nations and Nationalism*, vol. 7, no. 2 (2001), pp. 174–194.

even incoherence',[10] does not help us to understand the limits that cultural and institutional history may place on those who want to appropriate the nationalistic rhetoric to their own ends. As Balibar has also commented, identity may constitute, 'a retrospective illusion, but it also expresses constraining institutional realities'.[11]

It is becoming increasingly apparent that the extent to which the representation of national identity becomes a 'constraining institutional reality' is open for debate. The more a given identity constrains action the less appropriate it would be to explain political decision-making in rational-choice terms If actions are really constrained by the conceptual biases of a particular identity then the range of options within which rational choices can be made is extremely limited. Alternatively, if political identity is seen as flexible then one may want to look at the operation of the politician or institution that appropriates it, rather than the identity itself, as the centre of our explanation.

For this reason even if one is a constructivist, the rationalist/discursive divide can still be seen as a means of dividing social theories. A rationalist-constructivist might seem like something of an oxymoron but there is no real contradiction between them. One can accept the ontological point that identities are constructed and also accept the rationalist belief that identities are routinely the subject of manipulation so that no identity offers a particularly strong constraint on political decision-making.

Of course, the really difficult part will be to identify criteria for establishing the extent to which political discourses and identities put a constraint on political decision-making. This chapter will attempt a more modest task, highlighting the issue of constraint by trying to identify the areas where Albanian national identity has been particularly susceptible to conflict and multiple interpretations. First, however, it is necessary to explain why the rationalist argument needs any kind of cultural supplement at all.

10 Benedict Anderson, *Imagined Communities: Reflections on the Origin and the Spread of Nationalism* (London: Verso, 1991), p. 5.

11 Balibar, 'The Nation Form: History and Ideology', p. 132.

The Limitations of the Rationalist Argument

Although International Relations may have moved away from the purely rational choice analysis, there are still many areas of political analysis where it is commonplace. This is particularly true when discussing the European Union since the European project has consistently been sold on the basis of its claimed economic benefits.

There are fairly obvious reasons why such an explanation would seem appropriate to Albania. As one of the least economically developed countries in Europe, emerging from the shadow of an authoritarian and truly isolationist regime, the benefits of EU membership for Albania are considerable. Through improved access to a huge market, support in institutional reform and financial aid, Albania could reasonably expect to become a more prosperous, more democratic and more stable country as a result of becoming a member of the EU.

However, such explanations are never straightforward and there seem to be two reasons why a truly rationalist account will be insufficient. First, costs and benefits will undoubtedly be unevenly distributed but if Mustafa Nano is right then 90% of the population support membership.[12] If the rationalist argument is to be persuasive, we would have to believe that 90% of the population are fairly convinced that they would personally gain from European integration. One would also have to believe that these people have sufficient information and expertise to reasonably draw this conclusion.

Of course, one could argue that rational choices are never made with perfect information and that to exclude the rationalist analysis on this basis is to misunderstand the nature of rationalist theory. However, incomplete information is not simply a matter of calculating probabilities. It also forces us to ask questions about where dominant views come from. As Christopher Anderson has argued, the degree to which the population takes its lead from the interpretation of the

12 Mustafa Nano, 'Shqiptaret Bejne Sehir Europen [Albanians Idly Look at Europe]', in *Shekulli* (2 May 2004), at: http://www.shekulli.com.al/index.php?page=shownews&newsID=38258%20class=

political elites depends on how much those elites are trusted.[13] The way in which this trust is ensured and the political and rhetorical resources used to explain the benefits of integration then needs to become part of our analysis.

The second reason that purely rational/economic motives are insufficient to explain European identity and EU membership is that a purely rationalist expression of EU membership would not need a justification in terms of identity. If economic issues are the only consideration in people's calculations why not explain your desire to become a member of the EU in explicitly and solely these terms?

One way of countering this argument and offering a defence of rationalist explanations is to suggest that the intended audience for these declarations of European identity is not the Albanian population itself but rather the Brussels decision-makers. In the recent discourses surrounding EU membership cultural arguments have been writ large. Turkey's EU accession negotiations have been routinely peppered with talk of European culture. Delanty writes, 'the inclusion of Islamic and orthodox religious traditions will have implications for cultural identities that presuppose secular Christianity'.[14]

As a result, political elites and the general public in predominantly Muslim countries may feel it is necessary to exaggerate their European inclinations in order to enhance their opportunities for integration at some point in the future. Even if this is so, however, the simple fact that a given identity may serve some instrumental goal does not explain how it emerged in a particular way or how it operates. To understand its operation, and particularly its flexibility to political appropriation, it is necessary to look at the way the identity, or a component of it, has operated in a far wider range of contexts. This will be the goal of the rest of the chapter.

13 Christopher Anderson, 'When in' Doubt, Use Proxies: Attitudes toward Domestic Politics and Support for Integration', *Comparative Political Studies*, 31, no. 5 (1998), pp. 569–601.

14 Gerard Delanty, 'The Making of a Post Western Europe: A Civilizational Analysis.' *Thesis Eleven*, 72 (2003), p. 12.

Europeanness and Albanian Identity

The emphasis that contemporary Albanian political and intellectual elite have put on the Europeanness of Albania is evident from a range of sources. The well-known Kosovar Albanian academic and publicist Rexhep Qosja for example, shows no uncertainty in the fundamentally European character of the Albanian nation when he argues that 'Albanians today are the only European people that … still lag behind the other Balkan peoples in the process of European integration'.[15] Similarly, Albanian politician, Ilir Meta, in the day of the announcement of his new political party called The *Socialist Movement for Integration*, declared that 'we, the European Albanians, have the power for change, for not remaining victims of threats of abusive government, corruption and criminal world'.[16]

However, any attempt to analyse the longer term connection between Albanian national identity and discourses on Europe requires a more historically oriented analysis. The following sections will analyse the way in which the discussions of Europeanness and national discourse have emerged and transformed over three periods, the Albanian National Renaissance (late 19th century – 1912), the interwar period (1919–1939) (these two periods are put in one section) and the post World War II period under communism (1945–1990).

15 Rexhep Qosja, 'Shqiptaret kunder vetvetes [Albanians Against Themselves]' (8 October 2003), at: http://wwww.lajmet.com/Analiza/Rexhep_Qosja-8–Tetor-03.html, p. 1.

16 Ilir Meta, 'Fjala e Z.Ilir Meta ne diten e shpalljes se Levizjes Socialiste per Integrim [Speech of Mr. Ilir Meta in the Day of Declaration of the Socialist Movement for Integration], *Ilir Meta Online* (6 September 2004), at: http://www.ilirmeta.com/index.php?page=news&news=185

The Albanian National Renaissance

In the National Renaissance period the European Enlightenment and ethno-national romanticism ideas infiltrated the Albanian elite and provided the driving force for the creation of the Albanian national identity. As Pirro Misha has elaborated,

> The very idea of an Albanian nation germinated first in the minds of a handful of intellectuals living outside the country, mostly in Europe...The initial impulse and inspiration came from the European Enlightenment, as well as from the influence of the writings of a number of Western scholars, travellers, poets, ethnographers and philologists who were discovering this forgotten part of Europe, which for a long time has constituted a 'forbidden' land, generally referred to as 'European Turkey' or as 'the Near East', as if hinting at something already lost.[17]

While the ideas of Enlightenment Europe dictated the way in which Albania would become a prosperous state, economically and militarily strong, romanticism provided the nationalist mythology that would provide the necessary ingredients for achieving an independent Albania.

The pivotal figure of the period, Sami Frasheri, for example, suggests that European civilisation is prosperous because of its liberal politics and that the despotic politics that Albania suffered under the Ottoman rule fundamentally conflict with its development. As he says, 'The civilisation [European] has created such conditions that a tough-handed and uneducated approach does not produce good outcomes'.[18] As a result other intellectual figures of the period, like Zef Jubani, suggested economic and political reforms based on a European Model at the centre of which was a native bourgeoisie that would pay fewer

17 Pirro Misha, 'Invention of a Nationalism: Myth and Amnesia', in Stephanie Schwander-Sievers and Bernd Fischer (eds.), *Albanian Identities: Myth and History* (London: C. Hurst & Co. Publishers Ltd. 2002), p. 33.

18 Zija Xholi, *Mendimtare te Rilindjes Kombetare [Thinkers of National Renaissance]* (Tirane: 'Mihal Duri' Publishing House, 1987), p. 325.

taxes and would be encouraged to trade with Europe while focusing on industrial development at home.[19]

Of course, borrowing developmental ideas from Europe hardly makes one European. However, the geographical and historical position of Albania vis-à-vis Europe did allow this idea to become particularly firmly rooted in the minds of political and intellectual elites, not just as an aspirational model but as a national birthright.

Like all notions of national identity, establishing and maintaining this connection required a projection of Albanian nationalism into the European past. The historical Europeanness was routed in two main facts, that Albania is made up of descendents of ancient Illyrians and that it has an Indo-European language. Kostantin Cekrezi, an Albanian nationalist, wrote in 1919 that 'it is generally recognised today that the Albanians are the most ancient race in south-eastern Europe. All indications point to the fact that they are descendents of the earliest Aryan immigrants who were represented in historical times by the kindred Illyrians, Macedonians and Epirots'.[20]

The European nature of the Albanian language also played an important role in arguments for European national identity. In a rhetorical question, Pashko Vasa, a founding father of Albanian nationalism during the second-half of the 19th century takes pride in the ancientness of Albanian as a European language and its survival instincts. 'How did this ancient language, being the oldest of all known ancient languages in Europe, spoken by a population of only two million people, manage to exist like it was in its origins, without having a developed literature and civilisation to become distinguished?'[21]

As in modern times, even if one accepts that Albania is fundamentally European, this should not encourage one to ignore the strategic uses to which that identity was put. In the Renaissance period, Albanian intellectuals and politicians looked towards Europe as their

19 Ibid., p. 86.

20 Noel Malcom, 'Myths of Albanian National', in Stephanie Schwander-Sievers and Bernd Fischer (eds.), *Albanian Identities: Myth and History* (London: C. Hurst & Co. Publishers Ltd. 2002), p. 73.

21 Zija Xholi, *Mendimtare te Rilindjes Kombetare [Thinkers of National Renaissance]*, p. 143.

model for the development of Albania and used this as part of their justification for a wide range of social changes. Simultaneously, Albanian politicians used the European rhetoric in order to gain political and cultural recognition from the European powers.

Nonetheless, in spite of this apparent convergence of ideological and geo-strategic considerations neither the ideological component nor the political manoeuvring was as simple as this account might suggest. Pirro Misha captures well the contradictory inclinations of the Albanian elites regarding Europe that is seen as both an aspirational developmental model and a profound security threat.

> Europe is for the Albanians the land of aspirations, the incarnation of civilisation, power, the dream of wellbeing, the shelter in which to feel secure and protected. Yet, there are the contrasting images of 'Europe the faithless', Europe the inimical cause of many wrongs done to Albanians including their partition, Europe the immoral, the 'old whore', etc. Europe is both dreamed about and yearned for as well as conceived as being threatening, slippery and not to be trusted but rather to be avoided.[22]

These conceptual conflicts found concrete support in the power political confusions of the time. Albania's place in the Ottoman Empire combined with these uncertain feelings vis-à-vis the European Powers led some intellectuals of the time to emphasise the need to maintain the already existing oriental elements of Albanian national identity.

One illustration of this can be seen in the discussions concerning the choice of a national script. During the Renaissance, the existing perception was that the use of Latin script was for the European world, Arabic for the Turkic-Arabic world, whereas Greek was for the Byzantine-Orthodox world[23]. Even so, some considered that an Arabic script might be more appropriate for Albania than Latin. Faik Konitza, another pivotal figure of Albanian nationalism, and the minister of foreign affairs of Austro-Hungary discussed at length the practiceability of the use of the Arabic script for the Albanian language.

22 Pirro Misha, 'Invention of a Nationalism: Myth and Amnesia', p. 44.

23 Zija Xholi, *Mendimtare te Rilindjes Kombetare [Thinkers of National Renaissance]*, pp. 174–5.

Konitza argued that 'The Albanian alphabet based on the Turkish [Arabic] script, as proposed by the competent author of the comparative table, is comprehensible and practicable; it is very similar to the one I had envisaged'.[24]

This was conceivable for a range of reasons. Most obviously, as a predominantly Muslim country with strong historical connections to the Ottoman Empire, culturally speaking Albania could certainly justify an orientation in either direction. Equally, while the aspiration to modernity created a considerable inclination towards Europe within the Albanian nationalist movement, many Albanians who enjoyed political influence within the Ottoman Empire fought against this inclination for instrumental reasons. Konitza continues his correspondence with the Austro-Hungarian minister:

> Nonetheless, I have written to Tahir Pasha, a chief of the Albanian royal guard. He comes from Northern Albania, has a daily audience with the Sultan, enjoying his boundless trust. Implementing for the first time in practice Your Excellency's idea, I wrote to him in Geg [one of Albanian dialects] with a Turkish [Arabic] script, saying it would be in the best interest of His Excellency, the Sultan, to authorise the opening of Albanian schools.[25]

Of course, in the years between the World Wars when the Ottoman Empire had faded into the historical distance, the inclination to associate with the Islamic and ex-Ottoman world receded further. Dominated by prime minister and then self-proclaimed monarch, Ahmet Zogu (King Zog), this period saw Europe become the unquestioned benchmark of economic and cultural modernisation. As Jason Tomes has said Zog thought that 'like other Balkan states, it should repudiate the legacy of the Ottoman period and strive to catch up with the rest of Europe…. [H]is rhetoric was always of modernisation: roads, bridges, schools, literacy, public health, agronomy, tourism and industry'.[26] Furthermore, at a time when European ideals were once more in the

24 Bejtullah Destani (ed.), *Faik Konitza: Selected Correspondence* (London: The Centre for Albanian Studies, 2000), p. 22.

25 Ibid., p. 23.

26 Jason Tomes, 'The Throne of Zog (Albania's King Zog)', *History Today* (September 2001), at: http://www.findarticles.com/cf_O/PI/search.jhtml?key="Jason Tomes", p. 2.

ascendancy not only did he suggest that the modernisation process should adopt European institutional management and technological characteristics but, as far as possible, should become European culturally. Zog stated that his political plan was 'to civilise my people and make them as far as possible adopt Western habits and customs'.[27]

This cultural modernisation process drew on a similar discourse to the national renaissance intellectuals regarding the European ethno-cultural origins of Albanian identity. Tomes continues, 'According to Zogists, the Albanian throne had a 2,500-year history … asserting that ancient Macedonia, Epirus and Illyria were in some sense Albanian states, they devised a list of precursors for Zog … which included Achilles, Alexander the Great, Pyrrhus and Queen Teuta'.[28]

Thus, throughout the Renaissance period and between the World Wars, there was considerable consistency in the treatment of the Albanian nation as fundamentally European. However, at different times this characterisation was not without its contradictions and its opponents. The European discourse supported the aspiration to modernisation and development within the country and was used to try and persuade the Great European Powers to afford recognition to the political independence of the Albanian nation. However, the ambivalence that many Albanians felt towards European power vis-à-vis Albanian weakness, combined with the political realities of Albania's position in the Ottoman Empire, persuaded some to consider other options. That they were able to find discursive resources within Albanian culture to support alternative interpretation suggests a conflict that has been a consistent part of Albanian identity ever since.

27 Ibid.
28 Ibid., p. 3.

The Communist Period

In the analysis so far contradictions and imperfections in the national discourse generally played a secondary role to the fundamentally European national project. In contrast, during the communist period the Albanian political elite fundamentally rejected the connection between their nation and Europe, as the Europe of this period ceased to personify the modernist ideals to which they aspired. This occurred for three main reasons.

First, the rise of fascism in the West and its defeat by a particularly Albanian brand of Communism highlighted the insidious nature of capitalism and the superiority of communism. At the heart of this was the belief, commonly propagated within the Soviet sphere, that while Europe, and in particular Germany, represented the ideal of national and industrial success, the excesses best exemplified by the rise of fascism showed that Europe had become of a perversion of these Enlightenment ideals. As Theodor Adorno and Max Horkheimer argue in *The Critique of the Enlightenment*, 'The horde which so assuredly appears in the organization of the Hitler Youth is not a return to barbarism but the triumph of repressive equality... the free themselves finally came to form the "herd" which Hegel has declared to be the result of Enlightenment'.[29] Even when fascism was not seen as a direct descendant of European modernism, Western European liberal complacency and the self-indulgent excesses of the Weimar Germany were held responsible for allowing it to happen.

As a result the Albanian communist elite argued that capitalist Europe was a threat to Enlightenment humanistic values and to every nation that espoused them. As Zija Xholi clearly states, 'The wild rules of capitalism that directed the economic and political lives of European countries did not bring cooperation among governments but

29 Theodor Adorno and Max Horkheimer, *Dialectic of Enlightenment* (New York: Herber and Herber, 1972), p. 13.

contradictions and conflicts, disrespect for the political and moral autonomy of nations'.[30]

Simultaneously, the defeat of Nazism by the *Albanian* Communists rather than the Soviets helped to solidify the connection between nationalism and Communism in Albania to an extent that was probably not reflected to the same extent in other Eastern European states.[31] As Fatos Tarifa explains,

> In Albania, which was liberated with no assistance from the Red Army, the Communists seized power without outside aid....[they also] constituted the only political force opposing the fascist occupation from the beginning of World War II until its end...the war-time Partizan *esprit de corps* and the tie of nationalism...were of great importance in establishing the legitimacy basis of.... [Enver] Hoxha's Communist rules and in determining [its] iconoclastic and independent path in the decades to come.[32]

The third reason that Communism became so strongly attached to nationalism was that, at least in the aftermath of the Second World War, communism was routinely seen as a more reliable route to economic development while the depression of the 1930s had demonstrated capitalism's weakness.[33] Again, the connection between communism and nationalism was particularly prominent in Albania as Tarifa explains,

> In Albania, the smallest and poorest communist country in Eastern Europe, the communists attained a stronger support among the predominantly agrarian population than any other country right from the start... the strikingly rapid economic growth experienced in the 1950s and 1960s, which contrasted with the extremely low initial level seemed enormous, as well as considerable achievements recorded in the fields of social equality, housing, employment, literacy, health care, education, and culture, impressed the population.[34]

30 Zija Xholi, *Mendimtare te Rilindjes Kombetare [Thinkers of National Renaissance]*, p. 77.

31 Robert Tucker, 'Communist Revolutions, National Cultures, and Divided Nations.' *Studies in Comparative Communism*, 7 (1974), pp. 235–245

32 Fatos Tarifa, 'The Quest for Legitimacy and the Withering Away of Utopia', *Social Forces*, 76, no. 2 (1997), p. 446.

33 Daniel Chirot, 'What Happened in Eastern Europe in 1989?', in Daniel Chirot (ed.), *The Crisis of Leninism and the Decline of the Left: Revolutions of 1989* (Washington: University of Washington Press, 1991), pp. 9–10.

34 Tarifa, 'The Quest for Legitimacy and the Withering Away of Utopia', p. 455.

Finally, the attachment of communism and nationalism was further enhanced by the cultural support provided to Communism from a range of progressive and respected Western intellectuals. As Walter Lacquer argues, the support of writers like Henri Barbuse, George Bernard Shaw, Theodore Dreiser, Thomas Mann and even Albert Einstein helped to support the idea that Communist Eastern Europe and the USSR were the true descendants of European Enlightenment values.[35]

This is not to suggest that the Albanian elite disclaimed its ethno-cultural connections to a European past. For example, intellectual Ismail Kadare maintained the connection of the Albanian culture to its Illyrian roots even in work written during the communist period.[36] However, modern Europe was no longer seen as a contemporary projection of the ideals that European civilisation had long been seen to represent. As a result, during the communist period the argument was made that the roots of Albanianness were those of the 'ancient Europeans' a characterisation that obviously allowed them to be separated from the corrupt values of Western Europe of that time.

Equally, in terms of language, the communist regime sought to put more stress on the authenticity of the Albanian language as an expression of reconfigured communist national identity rather than as a connection to modern Europe.[37] In this context the longevity of the language, in the face of a European and Ottoman onslaught became a useful device for expressing Albania's historical independence.

The particular nature of Albanian communism and its isolationist approach to international politics further solidified the connection between communist and nationalist rhetoric. For the other Communist states in Eastern Europe there was always a tension between nationalism and Communism. Eastern European nationalists always saw that

35 Walter Lacquer, *The Dream That Failed: Reflections on the Soviet Union.* (Oxford: Oxford University Press, 1994).

36 Galia Valtchinova, 'Ismail Kadare's The H-File and the Making of the Homeric Verse', in Stephanie Schwander-Sievers, and Bernd Fischer (eds.), *Albanian Identities: Myth and History* (London: C. Hurst & Co. Publishers Ltd. 2002), p. 111.

37 Zija Xholi, *Mendimtare te Rilindjes Kombetare [Thinkers of National Renaissance]*, p. 143.

Soviet commitment to national autonomy was thin. While the Soviet Communist party never officially overturned its commitment to the autonomy of the nations that fell under its rule, it was always clear to nationalists that the ultimate goal of Soviet socialism was the dissolution of national divides.[38]

In contrast Albania's main communist ruler, Enver Hoxha employed a rhetoric that resonated with a strong nationalist discourse. Particularly after the beginning of Albanian isolationism from the Soviet Union in 1960 and its complete isolation that came from separation with China in 1978, he routinely attacked the idea that Albania was a simple member of the communist family. He once declared that the 'Titoites, the Soviet revisionists and those of the countries of Eastern Europe and Mao-Tse-Tung's China had ulterior, hostile, enslaving aims. We tore the mask from them and told them bluntly that Albania was not for sale for a handful of rags, or a few roubles, dinars or yuan'.[39]

Of course, this rhetoric served a particular purpose but highlighting the instrumental use to which it has been put does not undermine the discursive element of the explanation. Hoxha, like all political entrepreneurs, was limited in what he was able to justify by the rhetorical material available to him.

In general terms therefore it is possible to see that while the separation of Albanian nationalism from conceptions of modern Europe emerged for historically particular reasons they were also supported by changes and conflicts in the discourse concerning modernism. Prior to 1918, European liberal capitalism had been seen as the only successful expression of enlightened and humanistic development. After that date, and particularly following the disaster of fascism in Western Europe, this association became tainted and leaders like Hoxha were able to mobilise this conflict for their own ends.

38 Walter Kemp, *Nationalism and Communism in Eastern Europe and the Soviet Union: A Basic Contradiction?* (New York: St Martin's Press, 1999).

39 Enver Hoxha's speech quoted in Miranda Vickers, *The Albanians: A Modern History* (London: I.B. Tauris Publishers, 1999), p. 20.

Conclusion

In discussing the role of Europe in Albania's nationalist discourse we sought to make two points. First, we argued that a rationalist/discursive theoretical division continues to be useful. If identities and political spaces are constructed, there is still scope for disagreement over the extent to which a particular identity requires a specific action. Where a discursive space constrains actions within narrow parameters then rationalist argument seems largely inappropriate because the rational choices available to anyone so constrained are already extremely limited. However, where discourses are open to wide ranging interpretations, then there is considerable space for elite and materially driven discursive manipulation.

Second, we sought to highlight the inadequacies of both sides for explaining the relationship between Albanian identity and its conception of Europe. The second section therefore criticised the rationalist argument. The unanimity of support for EU membership and the desire to justify that membership in historical terms could not be explained by simple cost/benefit calculations.

In the final section of the chapter, the intention was to demonstrate the multiple and conflicting strands of the discourses concerning Europe to highlight where there may be space for political appropriation now and in the future.

It is possible to draw some tentative conclusions from this analysis. Most importantly, it seems as though contrary to much contemporary discourse, the connection between Albanian nationalism and Europeanness does not necessarily suggest that Albanian nationalism will remain unanimously European in the future. As our historical overview has shown, European aspirations have rarely been aligned in any simple sense. Even when there was no alternative model for economic and political development, Europe was seen as a potential threat to Albanian independence. It seems fairly obviously that any Albanian nationalist is likely to be ambivalent about joining a more powerful political institution. Therefore, it is possible that this historical ambivalence vis-à-vis European power and reliability could become a rhetorical resource for anti-Europeans in the future. If Europe falters, becomes insular and fails to deal with its own economic and military developmental difficulties then it may not be seen as an aspirational model and attachment to it may wane.

Bibliography

Adorno, Theodor and Max Horkheimer, *Dialectic of Enlightenment* (New York: Herber and Herber, 1972).

Anderson, Benedict, *Imagined Communities: Reflections on the Origin and the Spread of Nationalism* (London: Verso, 1991).

Anderson, Christopher, 'When in Doubt, Use Proxies: Attitudes toward Domestic Politics and Support for Integration', *Comparative Political Studies*, vol. 31, no. 5 (1998), pp. 569–601.

Balibar, Etienne, 'The Nation Form: History and Ideology', in Geoff Eley and Ronald Suny (eds.), *Becoming National: A Reader* (Oxford: Oxford University Press, 1996).

Campbell, David, *National Deconstruction: Violence, Identity and Justice in Bosnia* (Minneapolis: University of Minnesota Press, 1998).

Carey, Sean 'Undivided Loyalties: Is National Identity an Obstacle to European Integration?' *European Union Politics*, 3, no. 4 (2002), pp. 387–413.

Cederman, Lars-Erik, 'Nationalism and Bounded Integration: What It Would Take to Construct a European Demos', *European Journal of International Relations*, 7, no. 2 (2001), pp. 139–174.

Checkel, Jeffrey, 'Norms, Institutions and National Identity in Contemporary Europe', *International Studies Quarterly*, 43, no. 1 (1999), pp. 83–114.

Chirot, Daniel, 'What Happened in Eastern Europe in 1989?', in Daniel Chirot (ed.), *The Crisis of Leninism and the Decline of the Left: Revolutions of 1989* (Washington: University of Washington Press, 1991).

Deflem, Mathieu, 'The Myth of Postnational Identity', *Social Forces*, 75, no. 1 (1996), pp. 119–143.

Delanty, Gerard, 'The Making of a Post Western Europe: A Civilizational Analysis', *Thesis Eleven*, 72 (2003), pp. 8–25.

—— 'The Limits and Possibilities of a European Identity: A Critique of Cultural Essentialism', *Philosophy and Social Criticism*, 21 (1995), pp. 15–36.

Destani, Bejtullah (ed.), *Faik Konitza: Selected Correspondence* (London: The Centre for Albanian Studies, 2000).

Diez, Thomas, 'Europe's Other and the Return of Geopolitics', *Cambridge Review of International Affairs*, 17, no. 2 (2004), pp. 319–335.

Eley, Goeff and Suny, Ronald, 'Introduction: From the Moment of Social History to the Work of Cultural Representation', in Geoff Eley and Ronald Suny (eds.), *Becoming National: A Reader* (Oxford: Oxford University Press, 1996).

Katzenstein, Peter (ed.), *The Culture of National Security* (New York: Columbia University Press, 1996).

Kemp, Walter, *Nationalism and Communism in Eastern Europe and the Soviet Union: A Basic Contradiction?* (New York: St Martin's Press, 1999).

Lacquer, Walter, *The Dream That Failed: Reflections on the Soviet Union.* (Oxford: Oxford University Press, 1994).

Levinger, Matthew, and Lytle, Paula, 'Myth and of Mobilisation: the Triadic Structure of Nationalist Rhetoric', *Nation and Nationalism*, 7, no. 2 (2001), pp. 175–194.

Little, Richard and Smith, Steve (eds.), *Belief Systems and International Relations* (Oxford: Blackwell, 1988).

Malcom, Noel, 'Myths of Albanian National Identity', in Stephanie Schwander-Sievers and Bernd Fischer (eds.), *Albanian Identities: Myth and History* (London: C. Hurst & Co. Ltd., 2002).

Meta, Ilir, 'Fjala e Z.Ilir Meta ne diten e shpalljes se Levizjes Socialiste per Integrim [Speech of Mr. Ilir Meta in the Day of Declaration of the Socialist Movement for Integration], *Ilir Meta Online*(6 September 2004), at: http://www.ilirmeta.com/index.php?page=news&news =185

Misha, Pirro, 'Invention of a Nationalism: Myth and Amnesia', in Stephanie Schwander-Sievers and Bernd Fischer (eds.), *Albanian Identities: Myth and History* (London: C. Hurst & Co. Ltd., 2002).

Nano, Mustafa. 'Shqiptaret Bejne Sehir Europen [Albanians Idly Look at Europe]', in *Shekulli* (2 May 2004), at: http://www. shekulli. com.al/index.php?page=shownews&newsID=38258%20class=

Official Website of the Albanian President, 'President Moisiu's Speech in the Session Entitled "European Enlargement: The Dimensions and Architecture of This Enlargement'" (25 June 2004), at: http://www.president.al/shqip/info.asp?id=1216

Qosja, Rexhep, 'Shqiptaret kunder vetvetes [Albanians against Themselves]' (8 October 2003), at: http://www.lajmet.com/Analiza/Rexhep_Qosja-8–Tetor-03.html

Rakipi, Albert, Bumci, Aldo (eds.) *Albania and the European Union: Perceptions and Realities* (Tirana Albanian Institute for International Studies, 2003).

Rumelili, Bahar 'Constructing Identity and Relating to Difference: Understanding the EU's Mode of Differentiation.' *Review of International Studies*, 30, no. 1 (2004), pp. 27–47.

Snyder, Jack, *Myths of Empire: Domestic Politics and International Ambition* (London: Cornell University Press, 1991).

Tarifa, Fatos, 'The Quest for Legitimacy and the Withering Away of Utopia', *Social Forces*, 76, no. 2 (1997), pp. 437–473.

The Republic of Albania, Council of Ministers. 'Platforma e Strategjise per Integrimin Europian dhe Euroatlantik te Republikes se Shqiperise [The Platform of Strategy for European and Euroatlantic Integration of the Republic of Albania]' (December 1998), at: http://www.mfa.gov.al/shqip/strategjiaintegrimit.asp

Tomes, Jason. 'The Throne of Zog (Albania's King Zog)' in *History Today* (September 2001), at: http://www.findarticles.com.cf_O/PI/search.jhtml?key="Jason Tomes"

Tucker, Robert, 'Communist Revolutions, National Cultures, and Divided Nations.' *Studies in Comparative Communism*, 7 (1974), pp. 235–245.

Valtchinova, Galia, 'Ismail Kadare's The H-File and the Making of the Homeric Verse', in Stephanie Schwander-Sievers and Bernd

Fischer (eds.), *Albanian Identities: Myth and History* (London: C. Hurst & Co. Ltd., 2002).
Vickers, Miranda, *The Albanians: A Modern History* (London: I.B. Tauris Publishers, 1999).
Wendt, Alexander, 'Anarchy is What States Make of it: The Social Construction of Power Politics', *International Organization*, 46, no. 2 (1992), pp. 391–425.
Wendt, Alexander, *Social Theory of International Politics* (Cambridge: Cambridge University Press, 1999).
Xholi, Zija, *Mendimtare te Rilindjes Kombetare [Thinkers of National Renaissance]* (Tirane: 'Mihal Duri' Publishing House, 1987).

DONNACHA Ó BEACHÁIN

Transformation of Social Status: Ethnic Russians in Post-Soviet Kazakhstan[1]

The Nationalizing State

Since the collapse of communism in Eastern Europe and the Soviet Union, considerable academic interest has focused on how transitional elites have sought to legitimize their authority and establish durable nation-states from the debris of the Soviet empire. Brubaker has provided an influential definition of a nationalizing state by describing them as 'ethnically heterogeneous yet conceived as nation-states, whose dominant elite's promote (to varying degrees) the language, culture, demographic position, economic flourishing, and political hegemony of the nominally state-bearing nation'.[2] This certainly captures the reality in much of the former Soviet Union. Scholars such as

1 This article draws on arguments and information presented in shorter and different formats at two conferences. The first paper – 'The Politics of Language in Post-Soviet Kazakhstan' was delivered at the second international conference of the Eurasian Political Science Network entitled 'Political Science and State Authorities Interaction in the Formation of the Political Processes in the Russian Federation and the Newly Independent States', which took place at the Institute of Philosophy and Law, Yekaterinburg, Russian Federation from 6–8 February 2004. The second paper – 'The Kazakh Language and Slavic Migration' – was delivered at the CEP/SCOUT sponsored conference 'Language and Migration in a Changing World', which took place from 19–22 May 2004 at the Buryat State University, Ulan Ude, Republic of Buryatia, Russian Federation. I am grateful for the feedback from the audience and panelists, and to the conference organizers, Vitaly Merkushev in Yekaterinburg and Vsevolod Bashkuev in Ulan Ude.

2 Rogers Brubaker, 'National Minorities, Nationalizing States, and External Homelands in the New Europe', *Daedalus*, 124, no. 2 (1995), p. 109.

Taras Kuzio have rightly pointed out that this phenomenon is not much different in substance from the nation-building efforts in western Europe that saw official national cultures and languages like French, English and Spanish weaken or obliterate those of groups like the Manx, Bretons, Cornish, Basques and Scots.[3] What is being witnessed in much of the former Soviet Union from Tallinn to Tashkent is a form of remedial nation-building which seeks to belatedly catch-up with processes long experienced in the consolidated democracies of the western world.

In this essay, we examine Kazakhstan as an example of the post-soviet nationalizing state. Whereas the predicament may not be as dramatic as that which prompted Massimo d'Azeglio to proclaim in the 19th century that 'we have created Italy, now we have to make Italians', it is not substantially different either.[4] The collapse of the Soviet Union facilitated the emergence of the independent state of Kazakhstan but many doubted whether the 130 nationalities who resided there could be moulded into a political community of 'Kazakhstanis'.

It is not surprising that language has emerged as a key aspect of this nationalizing process among the newly independent states as it has been argued that languages are like animals in that they need and defend their territories.[5] As a rule, language revival will contain elements of restoration (backward looking) and/or transformation (forward

3 Taras Kuzio, 'Nationalizing States' or Nation-building? A Critical Review of the Theoretical Literature and Empirical Evidence', *Nations and Nationalism*, 7, no. 2 (2001), pp. 135–154.

4 After quoting d'Azgelio, Alter comments that the former Piedmont Prime Minister was 'acutely aware that political unification in the national state did not guarantee the existence of a nation', in Peter Alter, *Nationalism* (London: E. Arnold, 1989), p. 23. A more recent example is provided by South African government minister Dr. Essop Pahad who told the National Assembly on 11 May 2001 that 'now that we have a democratic South African state, we must all become South Africans, proud citizens of a South Africa which revels in its multiplicity of identities and yet seeks to connect with its African core and destiny'. Government Communication and Information System, at: http://www.gcis.gov.za/media/minister/010511.htm [accessed 10 October 2005].

5 Jean Laponce, *Languages and Their Territories* (Toronto: University of Toronto Press, 1987); Jean Laponce 'Do languages behave like animals', *International Journal of the Sociology of Languages*, 103 (1993), pp. 19–30.

looking).[6] A national language does not necessarily mean one spoken by everyone in a nation or state or even a majority of the population (though this is often assumed). Rather, it is the language given special status by the state. Minority languages are described thus not because of their numerical inferiority but because of their non-national, non-official status. Kazakhstan, therefore, provides an interesting case study as we must consider Russian as a minority language though it spoken by more citizens than the national language, Kazakh. That said, it is not the most daunting task every faced by state language planners. In Western Europe, Ireland provides a solitary and perhaps uninspiring example of a state where the government has attempted to legislatively revive a national language after centuries of colonial attrition, at the expense of an international language (English) spoken by the vast majority of Irish citizens on a daily basis.[7] A more extreme example can be found in the Philippines where the 1976 and 1987 Constitutions legally established a national language which does not actually exist (Pilipino) but is one that the government is eager to manufacture and sell to a culturally insecure population.[8] Despite the occasional absurdities, few scholars doubt that the state and its dominant political class play a crucial role in determining which languages will flourish or wilt by providing a supportive linguistic ecology.[9] Most states – including civic ones – have an ethno-cultural core and

6 Abdelâli Bentahila and Eirlys Davies, 'Language Revival: Restoration or Transformation', *Journal of Multilingual and Multicultural Development*, 14 (1993), pp. 355–374. See also R.G. Crocombe, *The South Pacific: An Introduction* (Christchurch: Institute of Pacific Studies, 1989), p. 47 who estimates that of 1200 languages of the Pacific region, no more than about 12 will survive.

7 Donnacha Ó Beacháin, 'The Problems of Language Revival in Ireland and Kazakhstan', in *Kazakhstan in the Age of Globalization* (Almaty: Academy of Labour and Social Relations, Vol. 1, 2004), pp. 37–47.

8 Robert Kaplan and Richard Baldauf Jr., *Language Planning From Practice to Theory* (Clevedon: Multilingual Matters, 1997), pp. 15–16.

9 Mühlhäusler suggests that unless the necessary linguistic ecology to support endangered languages is put in place, about 90% of the world's languages will have disappeared within a few generations. Peter Mühlhäusler, 'The Ecology of small languages' in R. Baldauf (ed.), *Backing Australian Languages* (Canberra: National Languages and Literacy Institute of Australia, 1995), pp. 1–14.

Kazakhstan is unlikely to be an exception. Despite the honeyed words of political leaders, plans for language transformation in Kazakhstan and other post-Soviet states are not without profound implications in all spheres of life for

> while language planning sets out to study and control various sociological factors which influence language change, its very character as a form of 'interest-bound' modern social planning has led, in many cases, to a failure to tackle the hidden agendas – political, social, educational and otherwise – of particular forms of government, economic relations, politics and social organization ... That is, as a discourse of government policy, language planning has tended to avoid directly addressing larger social and political matters within which language change, use and development, and indeed language planning itself, are embedded.[10]

In this article, I will explore the hidden agendas behind the policy of 'Kazakhization' and concentrate on one of the 'larger social and political matters' in particular; the flight of ethnic Russians (along with smaller but significant numbers of Germans and Ukrainians) from Kazakhstan since 1991.

The Diminishing Russian Community

The process of Slavic settlement in Kazakhstan was dramatic. The first census held in the Russian Empire in 1897 revealed that the population of Kazakhstan was 4.16 million, of whom 454,402 were Russian (10.9%) and 79,573 were Ukrainian (1.9%). Tsarist Russia's rapid settlement policy overseen by Stolypin between 1911 and 1913 saw the Slavic population rise to 1.5 million or 30% of the population. The first Soviet census of 1926 indicated that there were 1,279,979

10 Allen Luke et al, 'On the Limits of Language Planning: Class, State and Power', in Richard Baldauf and Allen Luke (eds.), *Language Planning and Education in Australasia and the South Pacific* (Clevedon: Multilingual Matters, 1990), p. 27.

Russians and 860,822 Ukrainians (19.68% and 13.23% respectively).[11] The relative growth in strength of Russians during the 1930s can be explained by the brutal impact of the Soviet policy of imposed collectivization. In 1928, only two per cent of Kazakh households were collectivized; by April 1930 this figure had risen to 50.5% and the process was completed by the end of 1933. The Stalinist purges of the late 1930s also took their toll so that during the 1930s, almost two million Kazakhs are estimated to have died through starvation, disease, and executions while it is thought that over a million fled to neighbouring countries.[12] Indeed, so damning were the results of the 1937 census which showed a 41% decline in the Kazakh population that Stalin suppressed the census and it was not made public until the late 1980s.[13]

The ramifications of this assault on the Kazakh population could be felt decades later. In 1959, for example the Kazakh population was still 900,000 less than it had been in 1926.[14] During the 1940s, Kazakhstan was a dumping ground for deported populations, particularly from Russia and Ukraine, and in all 800,000 of these 'special settlers' (*spezposelentzy*) were sent by Stalin to the region, many of whom remained after his death in 1953 and the end of the policy of involuntary resettlement of ethnic groups. In addition, during World War II, huge numbers of factories and personnel were moved to Central Asia to be saved from the advancing Germans (90 factories and 1 million people were moved to Uzbekistan alone) and, again, many of these

11 Peter Sinnot, 'Population Politics in Kazakhstan', *Journal of International Affairs*, 56, no. 2 (Spring 2003), pp. 105–108.

12 The number that died and fled can never be established with exactitude and this is reflected in the diverse statistics in relevant academic works. The highest estimate is that 3.3 million Kazakhs died and 1.2 million were driven into exile by famine during the early 1930s. Martha Olcott, 'Ceremony and Substance: 'The Illusion of Unity in Central Asia', in Michael Mandelbaum (ed.), *Central Asia and the World: Kazakhstan, Uzbekistan, Tajikistan, Kyrgyzstan and Turkmenistan* (New York: Council of Foreign Relations Press, 1994), p. 19.

13 Robert Conquest, 'Academe and the Soviet Myth', in John Moore (ed.), *Legacies of the Collapse of Marxism* (Fairfax: George Mason University Press, 1994), p. 235.

14 Shirin Akiner, *The Formation of Kazakh Identity: From Tribe to Nation State* (London: The Royal Institute for International Affairs, 1995), p. 45.

settlers remained after the circumstances which occasioned their arrival in Central Asia had ended.[15]

The next and final major influx of Slavs to Kazakhstan coincided with Nikita Khrushchev's major plan to dramatically increase the area of land in Kazakhstan under cultivation. This policy of reclamation of the 'Virgin Lands' brought a new wave of Russians to northern Kazakhstan so that the area under cultivation increased by 250% to 20.6 million hectares between 1954 and 1955. The impact of the Virgin Lands policy was immediately felt, and the results of the 1959 census made clear that, for the first time, Slavs now constituted the majority of the population of Kazakhstan (50.86%). From that date, however, the percentage of Slavs slowly declined despite increasing in absolute terms. Results from the 1970, 1979, and 1989 censuses charted the decline, which can be attributed to a rise in the Kazakh birth rate combined with a corresponding decline in the size of Russian families. The last Soviet census of 1989 estimated the Slav percentage of the population at 44%, a figure which included 6,227,549 Russians (37.8% of total population).[16]

The industrialization of Kazakhstan was Russian led. Slavs from throughout the Soviet empire descended on Kazakhstan, bringing the necessary skills and occupying the areas where the resources existed for industrial production of raw materials. As a result, urbanization tended to be concentrated in the north of Kazakhstan. As late as 1979, only 20.8% of the urban population was Kazakh while 21% of the industrial workforce was composed of the titular nationality.[17]

Between 1993 and 1999, 1,123,960 Slavs left Kazakhstan (almost 300,000 in 1994 alone) and they were followed by almost half a million ethnic Germans. In the decade that followed the last Soviet census of 1989, the Russian population fell from 37.8% to just 29.96% while the European population (Russian, Ukrainian, German, Polish,

15 Valery Tishkov, *Ethnicity, Nationalism and Conflict in and after the Soviet Union: The Mind Aflame* (London: Sage, 1997), p. 116.

16 See Bhavna Dave, 'Minorities and Participation in Public Life: Kazakhstan', Working Paper, Commission on Human Rights, Sub-Commission on Promotion of Human Rights, United Nations (5 May 2003), pp. 2–4.

17 Anatoly Khazanov, 'The Ethnic Problems of Kazakhstan', *Central Asian Survey*, 14, no. 2 (1995), p. 242.

Belarusian, and Greek) declined from 49.8% to 39%. During the same period, the number of ethnic Kazakhs grew by 1.5 million pushing their numbers above the critical 50% mark (rocketing from 39.7% to 53.4%). Kazakhs who had been forced to leave during the Stalin years were encouraged to return home, an offer that one hundred thousand have thus far accepted.[18]

There are a number of factors which can explain the decline. Firstly, Russians have smaller families than Kazakhs. Moreover, in 1995, the Total Abortion Rate (TAR), for Russians was 2.74 whereas it was only 1.11 for Kazakhs. By 1999, this figure had been reduced to 1.75 and 1.06 respectively.[19] Many left for Russia hoping that it would develop as a more prosperous state. The mass migration of Russians can also be attributed to the policy of Kazakhization which has elevated Kazakhs at their expense, largely through the promotion of the Kazakh language. It is to this factor that we will now focus our attention.

State Policy of 'Kazakhization'

The over-representation of Kazakhs in public life has its roots in the *korenizatsiia* (indigenization) policies[20] of the Soviet regime of the 1930s, and was particularly evident during the years of First Secretary Kunauv in the 1970s and 1980s. When, in 1986, Gorbachev sought to

18 See Sinnott, pp. 103–125.

19 Charles Westoff, 'The Substitution of Contraception for Abortion in Kazakhstan' from Population Resource Center, Washington D.C. and Princeton, N.J. at: http://www.prcdc.org/summaries/newabortion/newabortion.html [accessed 10 October 2005].

20 See Terry Martin, *The Affirmative Action Empire: Ethnicity and the Soviet State, 1923–1939* (Ithaca: Cornell University Press, 2001); Terry Martin 'An Affirmative Action Empire: The Soviet Union as the Highest Form of Imperialism', in Ronald Suny and Terry Martin (eds), *A State of Nations: Empire and Nation-Making in the Age of Lenin and Stalin* (Oxford: Oxford University Press, 2001), pp. 67–90.

undermine endemic corruption in Kazakhstan and appointed a Russian as the First Secretary of the Communist Party of Kazakhstan for that purpose, the result was the first serious ethnic challenge to Gorbachev's rule.[21] Ten thousand riot-police had to be mobilized to quell angry rioters in Almaty with the result that at least three people died and many more were injured.[22]

In Soviet times, however, over-representation at the level of the Soviet Socialist Republics was of limited significance for, as Stalin noted, there was no contradiction between Soviet federalism and a unified political and economic system as it did not entail the devolution of substantial powers.[23] The process of over-representation has accelerated since independence, but now the Kazakhstani state does enjoy real power. One semi-official Kazakhstani report conducted within three years of independence found that Slavs, who then constituted 43% of the population, made up only 22.9% of officials in the first and second echelon executives in the Cabinet of Ministers and presidential apparatus. Other minorities, who made up 12.1% of the population and of whom Germans were the most significant group, had 3.1% of positions. The remaining three quarters of posts were filled by Kazakhs, though they were significantly smaller in number than the aforementioned ethnic groups combined.[24] When elections to

21 Gorbachev's appointee, Gennadi Kolbin, was not an ethnic Russian from Kazakhstan but was born in the Russian Federation and would thus have been considered a total outsider. While Gorbachev saw this as a virtue in fighting corruption, it was viewed in Kazakhstan as a repudiation of the political machine dominated by ethnic Kazakh Dinmukhamed Kunaev who had been First Secretary for over a quarter of a century. See Martha Olcott, *The Kazakhs* (Second Edition, Stanford: Hoover Institution Press, Stanford University, 1995), pp. 249–253.

22 The event to this day is shrouded in mystery and estimates of the number of the dead range from three (official) to two hundred (unofficial).

23 Martin, 'An Affirmative Action Empire', p. 75.

24 Figures quoted in Pål Kolstø and Irina Malkova, 'Is Kazakhstan being Kazakified', *Analysis of Current Affairs*, 9, no. 11 (November 1997), p. 1. Similar figures are provided by Ronald Suny who writes that by 1994, 74% of top administrative positions were occupied by Kazakhs. Ronald Suny 'Southern Tears: Dangerous Opportunities in the Caucasus and Central Asia', in Rajan

the new bi-cameral parliament were held in December 1995, Kazakhs outnumbered Russians by more than two to one in both chambers.[25] This pattern has been repeated in subsequent elections, most recently in the parliamentary elections of September/October 2004 when ethnic Kazakhs constituted almost 80% of candidates and elected members of parliament.[26]

For some Kazakhs involved in the debate, the figures indicating large-scale emigration of Russians and other Europeans, modest immigration of ethnic Kazakhs from abroad (particularly China and Mongolia), and the higher birth rate of Kazakhs, can be combined to justify Kazakh over-representation in state institutions. Azimbai Galiev has claimed that

> while the major ethnic groups have different degrees of representation in the examined structures, the differences are not so large that they give cause for concern. The dynamics of ethnic representation, in our view, *go in the same direction* as the ethno-demographic development in the country.[27]

It is not as simple as that, of course. One would expect a considerable time lag, possibly a generation, before representation in administration would catch up with changes in the demographic composition of society. What we have here is the explanation of existing imbalances not on the basis of the actual numbers of Russians, but on their anticipated number in the years to come.

Menon, Yuri Fedorov and Ghia Nodia, *Russia, the Caucasus and Central Asia* (Armonk: M.E. Sharpe, 1999), p. 169.

25 Twenty six Kazakhs and twelve Russians were elected or appointed to the upper house while in the Lower House, there were 42 Kazakhs, 19 Russians, and 5 members of other nationalities.

26 There are sixty Kazakhs in the new parliament (78%), fifteen Russians (19.5%) and one Tatar. One deputy did not reveal his ethnicity. Russians obtained a majority in only one of the fourteen regions of Kazakhstan. Based on information made available by the Central Election Committee of Kazakhstan. See Donnacha Ó Beacháin, 'Parliamentary Elections in Kazakhstan', *Electoral Studies*, 24. no. 4 (December 2005), pp. 762–770.

27 Quoted in Pål Kolstø: 'Anticipating Demographic Superiority: Kazakh Thinking on Integration and Nation Building', *Europe-Asia Studies*, 50, no. 1 (January 1998), pp. 51–69.

A variation of this rationalization is to be found in the writings of Kazakh essayist and senior member of President Nazarbaev's analytical centre, M. Tatimov. Using the criterion of demographic development, Tatimov has divided the world into 'old' and 'young' nations.[28] If the demographic pyramid is weighted in favour of the older age cohorts, then it can be considered to be an 'old' nation, while 'young nations' are dominated numerically by the youth. In this typology, Germans, Italians, and Spanish are 'old' nations.[29] Where two 'old' nations predominate on a given territory, they tend, according to Tatimov, to engage in a cold war for control, as is the case in Ukraine, Latvia or Estonia. No such icy relations leading to a frozen conflict are anticipated in Kazakhstan however as, quite simply, the Russians are 'old' and the Kazakhs are 'young'. All that needs be done is to sit back and let mother nature do the rest. In this battle of the bedrooms, the younger and more virile Kazakh nation will emerge victorious.

As the Slavs of Kazakhstan are in the main located in the provinces adjacent or close to Russia, the Kazakh administration feared that their geographical proximity to the 'motherland' could spur separatist sentiments. Moreover, the Kazak border with Russia is 6846 km long – quite impossible to patrol effectively. Fearing possible separatism, the Kazakh government has sought to eliminate all manifestations of Russian control at a local level. In 1997, a major territorial-administrative reform was implemented. Only areas where Slavs were concentrated were affected by the changes and thus the intention was clear. Areas which had Russian majorities were added to areas with large concentrations of Kazakhs so as to blunt the potential influence of the Russian population. Moreover, *oblast* centres in Northern Kazakhstan were only transferred to cities where ethnic Russians predominated. With the bulk of administrative positions (80% and rising) being filled by Kazakhs, the decision was made with a view to attracting Kazakhs to the predominately Russian oblasts and

28 Ibid.

29 Donald Rumsfeld introduced a similar notion when he spoke deridingly of 'old Europe' which, crippled by infirmity it seems, was unwilling to participate in the youthful exigencies of war. The 'youthful' United States had no such qualms, it was implied.

thus altering the ethno-demographic situation. The results of the 1999 census indicate that this policy has been successful. Compared to the last Soviet census conducted in 1989, the Akmola *oblast* saw the share of Kazakhs rise from 22.4% to 37.5%. Figures for the other regions are Eastern Kazakhstan *oblast* 48.5% (27.2%); Karaganda *oblast*, 27.5% (17.1%); Kostanai *oblast*, 30.9% (22.8%); and Northern Kazakhstan *oblast*, 29.6% (18.6%).

The most visible result of this policy of re-colonization has been the moving of the state capital from Almaty to Astana in 1997, and the jury is still out on whether this will be viewed as an act of Presidential vision or folly. The decision to move from Almaty with its mild climate and picturesque setting to the new conglomeration of Astana in the barren and inhospitable steppes was something of a mystery. Reminiscent of the Soviet days when populations were unceremoniously uprooted and moved depending on the whims of the communist leadership, the trek to the new capital has proved very unpopular with those officials and functionaries who are compelled to make it.[30] The official explanation for the move – which is estimated to have cost $1.5 billion in construction costs alone – is that Almaty lies in an earthquake zone and that placing the capital in the north would assist in the development of new jobs and opportunities in a hitherto neglected region.[31]

While not common, capital relocations are not as infrequent as sometimes thought: there have been a dozen such changes since Brasilia replaced Rio de Janeiro as Brazil's capital in 1956, the most recent being the move in 2000 of Malaysia's capital from Kuala Lumpur to Putrajaya. Sometimes they seek to signify the beginning of a new era or a return to a former one (both objectives played a part in the move of Germany's capital to Berlin in 1990). In his study of the political geography of capital relocation, Edward Schatz suggested that the moving of a capital occurs usually in authoritarian and post-

30 See 'Kazakhstan's Unpopular New Capital', *The Economist*, 26 July 1997, pp. 35–36.

31 In this, the rationale is similar to the placing of the Brazilian capital in Brasilia and the Nigerian capital in Abuja.

colonial contexts.[32] Rational-technical reasons (administrative efficiency, economic growth etc.) are often offered to explain the relocation but these are often for public consumption, particularly international opinion, but obscure the real motivations. In Malawi and the Ivory Coast, for example, capitals were moved closer to the centre of the President's ethnic power base so as to consolidate their rule. In Botswana, conversely, the relocation was motivated by a desire to bring the locus of power to potential opponents of the new state. Similarly, it is plausible to argue Astana's eclipse of Almaty stemmed from the intention to place a Kazakh Trojan horse within the Russian citadel.[33] Government personnel, mainly Kazakh, would be moved into the region and would hopefully help reverse the demographic balance. By moving the capital to northern Kazakhstan Nazarbaev may have hoped to exert tighter control over an alternative power base and to quell suggestions that the region might be transferred to Russia due to the overwhelmingly Slav composition of the population.

The Politics of Language

During Soviet times, Russian was the language of government and prestige. To advance up the social ladder education through the medium of Russian, provided in a plethora of Russian schools, was imperative. In the new political landscape, it is the Kazakh educated pupils who welcome the strict application of the new language policies as it opens up job opportunities previously the exclusive reserve of Russian speakers. Some government efforts appear to be aimed at promoting English as a second language at the expense of Russian. Visas in Uzbekistan and Kazakhstan are issued in the official language and

32 Edward Schatz, 'When Capital Cities Move: The Political Geography of Nation and State Building', Working Paper 303, Helen Kellogg Institute for International Studies, University of Notre Dame, February 2003.

33 Judith Matloff, 'Puzzle Over Capital Move in Central Asia', *Christian Science Monitor*, 91, no. 47 (2 March 1999), p. 7.

in English only. Official signs are often bi-lingual with Russian excluded.

Article 1 of the first constitution of Kazakhstan forbade discrimination against any citizen, a provision which was reaffirmed in the present constitution, Article 14 of which proclaims:

> Everyone is equal before the law. No one can be subjected to any discrimination for reasons of origins, social position, property status, sex, race, nationality, language, faith, political and religious convictions, place of residence or any other circumstances.

However, Article 114 of the first constitution and Article 41 of the second constitution make it compulsory that the President of the Republic be able to speak Kazakh.[34] This clearly interferes with the democratic process as it prohibits citizens who do not speak Kazakh offering themselves for elections to the highest office.

Subsequent laws have reinforced these constitutional provisions. One regulation, adopted in July 1997, declared that 'it is the duty of every citizen of the Republic of Kazakhstan to master the state language'.[35] Broadcasts on TV and radio channels in Kazakh must be equal to that of all other languages (though in practice, Russian is the only language concerned).[36] As is often the case, this measure has been taken neither with the consultation of the bodies involved (which have displayed a lack of interest in producing high quality productions in Kazakh) nor the financial resources necessary to make them a success. In 1998, It was decreed by the President that government paperwork be in Kazakh.[37] Originally, it was anticipated that this policy would be implemented immediately after the adoption of the

34 Article 90 of the Uzbek Constitution, Article 43 of the Kyrgyz Constitution, and Article 65 of the Tajik Constitution contain similar requirements for the office of the President. There is no such constitutional requirement for the Turkmen president though there has been intensive discrimination against Russian speakers in Turkmenistan.

35 Law on Languages in the Republic of Kazakhstan, Article 4.

36 Law of the Republic of Kazakhstan, July 11 1997, no. 151–1, On Languages in the Republic of Kazakhstan, Chapter III, Article 18.

37 Presidential Decree, Republic of Kazakhstan, 5 October 1998, no. 4106, On the State Programme for the Functioning and Development of Languages.

constitution but the lack of competent staff and adequate provisions for language instruction has meant that the deadline has been continually extended. However, the process has begun in earnest and appears irreversible. For some Russians, it is as if their language and culture have been given a sentence of death though a stay of execution is continually being afforded. Numerous Slavs, uncertain of when the day will finally arrive when Russian is no longer sufficient to work in many areas of life, have voted with their feet.

But while there has been a legal revolution, with a myriad of laws being promulgated and decreed, much less effort has been created to enable these laws to take effect. Often this leaves non-Kazakh speakers with the barriers that the legislation envisages but not the means to overcome them due to the dearth of trained teachers and adequate teaching materials. Russian is the language spoken by the greatest number of people living in Kazakhstan. Almost all Russians do not speak Kazakh whereas the vast majority of Kazakhs speak Russian and many ethnic Kazakhs (approximately one third) do not speak Kazakh. In the last census, conducted in 1999, 99.4% of Kazakhs claimed that Kazakh was their native language.[38] This figure is inflated, more a demonstration of patriotic fervour than an accurate reflection of linguistic competence.

Moreover, there is little evidence that language habits are changing. A survey conducted in 1996 found that 42.5% of adult Kazakhs had received their education in Russian and the remainder in Kazakh. As for their children, 40.1% were being educated in Russian while 66.4% were being educated in Kazakh, indicating that the attractions of Russian remain strong though knowledge of Kazakh will increase over time. It also suggests that there will continue to be many Russophone Kazaks. Less success is evident among Russians and other minorities. Ninety nine per cent of Russians had been educated through the medium of their mother tongue while 98.2% of their children were being educated likewise. Among other minorities, the figures indicate a rise in the number of people being educated through the medium of

38 Dave, 'Minorities', p. 5.

Russian (from 83.1% to 89.3%).[39] Therefore, there is little evidence that patterns of language use will be substantially altered during the next generation.

It should be borne in mind that while the Kazakhstani Government's language policies may seem authoritarian and discriminatory, they are no more than the reverse of the language policies imposed by the Soviet Union. Russians are not (as in the Baltic states) being told that they will lose citizenship should they decide not to become competent in Kazakh, merely that their chances of rising in certain areas of public life will be circumscribed. Kazakh will now be the language of political, administrative, and (to a lesser though still significant extent) social mobility.

Russian Interference

While the response of ethnic Russians in Kazakhstan to 'Kazakhization' has been relatively muted, political entrepreneurs in Russia have exploited their position for domestic electioneering. One of the most well-known and controversial advocates of 'Russian' Kazakhstan being incorporated into a greater Russia was Alexander Solzhenitsyn. In his 1990 work 'How Shall We Re-conquest Russia', he argued that Russia should free itself of 'expansionist great power thinking and imperial befuddlement', leave the dissident republics to go their own way, and concentrate on ruling the culturally Russian parts of the Soviet Union.

Though derided at the time by doctrinaire communists and nationalists for advocating a 'small Russia', it did not escape the notice of many that in his definition of what constituted 'Russian' territory,

39 Pål Kolstø and Irina Malkova, 'Is Kazakhstan being Kazakified', *Analysis of Current Affairs*, 9, no. 11 (November 1997), p. 3. The poll was conducted in September 1996 in ten oblasts with one thousand respondents.

Solzhenitsyn included Belarus, Ukraine, and Kazakhstan.[40] Despite the fact it was the Russian political elite, with Boris Yeltsin at the helm, who broke the link with the Russian communities throughout the Soviet Union by instigating the break-up of the Soviet Union, Solzhenitsyn's views have had considerable influence on Russian decision makers.[41] In November 1992, President Boris Yeltsin issued a decree 'On the Protection of the Rights and Interests of Russian Citizens outside the Russian Federation', an attempt to assert Russia's affinity with ethnic Russians in the 'near abroad' and to assume responsibility for their protection.

In the Russian Federation the best known advocate of the rights of the diaspora is undoubtedly Vladimir Zhirinovsky who hailed from Almaty, where he was born in 1946 and where he lived until exiting to Moscow to study at the Institute of Oriental Languages. A political chameleon, who has lost much of his credibility and charm since the heady days of the early 1990s, Zhirinovsky was a strong force in post-communist Russia and a serious contender for the Presidency. His support peaked at 23% of the Russian vote in 1993, the same year that almost 400,000 Russians left Kazakhstan. Zhirinovsky set himself up as the spokesman for the rights of Russians everywhere but more particularly, the twenty five million strong diaspora who found themselves on the wrong side of the border when the Soviet Union collapsed. His childhood, or that which he projected for public consumption, was a desolate tale of a Dickensian character, and found a receptive audience among many underprivileged Russians.

What made Zhirinovsky's rhetoric dangerous from the perspective of Kazakhstan is how he blamed his early misfortunes on the Kazakhs. His autobiography, *Last Thrust to the South* (which refers to his stated objective of re-creating a Russian empire with imperial borders that stretch to the Indian Ocean) is littered with tales of self pity,

40 Solzhenitsyn's brochure was published in *Komsolskaya Pravda* and *Literaturnaya Gazeta* in September 1990. See Francis Fukuyama, 'Varieties of Russian Nationalism', in Moore (ed.), *Legacies*, pp. 59–60.

41 See Eduard Ponarin, 'Alexander Solzhenitsyn as a Mirror of the Russian Counter-Revolution', PONARS Policy Memo 150 (St. Petersburg: European University at St. Petersburg, October 2000).

envy, and blame. His resentment of Kazakh preferential treatment was learnt on his mother's knee where he was told how Russians did all the work while Kazakhs reaped the material rewards. 'I would ask Mum, "Why do we have such bad housing conditions? Why can't we get an individual apartment" Mum replied: "We aren't Kazakhs ... Kazakhs get priority"'.[42] Combined with this resentment, was a distain for the Kazakh nation and their notions of independent statehood:

> I was born in Central Asia myself, you see. We regard it as Russia, not Central Asia. Initially, it was populated by Russians only, and Russians brought civilization there. The Kazakhs lived in nomad tents. They had no electricity, nothing, and all they had was cattle, sheep breeding. Like all primitive communal tribes. There was no state there.[43]

As parliamentary elections loomed in 1993, Zhirinovsky claimed that 'Kazakhstan is an artificial creation that can thrive only under Russian domination'[44] and a few months later he stated on Russia's World Service Radio that 'the frontiers of the Soviet Union as of 1975, recognized by the world community, will be restored and Russian flags will fly over cities in Kazakhstan'.[45]

The dangers were obvious. Russians were drained of their imperial pride, stripped of dignity, robbed by pirate capitalists, duped by political promises – all ingredients which led to imperial nostalgia and nationalist extremism. Comparisons with the rise of the Nazis in Germany are observable. Zhirinovsky's bitter reminiscences of life in Almaty are chillingly redolent of Hitler's autobiographical memoirs of his time as a struggling artist in Vienna. The exaggerated image of Russians in the 'Near Abroad' labouring under the yolk of pervasive discrimination and petty indignities mirrors Hitler's fixation with the

42 Quoted in Graham Frazer and George Lancelle, *Absolute Zhirinovsky: A Transparent View of the Distinguished Statesman* (London: Penguin, 1994), p. 23.

43 Quoted in David Remnick, *Resurrection: The Struggle for a New Russia* (New York: Vintage, 1998), pp. 97–98.

44 *Frankfurter Allgemeine*, 16 December 1993. Quoted in Frazer and Lancelle, *Zhirinovsky*, p. 23.

45 ITAR-TASS, World Service Radio, 2 April 1994. Quoted in Frazer and Lancelle, *Zhirinovsky*, p. 10.

fate of the *Auslandsdeutsche* in Czechoslovakia and Poland.[46] This sympathy is articulated in a readiness to unite all ethnic kin as one political unit so that there can be an *Anschluss* for Kazakhstan just as there was for Austria. The parallels were not lost on President Nazarbayev when it became clear that as Zhirinovsky's popularity rose, the Russian Government felt obliged to compete with his pan-Russian policies. When, on the eve of Russia's 1993 parliamentary election, the Russian Foreign Minister Kozyrev threatened that Moscow would take tough action if necessary to protect the rights of Russians in the former Soviet Republics, Nazarbayev reacted angrily, saying that 'when someone talks about the protection of Russians not in Russia but in Kazakhstan, I recall the times of Hitler, who started with protecting the Sudeten Germans'.[47]

Interest in the diaspora legitimated the instinctive desire of many in the Russian political elite to interfere in the affairs of the new post-Soviet Republics. Instead of stating explicitly that they viewed the new states as a natural sphere of influence, Russia could couch its interests in humanitarian terms. In this way, they portrayed their concerns as stemming from a desire to see civil-political rights observed rather than being the product of neo-imperial designs. These internal debates within the Russian political elite, while often politically expedient and rewarding, made little impact on the daily lives of Russians in Kazakhstan. Far from promoting the cause of Russians in Kazakhstan, Zhirinovsky and others did great harm. They did not afford Russians in Kazakhstan any tangible assistance that might ameliorate

46 It should be noted that Western democracies like France and Britain have also pursued disastrous policies motivated by concern for their settler populations. See Miles Kahler, 'Empires, Neo-Empires, and Political Change: The British and French Experience' in Karen Dawisha and Bruce Parrot, *The End of Empire?: The Transformation of the USSR in Comparative Perspective* (Armonk: M.E. Sharpe, 1997), pp. 286–312. See also Michael Fry, 'Decolonization: Britain, France and the Cold War' in the same volume pp. 121–154, particularly pp. 139–141.

47 Reuters, 24 November 1993 quoted in 'Chronology of Russians in Kazakhstan' at Minorities at Risk, University of Maryland Centre for International Development and Conflict Management, at: http://www.cidcm.umd.edu/inscr/mar/chronology.asp?groupId=70501 [accessed 10 October 2005]

their position though their rhetoric exposed ethnic Russians to the danger of being objects of suspicion and hostility among their fellow citizens in Kazakhstan.

Conclusion

When Kazakhstan became independent, President Nursultan Nazarbayev was faced with a complex task. Unprepared for independence, he had to balance the need to legitimize the state and his own power through a process of nation-building without severely alienating the numerically large non-Kazakh population, without whose co-operation his projects could not be implemented. Kazakhstan would have to be a home for the Kazakhs, the product of a daily affirmation of self-determination, reflecting their culture and values, and at the same time it had to be a multi-ethnic state, diverse in language and culture, a state which valued citizenship at least as much as ethnicity. It was a demanding undertaking and the imperfections and incompleteness of the results are as much due to the enormity of the challenge, and insufficient resources to implement policies effectively, as it can be attributed to the Kazakhstani President, who has at varying times had to be both delicate and firm, nationalist and cosmopolitan, robust and conciliatory. The risk of conflict along ethnic fault lines was ever present.

Initially, it appeared that the Slavs of Kazakhstan (of whom the Russians constitute the vast majority with smaller numbers of Ukrainians, Belarusians, and Poles) could be a major destabilizing force. The policy of the Kazakhstani President has been one of 'Kazakhization'. Ethnic Kazakhs have been encouraged to migrate from their homes in China, Afghanistan, Russia, Mongolia, Iran, Turkey and the other Central Asia republics.[48] The ratio of Russians to Kazakhs in elite political and economic positions is steadily diminishing. In Soviet times,

48 Edward Schatz, 'Framing Strategies and Non-Conflict in Multi-Ethnic Kazakhstan', *Nationalism and Ethinc Politics*, 6, no. 2 (Summer 2000), p. 84.

Russians may have been underrepresented in the Kazakh Soviet Socialist Republic, but they were amply represented in the political structures of the USSR. Without the external and powerful check provided by the Soviet leadership in Moscow, Russians in Kazakhstan are effectively on their own.

The Kazakhstani Government has determined that the Kazakh language will play a pivotal role in the 'Kazakhization' of society and government policy has been sketched out largely without public discussion or consultation. Language laws, and the entire nation-building project, have been both unifying and divisive. They are deemed necessary to create a coherent national Kazakh identity on which the legitimacy of the state will be based while, at the same time, they accentuate existing inter-ethnic (and sometimes intra-ethnic) divisions.[49] With legislation as a new growth industry, the more difficult endeavour of translating official edicts into tangible realities remains unresolved. It has been largely left to individual actors and localities who are ill-equipped and lacking the necessary resources. As yet, these deficiencies have reduced the government campaign on occasions to little more than a 'paper war'.

The policy of Kazakhization in large part depends on Russian migration for its success. Not only has the government done little to stem the tide but it has made ambitious projections for the ethnic Kazakh percentage of the population and language proficiency without making any predictions of a demographic explosion on behalf of the Kazakh populace. Therefore, it is expected, and quietly endorsed, that Russians should leave so as to facilitate the process of Kazakhization. Rather than fight, the Russians have simply left. Throughout the 20th century, Russians emigrated to Kazakhstan and played a defining role in its development. The transformation of their status since the collapse of the Soviet Union has occasioned an exodus that may also fundamentally change the character of the newly independent Central Asian state.

49 Intra-ethnic divisions refer to divisions between those ethnic Kazakhs who speak Kazakh and those who do not.

Bibliography

Akiner, Shirin, *The Formation of Kazakh Identity: From Tribe to Nation-State* (London: The Royal Institute of International Affairs, 1995).

Alter, Peter, *Nationalism* (London: E. Arnold, 1989).

Bentahila, Abdelâli and Davies, Eirlys, 'Language Revival: Restoration or Transformation', *Journal of Multilingual and Multicultural Development*, 14 (1993), pp. 355–74.

Brubaker, Rogers, 'National Minorities, Nationalizing States, and External Homelands in the New Europe', *Daedalus* 124, no. 2 (1995), pp. 107–132.

—— 'Nationalizing States in the Old 'New Europe' – and the New', *Ethnic and Racial Studies*, 19, no. 2 (April 1996), pp. 411–37.

Conquest, Robert, 'Academe and the Soviet Myth', in John Moore (ed.), *Legacies of the Collapse of Marxism* (Fairfax: George Mason University Press, 1994), pp. 29–37.

Crocombe, R.G., *The South Pacific: An Introduction* (Christchurch: Institute of Pacific Studies, 1989)

Dave, Bhavna, 'Minorities and Participation in Public Life: Kazakhstan', Working Paper, Commission on Human Rights, Sub-Commission on Promotion of Human Rights, United Nations (5 May 2003).

Dawisha, Karen and Parrot, Bruce, *The End of Empire?: The Transformation of the USSR in Comparative Perspective* (Armonk: M.E. Sharpe, 1997).

Frazer, Graham and Lancelle, George, *Absolute Zhirinovsky: A Transparent View of the Distinguished Statesman* (London: Penguin, 1994).

Fukuyama, Francis, 'Varieties of Russian Nationalism', in John Moore (ed.), *Legacies of the Collapse of Marxism* (Fairfax: George Mason University Press, 1994), pp. 35–79.

Fry, Michael, 'Decolonization: Britain, France, and the Cold War', in Karen Dawisha and Bruce Parrot (eds.), *The End of Empire?*

The Transformation of the USSR in Comparative Perspective (Armonk: M.E. Sharpe, 1997), pp. 121–154.

Kahler, Miles, 'Empires, Neo-Empires, and Political Change: The British and French Experience' in Karen Dawisha and Bruce Parrot (eds.), *The End of Empire? The Transformation of the USSR in Comparative Perspective* (Armonk: M.E. Sharpe, 1997), pp. 286–312.

Kaplan, Robert and Baldauf, Richard Jr., *Language Planning From Practice to Theory* (Clevedon: Multilingual Matters, 1997)

Khazanov, Anatoly, 'The Ethnic Problems of Kazakhstan', *Central Asian Survey*, 14, no. 2 (1995), pp. 243–264.

Kolstø, Pål and Malkova, Irina 'Is Kazakhstan being Kazakified', *Analysis of Current Affairs*, 9, no. 11 (November 1997), pp. 1 and 3–4.

Kolstø Pål, 'Anticipating Demographic Superiority: Kazakh Thinking on Integration and Nation Building', *Europe-Asia Studies*, 50. no. 1 (January 1998), pp. 51–68.

Kuzio, Taras: '"Nationalizing States" or Nation-building? A Critical Review of the Theoretical Literature and Empirical Evidence', *Nations and Nationalism*, 7, no. 2 (2001), pp. 135–154

Laponce, Jean, *Languages and Their Territories* (Toronto: University of Toronto Press, 1987).

Laponce, Jean, 'Do Languages Behave Like Animals', *International Journal of the Sociology of Languages*, 103 (1993), pp. 19–30

Luke, Allen, McHoul, Alec and Mey, Jacob, 'On the Limits of Language Planning: Class, State and Power' in Richard Baldauf and Allen Luke (eds.), *Language Planning and Education in Australasia and the South Pacific* (Clevedon: Multilingual Matters, 1990), pp. 25–44.

Mandelbaum, Michael (ed.), *Central Asia and the World: Kazakhstan, Uzbekistan, Tajikistan, Kyrgyzstan and Turkmenistan* (New York: Council of Foreign Relations Press, 1994).

Martin, Terry, *The Affirmative Action Empire: Ethnicity and the Soviet State, 1923–1939* (Ithaca: Cornell University Press, 2001).

Matloff, Judith, 'Puzzle Over Capital Move in Central Asia', *Christian Science Monitor*, 91, no. 47 (2 March 1999), p. 7.

Mühlhäusler, Peter, 'The Ecology of Small Languages', in Richard B. Baldauf, *Backing Australian Languages* (Canberra: National Languages and Literary Institute of Australia, 1995) pp. 1–14.

Mesbahi, Mohiaddin (ed.), *Central Asia and the Caucasus after the Soviet Union: Domestic and International Dynamics* (Gainesville: University Press of Florida, 1994).

Minorities at Risk 'Chronology of Russians in Kazakhstan' from the University of Maryland Centre for International Development and Conflict Management, at: http://www.cidcm.umd.edu/ inscr/ mar/chronology.asp?groupId=70501

Moore, John (ed.), *Legacies of the Collapse of Marxism* (Fairfax: George Mason University Press, 1994).

Ó Beacháin, Donnacha, 'The Problems of Language Revival in Ireland and Kazakhstan', in *Kazakhstan in the Age of Globalization* (Almaty: Kazakhstan Academy of Labor and Social Relations, Vol. 1, 2004), pp. 37–47.

—— 'Parliamentary Elections in Kazakhstan', *Electoral Studies*, 24, no. 4 (December 2005), pp. 762–770.

Olcott, Martha, 'Kazakhstan', in Mohiaddin Mesbahi (ed.), *Central Asia and the Caucasus after the Soviet Union: Domestic and International Dynamics* (Gainesville: University Press of Florida, 1994), pp. 119–132.

—— *The Kazakhs* (Second Edition; Stanford: Hoover Institution Press, Stanford University, 1995).

Ponarin, Eduard, 'Alexander Solzhenitsyn as a Mirror of the Russian Counter-Revolution', PONARS Policy Memo 150 (St. Petersburg, European University at St. Petersburg, October 2000).

Remnick, David, *Resurrection: The Struggle for a New Russia* (New York: Vintage, 1998).

Schatz, Edward, 'Framing Strategies and Non-Conflict in Multi-Ethnic Kazakhstan', *Nationalism and Ethnic Politics*, 6, no. 2 (Summer 2000), pp. 71–94.

—— 'When Capital Cities Move: The Political Geography of Nation and State Building', Working Paper 303, Helen Kellogg Institute for International Studies, University of Notre Dame, February 2003.

Sinnott, Peter, 'Population Politics in Kazakhstan', *Journal of International Affairs*, 56, no. 2 (Spring 2003), pp. 103–115.

Suny, Ronald, 'Southern Tears: Dangerous Opportunities in the Caucasus and Central Asia', in Rajan Menon, Yuri Fedorov and Ghia Nodia (eds.), *Russia, the Caucasus and Central Asia* (Armonk: M.E. Sharpe, 1999), pp. 147–176.

Suny, Ronald and Terry Martin (eds.), *A State of Nations: Empire and Nation-Making in the Age of Lenin and Stalin* (Oxford: Oxford University Press, 2001).

Tishkov, Valery, *Ethnicity, Nationalism and Conflict in and after the Soviet Union: The Mind Aflame* (London: Sage, 1997).

Westoff, Charles, 'The Substitution of Contraception for Abortion in Kazakhstan', from Population Resource Center, Washington D.C. and Princeton, N.J., at: http://www.prcdc.org/summaries/newabortion/newabortion.html [accessed 10 October 2005].

ZOLTÁN BERÉNYI

Weak Civic Culture in Hungary: An Examination of Some Consequences of Economic Inequality

Since the collapse of communism, Hungary is praised for its political stability and for the improving performance of its market economy. Although economic and political transformations can be regarded as remarkable, there are problems with the development of civic culture. After the collapse of communism it was thought that Hungary possessed the best opportunity to build a democracy with a strong civic culture.[1] During the first decade following the reestablishment of constitutional democracy in Hungary however, it has turned out that the initial expectations with regard to civic culture development were too optimistic. While four free elections were held successfully and the institutional structure of constitutional democracy remain secure, public opinion surveys indicate that there are still serious problems in the development of civic culture and in the functioning of democracy in Hungary.

The objective of this paper is to examine the development of civic culture. I will argue that radical pro-market economic reforms debilitated civil society in post-1990 Hungary. This in turn hindered the development of civic culture and weakened moral compassion and

1 Hankiss Elemér, *East European Alternatives* (Oxford: Oxford University Press, 1990); Szelényi Iván, 'A kelet-európai új osztály stratégia távlatai és korlátai: Az értelmiség útja az osztályhatalomhoz önkritikus felülvizsgálata', [Perspectives and boundaries for employing the Eastern European 'new class' strategy: exerting self-criticism over the way of the intelligentsia to the class power], in *Új osztály, állam, politika* (Budapest: Európa, 1990); Ágh Attila, 'Transition to Democracy in East-Central Europe: a Comparative View', in Szoboszlai György (ed.), *Democracy and Political Transformation: Theories and East-Central European Realities* (Budapest: Hungarian Political Science Association, 1991), pp. 103–122.

generosity. Economic inequality affects not only people's life chances in education and health, but also how they treat and identify each other, so having consequences for belonging, sharing and civic action.

In the next section, I will outline how civic culture is weak in terms of trust, corruption and honesty. The following section discusses how economic reforms and inequalities are in part a cause of poor civic participation and values. Finally, I will finish with some final remarks.

A Weak Civic Culture

Civic culture consists of various values such as trust, tolerance, honesty and respect for law and order. By looking at public surveys, I will show that there are problems in the Hungarian civic culture.

According to the January 2002 survey of the Social Research Institute in Hungary (TÁRKI), 55% of the citizens were dissatisfied with the performance of democracy. Only 45% of the citizens said that they were more or less satisfied with democracy.

Table 1: TARKI – Satisfaction with democracy

	%
Very satisfied	1,5
Rather satisfied	43,5
Rather dissatisfied	41,7
Very dissatisfied	13,3
Total	100,0
Average	2,33
Does not know, did not respond	12,4

Source: *'TÁRKI: Lakossági vélemények a mai és tíz év előtti társadalmi-politikai rendszerről. Közép-európai összehasonlítás'* [The opinion of the citizens about the social and political system of today and the previous one that collapsed a decade ago. A Central European Comparison.] available at: http://www.tarki.hu/kozvelemeny-h/velemeny/200202.pdf

Several studies revealed that trust in democratic institutions has been consistently low since 1990. Data in Table 2 and Table 3 indicates that institutions of the new constitutional democracy were not only unable to gain trust since 1990, but a significantly smaller number of citizens trusted them in 2000 than in 1991.

Table 2: Trust in institutions in Hungary in 1991 and 1994

Institutions	1991 (%)	1994 (%)
President	–	19
Army	47	44
Police	43	45
Law courts	44	46
Public administration	33	33
Government	26	21
Parliament	29	23
Churches	46	39
Media	40	30
Old labour unions	20	14
New democratic unions	25	23
Political parties	16	11

Source: Fricz Plasser and Peter A. Ulram 'Measuring Political Culture in East Central Europe. Political Trust and System Support', in Andreas Pribesky and Fricz Plasser (eds.), *Political Culture in East Central Europe* (Aldershot: Avebury, 1996), p. 17.

Table 3: Trust in institutions in Hungary in 2000

Institutions	2000 (%)
President	58
Police	27
Law courts	33
Public administration	26
Government	20
Parliament	18
Churches	38
Media	32
New democratic unions	20
Political parties	7

Source: Central European Opinion Research Group (TARKI), *Trust in Democratic Institutions 2000*, http://www.tarki.hu/kozvelemeny-h/velemeny/200006.pdf.

Political efficacy figures also indicate that only a very low proportion of the citizenry thinks that they can indeed exert real influence on the activity of the government. A national survey conducted in 1994 indicated that when respondents were asked whether they could do anything against a governmental decision that was against the interests of the citizenry, only 11% of Hungarians responded positively.[2] Another research showed that only 27% of the citizens thought that they could influence how the government ran things. This figure is low by European standards.[3]

Data from international comparative surveys indicates that although about 75% of the Hungarian citizenry rejected the notion of the

2 László Bruszt and János Simon, 'Az Antall-korszak után, a választások elõtt – a vagy demokráciánk és pártjaink az állampolgárok szemével' [After the Antall era, before the elections – our democracy and our parties through the eyes of citizens] in S. Kurtán, P. Sándor and L. Vass (eds.), *Magyarország politikai évkönyve* (Budapest: Demokrácia Kutatások Magyar Központja Alapítvány, 1994), pp. 774–802.

3 Fricz Plasser and Peter Ulram 'Measuring Political Culture in East Central Europe. Political Trust and System Support', in Fricz Plasser and Andreas Pribesky, pp. 3–35.

dissolution of parliament and the abolition of parties, about 25% of them were still ready to support authoritarianism in 1993 and this figure rose to 30% in 1994.[4] Later surveys in 1996 and 1997 indicated a growth of intolerance and a rise of support for right or left wing dictatorship in Hungary.[5] Despite the fact that the majority of the citizenry rejected authoritarianism, these data indicate serious problems in building an attachment to democratic values, and difficulties in the development of democratic political culture in post-1989 Hungary.

It is not only political institutions that citizens do not trust in Hungary. Several studies indicate that citizens do not trust horizontal networks of social interaction and that trust in civic organizations is just as low as in political institutions.[6] Besides the declining trust in civil organizations, Adam Seligman and Katalin Füzér in the mid-90s found that the level of interpersonal trust and tolerance remained low. They found that trust remained

> articulated along rather restricted venues. In contemporary Hungary we find an increasing intolerance towards any otherness: ethnic, religious minorities, Gypsies, Jews, Arabs, Chinese, blacks... In Hungary there is not, as in many modern societies a sense of basic trust that connects all citizens... Rather, trust is woven around restricted boundaries.[7]

After conducting a research on values in post-1990 Hungary, András Sajó found that

4 Fricz Plasser and Peter Ulram, p. 46.; Richard Rose and Catherine Haerpfer, *New Democracies Barometer III: Learning from What is Happening* (Glasgow, 1994).

5 Fábián Zoltán, 'Az autoritarianizmus, az előítéletek és a politikai-ideológiai tagoltság kapcsolata Magyarországon a posztkommunista átalakulás idején' [The relation between authoritarianism, prejudice and political ideological division during the post-communist transformation in Hungary], unpublished doctoral thesis, Budapest: MTA Pszichológiai Intézet, 1997.

6 William Misher and Richard Rose, 'Trust, Distrust and Skepticism: Popular Evaluations of Civil and Political Institutions in Post-Communist Societies', *The Journal of Politics*, 59, no. 2. (1997), pp. 418–451.

7 Adam Seligman and Füzér Katalin, 'The Problem of Trust and the Transition from State Socialism', *Comparative Social Research*, 14, no. 1 (1994), pp. 193–221.

> there is a little understanding of the concept of fundamental right; people tend to accept a limitation on rights if justified by public interest or welfare, as long as these limitations are related to other people's rights. There is neither a tradition nor trust in public participation.[8]

In 1997 a national survey indicated that 82% of the respondents considered 'law breaking as acceptable if it promotes individual achievement', which showed a shocking level of the acceptance of law breaking.[9] This figure has improved by 2001, but was still the highest among the former Eastern bloc countries (77%). The proportion of those who agreed with the statement that breaking the law is necessary for individual achievement was especially high (82%) among the young generation (18–29 years old), those who lived their adult life in the new democracy, and learned 'how things are done' today.

In summary, these data show general dissatisfaction with democracy; low level of trust in political and civil institutions; low level of political efficacy; alarmingly low level of respect for law; low level of interpersonal trust; rising level of intolerance and prejudice. Thus, these figures clearly indicate that there are problems in the development of civic culture in post-communist Hungary.

Poor Participation in Civil Society

Despite these figures, writers suggest that civil society has become stronger in Hungary since 1990.[10] Proponents of this view argue that the growing number of registered civil organizations supports a strong

8 Sajó András, 'Legal Socialization in Hungary', *Comparative Social Research*, 14, no. 1 (1994), pp. 97–109.

9 Sík Endre and Tóth István György (eds.), pp. 208–220.

10 Sárközy Tamás, *A privatizáció joga Magyarországon* (1989–1993), [Privatisation law in Hungary 1989–1993] (Budapest: Akadémiai Kiadó, 1993); Kuti Éva, *The Nonprofit Sector in Hungary* (Manchester: Manchester University Press, 1996); Körösényi András, *The Hungarian Political System* (Budapest: CEU Press, 1999).

civil society.[11] At the same time, they also claim that the problems of democratic political culture and civic culture have nothing to do with civil society. By civil society, they only mean non-profit organizations, and argue that interest representation organizations and pressure groups should not be considered as part of civil society.

However, I will argue that it is mistaken to claim that the number of registered civil organizations is the main indicator for the strength of civil society. Instead, the strength of civil society in a democracy can only be measured by looking at how it is able to function and how it is able to fulfil its role.

I will elaborate the concepts of democracy and civil society. I propose the definition of democracy as put forward by Almond and Verba in their work on the civic culture. They understand democracy as a political system in which the government is elected by the majority of the voters at regularly held, free elections, and where citizens control the government through institutionalized channels of mass political participation.[12] The performance and the quality of democracy thus depends on how effective is this control. However, this model has to be complemented, as Finer notes,

> in all liberal democracies there exists, not one but two channels of popular representation. Political parties and the electoral process are one; pressure groups provide the other. The concept of pressure groups includes the major interest organizations in a country as well as the more numerous and smaller promotional groups.[13]

In a democratic political system institutionalized channels of mass political participation must occur through political parties as well as pressure groups.

Civil society is a sphere where citizens learn norms, they form their ideas about good and bad, gain attachment to certain values, form their opinion about democratic political institutions, about civil organ-

11 On 1 January, 2003 the number of registered civil organisations was 53,022. Hungarian Central Statistical Office, available at: http://portal.ksh.hu/pls/ksh/docs/hun/xftp/idoszaki/pdf/nonprofagy03.pdf, p. 1.

12 Gabriel Almond and Sidney Verba, *The Civic Culture. Political Attitudes and Democracy in Five Nations* (Boston: Little Brown, 1965), p. 326.

13 Samuel Finer, *Comparative Government* (London: Allen Lane, 1979), p. 152.

izations, about the government and ultimately, about the democratic system itself. In effect, civil society has two crucial functions to perform in a democracy: one of them is to facilitate interest realization and mediation; the other one is to foster democratic political socialization.

Its performance in democratic political socialization and in interest mediation shows the real strength of Hungarian civil society. The strength of civil society cannot be identified by the number of registered organizations, or the number of people working in them by civil associations. The Hungarian civil society can be measured in three respects. First, strength of civil society can be measured by examining to what extent horizontal networks enable citizens to take decisions at local, regional and national levels, and to realise their interests. Second, the strength can be measured by examining to what extent civil society fosters the development of norms of reciprocity and trust, decreases incentives for selfish behaviour and builds up trust in horizontal networks of social interaction. Third, the spread of civility or public civicness, that is equitable and fair treatment of others, generalized interpersonal trust, tolerance and cooperation towards citizens, are also indicative of the strength of civil society in Hungary.

As we saw in the previous section, the first 15 years in Hungary witness a weak set of civic values. During that time, horizontal networks of social interaction were unable to gain the trust of the citizenry. Instead, trust in civil organizations was just as low as in political institutions. Norms of reciprocity and trust have not become a general standard in social interactions. Instead of the development of generalized interpersonal trust, public surveys indicate that people tend to distrust others. Norms of reciprocity and trust remain restricted in immediate group boundaries, and the level of cooperation has dropped. Instead of tolerance towards fellow citizens, intolerance towards minorities and refugees has spread in the past decade.

In sum, we can say that it is not public civicness, but the lack of civility that spread in post-1990 Hungary. At this point a question emerges: what is the reason of that? In the field of democratic political socialization several studies have pointed out that there is a relationship between levels of civic engagement and interpersonal trust.[14] The greater the trust the citizens hold for others, the more likely they are to participate; the more citizens participate in their communities, the more they learn to trust others. People who participate extensively in their communities are likely to have highly positive beliefs about the helpfulness, trustworthiness and fairness of others. Moreover, there are scholars who argue that trust in other people and democratic institutions go together.[15]

We can perhaps better understand the poor development of civic culture by looking at the level of participation in civil organizations in post-1990 Hungary. Despite the fact that the number of registered civil organizations is high, participation in civil organizations was extremely low. In the 1990s, 20% of the country's adult population had a membership in civil associations.[16] Comparing the level of civic participation with similar data in countries of Western Europe shows a relatively low level of Hungarian participation rate.[17]

However, further analysis of the active participation of members shows that people by no means proved to be highly active in civil organizations. Only 7% of the country's adult population was really ac-

14 Dietlind Stolle and Thomas Rochon 'Are All Associations Alike?', *The American Behavioral Scientist* (September 1998), pp. 47–65; Robert Putnam, *Making Democracy Work* (Princeton: Princeton University Press, 1993); John Brehm and Wendy Rahn, 'Individual-Level Evidence for the Causes and Consequences of Social Capital', *American Journal of Political Science*, 41, no. 3 (1997), pp. 999–1023.

15 Ronald Inglehart, *Culture Shift* (Princeton: Princeton University Press, 1990); Edward Muller and Mitchell Seligson, 'Civic Culture and Democracy. The Question of Causal Relationships', *American Political Science Review*, 88 (1994), pp. 635–52.

16 Sebestyén István, *A nonprofit szféra a legfrissebb adatok tükrében* [The nonprofit sphere in the light of recent figures] (Budapest: Budapesti Művelődési Központ, 1994) , p. 84.

17 The percentage of active volunteers among the adult population in 1997 was: Austria – 26%; Belgium – 28%; Denmark – 26%; France – 23%; Germany – 31%; Ireland – 27%; Italy – 23%; Netherlands – 37%; Sweden – 39%; United Kingdom – 16%. In L. Kenworthy, 'Civic Engagement, Social Capital and Economic Cooperation', *The American Behavioral Scientist*, 40, no. 5 (1997), p. 649.

tive in these organizations. They spent only about 0.16 per cent of their total available time and less than one per cent of their free time undertaking voluntary work.[18]

Why has participation been so low? In part, the answer lies in the poverty of many individuals, who lack the time and resources to participate. Since 1990 the Hungarian government began to marketize the economy;[19] proponents of radical economic reforms argued that the market economy would produce societal changes that would rule out a 'return to the past'. However, as Reisinger points out,

> market relations stress competition among citizens, not common action ... [However, after the fall of communism] Eastern European countries did not have a dense network of political and social organizations present in Western societies to offset the competitive realm of market economy. So, while successful marketization of some degree will be crucial to democratization, marketization alone will not lead to a civil society supportive of democracy. Equally crucial will be the establishment of interest groups and social organizations and, through their operation, the creation of centripetal, not centrifugal, social forces.[20]

Under conditions of accelerating marketization and privatization, a rapid polarization of society emerged, that is, a accumulation of wealth for some and widespread poverty for others.

National survey showed that in the past decade the range of social groups threatened by poverty has expanded in Hungary. With the exception of a very narrow upper stratum, generally, all social groups have suffered from spiralling inflation and a drastic drop in real incomes. National surveys indicated that in the first five years of the 1990s, real incomes dropped by 31%, then in 1996, a further drop of 16% occurred, followed by a further drop of 5.7% in 1997. The

18 Czakó, Ágnes., *et. al.* (eds.), *Individual Giving and Volunteering* (Budapest: Központi Statisztikai Hivatal – Nonprofit Kutatócsoport, 1995), p. 13.

19 Petschnig M. Zita, *Örökségtől örökségig* (From heritage to heritage) Budapest: Századvég Kiadó, 1994; Lengyel László, 'Külpolitika vagy nemzetpolitika,' (Foreign policy or national policy), in Gombár Csaba (ed.), *Kormány a mérlegen 1990–1994* (Budapest: Korridor, 1994), pp. 346–369.

20 William Reisinger, 'Establishing and Strengthening Democracy,' in Robert Grey (ed.), *Democratic Theory and Post-Communist Change* (New Jersey: Prentice Hall, 1997), p. 65.

same research also revealed that between 1990 and 1997 it was the middle class, whose income decreased the most.[21] As education and income levels prove to be the crucial factor in determining the level of civic participation in Hungary, impoverishment impeded higher participation.[22]

More effective protection of the real value of wages and lower taxes on small and medium enterprises might have had moderated the spread of poverty in post-1990 Hungary. For this to happen, vested interest groups would require adequate involvement in macroeconomic decision-making process. However, the government and the parliament, instead of fostering the participation of labour organizations in economic and social policymaking, strove to decrease their bargaining capacity and successfully blocked the access of employees' and employers' organizations. The Interest Reconciliation Council (IRC), which could have been the institution for channelling social interests into policy making failed to fulfil its function. The main reasons for this failure were that it was not legally independent from the government and its agreements were not legally binding on the government and the parliament. In 1995 the parliament modified the Labour Code and new regulations placed more burden on employees at workplaces. The modification proposal was submitted to the parliament by a socio-liberal government. Although employee and employer organisations in the IRC strongly protested against the proposal, the government ignored them and submitted its proposal to the legislature.[23]

21 Spéder Zsolt, 'Szegénység' ['Poverty'] in Sík Endre and Tóth István György (eds.), *Magyar Háztartás Panel – Műhelytanulmányok 9. Zárótanulmány* (Budapest: BKE-TÁRKI, 1998), p. 35.

22 Utasi Ágnes, *Lyfestyles, Contact Capital and Hungary's Elite* (Budapest: Institute for Political Science of the Hungarian Academy of Science, 1996); Rabi Béla, 'A civil szervezeteket érintő törvényelőkészítési munkák és törvények néhány ellentmondása' ['On some contradictions regarding drafting legal regulations and enacted laws'], in Slézia Gábor (ed.), *Civil Budapest '94 – Sikermodellek és problémák a civil szevezetekben* (Budapest: Budapesti Mûvelõdési Központ, 1994), pp. 39–49.

23 Berényi Zoltán, *Constitutional Democracy and Civil Society in Post-Communist Hungary* (Budapest: Institute for Political Science of the Hungarian Academy of Science, 1999) p. 123.

The reason of this hostile behaviour of the government towards labour organisations was that it did not want to allow employees' and employers' organizations to place limits on its economic policy-making. Struggling with the problem of rapid and drastic decline in membership, labour organisations were unable to prevent the government in imposing subsequent restrictions on their rights.

As a result, during the first decade of post-communism in Hungary produced a situation in which those groups most vulnerable to the macroeconomic stabilization policy were deprived the ability to represent their own interests. Marketization in these conditions brought about accelerating social polarization and accelerating growth of income inequality. In 2003, among the countries of Central Europe income inequalities were the highest in Hungary. The wealthiest 10 per cent of the population had real income 8.4 times higher than the poorest 10 per cent.[24] The government not only failed to promote the development of a strong middle class, but in the mid-1990s effectively fostered its erosion.

Growing income inequality, high level of unemployment, drastic decline in real incomes and rising poverty levels diminished trust in institutions as well as interpersonal trust. Scarcity increased the risk of misplaced trust; hard times made people less sympathetic, compassionate and generous in their treatment of others, who viewed as competitors in the economic struggle of making ends meet. When resources are unequally distributed, people tend to feel ashamed, humiliated, exploited, leading to their faith in fellow citizens diminishing. I argue that two factors played a crucial role in the development and maintenance of this state of affairs in the early years of post-communist transition in Hungary. One of the factors is a culture of informality and distrust which developed during the years of communism. This decisively determined the way citizens interacted with each other and with formal institutions in the early years of post-communism. Communism created an atmosphere where distrust pervaded society, where obligations outside one's kinship relations were

24 Tóth István György Jövedelemeloszlás ['Income distribution'], in Szívós Péter and Tóth István György (eds.),*TÁRKI monitor jelentések 2003* available at: http://www.tarki.hu/adatbank-h/kutjel/pdf/a530.pdf, p. 36

more or less subjected to informal bargaining and where laws were not taken seriously if there was a chance to break them without being subject to sanctions. By the development of an informal economy, *informal individual* bargaining emerged, and any form of collective action based on solidarity met with immediate and severe repression. In this atmosphere citizens learned that it is not by collective action based on trust and solidarity but by informal, individual bargaining that much can be achieved. This socialization emerged from the rule of communism, creating a high level of distrust and a low level of solidarity and trust in collective action.

After 1989 citizens became formally free to form civil organisations and to make the new democratic institutions work. However, while the new democratic institutions were relatively easy to legislate into existence, the culture of distrust and disrespect for the law, the lack of civic solidarity and a preference for informality were incomparably more difficult to change. These cultural norms could only change if individuals had directly experienced how formal institutions and civil organisations could bring success. With no evidence showing that collective action can bring more success than informal and individual bargaining, citizens were reinforced in their previous belief. Instead of trying to make democratic principles work, individuals continued to resort to informal compromises and to avoid collective action. It is not surprising therefore that in these conditions in post-1990 Hungary citizens did not become highly active in civil organizations, and as a result these organizations were unable to gain political and moral power.

Conclusion

Social scientists argue that a weak civil society allows corruption and informal mechanisms of interest mediation and representation.[25] The state bureaucracy becomes riddled with networks of clientelism favouring some groups over others; and an informal economy blossoms, so escaping the disciplinary mechanisms of the state. The result is in part disrespect for law and a lack of proper regard for others throughout the state administration and the wider society.

During the past 15 years in Hungary, the political system has failed to incorporate vested interests and special groups into a decision-making process. In part, the economic reforms have generated social inequalities leading to political exclusion.

Bibliography

Ágh, Attila, 'Transition to Democracy in East-Central Europe: a Comparative View', in Szoboszlai György (ed.), *Democracy and Political Transformation: Theories and East-Central European realities* (Budapest: Hungarian Political Science Association, 1991).

Almond, Gabriel and Verba, Sidney, *The Civic Culture. Political Attitudes and Democracy in Five Nations* (Boston: Little Brown, 1965).

Az anómia elterjedtsége és a normaszegés elfogadottsága három visegrádi országban – Magyarország, Csehország és Lengyelország – kelet-közép-európai összehasonlítás (2001) [The extent of an-

25 Nicos Mouzelis, 'Modernity, Late Development and Civil Society', in John Hall (ed.), *Civil Society. Theory, History, Comparison* (Cambridge: Polity Press, 1995), pp. 224–250; William Reisinger, 'Establishing and Strengthening Democracy', in Robert Grey (ed.), *Democratic Theory and Post-Communist Change* (New Jersey: Prentice Hall, 1997), pp. 52–74.

omie and the acceptance of norm-breaking in three Visegrád countries – Hungary, Czech Republic and Poland – Eastern Central European Comparison], available at: http://www.tarki.hu/kozvelemeny/ceorg/2001_02.pdf

Berényi, Zoltán, *Constitutional Democracy and Civil Society in Post-Communist Hungary* (Budapest: Institute for Political Science of the Hungarian Academy of Science, 1999).

Bemutató [Presentation] available at: http://www.tarki.hu/research/monitor/monitor2003/bemutato2004.pdf

Bihari, Mihály, 'Rendszerváltás és hatalomváltás Magyarországon 1989–1990', [Regime change and the change of power in Hungary, 1989–1990] in Kurtán Sándor, Sándor László and Vass László (eds.), *Magyarország politikai évkönyve 1991* (Budapest: Ökonómia Alapítvány – Ecomix Rt, 1991).

Brehm, James and Rahn, W, 'Individual-Level Evidence for the Causes and Consequences of Social Capital', *American Journal of Political Science*, 41, no. 3 (1997), pp. 999–1023.

Bruszt, László and Simon, János (1994). 'Az Antall-korszak után, a választások elõtt – avagy demokráciánk és pártjaink az állampolgárok szemével' [After the Antall era, before the elections – our democracy and our parties through the eyes of citizens] in S. Kurtán, P. Sándor and L. Vass., *Magyarország politikai évkönyve – 1994* (Budapest: Demokrácia Kutatások Magyar Központja Alapítvány), pp. 774–802.

Central European Opinion Research Group (TARKI), Trust in Democratic Institutions (2000) at: http://www.tarki.hu/kozvelemeny-h/velemeny/200006.pdf.

Czakó, Ágnes, *et al.* (eds.), *Individual Giving and Volunteering* (Budapest: Központi Statisztikai Hivatal – Nonprofit Kutatócsoport, 1995).

Elekes, Zsuzsa, Paksi, Béla and Spéder, Zsolt, 'Elégedettség, lelki problémák, elidegenedettség, anómia', [Satisfaction, emotional problems, alienation, anomie], in Sík Endre and Tóth István György (eds.), *Magyar Háztartás Panel – Műhelytanulmány 9. Zárótanulmány* (Budapest: BKE-TÁRKI, 1998).

Fábián, Zoltán, 'Az autoritarianizmus, az előítéletek és a politikai-ideológiai tagoltság kapcsolata Magyarországon a posztkommunista átalakulás idején' [The relation between authoritarianism, prejudice and political ideological division during the post-communist transformation in Hungary] unpublished doctoral thesis, Budapest: MTA Pszichológiai Intézet, 1997.

Finer, Samuel, *Comparative Government* (London: Allen Lane, 1979).

Hankiss, Elemér, *East European Alternatives* (Oxford: Oxford University Press, 1990).

Hungarian Central Statistical Office, available at: http://portal.ksh.hu/pls/ksh/docs/hun/xftp/idoszaki/pdf/ nonprofagy03.pdf

Inglehart, Robert, *Culture Shift* (Princeton: Princeton University Press, 1990).

Kenworthy, Lane, 'Civic Engagement, Social Capital and Economic Co-operation', *The American Behavioral Scientist*, 40. no. 5 (1997), pp. 645–657.

Körösényi, András, *The Hungarian Political System* (Budapest: CEU Press, 1999).

'Korrupció' [Corruption] *Heti Világgazdaság*, 22. November 1997.

Kuti, Éva, *The Nonprofit Sector in Hungary* (Manchester: Manchester University Press, 1996).

Lengyel, László, 'Külpolitika vagy nemzetpolitika', [Foreign policy or national policy], in Gombár Csaba, et al. eds., *Kormány a mérlegen 1990–1994* (Budapest: Korridor, 1994).

Misher, Willem, and Rose, Richard., 'Trust, Distrust and Skepticism: Popular Evaluations of Civil and Political Institutions in Post-Communist Societies', *The Journal of Politics*, 59, no. 2. (1997), pp. 418–451.

Mouzelis, Nicos, 'Modernity, Late Development and Civil Society', in John A. Hall (ed.), *Civil Society. Theory, History, Comparison* (Cambridge: Polity Press, 1995), pp. 224–250.

Népszabadság, 2. April 2001.

Petschnig, Mária. Z., *Örökségtõl örökségig* [From heritage to heritage] (Budapest: Századvég Kiadó, 1994).

Plasser, Fricz and Ulram, Peter A. 'Measuring Political Culture in East Central Europe. Political Trust and System Support', in Andreas Pribesky and Fricz Plasser (eds.), *Political Culture in East Central Europe* (Aldershot: Avebury, 1996).

Rose, Richard and Haerpfer, Catherine, *New Democracies Barometer III: Learning from What is Happening* (Glasgow, 1994).

Putnam, Robert, *Making Democracy Work* (Princeton: Princeton University Press, 1993).

Rabi, Béla, 'A civil szervezeteket érintő törvényelőkészítési munkák és törvények néhány ellentmondása' [On some contradictions regarding drafting legal regulations and enacted laws], in Slézia Gábor (ed.), *Civil Budapest '94 – Sikermodellek és problémák a civil szervezetekben* (Budapest: Budapesti Művelődési Központ, 1994).

Reisinger, William, 'Establishing and Strengthening Democracy', in Robert Grey (ed.), *Democratic Theory and Post-Communist Change* (New Jersey: Prentice Hall, 1997).

Sajó, András, 'Legal Socialization in Hungary', *Comparative Social Research*, 14, no. 1 (1994), pp. 97–109.

Sárközy, Tamás, *A privatizáció joga Magyarországon (1989–1993)*, [Privatisation law in Hungary 1989–1993] (Budapest: Akadémiai Kiadó, 1993).

Sebestyén, István, *A nonprofit szféra a legfrissebb adatok tükrében* [The non-profit sphere in the light of recent figures] (Budapest: Budapesti Művelődési Központ, 1994).

Seligman, Adam and Füzér, Katalin, 'The Problem of Trust and the Transition from State Socialism', *Comparative Social Research*, 14, no. 1 (1994), pp. 193–221.

Seligson, Adam, 'Civic Culture and Democracy: The Question of Causal Relationships', *American Political Science Review*, 88 (1994), pp. 635–52.

Social Portrait of Hungary, Budapest: Hungarian Central Statistical Office, 1996.

Spéder Zsolt, 'Szegénység' [Poverty] in: Sík Endre – Tóth István György (eds.), *Magyar Háztartás Panel – Műhelytanulmányok 9. Zárótanulmány* (Budapest: BKE-TÁRKI, 1998), p. 35.

Stolle, Dietlind and Rochon, Thomas, R. 'Are All Associations Alike?', *The American Behavioral Scientist* (September 1998) pp. 47–65.

Szelényi, Iván, 'A kelet-európai új osztály stratégia távlatai és korlátai: Az értelmiség útja az osztályhatalomhoz önkritikus felülvizsgálata', [Perspectives and boundaries for employing the Eastern European 'new class' strategy: exerting self-criticism over the way of the intelligentsia to the class power], in *Új osztály, állam, politika* (Budapest: Európa, 1990).

Szívós, Péter and Tóth, István Gy., 'A háztartások jövedelmi szerkezete, szegénység, jövedelmi támogatások', [The income structure of households, poverty and income supports] in: Tóth István György (ed.), *Magyar Háztartáspanel – Zárótanulmány – 1998* (Budapest: BKE-TÁRKI, 1998).

—— *A háztartások jövedelmi szerkezete, egyenlőtlenségek, szegénység és jóléti támogatások Magyarországon* [The income structure of households, inequalities and poverty in Hungary] (Budapest: BKE-TÁRKI, 1998).

'TÁRKI: Lakossági vélemények a mai és tíz év előtti társadalmi-politikai rendszerről. Közép-európai összehasonlítás' [The opinion of the citizens about the social and political system of today and the previous one collapsed a decade ago. A Central European Comparison.] Available at: http://www.tarki.hu/kozvelemeny-h/velemeny/200202.pdf

Tóth István György 'Jövedelemeloszlás' ['Income distribution'], in Szívós Péter and Tóth István György (eds.), *TÁRKI monitor jelentések 2003* available at: http://www.tarki.hu/adatbank-h/kutjel/pdf/a530.pdf,

Utasi, Ágnes, *Lifestyles, Contact Capital and Hungary's Elite* (Budapest: Institute for Political Science of the Hungarian Academy of Science, 1996).

Voszka, Éva, 'Az állam és tulajdon szivárványos viszonya', [State and property – a colorful relationship] in Gombár, Csaba – Hankiss, Elemér and Lengyel, László (eds.), *És mi lesz, ha nem lesz?* (Budapest: Korridor, 1997).

—— *A redisztribúció újjáéledése*, [The revival of redistribution] (Budapest: Akadémia, 1993) at: http://www.tarki.hu/research/monitor/monitor2000/m2000_01.pdf

STEPHAN E. NIKOLOV

The Constrained Development of Non-Profit Organisations in Bulgaria

This work examines the development of the civil society sector in post-communist Bulgaria. It puts forward a thesis that the post-communist environment, with legacies of weak ties of free association and inclination to corrupt practices, on the one side, and undeveloped legal framework, on the other, creates the conditions under which civil society organisations tend to become dependent on governmental and foreign aid for their survival and redistribute the benefits among their own members – quite contrary to the mission of providing scare public goods and monitoring state activity.

After decades of absence from both the scholarly debate and the public discourse, civil society experienced a remarkable renaissance in recent years, when, 'all of a sudden, it has been taken out and thoroughly dusted, and has become a shining emblem'.[1] At present, however, civil society is given many different meanings by different authors. Various authors suggested categorisations of the manifold traditional and contemporary meanings of civil society.[2] Typically, concepts of civil society have both a particular empirical referent and

1 Ernest Gellner, *Conditions of Liberty: Civil Society and its Rivals* (London, 1994), p. 1.

2 Among the plethora of authors that contributed to the elaboration of the concept we may quote at least several – Adam B. Seligman, *The Idea of Civil Society* (Princeton, N.J., Princeton University Press, 1992), 201ff.; Victor Perez-Diaz, *The Return of Civil Society: The Emergence of Democratic Spain* (Cambridge, MA. Harvard University Press, 1993), 55ff.; Jeffrey Alexander, *Real Civil Societies: Dilemmas of Institutionalisation* (London: Sage, 1998), 3–8; John Keane, *Civil Society: Old Images, New Visions* (Cambridge: Polity, 1998. Translated into Bulgarian, Sofia, 2002), 36ff. To mention also the Bulgarian author G. Fotev, *Grazhdansko obshtestvo [Civil Society]* (Sofia: Publishing House of the Bulgarian Academy of Sciences, 1992).

a philosophically normative claim. We will refer to one useful categorisation on the basis of socio-analytical meanings of civil society.[3] In the tradition of this concept as one opposing the state, individual human rights are advanced and prioritised, but a significant role is devoted also to the public opinion as an expression of the 'collective will', making of which appears to be the main purpose of the political activity.[4]

Ralf Dahrendorf, who bases his modern understanding of civil society mainly on the 18th century heritage, underlines *association* as the

> word [that best] describes… the 'parts, interests and classes of citizens' which civil society is about… The creative chaos of associations coalesces as if guided by an invisible hand into the setting in which the greatest number find the greatest life chances. In economic terms, the market describes that setting; in political terms it is the public. [...] The market and the public are where the associations of civil society interact.[5]

Here, no explicit reference is made to the state and its potential to threaten the free association and interaction within civil society. Other authors, who conceive of the state as the central referent of civil society, in both a threatening and an enabling capacity, more explicitly emphasise the distinction between the two. As John Keane put it in a recent definition, civil society is

> an ideal typical category [...] that both describes and envisages a complex and dynamic ensemble of legally protected non-governmental institutions that tend to be non-violent, self-organising, self-reflexive and permanently in tension

3 Pérez-Díaz, p. 211.

4 A more detailed account of the theoretical premises of the concept of civil society can be found in Michael Ignatieff, 'On Civil Society', *Foreign Affairs*, 74, no. 2 (March/April 1995); Ernest Gellner, 'Civil Society in Historical Context', *International Social Science Journal*, 129 (1991); E. van der Zweerde, Civil Society, *Encyclopedia of the Developing World*. Ed. Thomas M. Leonard. New York, London: Routledge, 2006, pp. 346–8.

5 Ralf Dahrendorf, *After 1989: Morals, Revolution, and Civil Society* (New York: St. Martin's Press, 1997), p. 78.

> with each other and with the state institutions that 'frame', constrict and enable their activities.[6]

We shall use this definition as a basis for further discussion of the relationship between civil society and democracy. In our understanding, 'civil society' is much more that the quantitative aggregate of the formally registered nongovernmental organizations (NGOs); it also covers informal demonstrations of public opinion, public will, and so on. In this sense, civil society is not only confined to the so called the 'third sector', which is considered to be the domain of the NGOs, but overlaps the state (through political elections, parties and campaigns) and the market (through interest groups and trade associations). We shall also use terms 'nonprofit organizations' and 'nongovernmental organizations' when referring to organizations in civil society.[7]

In this paper, I will discuss the development of civil society before and during the communist period, and then I will analyse how non-profit organisations have fared during the postcommunist period. Finally I will conclude with some remarks.

Theoretical Ideas on Non-Profit Organisations

During the 1980s, a dominant idea in the social science discourse was that communist societies' increasing internal tensions were because of the confrontation between the political structure (i.e., the Communist Party/State) and civil society. The state began to face the powerful dynamics of the society. The emergence and development of the so-called 'second society' (known also as a 'grey zone') was a significant indicator of the changes occurring in the society. This 'grey zone' was relatively independent from political control, and had the potential for

6 Keane, p. 6.

7 See, for more details, Radhamany Sooryamoorthy, 'Non-Governmental Organizations (NGOs)', in Thomas M. Leonard (ed.), *Encyclopedia of the Developing World* (London: Routledge, 2006), pp. 1150–51.

self-organisation.[8] It included shadow economy, various forms of dissent and, 'underground' culture, *samizdat*, etc.).

However, while there was a certain leeway for some forms of private initiative against the dogmas of the Marxist political economy, which were aimed at reanimation of the ailing financial and production system, this was not the case everywhere. Terror against dissidents and unofficial culture was by far not eased, especially in the countries of the former USSR, Bulgaria and Romania. At the same time, processes of shattering the state's dominant role in all fields of society acquired irreversible character in most of Central European countries. This signified a failure of the totalitarian Communist State's attempt to organise the whole society 'like a large factory'.

One of the acknowledged authors in the field, Lester Salomon, describes the mutual conditioning of the state, market and civil society. He uses the term the 'third sector' to depict a vague domain, which is neither the state, nor the market, and which encompasses a vast spectrum of phenomena and structures, including various forms of public opinion and civic initiative, mass media, and civic organisations. He considers the 'third sector' to cover the whole universe of the civil society, which is too broad. Salomon explains formation of non-profit, or civic, organisations as a result of inherent limitations of both the market system and the state, 'market and government failures'.[9] With respect to the market, this kind of argument has been applied to the non-profit sector most explicitly by Burton Weisbrod,[10] who referred to these limitations as 'market failures'.

8 David Ost, 'The Politics of Interests in Post–Communist Eastern Europe', *Theory and Society*, 22, no. 4, 1993; George Schöpflin, Culture and Identity in Post-Communist Europe, in *Developments*, in Stephen White (ed.), *East European Politics* (London: Macmillan Press, 1993).

9 Lester Salamon, *America's Nonprofit Sector. A Primer.* (Baltimore. MD: John Hopkins University Press 1992), pp. 7–10. See also De Odem, 'Of Market Failure, Voluntary Failure, and Third-Party Government: Toward a Theory of Government-Non-profit Relations in the Modern Welfare State', *Journal of Voluntary Action Research*, 16, nos. 1–2 (1987), pp. 29–49.

10 Burton Weisbrod, *The Voluntary Nonprofit Sector*. (Lexington, MA: Lexington Books, 1978). Basically, this means that the market is excellent for handling things that are consumed individually, such as shoes, cars, clothing, and food. Consumer choices in the marketplace send signals to producers about the prices

Those failures are to be compensated for by introducing some kinds of non-market mechanisms. One such mechanism is the government, which imposes taxes on individuals, thus compelling everyone to share in the cost of collective goods. Another type is the non-profit organisations. Non-profit organisations allow individuals to pool their resources to produce collective goods they mutually desire. Through non-profit organisations individuals can provide kinds and levels of collective goods they desire.

Finally, the reason for existence of civic non-profit organisations has to do not so much with the efficiency of these organisations or the service functions they perform. It has to do with the role they play in promoting social values, such as freedom and pluralism. Civic organisations bolster individual initiative for public good. This elucidates the reason why most of the principal reforms in human history originated in the realm of the civic initiative and activity, such as civil rights, environmental protection, workplace safety, child welfare and women's rights. As Tocqueville put it most properly and flawlessly more than a century and a half ago,

> among the democratic nations... all the citizens are independent and feeble; they can do hardly anything by themselves, and none of them can oblige his fellow men to lend him their assistance. They all, therefore, become powerless if they do not learn voluntarily to help one another.[11]

Thus, voluntary associations ensure the capacity for joint action and human solidarity in democratic societies,

> If men living in democratic countries had no right and no inclination to associate for political purposes, their interdependence would be in great jeopardy,

that will be paid and the quantities of such items that can be sold at those prices. However, there exists a no less important substance, which, by contrast, can only be used up collectively – such as clean air and water, national security and defence, or safe neighbourhoods. Mechanisms of the market are not able to handle well these so-called public goods. They involve a serious 'free-rider' problem because, once produced, everyone can benefit from them even without contributing in meeting the cost – paid by his or her neighbour.

11 Alexis de Tocqueville, *Democracy in America*. (New York: Vintage Books. 1985 [1835]), p. 114.

> but they might long preserve their wealth and their cultivation; whereas if they never acquired the habit of forming associations in ordinary life, civilisation itself would be endangered.[12]

This last description not only reveals the reasons that made civil society to exist, but explains also how crucial it is to have this vibrant sector in a democratic society. All this is especially relevant for post-communist countries in order to improve deficiencies and fill the gaps left by a democratic government and a market economy. It is expected that civil society should 'mediate and balance the power of state and market, to provide a moral check on the market and, likewise to maintain the democratic integrity of the state'.[13] Lacking the authority of the state and driven by the value-based rather than profit-based motivation and purpose, civil society structures represent networks of citizens freely participating in associations. Those networks strive 'to change the status quo in the interest of some assumed public good'[14] – or, put even more visionary 'to serve underserved or neglected populations, to expand the freedom of or to empower people, to engage in advocacy for social change, and to provide services'.[15]

12 de Tocqueville, p. 118.

13 James Howell and J. Pierce, 'Civil Society: Technical Instrument or Social Force for Change?', in D. Lewis and T. Wallace (eds.), *New Roles and Relevance: Development NGOs and the Challenge of Change* (Hartford, CT: Kumaritan Press, 2000), pp. 75–88.

14 Charles Charfield, 'Intergovernmental and nongovernmental associations to 1945', in J. Smith *et al.* (eds.), *Transnational Social Movements and Global Politics: Solidarity beyond the State* (New York: Syracuse University Press, 1997).

15 McCarthy *et al.*, *The Nonprofit Sector in the Global Community: Voices from Many Nations* (San Francisco: Jossey-Bass, 1992), p. 3

Non-Profit Organisations in Bulgaria

It is now the third time civil society in Bulgaria has been reinvigorated. Without even knowing the term *civil society*, the ancestors in the 19th century created various self-sustaining, reliable and independent civic structures. This primeval Balkan civil society developed separately from the European trend that commenced with the French Enlightenment. Bulgarian *chitalishta,*[16] church and school boards, monastery *ephoréias,*[17] professional guilds with their *lonjas*[18] managing the socio-economic relations of craftsmen from various branches, were distinctive forms of social organisation.

However, adjusted to the conditions of the Ottoman rule, these civic structures appeared to be unprepared and inadequate within the thoroughly changed state of the independent country after the collapse of the Ottoman Empire. It required a quite different type of organisation, style and even pace of work and operation, as independent Bulgaria strived to become a modern European industrialized nation. Organizations attempted to develop without losing their national identity and specificity. However, the period between the end of the 19th century until the end of the Second World War in 1944 turned out to be too short for growth and reinforcement. Oddly enough, many of the charities, which were earlier outlawed for being connected to the 'Anglo-American plutocracy' and other 'hostile ideologies', were banned for being 'pro-fascist'. Under the Stalinist dictatorship, only organisations, whose articles stated that they were 'contributing to the struggle for the final triumph of communism,'[19] had the right to exist. This related even to the philatelic and numismatic societies, which under other normal circumstances were removed from politics. The

16 Literally, 'reading clubs which are voluntarily set up and funded by the local population. They consist of libraries, amateur music, dance, and theatre groups, as well as instruction on various practical skills and popular learning.

17 From Greek, 'board of trustees', which is sustained by bequeathed or donated funds.

18 Turkish from Italian, 'general meeting of the masters from certain vocation'.

19 See for more details Stephan Nikolov, *Blagotvoryashtiyat Sektor* [The Benevolent Sector]. (Sofia: RIK Litera, 1999), esp. pp. 11–12, 47–48.

control of the Communist Party over everyday behaviour, professional activities, artistic and academic production of the intellectuals was quite intense in Bulgaria. In order to have her career, artists, writers and academics were forced to become members of the Communist Party, or not belong to closed clubs of the 'non-party communists'.[20]

In addition, this delayed rise of civil society in Bulgaria resulted also from a number of historical factors, common for the South Eastern Europe (the Balkans). Distorted views about 'the world around' to a great degree detained society's development and narrowed its worldview. Under these circumstances, the very notion of civil society appeared to be unaccustomed and seemingly inappropriate, seen as something alien and suspicious, which permitted power to be monopolised by the political and other elites. These urban elites, which relied on the state for their careers and incomes, dominated the large and generally uneducated rural masses. For the latter politics with its complicated procedures was something distant and inexplicable according to traditional agrarian community values.[21] Many ordinary people were not able to differentiate political parties, various interest groups, and numerous charitable organizations. This confusion fostered negative attitudes and suspicions toward charities and charitable efforts.

However, though through a slow and cumbersome process, civil society gained foothold in Bulgaria. It still has to go a long way in

20 Even the Eastern Orthodox Church, historically and traditionally submitted to the secular authorities, turned into a specific department of the *nomenclature*; no members of the high clergy could be elected without the approval of the Communist Party. As early as 1949, an official Eastern Orthodox publication depicted the communist regime as 'a requirement of the Christian consciousness and Christian social spirit' (D. Penov, *Hristiyanstvoto za kapitalizma i sotsializma* [Christianity about Capitalism and Socialism], in *Pravoslaven pastir*, no. 6 (1949), p. 137). This statement could never be made by a Polish Catholic archbishop. At the same time, there were a series of fabricated trials against Catholic and Evangelist clergy, who were accused of being 'agents of the world imperialism', CIA spies, and so on, to exile them in labour camps. There were, indeed, victims and martyrs among Orthodox clergy, especially among ordinary priests. The Islamic boards of trustees and ruling bodies were also penetrated.

21 See, for more details, Victor Roudometof and Stephan E. Nikolov, 'Roots of the Balkan Political Model: Pernicious Combination between Nationalism and Underdevelopment', *Sociologicheski Problemi*, nos. 3–4 (1999), pp. 146–163.

order to grow into a genuine partnership with the state. Its source comes from the so-called 'third sector' – the non-profit organisations. Most of them were founded and developed during the last ten years. As observable and identifiable objects, most authors concentrate their attention on these organisations, though they are only a part of a large, complex, and heterogeneous class of phenomena. If we consider the growing number and diversity of NGOs, the large number of Bulgarian citizens involved and the development of the legislative and institutional framework protecting NGOs, then we can conclude that there is a significant progress in the rise of civil society.

The distribution of NGO in Bulgaria, with the majority of organisations concentrated in the largest cities and towns, draws parallel with another least developed Balkan state, Albania.[22] Both local businesses and the state fail to provide any significant support to the non-profit sector because government lacks funds. Companies prefer to fund advertising, such as topless competitions and TV shows. Furthermore, governmental agencies lack ideas about how to work with NGOs. Government funding of the NGOs is almost non-existent, and the civil servants are reluctant to provide any tax incentives that may incite more Bulgarian businessmen to extend support to help ailing medical care, foster care homes, culture and research. One consequence is that the Bulgarian non-profit sector relies almost on foreign donors. Those who fail to secure grants are doomed, while the others that are successful become eternal parasites.

Civic organisations not only fail to perform the expected function of monitoring and controlling a political and economic sphere in order to prevent corrupt practices, but appear to be distributive coalitions, special interest groups, embezzling huge resources to enrich themselves and their retinue. In a series of articles Minev and Jeliazkova criticise some foreign-funded foundations in Bulgaria, and reveal that they lack integrity, and divert foreign funds to a circles of partners and

22 Jenny Hyatt, *An Introduction to the Non-Profit Sector in the Balkans* (Kent, MA: Charities Aid Foundation, 2000); Tina Mavrikos-Adamou, 'The Development of Civil Society in Southeastern Europe', in George Kourvetaris (ed.), *The New Balkans: Disintegration and Reconstruction* (Boulder: East European Monographs, 2002), p. 281.

friends.[23] Their articles displaying a cynical picture of the so called 'third sector' were published in one of the highest circulation newspapers. There was no reaction from any organisations from the Third Sector organisations, or from the Union of Bulgarian Foundations and Associations, Democracy Network, or the parliamentary Committee for the Civil Society.

People started to distrust public organisations. According to an April 2003 survey of the National Centre for Public Opinion Research, 33% Bulgarians believe that there are extraterrestrial beings, while only 15% trust the political parties in Bulgaria.[24] The General Auditing Office's head stated that a third from the nearly 300 (*sic*) registered political parties are nothing more than disguised businesses.[25] There is no openness in the process of deciding which organisations and which activities should be supported by scarce public sources, some 4.3m Bulgarian Levs (approx. 2.2m Euro).

Aid from and co-operation with the Western organisations and institutions are crucial for the existence and sustainability of NGOs, and finding ways and means for survival is crucial. Only 27% of the interviewed in an USAID sponsored study reported that a minor part of their resources came from internal sources. In the same study from an opinion poll conducted by one of the leading agencies in the field, MBMD, a third of respondents in a nationally representative sample in January 2003 revealed negative or indeterminate attitude toward the existing NGOs.[26]

Similar facts made a young British student of Bulgarian background to call the post-communist transition in Bulgaria 'institutionalisation of the practices of disorder and chaos'.[27] The student wrote that the population perceives the whole spectrum of the political elite as 'all the same' – i.e., corrupted and vacillating. At the same time, 'the government is accountable to the people only in a notional

23 *Trud* daily, 26, 28, and 30 September 2002.

24 *Standart* daily, 9 May 2003.

25 *Trud* daily, 7 June 2003; *Novinar* daily, 9 June 2003; *Standart* daily, 10 June 2003.

26 Quoted in *Dnevnik* daily, 27 July 2003.

27 Emilian Kavalski, 'Bulgaria: the State of Chaos', *Southeast European Politics*, 4, no. 1 (2003), pp. 70, 41–74, 86.

and very abstract (if not populist) sense, while the people do not feel responsible for the governments' actions' (i.e., there is a clear distinction between 'us' and 'them')'.[28] Bulgarians appeared to be too disturbed and confused after a decade and a half of fruitless transition that brought more hardships than comfort for the large population. This contributed for the ever-increasing distrust toward the institutions of civil society in Bulgaria. The two most recent national parliamentary elections, in June 2001 and 2005, demonstrated persuasively this large distraction and frustration. Voters not only massively disregarded major old parties that dominated the political scene since 1990 but rejected as well the newly established 'popular movements' that aimed at replacing traditional political parties. A political novice – the former king that spent most of his life in exile, overwhelmingly won the elections.[29] He returned back home only a couple of months before the elections and was not able even to establish his own political party, the National Movement Simeon II.

Four years later, things have not changed a lot – at least in a positive direction. Bulgaria saw the next democratic elections, which proved further disappointment, distrust, and lack of stable democratic values among the population. Despite authorities' efforts in introducing a sort of lottery to persuade people to vote, almost half of the eligible voters abstained. Not only no clear or viable majority emerged as a result of the voting, but situation from 2001 repeated even more acerbically. Again within a two months' time, a quasi-fascist coalition, called 'Attack', appeared almost from scratch and succeeded to enter the parliament with some 20 members. 'Attack' skilfully exploited ordinary Bulgarians' fears and qualms. Among other claims, the party urge to create labour camps for the Gypsy population and overall 'de-Turkization' and 'de-Gypsization' of the country.

28 Kavalski, p. 51.
29 Simeon II's bid was supported by a coalition of two marginal parties, but later he formalized the loose coalation to form the National Movement Simeon II. Simeon himself never was in the election ballots.

'Attack' is another proof of the absence of a developed civil society that promotes people's interests and needs.[30] In order to achieve this, a long-term strategy should address the larger issue of democratisation using the NGOs as vehicles for building the political culture. It is necessary to understand that neither the state nor the various organisations alone are able to build a democratic civil society. It is necessary, first, to pay more attention to what extent historical legacies shape opportunities for the civil society development; second, to review the role of political-economic systems, ideologies, and social networks in both enabling and constraining voluntary action and civic initiative; and third, to search for legitimacy in providing social services under conditions of uncertainty.

Conclusion

In this work I have tried to examine the development of the civil society sector in post-communist Bulgaria. It is now the third time civil society in Bulgaria has been reinvigorated. The lack of development of civil society in Bulgaria is the result of a number of historical factors, some specific to the country, and others common to South Eastern Europe.

Civil society still lacks a genuine partnership with the state. The theory of civil society is far from being exhausted as a source of explanation and understanding. Civil society theory needs to be anchored in specific empirical investigations without losing the concept's universal meaning and significance.

30 For more details see Michael Haynes and Rumy Husan, 'Market Failure, State Failure, Institutions, and Historical Constraints in the East European Transition', *Journal of European Area Studies*, 10, no. 1 (2002), pp. 105–129.

Bibliography

Alexander, Jeffrey C., *Real Civil Societies: Dilemmas of Institutionalisation* (London: Sage, 1998).

Bunce, Valerie, 'The Historical Origins of the East-West Divide: Civil Society, Political Society, and Democracy in Europe', in Nancy Bermeo *et al.* (eds.), *Civil Society before Democracy: Lessons from Nineteenth Century Europe* (Latham, MD: Rowman and Littlefield Publishers, 2000).

Burtt, E. A., *The English Philosophers from Bacon to Mill* (London: Modern Library, 1989).

Cellarius, Barbara A., and Caedmon Staddon, 'Environmental Nongovernmental Organisations, Civil Society, and Democratisation in Bulgaria', *East European Politics and Societies*, 16, no. 1 (2002), pp. 182–222.

Charfield, Charles, 'Intergovernmental and nongovernmental associations to 1945', in J. Smith, C. Chartfield and R. Pagnucco (eds.), *Transnational Social Movements and Global Politics: Solidarity beyond the State* (New York: Syracuse University Press, 1997).

Dahrendorf, Ralf, *After 1989: Morals, Revolution, and Civil Society* (New York: St. Martin's Press, 1997).

Fotev, Georgi, *Grazhdansko obshtestvo* [*Civil Society*] (Sofia: Publishing House of the Bulgarian Academy of Sciences, 1992).

Friedberg, James, and Branimir Zaimov, 'Politics, Environment and the Rule of Law in Bulgaria', in Krassimira Paskaleva et al. (eds.), *Bulgaria in Transition: Environmental Consequences of Political and Economic Transformation* (Aldershot: Ashgate, 1998).

Gellner, Ernest, 'Civil Society in Historical Context', *International Social Science Journal*, 43, no. 3 (August 1991), pp. 495–510.

—— Conditions of Liberty: Civil Society and Its Rivals. (London: Penguin,1994).

Hansmann, H., 'Why Are the Nonprofit Organizations Exempted from Corporate Income Taxation', in Michelle White (ed.), *Nonprofit*

Firms in a Three-Sector Economy (Washington, D.C.: The Urban Institute Press, 1981).

Haynes, Jeff, *Democracy and Civil Society in the Third World* (Cambridge: Polity Press, 1997).

Haynes, Michael, and Rumy Husan, 'Market Failure, State Failure, Institutions, and Historical Constraints in the East European Transition', *Journal of European Area Studies*, 10, no. 1 (2002), pp. 105–129.

Howell, James and J. Pierce, 'Civil Society: Technical Instrument or Social Force for Change?', in D. Lewis and T. Wallace (eds.), *New Roles and Relevance: Development NGOs and the Challenge of Change* (W. Hartford, CT: Kumaritan Press, 2000), pp. 75–88.

Hyatt, Jenny, *An Introduction to the Non-Profit Sector in the Balkans* (Kent, MA: Charities Aid Foundation, 2000).

Ignatieff. M., 'On Civil Society. Why East European's Revolutions Could Succeed', *Foreign Affairs*, 74, no. 2 (March/April 1995), pp. 128–136.

Kavalski, Emilian, 'Bulgaria: the State of Chaos', *Southeast European Politics*, 4, no. 1 (2003), pp. 68–90.

Keane, John, *Civil Society: Old Images, New Visions* (Cambridge: Polity Press, 1998; translated into Bulgarian Sofia, 2002).

Kuti, Éva, 'Different Eastern European Countries at Different Crossroads', *Voluntas*, 10, no. 1 (1999), pp. 26–41.

Linz, Juan and Alfred Stepan, *Problems of Democratic Transition and Consolidation – Southern Europe, South America, and Post-Communist Europe* (Baltimore: Johns Hopkins University Press, 1996).

McCarthy, Kathleen, Virginia Hodgkinson and Russi Sumariwalla, *The Nonprofit Sector in the Global Community: Voices from Many Nations* (San-Francisco, CA: Jossey-Bass, 1992).

Mavrikos-Adamou, Tina, 'The Development of Civil Society in Southeastern Europe', in George A. Kourvetaris, Victor Roudometof, Kleomenis Koutsoukis and Andrew G. Kourvetaris (eds.), *The New Balkans: Disintegration and Reconstruction* (Boulder: East European Monographs, 2002), pp. 274–292.

Minev, Doukhomir et al., *Promenyashtite se liza na demokrazijata* [*Changing Faces of Democracy*] (Sofia: Perspektiva Foundation, 2000).

Minev, Doukhomir, Maria Jeliazkova, 'Bulgaria: razhdaneto na kapitalizma i na ikonomicheskata racionalnost' ['Bulgaria: Birth of Capitalism and of the Economic Rationality'], *Sociologicheski problemi*, nos. 3–4 (2000), pp. 118–147.

Nikolov, Stephan E., *Blagotvoryashtiyat Sektor* [*The Benevolent Sector*] (Sofia: RIK Litera, 1999).

Olson, Mancur. *The Rise and Decline of Nations: Economic Growth, Stagflation and Social Rigidities* (New Haven: Yale University Press, 1982).

Ost, David, 'The Politics of Interests in Post-Communist Eastern Europe', *Theory and Society*, 22, no. 4 (1993), pp. 453–486

Parrott, Bruce, 'Perspectives on Postcommunist Democratization', in Karen Dawisha and Bruce Parrott (eds.) *Politics, Power, and the Struggle for Democracy in Southeast Europe* (Cambridge: Cambridge University Press, 1997).

Penov, D., 'Hristiyanstvoto za kapitalizma i sotsializma' ['Christianity about Capitalism and Socialism'], *Pravoslaven pastir*, no. 6 (1949).

Pérez-Diaz, Victor, *The Return of Civil Society: The Emergence of Democratic Spain* (Cambridge, MA, Harvard University Press, 1994).

Potůček, Martin, 'The Uneasy Birth of Czech Civil Society', *Voluntas*, 11, no. 2 (2000), pp. 107–121.

Regulska, J., 'NGOs and their Vulnerabilities during the Time of Transition: The Case of Poland', *Voluntas*, 10, no. 1 (1999), pp. 61–72.

Roudometof, V. and Stephan E. Nikolov, 'Korenite na balkanskiya politicheski model: Pagubno suchetanie mezhdu nacionalism i nedorazvitost' ['Roots of the Balkan Political Model: Pernicious Combination between Nationalism and Underdevelopment'], *Sociologicheski Problemi*, no. 3–4 (1999), pp. 146–163.

Salamon, Lester, 'Of Market Failure, Voluntary Failure, and Third-Party Government: Toward a Theory of Government-Non-profit

Relations in the Modern Welfare State', *Journal of Voluntary Action Research*, 16, no. 1–2 (1987), pp. 29–49.

—— *America's Nonprofit Sector. A Primer* (Baltimore: Johns Hopkins University Press, 1992).

Seligman, Adam, *The Idea of Civil Society* (Princeton, Princeton University Press, 1992).

Schöpflin, George, 'Culture and Identity in Post-Communist Europe', in *Developments in East European Politics* (London: Macmillan Press, 1993), pp. 16–34.

Sooryamoorthy, Radhamany. 'Non-Governmental Organizations (NGOs)', in *Encyclopedia of the Developing World*. Ed. Thomas M. Leonard. New York, London: Routledge, 2006, pp. 1149–56.

Sotiropoulos, Dimitri, 'A Colossus with Feet of Clay: The State in Post-Authoritarian Greece', in Harry Psomiades and Stavros Thomadakis (eds.), *Greece, the New Europe, and the Changing International Order* (New York: Pella Publishing, 1993).

Tempest, Clive, 'Myths from Eastern Europe and the Legend of the West', in Roberth Fine & Shirin Rai (eds.), *Civil Society: Democratic Perspectives* (London: Frank Cass, 1997).

Tocqueville, Alexis de, *Democracy in America* (New York: Vintage Books (1985 [1835]).

Weisbrod, Burton, *The Voluntary Nonprofit Sector* (Lexington, MA: Lexington Books, 1978).

Zweerde, E. van der. 'Civil Society', in Thomas Leonard (ed.), *Encyclopedia of the Developing World* (London: Routledge, 2006), pp. 346–8.

Culture

SARAH AMSLER

Knowledge, Freedom and Post-Soviet Imperialism: The Case of Social Science in Kyrgyzstan

Communism, Capitalism and the Progress of Reason

Questions about the autonomy of scientific knowledge have long been tied to questions about the political, cultural and economic organisation of society itself; and in particular, to degrees and styles of freedom and repression. While Pierre Bourdieu's classic analysis of the academic disciplines demonstrated the implicit heteronomy of the modern European academy under capitalism[1] and Michel Foucault's studies of power/knowledge established the possibility of an inverse relationship between knowledge production and human freedom,[2] other sociologists of science have argued that scientific knowledge becomes progressively more autonomous under conditions of economic and political liberalism.[3] This last approach gained particular credence in Anglo-American sociology during the Cold War, when questions about the relationship between science and political economy tran-

1 Pierre Bourdieu, *Homo Academicus* (Cambridge: Polity Press, 1988).

2 Michel Foucault, *Madness and Civilisation: A History of Insanity in the Age of Reason* (London: Tavistock, 1967); Michel Foucault, *The History of Sexuality: Vol. 1, an introduction* (Harmondsworth: Penguin, 1978); Michel Foucault, *Power/Knowledge: Selected Interviews and Other Writings*, edited by C Gordon (New York: Pantheon Books, 1980).

3 Robert Merton, 'Science and the social order', in P. Sztompka (ed.), *Robert K. Merton on Social Structure and Science* (Chicago: University of Chicago Press, 1938 [1996]); Robert Merton, 'The ethos of science', in P. Sztompka (ed.), *Robert K. Merton on Social Structure and Science* (Chicago: University of Chicago Press, 1943 [1996]).

scended the realm of theory and came to represent the success or failure of broader capitalist and communist utopias.[4]

Not surprisingly, therefore, the collapse of the Soviet regime was met with enthusiasm by scholars on both sides of the Atlantic who believed that the dismantling of authoritarian social structures would lead inevitably to the autonomisation – and hence the genuine progression – of scientific knowledge. This, in turn, was expected to contribute to the rationalisation and de-ideologicisation of social development.[5] This hope was particularly intense among social scientists in the peripheral regions of the former Soviet empire, such as the Baltics and Central Asia, where movements for limited intellectual and academic independence from the Soviet centre (i.e., Moscow, St. Petersburg and Novosibirsk) had emerged during the late socialist period.[6] In the Kyrgyz Republic, which will be the primary focus of this chapter, it was believed that the 'revolutionary renewal of Soviet society on the whole and in the union republics in particular' would enable social scientists to gain control over the 'structure, work, concepts and financial organisation' of their field;[7] in other words, control over the means of their own intellectual production.[8] The increasing

4 Noam Chomsky (ed.), *The Cold War and the University* (New York: New Press, 1997).

5 K. Bekturganov, T. Omurbekov, T. and A. Tishin, 'Komu vygoden populism v sotsiologii' [Who benefits from populism in sociology?], *Slovo Kyrgyzstana*, 11 May 1994; J. Eades and C. Schwaller (eds.), 'Transitional Agendas: Working Papers from the Summer School for Soviet Sociologists,' Centre for Social Anthropology and Computing, University of Kent at Canterbury, 1991; S. Ismailova, 'Sotsiologicheskoe obrazovanie: problemy stanovleniia i perspektivy' [Sociological education: problems of its creation and perspectives], *Kut Bilim*, 31 May: 6 1995; Kusein Isaev, 'Demokratsiia i vlast'' [Democracy and power], *Erkin-Too*, 30 September 1995.

6 Sarah Amsler, *From Truth in Strength to Strength in Truth: Sociology, Knowledge and Power in Kyrgyzstan, 1966–2003*. PhD thesis, London School of Economics and Political Science, 2005.

7 Kusein Isaev, 'Sotsiologiia v Kyrgyzstane: sostoianie i perspektivi,' *Izvestiia* – Obshchestvennye Nauki, Akademii Nauki Respublik Kirgizstana vol. 2 (1991), p. 32.

8 David Swartz, *Culture and Power: The Sociology of Pierre Bourdieu* (Chicago: University of Chicago Press, 1997), p. 255.

liberalisation of society, in terms of ideology, political institutions and economics, was expected to be unproblematically liberating for scientific life.

This chapter argues, however, that the collapse of Soviet authoritarianism and expansion of formal democracy and capitalism into the region has in fact not heralded the simple autonomisation or development of social science, but has instead initiated a rather more ambiguous formation of neo-colonial knowledge production in Kyrgyzstan. It suggests that while functionalist interpretations of the science-society relationship may provide useful points of discussion about the normative role of scientific knowledge, they are inadequate for understanding the organisation of science within a scientific world system.[9] For in post-colonial societies such as Kyrgyzstan, which are heavily dependent on foreign lending and development aid and politically subordinate to donor countries such as Russia and the US, the autonomy or heteronomy of science has as much to do with the structure and culture of imperialism as it does to do with creating a democratic ethos of science. The chapter therefore explores the promises and realities of post-Soviet sociology in Kyrgyzstan through the lens of academic imperialism, a concept which is borrowed from post-colonial scholarship and which has more recently been employed to analyse the relationship between the autonomy of scientific knowledge and the globalisation of capitalism.[10] It is argued that this concept not only addresses obstacles to scientific autonomy at the level of intellectual practice and institutions, but also at the level of political economy – all of which must be engaged in the struggle to establish 'social

9 Thomas Schott, 'Soviet science in the scientific world system: was it autarchic, self-reliant, distinctive, isolated, peripheral, central?', *Knowledge: Creation, Diffusion, Utilization*, 14, no. 4 (1992), pp. 410–39; Thomas Schott, 'Ties Between Center and Periphery in the Scientific World-System: Accumulation of Rewards, Dominance and Self-Reliance in the Center,' *Journal of World Systems Research*, 4 (1998), pp. 112–144.

10 Claude Ake, *Social Science as Imperialism: The Theory of Political Development* (Nigeria: Ibadan University Press, 1982); S. Alatas, 'Intellectual imperialism: definition, traits and problems', *Southeast Asian Journal of Social Sciences*, 28 no. 1 (2000), pp. 23–45.

conditions of the possibility for rational thought' in social scientific activity.[11]

The Promises of Social Science Reform in Kyrgyzstan

Since the emergence of sociology as a 'technical branch' of Marxist-Leninst philosophy in the Soviet Central Asian republics in the 1950s, questions about the relationship between social science and society, and in particular about the relationship between intellectual autonomy and political engagement, have shaped the agenda of the academic field (Amsler 2005). From its inception, the development of sociology was explicitly linked to the development of society; hence, the reform of the social sciences has historically been integrated into broader social reforms. As one Kyrgyzstani sociologist argued, even during perestroika people were 'looking [to sociologists] for the optimal methods to deal with the transition to the market economy, the process of perestroika, democratisation, and the wider participation of workers in state governance'.[12]

The project to reform social science in order to reform society accelerated during the late 1980s, and became intertwined with the new politics of the 'nation'. Even as the Communist Party and Soviet government put forward resolutions to increase the role of Marxist-Leninist sociology in the construction of communism both in Moscow and on the periphery, Kyrgyzstani academics and politicians were beginning to re-evaluate Soviet definitions of economic and social development.[13] During this time they elaborated a number of different

11 Bourdieu quoted in Swartz, p. 255.

12 Isaev, 'Sotsiologiia v Kyrgyzstane'.

13 T. Koichuev, 'Ideologiia obnovleniia i razvitie obshchestvennyh nayk v Kirgizskoi SSR' [The ideology of renewal and the development of social science in the Kirgiz SSR], *Izvestiia akademii nauk Kirgizskoi SSR*, vol. 2 (1988), p. 5; V. Sherstobitov, 'Vysokoe prednaznachenie obshchestvennykh nauk' [The highest mission of the social sciences], *Izvestiia akademii nauk Kirgizskoi SSR, Obshchestvennye nauki*, vol. 1 (1987), pp. 3–8.

alternatives to dominant Soviet models, including more national autonomy, full republican sovereignty, and gradual integration into the capitalist world market.

These alternatives also extended into the organisation of social science itself. Just before independence, following earlier trends in the Baltic republics, Kyrgyzstani sociologists proposed to form their own autonomous national branch of the Soviet Sociological Association, which would focus on new priorities such as nationhood, ethnicity, the national working class, and the development of new national economic institutions.[14] By establishing more political autonomy, it was argued, sociologists would ensure more intellectual autonomy. Through this, they felt they could be more influential in developing policies that were relevant to social realities in Kyrgyzstan (as opposed to the Soviet centre) and that would elevate their status as intellectuals and professionals within the union. For a time, it seemed that the 'conditions of an independent Kyrgyzstan provided [...] the possibility for the gradual development of a national sociology,' and with it, the possibility of better and more autonomous scholarship and practice.[15] Echoing scholars in other newly independent societies before them, Kyrgyzstani sociologists spent much of the next decade asking, 'how can the special skills of social scientists contribute to meeting the issues presented by demands for rapid and fundamental social change, often in circumstances of acute political tension?'.[16]

This question, however, has not been the exclusive propriety of social scientists in Kyrgyzstan. Interest in the reform, development and practical application of social science in post-Soviet Kyrgyzstan in fact extends beyond the geopolitical and ideological borders of the republic. Since 1991, international organisations and foreign governments have invested millions of dollars in supporting and influencing

14 Kusein Isaev, 'Pervaia konferentsiia sotsiologov v Kirgizii' [The first conference of sociologists in Kyrgyzstan], *Sotsis*, vol. 7 (1990).

15 Kusein Isaev, 'Sotsiologiiany saiasii soiku kylgylary bar' [They want to make a political prostitute out of sociology], *Asaba*, 6 March 1998.

16 Bryce Wood, 'Notes on Conference Proceedings,' *Social Science in Latin America: Papers Presented at the Conference on Latin American Studies Held at Rio de Janeiro March 29–31, 1965*, edited by Manuel Diégues Júnior and Bryce Wood (New York: Columbia University Press, 1967), p. 323.

the development of social science in the former Soviet Union;[17] bodies such as the Open Society Institute, USAID, and UNESCO, and the Ford, Eurasia and Rockefeller Foundations have become the primary benefactors of scientific research and activity in Kyrgyzstan.[18] Their considerable investment is based on the philosophy that institutionalising new models of social science is a modern solution to social problems brought on by underdevelopment and anti-modern ideology; and even that 'policy-relevant research is of central importance to the issue of democratic and peaceful co-existence of multi-ethnic groups in the Central Asian countries'.[19] It is also more implicitly based on an Orientalist assumption that knowledge produced in cooperation with the 'west' is somehow superior to that articulated solely in 'Soviet' or 'Kyrgyz' space. At the international level, the development of sociology in Kyrgyzstan is thus often synonymous with its westernisation, and evaluated in terms of its evolution to pre-established 'international standards' of scientific practice.[20]

17 Blair Ruble, Forward to the *Humanities and Social Sciences in the Former Soviet Union: An Assessment of Need*, unpublished report commissioned by the Carnegie Corporation of New York and John D. and Catherine T. MacArthur Foundations, prepared by the Kennan Institute, Woodrow Wilson Center, Washington DC, 1 August 1999.

18 For discussion about the role of such organisations in social science in the Third World, see Dan Chekki, *American Sociological Hegemony: Transnational Explorations* (1997) p. xxx; Chomsky, *Cold War and the University*; Irene Gendzier, *Managing Political Change: Social Scientists and the Third World* (Boulder: Westview Press, 1985); Harry Hiller, 'Universality of science and the question of national sociologies', *The American Sociologist*, vol. 14 (1979); Paul Lamy, 'The globalization of American sociology: excellence or imperialism?', *The American Sociologist*, 11 (1976); and William Foote Whyte, 'The role of the US professor in developing countries', *The American Sociologist* (February 1969)

19 UNESCO. 1999. 'Management of Social Transformations (MOST).'

20 This refers to a specifically political and economic project, which must be distinguished from movements within the global academic community to establish a school of 'global sociology' and to democratise intellectual practice (see Saïd Amir Arjomand (ed.) 'International Sociology into the New Millennium', *International Sociology*, 15, no. 1 (2000), pp. 5–10; Barry Smart, 'Sociology, Globalization and Postmodernity: Comments on the "Sociology for One World" Thesis', *International Sociology*, 9, no. 2 (1994), pp. 149–159; Gören

Reforms from the Bottom up and Top down

This double-barrelled project to reform social science from within as an 'indigenous institution' and from without as foreign 'development' project has created contradictions in the social organisation of science itself. On the one hand, it enables the continued production of social scientific work in the republic. However, while the opening of Soviet borders (both territorial and intellectual) provided the opportunity for unprecedented scholarly exchange and the expansion of collective knowledge, in Kyrgyzstan it also paved the way for many programmes that have 'had the effect of skewing the nature of East-West collaboration [and] fostering tendencies toward one-way, rather than mutual, learning'.[21] This, in turn, has frequently led to the polarisation of 'Western' and 'local' scholars into contending camps that work in parallel sets of institutions, each with a different relationship to state(s) and society.[22] Furthermore, 'policy relevant research' oriented towards increasing the efficiency of formally democratic and capitalist institutions has increasingly obscured critical inquiries into the underlying dynamics, problems and possibilities of Kyrgyzstani society.

As a result, it is seldom recognised that the politics and practices of social science in Central Asia are not particular to the post-Soviet or post-socialist experience. In fact, they share many similarities with patterns of institutionalisation, discourses and practices of social sci-

Therborn (ed.), 'From the Universal to the Global', *International Sociology*, 15, no. 2 (2000), pp. 149–150). While these works purposefully engage with difficult questions about the universality or particularity of certain types of social scientific knowledge, and the benefits and limitations of 'national' and 'international' scientific institutions, the social science debate conducted within the development aid community is predominately normative and based on Euro- or Americo-centric theories of the progress of reason.

21 Susan Bronson, Nancy Popson, and Blair Ruble, 'Sustaining Intellectual Communities: A Strategy for Rebuilding the Social Sciences and Humanities in the Former Soviet Union from Within', *The Humanities and Social Sciences in theFormer Soviet Union: An Assessment of Need*, a report prepared by the Kennan Institute, Woodrow Wilson Center, for the Carnegie Corporation of New York and the MacArthur Foundation (Washington, DC, 1999).

22 Amsler, *From Truth in Strength to Strength in Truth.*

ence observed in newly independent nations in Africa and Latin America during the middle of the last century. Comparative analyses of the development of social science in these societies suggest that the disintegration of Soviet communism was not a rupture in the history of either international social science or western imperialism; not the watershed it is assumed to have been. Instead, it has enabled the continuation of what Doty calls 'imperial encounters' between hegemonic world powers (in the post-Soviet period, the US) and weaker, necessarily dependent, neocolonial societies that are neither truly 'colonised' nor genuinely 'independent' (such as Kyrgyzstan).[23] The contemporary post-Soviet social science development project can therefore be understood within a broader history of power and knowledge, one that in many senses 'recapitulates what's gone on in our Third World domains for a long time and falls into place in a much longer story'.[24]

Theories of Academic Imperialism

The concept of 'academic imperialism' was developed in the late 1960s and early 1970s to describe the economic, political and cultural forces shaping the uneven development of academic disciplines and social research in newly independent societies in both Latin America and Africa. It was also part of a wider critique of the rationalist glorification of 'scientific development' and of a growing tendency at the time to import 'western scientific solutions' to abstract or non-existent social problems in the Third World. Even before Johan Galtung for-

23 Roxanne Doty, *Imperial Encounters: The Politics of Representation in North-South Relations* (Minneapolis: University of Minnesota Press, 1996), p. 3.

24 Noam Chomsky, *Chomsky on MisEducation* (Oxford: Rowman and Littlefield, 2000), p. 43; see also Cassandra Cavanaugh, 'Central Asia's Colonial Past and Why it Matters', *Central Asia Monitor*, 5–6 (2001), pp. 9–17.

mally introduced the idea in his 'structural theory of imperialism,'[25] critical sociologists had used the term to describe the development of social science in the Third World.[26] A volume of increasingly theoretical and analytical work about the topic, including the controversial 'globalisation' of American sociology,[27] later sprung up in the 1980s in India[28] and Africa.[29] More recently, Shils' theory of 'academic centrality' in international social science[30] has been used to analyse the intellectual domination of the West and the asymmetric relations between Third World scholars and their US and Western European colleagues,[31] sometimes even with reference to a 'scientific world system'.[32] Some writers have redefined academic imperialism in more discursive ways, framing it in Gramscian terms as a new form of 'global intellectual hegemony'.[33] Finally, there have recently been a number of critical studies on the relationship between academic knowledge, development practice and globalisation/imperialism in the South.[34]

25 Johan Galtung, 'A Structural Theory of Imperialism', *Journal of Peace Research*, 2 (1971), pp. 81–117.
26 Whyte, 'The role of the US professor'; Wood, 'Notes on conference proceedings', p. 330.
27 Chekki, *American Sociological Hegemony*.
28 Rahmad, *Intellectual Colonisation*.
29 Ake, *Social Science as Imperialism*.
30 Edward Shils, 'Tradition, Ecology and Institution in the History of Sociology', *Daedalus*, 99 (Fall 1970).
31 Abdalla Bujra, 'Whither Social Science Institutions in Africa: A Prognosis', *Africa Development*, 19 (1994), pp. 119–166.
32 Schott, 'Ties between center and periphery'.
33 G. Brosovic, 'Global Intellectual Hegemony and the International Development Agenda', *International Social Science Journal*, 166 (December 2000).
34 Frederick Cooper and Randall Packard, *International Development and Social Science: Essays on the History and Politics of Knowledge* (California: University of California Press, 1997); Arturo Escobar, 'Anthropology and the Development Encounter: The Making and Marketing of Development Anthropology', *American Ethnologist*, 18, no. 4 (1991), pp. 658–682; Norman Long and Ann Long (eds.), *Battlefields of Knowledge: The Interlocking of Theory and Practice in Social Research and Development* (London: Routledge, 1992); Michael Watts, 'Development I: Power, Knowledge, Discursive Practice', *Progress in Human Geography*, 17 (1993).

Although there is thus a substantial body of material about the subject, discussions about academic imperialism are quiet, even silent, in post-Soviet development discourse, where ironically the classical forms of this phenomenon have been reproduced. This is due to a number of related factors, including a perception of ideological unipolarity or the 'end of ideology' in post-socialist societies and the dominance of neo-liberal discourses of development via development institutions in Central Asia. In addition, the very relationships of academic imperialism have prevented scholars from drawing inferences between their experiences and those of intellectuals in other post-colonial societies. I would therefore like to introduce the central tenets of this concept in order to frame contemporary debates about the autonomy of social science in Kyrgyzstan in the alternative context of power, knowledge and imperialism. After commenting briefly on why scientific colonisation occurs in newly independent nations, I will point out its main structural and cultural features (as defined in the literature from India, Latin America, and Africa) and demonstrate how these have been reflected in contemporary developments in social science in Kyrgyzstan today.

Cultural Dependence in Kyrgyzstani Social Science

The central hallmark of academic imperialism is not, as sometimes suspected, the political motivations of colonising agents, but rather the structural and cultural inequalities which shape the kinds of discourse and volume and meaning of intellectual work that is produced in and about a particular society. These inequalities, particularly the intellectual dependence of post-colonial societies and the intellectual hegemony of dominant ones, emerge most frequently when one scientific or intellectual community becomes unable, unwilling or disallowed to support itself and becomes structurally or culturally dependent on others. This is one reason why newly independent nations, particularly those in which ex-colonial powers withdraw financial support for science and education, have historically been so vulnerable to academic imperialism.

Such is the case in Kyrgyzstan. Relations of dominance and dependence are common where there are divisions between centre and periphery. Contrary to assertions that there was neither centre nor periphery in Soviet science, a number of scholars have recently argued that the centre-periphery relationship was in fact one of its most prominent characteristics.[35] Since 1991, Kyrgyzstani scholars have had to work in conditions of extreme poverty and (enthusiastically or reluctantly) to accommodate the demands of external funding agencies into their work.[36] The independence from the Soviet Union which initially created intellectual breathing room also led to an almost total collapse of the country's educational and scientific institutions, a decline in academic standards and the disintegration of sociology's emerging structure and raison d'être. Many prominent and accomplished ethnic Russian scholars emigrated, and many more left the dilapidated academy in search of livelihoods elsewhere. For those that remained, intellectual labour grew increasingly beleaguered as state support for research and education was withdrawn; the Kyrgyz government now gives only token support for scientific activities.[37] In addition, Kyr-

35 S. Eisenstadt, 'Centre–periphery relations in the Soviet empire: some interpretive observations', in A. Motyl (ed.), *Thinking Theoretically About Soviet Nationalities: History and Comparison in the Study of the USSR* (New York: Columbia University Press, 1992); G. Nesvetailov, 'Centre–periphery relations and the transformation of post-Soviet science', *Knowledge and Policy: The International Journal of Knowledge Transfer and Utilization*, 8, no. 2 (1995), pp. 53–67; Schott, 'Soviet science in the scientific world system'.

36 Mehrigiul Ablezova, Interview by the author. Tape recording. American University–Central Asia. Bishkek, Kyrgyzstan. 20 March 2003; Yuri Blum, 'Pravda–ne v sile, no sile–v pravde' [Truth is not in strength, but strength is in truth], *Slovo Kyrgyzstana*, 6 February 1993, p. 7; R. Osmonalieva, Interview with Kusein Isaev, 'Nauka–glavnaia sila, na kotoroi rastsvetaet obschestvo' [Science is the main force upon which society flourishes], *Kut Bilim*, 18 January 1995, p. 4; Ainoura Sagynbaeva, Interview by the author. Tape recording. SIAR Bishkek. Bishkek, Kyrgyzstan. 22 May 2003.

37 State investment in education declined dramatically after Kyrgyzstan declared independence. Egorov (2002: 61) reported that government spending for research and development declined from 0.73% of the GDP in 1990 to 0.14% in

gyzstani social scientists were severed from the major Soviet (now Russian) academic institutions they had only recently been more fully included in, and have met with significant resistance from some sectors of government and society.[38] In short, national independence left social scientists in the republic with few material, political or intellectual resources, and thus at significant risk of becoming dependent on foreign funding agencies.

Of course, financial dependence does not necessitate intellectual dependence or domination. It is therefore important to move beyond the mere material forms of sponsorship to examine the structural and cultural consequences of this dependence and the larger political structures that funding is embedded within. We must also consider the discourses that surround this relationship and understand 'how certain representations [of aid and support] underlie the production of knowledge and identities and how these representations make various courses of knowledge possible'.[39] How much autonomy *do* social scientists in Kyrgyzstan have, formally and substantively, in determining the nature and political meaning of their work within these structures?

There are many symptoms of intellectual dependence in a given society, the level of which 'varies with the power, wealth, and resources of the nation state within which national social science communities are located'. These are detailed in Lamy, who argues that

> a national social science community is *culturally dependent* to the extent that definitions of what should be studied and how (theory and methods), and cri-

1999; Glenady (1995) supports this with her figure of 0.18% in 1994. According to the Kyrgyz National Statistics Committee, in 2000 the state allocated 3.1% of its annual GDP to education–less than half the amount it allocated in 1995 (Reeves 2003: 9). At the 2001 general meeting of the Kyrgyzstan Academy of Science, president Janybek Jeenbaev claimed that the 17 million soms ($345,000) allocated to the Academy by the government was 'not enough to achieve good scientific results' (Radio Free Europe, 2001). In 2002, a local newspaper reported that state universities received only 10–15% of their expenses from the state budget (Osorov 2002). See also Sydykov (1995) on the need to establish a union of scientists to protect the interests of scholars.

38 See Kyrgyz-Press International and Sydykova, 'U sotsiologii trudnoe proshloe'.

39 Doty, *Imperial Encounters*, p. 5.

> teria of desirable scholarly activity (role models and standards of excellence) are those of another national social science community where these are not shared by social science communities in general.[40]

Kyrgyzstani social science exhibits many of these characteristics. International organisations have invested considerably over the past decade specifically to help academics in Central Asia use science and education to 'create and nurture open societies'[41] and to promote regional stability and democratisation.[42] This underlying politico-economic agenda has significant influence on the types of institutions these organisations establish and support, the sorts of scholarship they sponsor and fund, the themes of research they encourage and publish, and the forms of institutionalisation they promote and organise. Through training, exchange and partnerships organised by the Academy for Educational Development, for example, the US Agency for International Development (USAID) trains thousands of 'mid-to-senior level leaders and professionals *in areas directly relevant to the*

40 Lamy, 'The Globalization of American Sociology', p. 107.

41 An 'open society,' according to OSI, is a society in which no individual holds claims to absolute truth, and which is 'characterized by the rule of law, respect for human rights, minorities and minority opinions, the division of power, and a market economy.' (From the OSI web site, 'Concept of Open Society,' www.osi.hu/index_files/promo.html.) This definition of an open society posits that democracy and capitalism are necessarily interdependent – and it implies that the creation of a narrow form of democratic *and* capitalistic society is the single way to achieve an *open* society, which is further equated with a *just* society and a *stable* society, and likened to ideals of the *good* society. This can be contrasted with other definitions of the open society, such as the existentialist concept of an 'open future' in which all individuals are truly free to make independent and creative choices about what kind of society they would like to live in and create. See Hazel Barnes, *An Existentialist Ethic* (Chicago: University of Chicago Press, 1967).

42 USAID claims that American aid for democratic institution building is important because 'any *negative action* on the part of Kyrgyzstan would seriously affect regional stability and pose a threat to American economic and political interests in Central Asia.' (From the home page of USAID Kyrgyzstan's programs, accessed via the Internet at www.usaid.gov/country/ee/kg, emphasis mine.)

transition to democracy and a free-market economy'.[43] The affiliated Eurasia Foundation 'makes small grants on an ongoing basis to support the *transition from centrally planned to market economies.*[44] In addition, the Open Society Institute sponsors activities and reforms that contribute to the development of an 'open society,' as described above. According to one expatriate scholar, however, 'the Soros foundations are supporting the social sciences and humanities, but they seem to be pushing their own agenda as there seems to be little or no consultation with local scholars... There is no interest in training the liberal arts variety of social science scholars, only diplomats and lawyers'.[45] Baruch Kimmerling defines these non-choices as 'framework decisions,' or 'frequently implicit decisions that must be made when approaching a research topic.' These are often 'value laden and are made in the absence of any empirical consideration,' and are 'not usually open to debate or to intellectual bargaining'.[46]

Other types of research questions – regarding alternatives to liberal capitalism, Soviet history, studies of China or Persia, Islam or Christianity (other than in terms of threat or 'tradition'), revolutionary social change, or Russian or American hegemony – have therefore been marginalised, as have academic disciplines such as Kyrgyz and Soviet literature, culture and the arts, sanskritology, linguistics, philosophy and history. As Kyrgyzstani ethnographer Abylabek Asankanov commented, although much historical, archaeological and anthropological work must be done in Kyrgyzstan, 'in order to be able to do it well, people must be trained to be able to access sources in the Chinese, Arabic, and Persian languages. IREX, ACTR/ACCELS, and the MacArthur Foundation have offered no help in these areas'.[47] Since the early 1990s, sociologists have also emphasised the importance of studying migration, youth culture, agricultural communities,

43 USAID Kyrgyzstan Activity Data Sheet, at http://www.usaid.gov/pubs/cbj 2002/ee/kg/116–042.html

44 The Eurasia Foundation, at http://www.eurasia.org

45 See Ruble, *Humanities and Social Sciences in the Former Soviet Union.*

46 Baruch Kimmerling, 'Sociology, Ideology, and Nation-Building: The Palestinians and their Meaning in Israeli Sociology', *American Sociological Review*, 57 (1992).

47 See Ruble, *Humanities and Social Sciences in the Former Soviet Union.*

regional relations, and the consequences of western intervention in the region. However, with the state providing only meager support to those projects that support its interests and western organisations supporting only those in line with their own, Kyrgyzstani social scientists have neither autonomy nor institutional support. Those who have the means to work independently are silently but effectively censored by their exclusion from these systems of sponsorship. As one sociologist noted, 'there are people doing sociology... It is another thing that their knowledge and work is not demanded in our conditions, due to the fact that our establishment is not interested in sociological knowledge'.[48]

Such debates have often polarised scholars into binary categories which symbolise competing constellations in the sociology of knowledge and which come to represent movements for 'internationalising' or 'universalising' knowledge production, on the one hand, and 'indigenising' it on the other. This struggle to negotiate the local and global, universal and particular, dominated and dominant, has historical precedent beyond Central Asia. As Pertierra commented in his study of social science in the Philippines, 'the interest in indigenising social science is shared by a host of other countries from India to Canada, indicating that the process has global roots... The global roots for such distinctive and emerging national traditions are a consequence of decolonization and illustrate the internal and external conditions for a social science practice'.[49] Generally speaking, as critical scholars in post-colonial societies realise that 'the uncritical adoption of theoretical perspectives and methods which have arisen in responses to the conditions and problems in another society does not always help to generate relevant knowledge about your own',[50] they often begin to search for more 'nationally relevant' alternatives.[51]

48 Sydykova, 'U sotsiologii trudnoe proshloe'.

49 Raul Pertierra, *Explorations in Social Theory and Philippine Ethnography* (Diliman, Quezon City: University of the Philippine Press, 1997), p. 4.

50 Lamy, 'Globalization of American Sociology', p. 109.

51 One of the most visible examples of this in recent history is the way that African scholars formed 'social science community-led' institutions for teaching and research in resistance to the dominant 'western-led' institutes that legitimated 'modernisation' in the 1970s and neoliberal structural adjustment

Although there have been few organized movements to indigenise social scientific knowledge in Kyrgyzstan,[52] the impetus is expressed through the activities of individuals and small groups of like-minded sociologists. One of the most vocal proponents of this has been Kusein Isaev, who was active in organising sociologists and popularising the discipline throughout the late 1980s and 1990s. His writings and interviews include treatises on the virtue of sociology and the tragedy of its subjugation beneath ideology; foreign, state and personal interests; he is also critical of the republic's geographical and intellectual isolation. In his estimation, scholars who had been trained only in the 'Soviet' tradition were ignorant of characteristics specific to the region, and paid no attention to life in mountain conditions, the role of family traditions in the republic or the communal foundations of knowledge. It was these questions, he claims, that made the social needs of Kyrgyzstan very different from those in the central regions of Russia or the Ukraine – or, indeed, in the US or Europe. Nevertheless, sociological questions that emanate from these societies have historically dominated the national research agenda. Isaev has argued that many of the problems facing Kyrgyzstani society could be alleviated or solved if sociology and sociological research – mainly for the purpose of identifying and defining social problems – was afforded more social relevance within the state itself.

programmes during the 1980s. According to one study, these new 'indigenous' institutions emerged for three reasons. First, 'the main concern was that if [UNESCO social science initiatives] remained unchallenged, then there was great danger that establishment, i.e. governments, would in effect gain control over social science in Africa.' Scholars would be forced to legitimise the status quo as opposed to having the freedom to influence or change it. Second, scholars wanted to 'counter the strong influence of former colonial powers in universities and research institutes.' And finally, African social scientists felt responsible for helping to influence policy-making and felt that they could have a positive influence on their government leaders (Bujra, 'Wither social science institutions in Africa', p. 143).

52 Kusein Isaev, 'Pervaia konferentsiia'.

Structural Dependence in Kyrgyzstani Social Science

However, Kyrgyzstani social scientists remain structurally dependent on foreign financial and institutional resources. Structural dependence, an aspect of academic imperialism, is directly related to the financial and institutional crises that often accompany decolonisation and/or independence; it is characterised by severely asymmetrical relationships between researchers, scientific communities and nations, and manifests itself in a number of ways. First, such programmes for the development of social science in post-colonial societies and in Kyrgyzstan often reject, *a priori*, pre-existing knowledge forms in order to replace them with those assumed to be more 'modern,' 'international,' 'western,' or 'scientific', and therefore 'progressive.' These models of academic reform are specifically based on the assumption of unequal power relationships of 'donor' and 'recipient,' 'expert' and 'learner,' or 'researcher' and 'subject.' One report by a leading US research institute found that in the former Soviet Union as a whole, 'in the case of most East-West collaborations, the intellectual agenda is set by the Western agency or institution. Even in scholarship programs that award grants to individuals, the priorities have, for the most part, come from the Western funder, and have not grown directly out of local interests and priorities'.[53]

As in other newly independent countries at other times in history, foreign academic consultants in Kyrgyzstan often 'assume the role of representatives of a "superior" scientific establishment generously coming to instruct and improve indigenous academic centres'.[54] This is why, for example, Chilean educator Gustavo Lagos once declared that post-colonial educational reforms in his country should 'take into account the necessity of formulating educational policies consistent with the realities in which they are applied and repudiat[e] programs imported from regions whose special characteristics have nothing to

53 Bronson *et al.*, 'Sustaining intellectual communities', p. 21.
54 Hiller, 'Universality of science', p. 127.

do with those of the recipient peoples.'[55] As Murad Esenov pointed out, egalitarian intellectual interaction in and about Central Asia is vital. However, 'assistance differs. If it is rendered on some particular conditions it is unacceptable. If it promotes development, then that is quite different. Indeed, nobody knows the situation here better than we do. However, cooperation with Western political scientists is relevant. It is necessary to discuss, to enrich ourselves with others' experiences and knowledge. Nevertheless, I believe it unreasonable to strictly follow all their recommendations.'[56]

Second, in structurally dependent scientific communities the distribution of intellectual production is skewed. The bulk of research about Central Asian societies, for example, has originated from western scholars located *outside* the country.[57] In Kyrgyzstan, concern about asymmetrical power relations among researchers and research communities has also been tied to another, more marginal issue: the use of social research in strategic intelligence. 'After 1994,' says Isaev, 'we [the national sociological union] did not conduct any mass surveys in the republic, and now international funds finance only those groups that do not lay claim on publication of their research.' He directly accuses these groups of being, in the words of his interviewer, 'some sort of foreign intelligence or reconnaissance,' and says 'the monitoring for foreigners support that kind of information that could be explosive for Kyrgyzstan. It is strategic data. Neither the govern-

55 Gustavo Lagos, 'The revolution of being: a preferred world model.' in Heraldo Munoz (ed.), *From Dependency to Development: Strategies to Overcome Underdevelopment and Inequality* (Boulder: Westview Press, 1981), p. 159.

56 See Murad Esenov, 'No One Knows the Central Asian Situation Better Than We', *The Central Asian Post*, 20 November 1997. Similar arguments made about contemporary Kyrgyzstan, however, risk being considered reactionary or uninformed about the universal value of scientific 'facts'. This, too, is not unusual in the politics of post-colonial sociology; for example, 'in attempting to develop a degree of structural and cultural independence, sociologists in Canada have been accused of racism and ethnocentrism' (Lamy, 'The Globalization of American Sociology', p. 111).

57 In Galtung's terms, this means that 'the center of gravity for the acquisition of knowledge about the nation is located outside the nation itself' ('Structural theory of imperialism', p. 296).

ment nor different state structures know about this. And these are the people who give us huge grants'.[58]

The converse of this prevalence of 'externalised knowledge' is that 'few comprehensive studies of the colonizer are carried out by people in the colony,' or rather simply that scholars in 'developing' countries 'learn' from 'teachers' from the 'developed' ones – they do not 'study' them critically.[59] In other words, educational and scientific 'exchanges' are actually structured as unequal transfers of knowledge and intellectual technique in which 'the Center always provides the teachers… and the Periphery always provides the learners'.[60]

In addition, many Kyrgyzstani students and scholars that do study in the West are lost to 'brain drain', both within and outside the republic; so much so that exchange programmes have begun placing terms of 'in-country service' as conditions for overseas study. This serves another purpose as well, as it attempts to 'replenish' the indigenous academic cadre, both in numbers and in the percentage of people who have earned coveted western qualifications. Some university students, however, have wondered whether they are actually 'trained to aspire to American goals that are easiest to reach… in America.'[61] Again, this question is not unique to Kyrgyzstan. Some Latin American social scientists who returned to their home countries after studying abroad 'became accustomed to styles of work which their own national resources cannot support. In their efforts to maintain this academic lifestyle, they become preoccupied with meeting the criteria of funding agencies,' thus actually reinforcing dependencies that they had intended to sever.[62]

A third aspect of structural dependency is that the national intellectual community recruits members and the bulk of its 'expert' trainers from foreign (particularly US and Western European) countries, and uses primarily foreign materials in teaching and training activities.

58 Sydykova, 'U sotsiologii trudnoe proshloe'.

59 Galtung, 'Structural theory of imperialism', p. 297.

60 Ibid., p. 93.

61 Baktygul Aliev, 'Is [American University in Kyrgyzstan] a Place of Losers?' *AUK Student Newspaper*, 1, no. 2, 3 November 1999.

62 Lamy, 'Globalization of American Sociology', p. 108.

In colonial and post-colonial societies, the importation of intellectual technology is often premised on deep-seated assumptions of cultural and intellectual inferiority and/or superiority, or on reifications of 'western' knowledge as 'modern' and 'objective' and 'indigenous' knowledge as 'backward' and 'ideological'. In one post-colonial context after another, however, scholars have reported that imported specialists are ill-qualified. In Kyrgyzstan, as across the former Soviet Union, the 'experts' who are 'rushing in to help convert the higher education systems (among other systems) from the Soviet model to the Western (USA?) model of organizing, teaching, evaluating and researching have little or no knowledge of the cultures, languages, or histories of the societies in which they are working'.[63]

Finally, much of the research conducted by social scientists in post-colonial nations is underwritten by foreign countries and organisations that either determine research agendas or place 'conditions' on researchers themselves. These take the form of both formal conditions (such as conducting research that is commensurate with existing international development policies in the region) and more informal constraints, whereby scholars adjusted their own research interests to meet the needs, often policy-oriented, of grant-giving organisations. As 'means turn to ends, and, with this shift, the entire research enterprise becomes more surely controlled by US sources than if the latter had dictated its activities in the first place'.[64] This, in turn, fosters the further development of cultural dependency, as defined above – evidence of which, and resistance to, can be seen in the discourses and practices of social science in Kyrgyzstan today.

63 Paula Sabloff (ed.), *Higher Education in the Post-Communist World: Case Studies of Eight Universities* (New York: Garland Publishing, 1998), p. xii.

64 Alejandro Portes, 'Trends in International Research Cooperation: The Latin American Case', *The American Sociologist*, 10 (1975), pp. 131–140.

Academic Imperialism in Central Asia

Although references to academic imperialism are today often seen as 'anachronistic',[65] the current development and politics of social science in Kyrgyzstan, and the discourse surrounding it, indicates that some of its key mechanisms and forms are being reproduced in post-Soviet Central Asia. However, the answer to the question of whether social science in Kyrgyzstan is a colonial construct or an indigenous institution is, both and neither. Social scientists in Kyrgyzstan have historically pursued a variety of intellectual and political projects within colonial and now neocolonial conditions and structures; these have both offered them promises of development and simultaneously precluded autonomous practice. Academic work in Kyrgyzstan has been typical of that produced in 'imperial encounters' in which 'one entity has been able to construct "realities" that were taken seriously and acted upon and the other entity has been denied equal degrees or kinds of agency'.[66] The emergence of movements to indigenise the discipline both during and after perestroika, however, indicates that Kyrgyzstani social scientists have also negotiated their opportunities rather than simply submitting to their limitations.

Their experiences suggest that we must interrogate the notion that we now live in a 'post-imperialist' world, and ask whether imperialist phenomena (including academic imperialism) have migrated from the 'Third World' to complicit parts of the 'Second World' (i.e., post-socialist countries), and transformed from classic colonialism to what István Mészáros calls 'global hegemonic imperialism.'[67] Social science, as a disciplinary institution and a potential locus of discursive power, is embedded in and shaped by these activities at both national and international levels. More theoretically, we must explore how the-

65 Vijay Prashad, '"Ready Made Ideas"', a review of Noam Chomsky (ed.), *The Cold War and the University'*, *Frontline: India's National Magazine*, 15, no. 23 (1998).

66 Doty, *Imperial Encounters*, p. 3.

67 István Mészáros, *Beyond Capital: Towards a Theory of Transition* (London: Merlin Press, 1995).

ories of imperialism that were developed to analyse post-colonial societies during the 1960s and 1970s are applicable to the problems of cultural institutions in the post-Soviet world. Despite the dominance of discourses about 'globalisation' and the end of history, it is clear that scholars in Kyrgyzstan still work within institutional and intellectual milieus that resemble those defined as imperialist in post-colonial and world systems theories of knowledge production.

Bibliography

Ablezova, Mehrigiul, Interview by the author. Tape recording. American University–Central Asia. Bishkek, Kyrgyzstan. 20 March 2003.

Ake, Claude, *Social Science as Imperialism: The Theory of Political Development* (Nigeria: Ibadan University Press, 1982).

Alatas, S., 'Intellectual Imperialism: Definition, Traits and Problems', *Southeast Asian Journal of Social Sciences*, 28, no. 1 (2000), pp. 23–45.

—— 'Academic Dependency and the Global Division of Labour in the Social Sciences', *Current Sociology*, 51, no. 6 (2003), pp. 599–613.

Ali, Agha Shaukat, *The Modernization of Soviet Central Asia* (Lahore: Panjab University, 1964).

Aliev, Baktigul, 'Is AUK a Place of Losers?' *AUK Student Newspaper*, 1, no. 2, 3 November 1999.

Amsler, Sarah, *From Truth in Strength to Strength in Truth: Sociology, Knowledge and Power in Kyrgyzstan, 1966–2003*. PhD thesis (London School of Economics and Political Science, 2005).

Barnes, Hazel, *An Existentialist Ethic* (Chicago: University of Chicago Press, 1967).

Bekturganov, K., T. Omurbekov and A. Tishin, 'Komu vygoden populism v sotsiologii' [Who benefits from populism in sociology?], *Slovo Kyrgyzstana*, 11 May 1994.

Blum, Yuri, 'Pravda – ne v sile, no sile–v pravde' [Truth is not in strength, but strength is in truth], *Slovo Kyrgyzstana*, 6 February 1993, p. 7.

Booth, David, 'Development Research: From Impasse to New. An Agenda' in *Beyond the Impasse: New Directions in Development Theory*, ed. by Frans Schurrman (London: Zed Books, 1993).

Bourdieu, Pierre, *Homo Academicus* (Cambridge: Polity Press, 1988).

Bronson, Susan, Nancy Popson, and Blair Ruble, 'Sustaining Intellectual Communities: A Strategy for Rebuilding the Social Sciences and Humanities in the Former Soviet Union from Within' in *The Humanities and Social Sciences in the Former Soviet Union: An Assessment of Need*, a report prepared by the Kennan Institute, Woodrow Wilson Center, for the Carnegie Corporation of New York and the MacArthur Foundation (Washington, DC, 1999).

Brudniy, Aaron and Cholpon Chotaeva, 'Central Asia: Ways and Models of Development', *Central Asia and the Caucasus*, 6 (2000).

Bujra, Abdalla, 'Whither Social Science Institutions in Africa: A Prognosis', *Africa Development*, 19 (1994), pp. 119–66.

Cavanaugh, Cassandra, 'Central Asia's Colonial Past and Why it Matters,' *Central Asia Monitor*, 5–6 (2001), pp. 9–17.

Chekki, Dan, *American Sociological Hegemony: Transnational Explorations* (New York and London: University Press of America, 1987).

Chomsky, Noam, ed., *The Cold War and the University* (NY: New Press, 1997).

—— *Chomsky on MisEducation* (Oxford: Rowman & Littlefield, 2000).

Cooper, Frederick and Randall Packard, *International Development and the Social Science: Essays on the History and Politics of Knowledge* (CA: University of California Press, 1997).

DeYoung, Alan, 'On the Prospects for Secondary Education Reform in the Kyrgyz Republic', *Central Asia Monitor*, 4 (2001), pp. 5–15 and 5–6 (2001), pp. 46–58.

Doty, Roxanne, *Imperial Encounters: The Politics of Representation in North-South Relations* (Minneapolis: University of Minnesota Press, 1996).

Eades, J. and Schwaller, C., eds., 'Transitional Agendas: Working Papers from the Summer School for Soviet Sociologists' (Centre for Social Anthropology and Computing, University of Kent at Canterbury, 1991).

Egorov, I., 'Perspectives on the scientific systems of the post-Soviet states: a pessimistic view', *Prometheus*, 20, no. 1 (2002), pp. 59–73.

Eisenstadt, S., 'Centre-Periphery Relations in the Soviet Empire: Some Interpretive Observations' in *Thinking Theoretically About Soviet Nationalities: History and Comparison in the Study of the USSR*, ed. by A. Motyl (New York: Columbia University Press, 1992).

Esenov, Murad, 'No One Knows the Central Asian Situation Better Than We', *The Central Asian Post*, 20 November 1997.

Escobar, Arturo, 'Anthropology and the Development Encounter: The Making and Marketing of Development Anthropology', *American Ethnologist*, 18, no. 4 (1991), pp. 658–82.

Foucault, Michel, *Madness and Civilisation: A History of Insanity in the Age of Reason* (London: Tavistock, 1967).

—— *The History of Sexuality: Vol. 1, An Introduction* (Harmondsworth: Penguin, 1978).

—— *Power/Knowledge: Selected Interviews and Other Writings*, ed. by C. Gordon (New York: Pantheon Books, 1980).

Galtung, Johan, 'A Structural Theory of Imperialism', *Journal of Peace Research*, 2 (1971), pp. 81–117.

Gendzier, Irene, *Managing Political Change: Social Scientists and the Third World* (CO: Westview Press, 1985).

Glenady, C., 'The Republic of Kyrgyzstan: an overview of science, technology and higher education,' Report 77, April–May 1995. At: http://www.nsf.gov/home/int/europe/reports/77.html

Gosovic, Branislav, 'Global Intellectual Hegemony and the International Development Agenda', *International Social Science Journal*, 166 (2000), pp. 447–456.

Hiller, Harry, 'Universality of Science and the Question of National Sociologies', *The American Sociologist*, 14 (1979), pp. 124–135.

Ibraeva, Gulnara, Interview by the author. Written responses received via email, February 2003.

Isaev, Kusein, 'Pervaia konferentsiia sotsiologov v Kirgizii' [The first conference of sociologists in Kyrgyzstan], *Sotsis*, 7 (1990).

—— 'Sotsiologiia v Kyrgyzstane: sostoianie i perspektivi' [Sociology in Kyrgyzstan: its status and perspectives] *Izvestiia Obshchestvennye Nauki, Akademii Nauki Respublik Kirgizstana*, 2 (1991), pp. 27–34.

—— 'Kak sozdavalas' Kyrgyzskaia sotsiologicheskaia sluzhba' [How the Kyrgyz sociological service was created], *ResPublica*, 29 May 1993.

—— 'Demokratsiia i vlast'' [Democracy and power], *Erkin-Too*, 30 September 1995.

—— 'Sotsiologiiany saiasii soiku kylgylary bar' [They want to make a political prostitute out of sociology], *Asaba*, 6 March 1998.

—— 'The Prioritized Development of Education as a Condition of Social Progress in the 21st Century,' unpublished paper, 1999.

Ismailova, S., 'Sotsiologicheskoe obrazovanie: problemy stanovleniia i perspektivy' [Sociological education: problems of its creation and perspectives], Kut Bilim, 31 May 1995.

Kimmerling, Baruch, 'Sociology, Ideology, and Nation-Building: The Palestinians and their Meaning in Israeli Sociology', *American Sociological Review*, 57 (1992), pp. 446–460.

Koichuev, T., 'Ideologiia obnovleniia i razvitie obshchestvennyh nayk v Kirgizskoi SSR' [The ideology of renewal and the development of social science in the Kirgiz SSR], [Izvestiia akademii nauk Kirgizskoi SSR, 2 (1988).

Kyrgyz-Press International News Agency, 'Kyrgyz opinion survey on corruption alarms officials', Bishkek, 13 September 2000.

Lagos, Gustavo, 'The Revolution of Being: a Preferred World Model' in *From Dependency to Development: Strategies to Overcome*

Underdevelopment and Inequality, ed. by Heraldo Munoz (Boulder, CO: Westview Press, 1981).

Lamy, Paul, 'The Globalization of American Sociology: Excellence or Imperialism?' *American Sociologist*, 11 (1976), pp. 104–114.

Long, Norman and Ann Long, eds., *Battlefields of Knowledge: The Interlocking of Theory and Practice in Social Research and Development* (London: Routledge, 1992).

Merton, Robert, 'Science and the Social Order' in *Robert K. Merton on Social Structure and Science*, ed. by P. Sztompka (Chicago: University of Chicago Press, [1938] 1996).

—— 'The Ethos of Science' in *Robert K. Merton on Social Structure and Science*, ed. by P. Sztompka (Chicago: University of Chicago Press, [1942] 1996).

Mészáros, István, *Beyond Capital: Towards a Theory of Transition* (London: Merlin Press, 1995).

Moldobaev, Kubat, 'The Transformation of Societal Values in Kyrgyzstan'' *Central Asia Monitor*, 4 (1998).

Nesvetailov, G., 'Centre-Periphery Relations and the Transformation of Post-Soviet Science', *Knowledge and Policy: The International Journal of Knowledge Transfer and Utilization*, 8, no. 2 (1995), pp. 53–67.

Nove, Alex and J. A. Newth, *The Soviet Middle East: A Model for Development?* (London: Allen and Unwin, Ltd., 1967).

Osmonalieva, R., Interview with Kusein Isaev, 'Nauka–glavnaia sila, na kotoroi rastsvetaet obschestvo' [Science is the main force upon which society flourishes], *Kut Bilim*, 18 January 1998.

Osorov, Z., 'Higher Education is a Big Business', *The Times of Central Asia*, 18 October 2002, at: http://www.timesca.com

Patrick, John, 'Civic Education in Former Communist Countries of Central and Eastern Europe,' unpublished paper, 8 July 1994. U.S. Department of Educational Resources Information Center (ERIC) document no. D374056.

Pertierra, Raul, *Explorations in Social Theory and Philippine Ethnography* (Diliman, Quezon City: University of the Philippine Press, 1997).

Portes, Alejandro, 'Trends in International Research Cooperation: The Latin American Case', *The American Sociologist*, 10 (1975), pp. 131–40.

Prashad, Vijay, 'Ready Made Ideas,' a review of *The Cold War and the University*, ed. by Noam Chomsky, in *Frontline: India's National Magazine*, 15, no. 23 (1998), at: http://www.flonnet.com/fl1523/15230720.htm

Radio Free Europe Kazakh report from 22 September 2000, 'Association of Sociologists and Political Scientists marks fifth anniversary', at: http://www.rferl.org/reports/kazakh-report/220900.asp

Rahmad, Abdur, *Intellectual Colonisation: Science and Technology in East-West Relations* (New Delhi: Vikas Publishing House, Pvt. Ltd., 1983).

Reeves, Madeleine, 'The Role of Universities in the Transformation of Societies: Case Study of the American University–Central Asia.' Research report conducted for the Centre of Higher Education Research and Information (CHERI) of the Open University of Great Britain and the Association of Commonwealth Universities (ACU), with support from the Open Society Institute, 2003.

Rist, Gilbert, *The History of Development: From Western Origins to Global Faith* (London: Zed Books, 1997).

Ruble, Blair, Forward to the *Humanities and Social Sciences in the Former Soviet Union: An Assessment of Need*. Unpublished report commissioned by the Carnegie Corporation of New York and John D. and Catherine T. MacArthur Foundations, prepared by the Kennan Institute, Woodrow Wilson Center, Washington DC, 1 August 1999.

Sagynbaeva, Ainoura, Interview by the author. Tape recording. SIAR Bishkek. Bishkek, Kyrgyzstan. 22 May 2003.

Schott, Thomas, 'Soviet Science in the Scientific World System: Was It Autarchic, Self-reliant, Distinctive, Isolated, Peripheral, Central?' *Knowledge: Creation, Diffusion, Utilization*, 14, no. 4 (2000), pp. 410–39.

—— 'Ties Between Center and Periphery in the Scientific World-System: Accumulation of Rewards, Dominance and Self-

Reliance in the Center', *Journal of World Systems Research*, 4 (1998), pp. 112–44.

Sherstobitov, V., 'Vysokoe prednaznachenie obshchestvennykh nauk' [The highest mission of the social sciences], *Izvestiia akademii nauk Kirgizskoi SSR, Obshchestvennye nauki*, 1 (1987), pp. 3–8.

Shils, Edward, 'Tradition, Ecology and Institution in the History of Sociology,' *Daedalus*, 99 (Fall 1970), pp. 760–825.

Swartz, David, *Culture and Power: The Sociology of Pierre Bourdieu* (Chicago: University of Chicago Press, 1997).

Sydykov, X., 'V soiuze s naukoi' [In union with science], *Kut Bilim*, no date, 1995.

Sydykova, Zamira, Interview with Kusein Isaev, 'U sotsiologii trudnoe proshloe, a buduschee takoe zhe neopredelennoe, kak i nastoiaschee' [Sociology has had a difficult past and its future, like its present, is equally as uncertain], *ResPublica*, 25 February 1998.

UNESCO, 'Management of Social Transformations (MOST)', at: http://portal.unesco.org

Watts, Michael, 'Development I: Power, Knowledge, Discursive Practice,' *Progress in Human Geography*, 17 (1993), p. 257.

Whyte, William Foote, 'The Role of the U.S. Professor in Developing Countries', *The American Sociologist*, February (1969), pp. 19–28.

Wood, Bryce, 'Notes on Conference Proceedings' in Social Science in Latin America: Papers Presented at the Conference on Latin American Studies Held at Rio de Janeiro March 29–31, 1965, ed. by Manuel Diégues Júnior and Bryce Wood (New York: Columbia University Press, 1967).

ANNA HOROLETS

Media and Politics in Transitional Poland: Symbiosis or Adversary Relations?

Polish Transformation and the Media

One Public Debate about the Media

One of the largest non-governmental organisations in Poland – the Stefan Batory Foundation – together with the Catholic weekly *Tygodnik Powszechny* took the initiative of organising a series of public debates about the 'professions of public trust'. Journalists have been indisputably classified as one such profession. In the debate on June 13, 2002 not only journalists as a professional group but also the Polish media in general were exposed to expert and public scrutiny. The organisers suggested several issues for discussion. First, the role of the media as the 'fourth power' was regarded as an achievement of the transformation processes in Poland, yet one that engenders several potential threats. Second, the problem of political pressures on the media was addressed. Last but not least, the commercialisation of the media was presented as a threat to democracy.

Due to the fact that the majority of panellists were journalists themselves, the debate focused on the weakness of Polish democracy and political pressures put on media. The participants stipulated that the 'colonisation' of media by politicians is one of the most dangerous consequences of the lack of democratic consolidation after the changes of 1989. This essay is an attempt of verifying these claims, since they are spread not only among Polish journalists but also their Western counterparts. In the 2001 report the Committee to Protect Journalists it was stated that 'in Central Europe journalists work in a relatively safe environment yet must still contend with the politicised broadcasters, as well as with threats and legal intimidation from the politicians.'[1]

In the first part of the essay we attempt to verify claims of the intrusion of politics into the life world of media by introducing some contextual information about the directions and consequences of transformation in the spheres of economy, politics and law that have affected the Polish media. The second part of the essay is a case study of the 'European debate' in which both journalists and politicians constructed public discussion about the accession of Poland to the European Union. After considering the political and media dimensions of this debate, particular attention is paid to the mutual influence of media and political actors, as well as to the specific nature of media product. In the concluding remarks the institutional threats to the press freedom principle are juxtaposed to the threats of the internal logic of media discourse.

Poland: a Fragile Democracy?

Not attempting to discharge the claim that freedom of press is threatened in Poland, we would like to problematise it as presenting only one dimension of the problem. In order to discern other dimensions, one has to look at the presumptions that are taken for granted in the journalists' line of argumentation. The most striking is the idealisation of the principle of freedom of press and, more broadly, the idealistic view of the democratic society. When Polish journalists (as well as their colleagues from the West) stipulate that this principle is broken in Poland, it is taken for granted that there are places where this principle is fully implemented. What is more, being treated as almost sacred, this principle is taken to its extreme.

Yet, a vital question is whether there is a country where this principle is implemented fully and unambiguously. As has been repeatedly maintained by various schools of media and communication studies, the media are exposed to numerous dangers. These dangers stem from

1 *Attacks on the Press in 2001. A Worldwide Survey of the Committee to Protect Journalists* (New York: CJP, 2002), p. 364.

the conditions of globalising economy, particularly the monopolisation of the media.[2] Moreover, the dangers are inherent in the very nature of politics, as Gramsci's concept of hegemony reveals. According to Gramsci, intellectual elites, and journalists in particular play an important role in promoting ideology into a dominant position.[3] The Birmingham School of Cultural Studies strongly relied on his theory in elaborating a critical perspective on the relations between politics and media.[4] The dangers also stem from the development of consumer attitudes in society and the decrease of engagement in public affairs among the population. Habermas considered that these developments threaten the functioning of the democratic public sphere.[5] The criticism outlined above relativises the freedom of press principle. It can be taken as the background against which it would be possible to make a more objective assessment of the feasibility of this principle in Poland.

What is more, in order to speak about the feasibility of this principle one has to distinguish its various layers. The principle of the freedom of press can be treated as an ideal or myth, an aim toward which the whole society should aspire. Alternatively, it can be treated institutionally and legally as a principle of democratic society, prescribed and protected by law and implemented through a variety of democratic institutions. These two understandings are combined and mixed in the public debates about the situation of Polish media. The blending of the two often results in the distorted assessment of the magnitude and seriousness of the challenges faced by the contemporary Polish media. In order to overcome this distortion, one has to insert the journalists' vision of their situation into the institutional context of the transition to democratic order in Poland.

2 Peter Golding and Graham Murdok, 'Culture, Communication and Economy' in James Curran and Michael Gurevitch (eds.), *Mass Media and Society* (London: Edward Arnold, 1996), p. 25.

3 Antonio Gramsci, *Prison Notebooks* (London: Lawrence and Wishart, 1971).

4 Graeme Turner, *British Cultural Studies: An Introduction* (London: Unwin-Hyman, 1990).

5 Jürgen Habermas, 'Further Reflections on the Public Sphere', in Craig Calhoun (ed.), *Habermas and the Public Sphere* (Cambridge, Mass.: MIT Press, 1992), p. 447.

Changes in Economy

The economic dependency of media is arguably one potential threat to the press freedom principle as on the one hand owners can steer editorial policy, and on the other, the editorial policy is dictated by the imperative of achieving market success. However, this threat has to be measured against the communist past of the Polish media, where the ownership of media was monopolised by the state. Moreover, because the economic success of media did not play a significant role, the quality of media production was relatively lower than after 1989. Below are several examples of how the Polish media underwent economic transformation.

The post-communist economic changes affected most notably the system of ownership of the media. As a result of the changes in 1989, Polish private media has started developing from a scratch as a part of the transition from planned to market economy.

> More than 85 percent of the media have been privatised. There are more than 300 newspapers, 119 commercial radio stations (six national stations five of which are state owned), as well as ten commercial television stations.[6]

Although competition with the state media is stiff for private broadcasters and major newspapers, their position is improved by the fact that they are owned by well-financed foreign media companies. For instance, the emergence and success of the quality newspaper *Rzeczpospolita* is significantly due to the investments of foreign capital, although it has also used the structure of circulation through subscription, which it 'inherited' from its period of functioning as a government newspaper from 1982–89.

However, there are also other recipes for economic success. The most popular quality newspaper *Gazeta Wyborcza* (holding the third position in sales at the national press market after two popular tabloids) had a chance of receiving its starting capital from the state budget in 1989, since its initial aim was to promote the politicians gathered around the legendary 'Solidarity' movement in the first

6 *Freedom in the World: The Annual Report of Political Rights and Civil Liberties 1999–2000* (New York: Freedom House, 2000), pp. 392–393.

democratic elections. Alternatively, some communist newspapers, most notably *Trybuna*, continue their existence in a modified form, yet were still supported by financing from the Democratic Left Alliance (SLD), the post-communist party.

Fifteen years after the change, it is clear that some media have used opportunity emerging from the systemic change in the country. *Gazeta Wyborcza*, with roughly half a million copies in circulation, is the most vivid 'success story'. Yet others did not manage to meet all the challenges of the market economy. The bankruptcy of several opinion newspapers such as *Życie* is exemplary. The market economy both boosts and curtails the freedom of press principle. The multiplicity of ownership creates chances for the multitude of opinions, while the 'invisible hand of the market' is to blame for the fact that some pressures on media cannot be easily traced. Yet, most observers agree that not only economic reasons, i.e. the degree of the adjustment to the conditions of the free market, influence the survival capacity of the media in post-socialist countries.

Changes in Politics

Apart from economic change, Poland has undergone the transformation of its political system. Instead of an authoritarian state with a single ruling party, Poland has become a multiparty presidential-parliamentary democracy. Despite the fact that quite a number of parties emerged after 1989, only a few managed to achieve over ten percent of votes in any election. The instability of the party system is caused not only by the multitude of political actors but also by weak political consolidation.

The role of media as a mouthpiece of the ruling party – or alternatively, as a source of underground resistance – has changed to the role of a democratic public forum, with no censorship and no limitations put on the choices of political options. The existence of the multiparty system probably prevented the relative polarisation of the media along a single divide between two major political forces. At the same time, the political situation of the 1970–80s rendered the opposition press a special authority in society. After 1989 the newspapers, which had emerged as the underground opposition media, started lacking the moral pathos they had when the 'Solidarity' was in the opposition. However, due to the public disenchantment with politics and politicians, in some instances media may replace politicians in opinion shaping and spin-mastering of ideas, views and even policies. This tendency might also be due to the special role traditionally assigned to the intelligentsia in Central and Eastern Europe.

Nevertheless, both media and politicians seem to realise that there is an unavoidable interdependence between them. Politicians are important public figures who 'make events happen', thus becoming natural objects of news reports and opinion articles and programmes. As far as politicians are concerned, press conferences have long become routine. There seems to be a growing understanding of the importance of media as a shaper of public opinion, and politicians eagerly accept invitations to various talk shows or Tele-debates.[7] With increasing intensity and professionalism, Polish politicians engage in the practices of political marketing.

Changes in Law

Though the law regulating the rights and responsibilities of media has been improved significantly and adjusted to the new economic and political reality, is not yet unproblematic. The two main legal troubles curtailing the execution of the freedom of press principle are indicated by experts: 'criminal libel laws and monopolies over media ownership afflict most of Eastern European states.'[8] The prospect of the accession to the European Union has invigorated both civic initiatives of drafting laws and government legislative work, which is needed to adjust Polish law to that of the EU. However, organisations of journalists in Poland still express their deep concern about the legal situation of mass media in Poland.

7 Cf. Edwin Diamond and Stephen Bates, *The Spot: The Rise of Political Advertising on Television* (Cambridge, Mass.: MIT Press, 1988).

8 Attacks (2002), p. 364.

Goszczyński, the director of the Press Freedom Monitoring Centre, draws particular attention to some discrepancies in Polish criminal law as compared to Western European or American.[9] He stipulates that in the West, the public interest is prioritised over than the private good of a given politician. What is more, politicians are well aware that they are capable of minimising the effects of unfavourable publications by themselves. Politicians are used to shaping their positive images in the eyes of public opinion by using media, not the courts. Furthermore, Polish law offers better protection against defamation in the press for people occupying official positions than it does for regular citizens.

> A public official is not burdened by the costs of the juridical procedure, because the public prosecutor's office is obliged to prepare the process, the costs of which are covered from the state budget.[10]

Experts regard this situation as needing urgent changes.

The corruption affair, which was revealed in late 2002, brought to the fore yet another instance of the violation of press freedom though legislative process. The whole affair developed against the background of continuous attempts of the SLD to 'colonise' the public television network TVP. It is known as 'the network whose management has close ties to Poland's former communist SLD movement.'[11] Furthermore, another state body, which was meant to be a guardian of press freedom, became increasingly politicised.

> The National TV and Radio Council (KRRiT) is ostensibly independent of the government, but since its nine members are nominated by parliament, the senate, and the president's office, politics play a role in its composition.[12]

During the drafting of the law on media, numerous procedural breaches occurred, some of them inspired by the highest state officials. The credibility of the ruling party was seriously damaged by the fact

9 Andrzej Goszczyński, 'Politycy pod kloszem' [Politicians under protection], *Media Polska*, 6 (June 1998), pp. 16–20.

10 Goszczyński, 'Politycy pod kloszem', ibid., p. 18.

11 Attacks (2002), ibid., p. 392.

12 Freedom, ibid., p. 393.

that they tried to enforce the law, which in practice would serve the narrowly understood party interests of SLD by eliminating the potential rivals of public television.

As far as positive changes are concerned, the law on access to public information can be called a success. 'While journalists struggled under longstanding legal burdens, new court rulings favoured press freedom, and legislation was drafted to improve access to information.'[13] A statute about Access to Public Information was passed on September 6, 2001, and became valid on January 1, 2002. It facilitates access to public information, which has bearings on the transparency of the public sphere, imposing on public officials and institutions much wider obligations to provide information about their activities.

A brief look at some of the legal regulations concerning media shows that in the process of transformation, Poland has become neither paradise nor hell for journalists. Yet the belief in the predicament of media in Poland is widespread among journalists themselves (for example, the debate discussed at the beginning of the essay) and is being internalised by public opinion about media. The pessimism of journalists in evaluating the situation of media stems from the prevalence of the 'mythical' interpretation of the press freedom principle. This interpretation creates a sharp discrepancy between economic and political reality, to which media need to adjust, on the one hand, and the popular expectations from media on the other. While the former allows for a considerable scope of press freedom while posing some threats to it,[14] the latter assumes that if the principle is not implemented fully press freedom is endangered.

It seems to us that the only remedy to this problem is the differentiation between the institutional meaning of the press freedom principle and its 'mythical' interpretations. The implementation of the former should be regarded as a necessary, however minimal, requirement for the principle's feasibility, whereas the latter should be treated as an ideal.

13 *Attacks on Press in 2000: A Worldwide Survey of the Committee to Protect Journalists* (New York: CJP, 2001), p. 231.

14 Cf. Grzegorz Ekiert and Stephen Hanson (eds.), *Capitalism and Democracy in Central and Eastern Europe* (Cambridge: Cambridge University Press, 2003).

Europe: Media Issue or Political Issue?

The Polish public debate about joining the European Union, which was particularly intense during the five years of accession negotiations (1998–2002) between Poland and the EU, amalgamates some important features of the relationship between politics and media. It demonstrates that public debates are shaped not so much by competing political interests but by the logic of media production. Our intention is to use it as an illustration of the variety of ways in which Polish media and politics interact in constructing issues of public concern.

Europe in Collective Consciousness

The debate about the Polish belonging to Europe has continued for over two centuries.[15] It focuses on the choice of the optimal road of civilisational development. After the collapse of the socialist regime, the idea of a 'return to Europe' implied a farewell to the totalitarian state and the welcoming of a democratic social order.[16] Thus, Europe was synonymous with 'normality', for there was a consensus in society concerning the necessity of democratic change. The by-product of such an interpretation of Europe was its idealisation. Therefore, when Polish people observed the everyday routine of relations between the EU and Poland, first as an Associate State and from 1998–2002 as a Candidate Country, they were somewhat disenchanted with Europe. The decline of the positive sentiment towards Europe as a more general idea was followed by the decrease of support for European integration, which fell from about 80% in 1996 to almost 50% in

15 Jerzy Jedlicki, *A Suburb of Europe: Nineteenth Century Polish Approach to Western Civilization* (Budapest: Central European University 1999).

16 Ireneusz Krzemiński, 'The National Identity and European Consciousness of Poles', in Petr Drulak (ed.), *National and European Identities in EU Enlargement* (Prague: Institute of International Relations, 2001), p. 59.

1998 when the accession negotiations started.[17] It increased later on, yet remained oscillating around 55% from 1998–2002.

In terms of public support for making a public issue out of integration with the EU, opinions were quite ambiguous. On the one hand, tiredness with the omnipresence of the European problematic was expressed.[18] People seemed to disapprove of spending time on an issue which was 'clear enough for all'. On the other hand, the population felt under-informed in matters concerning European integration.[19]

Europe in Party Ideologies

As for the political landscape over five years of accession negotiations, there were several major forces at the time when negotiations started. As a result of the parliamentary elections of 1997, the 'Solidarity' Election Action (AWS) formed a ruling coalition with the Freedom Union (UW). The strongest opposition party in that period was the post-communist SLD.

Both the ruling coalition and the strongest opposition party have expressed their support for European integration, despite the fact that there were some Eurosceptical voices within the AWS. An observer would expect that European integration should acquire a status of widely accepted and supported national interest, as long as no major party challenged its rationale. However, de-politicisation did not occur. Politicians instrumentally used the issue as a means of articulating ideological differences. While European integration was pronounced one of the main tasks of the government of the AWS-UW coalition, it has become a matter of discontent inside the coalition.

17 CBOS. Komunikat z badań [Centre for Social Opinion Research. Research Communicate], 61 (March 1998).

18 Elżbieta Skotnicka-Illasiewicz, *Powrót czy droga w nieznane? Europejskie Dylematy Polaków* [Return or the Road to the Unknown? European Dilemmas of the Poles] (Warsaw: European Centre of University of Warsaw, 1997).

19 Beata Roguska and Marek Strzeszewski, *Zainteresowanie społeczne, wiedza i poinformowanie o integracji Polski z Unią Europejską* [Public Interest, Knowledge and the Degree of Being Informed About the Integration of Poland With the European Union] (Warsaw: ISP, 2002).

Moreover, the idea protecting national interests has been pushed to the extreme of Europhobic attitudes by the parties that gradually acquired some political importance from 1997–2001. One was nationalist Catholic party, the League of Polish Families (LPR). The other was a left-clinging populist party Self-Defence (*Samoobrona*). They built their political identity on the opposition to the idea of European integration. In a similar fashion, European integration has become a card, which the post-communist opposition used to win the parliamentary election of 2001. The idea was to obtain exclusive right to the 'symbolic ownership' of Europeanness among Polish politicians.[20] In this manner an issue of national consensus turned into an issue instrumentally used in political struggle, ironically still being called a matter of 'national interest' in official discourse. However, none of these effects would have been achieved if the media had not been mediating (as its very name suggests!) between the public and the political sphere.

Media Construction of the European Debate

The media took an active part in polarising the debate about the integration of Poland with the EU. As early as 1922, Lippman, a journalist himself, brilliantly showed that events that happen in 'objective reality' are scrutinised by journalists for their 'news value'.[21] A consensus on the need for joining the European Union, which characterised the early stage of transformation, provided almost none of the qualities Lippman mentioned. Therefore, some 'emotionally involving' or 'con-

20 Leszek Miller, 'Europejska szansa' [European Opportunity] in *Trybuna*, 27–28 July 1998, p. 2. Cf. Murray J. Edelman, *The Symbolic Uses of Politics* (Urbana: University of Illinois Press, 1985).

21 Walter Lippman, *Public Opinion* (New York: Harcourt, Brace and Co., 1965). According to Lippman, 'news values' include clear subject matter that can be conveyed without contradictions, conflicts, superlatives, the surprising, something a reader can identify with because it is close in either a physical or psychological sense, the personally affecting, and that which has consequences for the reader. Cf. Elisabeth Noelle-Neumann, *The Spiral of Silence: Public Opinion – Our Social Skin* (Chicago: University of Chicago Press, 1984), p. 147.

flict' subject matters had to be found within the issue of consensus.[22] The 'emotionally involving' themes were sought within several 'problem areas', including the civilisational backwardness of Poland, conflicts of interest between Poland and the EU in economy and international politics, cultural incomepatibility with particular emphasis on the contrast between the religiosity of Poles and the secular character of European societies, and negative national stereotypes.

These 'problematic areas' added necessary dramaturgy to the European debate and gave journalists an occasion of turning them into arguments either in favour of or against the perspective of joining the EU. We would like to avoid presenting one or the other interpretation as being more 'innocent' or 'virtuous'. Both simplify reality in some way, thus distorting it. Those promoting the idea of integration often did so at the price of exploiting the inferiority complex of Poles. The development path for Poland was presented as a painful yet necessary road from backwardness to civilisation. Alternatively, the supporters of European integration referred to the 'historical debt' that Europe needs to repay to Poland, thus creating a distorted picture of contemporary politics. Those who argued against integration with the EU did so by referring to nationalism, various phobias (racial, sexual and cultural) and many other negative standpoints typical of the far right or populist ideologies.

Both opposing standpoints on European integration were engaged in replacing real problems, such as economic development, healthcare, education, poverty or unemployment, with the replica of a problem labelled 'European integration'. The polarisation has also been supported by the ways in which the results of public opinion polls were presented, notably in the news. To make the complex multivariable research results accessible they were conveniently organised exactly according to this binary opposition. Here, we by no means would like to imply that all publications about the EU represented these extreme views. Some valuable observations by outstanding public figures appeared in media. Some media appealed for

22 Elżbieta Skotnicka-Illasiewicz, 'Konsens czy przyzwolenie?' [Consensus or Consent] in Janusz Mucha (ed.), *Społeczeństwo Polskie w perspektywie przystąpienia do Unii Europejskiej* (Warszawa: IFiS PAN, 1999), p. 70.

treating Europe as a 'common cause'.[23] Yet in such appeals, the blame for dividing society was ascribed exclusively to politicians, while the role of objective observer was reserved for media. Illuminating and multifaceted debates about Europe can be found in Polish press dailies like *Rzeczpospolita* and weeklies like *Tygodnik Powszechny*. However, these thought-provoking and informative publications sink in an ocean of many more operating through the mechanisms of binary oppositions that have been described above. Thus we insist that the predominant tendency was to stretch the debate between the two opposing poles.

Apart from the polarisation of public opinion, media representations of the European debate resulted in its confusion. Press news about the EU and the negotiation process were delivered in a dry tone.[24] Media used obscure and specialised language, making the subject inaccessible and alien to the audience.[25] Moreover, as far as agenda-setting is concerned, the most absurd features of the European bureaucracy, such as regulations defining the maximum length of cucumbers or limiting the loudness of the lawnmower, made the biggest news.[26] In this way the EU became gradually associated with bureaucracy, and thus has been completely dissociated from the ideal Europe, which had been the single possible destination of 'return' in 1989.

23 Bronisław Wildstein, 'Nie grajmy Europą' [Let's Not Play with Europe], *Rzeczpospolita*, 1 February 2002, p. 3.

24 This claim is made on the basis of discourse analysis of 6 Polish newspapers from 1998–2002 conducted by the author as a part of her PhD research on the media representation of Europe.

25 Maciej Łubieński, 'Polska – Unia Europejska. Analiza prasy codziennej' [Poland – European Union. The Analysis of Daily Press], in Lena Kolarska-Bobińska (ed.), *Polska Eurodebata* (Warsaw: ISP, 1999).

26 Mark Leonard, *Europa odkryta na nowo* [Europe Discovered Anew] (Warsaw: ISP, 1998).

The European Debate at the Junction of Media and Political Discourse Structures

As it was outlined above, there was a general political consensus about the need for Poland to return to Europe. However, anti-European moods and opinions were continuously and increasingly delivered by some broadcast and print media. The fact that they were not directly linked to any party (in most cases they represented indiscriminate 'conservative nationalist' views) did not prevent them from imposing anti-European rhetoric on the public discourse on the EU. Radio Maryja is one of the most influential media representing such views. It was founded by Redemptorist Fathers and is successful in economic terms. It is connected to the newspaper Nasz Dziennik, which is the print version of the group's extreme views. The targeting of under-privileged groups is facilitated by the simple and inclusive rhetoric of Radio Maryja. The presenters avoid professional journalistic jargon and often introduce interactive forms, which allow minimising the distance between the producer and the receiver of the message.

All these factors ensured that this broadcast became extremely popular (the fourth most popular radio station in Poland, among 119). Moreover, the conservative nationalist party LPR won almost 8% of votes in the 2001 parliamentary elections due to the support of this broadcast and similar print media. Overt mutual support existed between the LPR and *Radio Maryja* up to the very eve of the European Referendum in Poland in July 2003. Just before the referendum, radio unexpectedly moderated their propaganda against European integration. This might have been due to the fact that the owners did not want to act in open opposition to the Vatican, which welcomed the idea of European unification.

At the other the axis (stretching from opponents to supporters of European integration), the centrist party Freedom Union (UW) spoke with a single voice about the necessity of integration for Poland and was overtly pro-European. Moreover, their opinions found expression in the most popular national newspaper *Gazeta Wyborcza*. When the UW did not enter parliament in the 2001 elections, *Gazeta Wyborcza* continued to shape public opinion in a pro-European key. Taking into account its circulation of over half a million copies, they could not but affect the collective consciousness. The newspaper has proved to possess more effective mechanisms of winning their public than the political party, whose members played an important role in forming the editorial policy of this newspaper. Arguably, since the UW's failure in the 2001 parliamentary elections, its political views and programs were disseminated effectively through the newspaper. Before the referendum, *Gazeta Wyborcza* was a major actor in the pro-European campaign. It acted in broad agreement with other euro-enthusiastic forces in society, including major broadcasters and newspapers, parties (such as the Citizens' Platform (PO) and Law and Justice (PiS)) and non-governmental organisations (e.g., Schuman Foundation, Stefan Batory Foundation, Friedrich Erbert Foundation, Konrad Adenauer Foundation).

Concluding Remarks

The example of the European debate in Poland was used to demonstrate the fields of mutual support and consensus between the ideologies supplied by the media and politicians, respectively. It appears that no straightforward dependence between political parties and the media can be discerned in Poland. The media are influenced, in stronger or weaker form, by political as well as economic interest groups. They sometimes express ideas, which are congruent with parts of party ideologies. However, they can by no means be called mouthpieces of any given party.

To summarise, while the media in Poland have acquired relative independence from political parties and politicians, their total liberation from politics as such is probably not feasible since political events constitute a part of social reality, which the media cannot help representing. Our belief is that the threat of the politicisation of media is less severe in terms of direct pressures put on the media through economic and legal mechanisms. These pressures are noticeable and tangible and therefore can be straightforwardly addressed by interest groups in a democratic society. Therefore, there is hope that such pressures would sooner or later be moderated, if not totally eliminated. In this respect, the importance of belonging to broader institutions such as those of the European Union can be of crucial importance for Poland, for it might guarantee stricter observance of law and democratic procedures.

The danger which is less tangible yet quite real is the 'colonisation' of media by certain discourse strategies that are aimed at producing sellable 'news'.[27] If the media are oriented towards making 'national problems' out of issues,[28] politicians might become sophisticated enough to use this feature of the media to their own ends. By distracting public attention by scandals, 'national threats' and similar 'sensational' matters, politicians might be able to indirectly influence the formation of the news agenda. This influence can run in such a way that significant matters having an impact on the entire population (poverty, unemployment, intolerance, discrimination and so forth) would be suppressed by fictional 'sensations'. In our opinion, therein lies a true threat to the freedom of press, if one understands this principle as the ability of the media to assess and present matters according to their importance for the public and not exclusively according to their attractiveness as consumer products or propaganda devices.

Bibliography

Attacks on the Press in 2000. A Worldwide Survey of the Committee to Protect Journalists (New York: CPJ, 2001).

Attacks on the Press in 2001. A Worldwide Survey of the Committee to Protect Journalists (New York: CPJ, 2002).

27 Cf. Norman Fairclough, *Language and Power* (Harlow: Longman, 1989); Teun A. van Dijk, ed., *Discourse as Social Interaction: A Multidisciplinary Introduction to Discourse Analysis* (London: Sage, 1997).

28 Cf. Luthar, p. 25.

CBOS. Komunikat z badania [Centre for Social Opinion Research. Research Communicate], 61 (March 1998).

Diamond, Edwin and Bates, Stephen, *The Spot: The Rise of Political Advertising on Television* (Cambridge, Mass.: MIT Press, 1988).

Edelman, Murray, *The Symbolic Uses of Politics* (Urbana: University of Illinois Press, 1985).

Ekiert, Grzegorz and Hanson, Stephen (eds.), *Capitalism and Democracy in Central and Eastern Europe* (Cambridge: Cambridge University Press, 2003).

Fairclough, Norman, *Language and Power* (Harlow: Longman, 1989).

Freedom in the World. *The Annual Report of Political Rights and Civil Liberties 1999–2000* (New York: Freedom House, 2000).

Golding, Peter and Murdock, Graham 'Culture, Communication and Economy', in James Curran and Michael Gurevitch (eds.), *Mass Media and Society* (London: Edward Arnold, 1996), pp. 11–30.

Goszczyński, Andrzej, 'Politycy pod kloszem' [Politicians under protection], *Media Polska*, 6 (June 1998), pp. 16–20

—— 'Wojna o media' [War over media], *Newsweek Poland*, 26 May 2003, pp. 32–34.

Gramsci, Antonio, *Prison Notebooks* (London: Lawrence and Wishart, 1971).

Habermas, Jürgen, 'Further Reflections on the Public Sphere', in Craig Calhoun (ed.), *Habermas and the Public Sphere* (Cambridge, Mass.: MIT Press, 1992), pp. 421–461

Jedlicki, Jerzy, *A Suburb of Europe. Nineteenth Century Polish Approach to Western Civilisation* (Budapest: Central European University, 1999).

Krzemiński, Ireneusz, 'The National Identity and European Consciousness of Poles', in Petr Drulak (ed.), *National and European Identities in EU Enlargement. Views from Central and Eastern Europe* (Prague: Institute of International Relations, 2001), pp. 57–68.

Leonard, Mark, *Europa odkryta na nowo* [Europe Discovered Anew] (Warsaw: ISP, 1998).

Lippman, Walter, *Public Opinion* (New York: Harcourt, Brace and Co., 1965).

Luthar, Breda *et al.*, *The Victory of the Imaginary Left. The Relationship Between the Media and Politics in the 2000 Parliamentary Elections in Slovenia* (Ljubljana: Peace Institute, 2001).

Łubieński, Maciej, 'Polska–Unia Europejska. Analiza prasy codziennej' [Poland – European Union. The Analysis of Daily Press], in Lena Kolarska-Bobińska (ed.), *Polska Eurodebata* (Warsaw: ISP, 1999), pp. 277–296

Miller, Leszek, 'Europejska szansa' [European Opportunity], *Trybuna*, 27–28 July 1998, p. 2

Noelle-Neumann, Elisabeth, *The Spiral of Silence. Public Opinion – Our Social Skin* (Chicago: University of Chicago Press, 1984)

Roguska, Beata and Strzeszewski, Marek, *Zainteresowanie społeczne, wiedza i poinformowanie o integracji Polski z Unią Europejską* [Public Interest, Knowledge and the Degree of Being Informed About the Integration of Poland With the European Union] (Warsaw: ISP, 2002)

Skotnicka-Illasiewicz, Elżbieta, *Powrót czy droga w nieznane? Europejskie dylematy Polaków* [Return or the Road to the Unknown? European Dilemmas of the Poles] (Warsaw: European Centre of University of Warsaw, 1997)

——'Konsens czy przyzwolenie?' [Consensus or Consent], in *Społeczeństwo Polskie w perspektywie przystąpienia do Unii Europejskiej*, [Polish Society in the Perspective of Joining the EU] ed. by Janusz Mucha (Warsaw: IFiS PAN, 1999), pp. 66–75

Turner, Graeme, *British Cultural Studies: An Introduction* (London: Unwin-Hymam, 1990)

van Dijk, Teun (ed.), *Discourse as Social Interaction. A Multidisciplinary Introduction to Discourse Analysis* (London: Sage, 1997)

Wildstein, Bronisław, 'Nie grajmy Europą' [Let's Not Play around with Europe], *Rzeczpospolita*, 1 February 2002, p. 3

IVAN CHORVÁT

Family and Women in Central and Eastern Europe: The Significance of Traditional Roles after Socialism

This paper will focus on possible transformations of 'family' in post-communist countries of Central Europe (using the examples of Slovakia and the Czech Republic) under the influence of Western feminism. It attempts to show how feminist ideas are reflected in the writings of Slovak and Czech social scientists and how they influence local cultural settings.

Although the ideas of feminism gained much influence, support, and popularity in the West, they were not influential in former communist countries. This was not surprising because the communist regimes did not allow Western ideas to spread in those societies. Western feminists hoped that after the collapse of communist ideology the situation would change. However, I would argue that their expectations have not been fulfilled and feminist ideas remain weak in post-communist societies.

There is a whole range of reasons that can explain why women in Central and Eastern Europe have not been very receptive to feminist ideas. This paper discusses some of these reasons, especially those that are related to family life and family setting. The focus of attention will be on the countries of Central Europe, Slovakia and the Czech Republic.

However, to say that local social scientists are not receptive to western feminism is not to suggest that there is no thinking about gender issues. It is that their ideas differ from Western feminist perspectives, and their approach to women's issues is not in line with the developments of the Western women's movement in the 1960 and 70s. Central European writers build their discourse rather in terms of more recent Western neo-feminist trends of sexual difference, of the articulation of specific values of female subjectivity and identity.

The following section discusses the impact of the communist regime on the position of women as full-time workers and the value of the family. The next two sections examine the significance of the private sphere and the family during and after communism. In the last section, I set out some perspectives of feminism in Central Europe.

Women under the Communist Regime

Jirina Siklova, a prominent Czech feminist, believes that the feminist movement is not developing in the former Czechoslovakia because it has been discredited by the previous communist regime. The regime considered the emancipation of women to be almost a state ideology, which meant, in the eyes of the citizens, a disgrace of the women's movement. The fact that the emancipation of women was reduced not to the right to work but to the 'duty to work'[1] alongside benefits for women just because they were women, weakened rather than strengthened women's self-confidence. Women became the basic labour force that was called upon to create the socialist society in the 1950's.[2] It is therefore necessary to see what are the political implications of women's employment and women's emancipation in Central Europe because, as Fuszara rightly observes, the situation of women is different in countries where work is an individual and economic right and the best way of gaining a personal living or increasing wealth, from

1 The Constitution of socialist countries introduced 'the duty to work'. Those who did not work were considered social parasites.

2 Jirina Siklova, 'Rozumi zapad nasim zenam?' ['Does the West understand our women?'], *Listy*, no. 5 (1991), p. 15.

those countries where it is largely a duty aimed at increasing the wealth of the community.[3]

Thus the role of women at the beginning of the communist period in Central Europe was defined as a unity of economic, maternal and political functions. However, as Heitlinger points out, in response to the declining birth rate[4] there were important shifts in emphasis within that threefold role of women:

> The formerly unitary model of the 'ideal' socialist woman gave way to a broader, more graduated model, one that recognised the contribution women make to society by having and raising children, and that took into account age and life-cycle differences among women. Women were no longer expected to fulfil all roles simultaneously.[5]

In 1970s the Czechoslovak government introduced new legal arrangements that were designed to help women in their multiple roles, to support families, especially young ones, and to encourage them to have more children. Some new measures were adopted, such as mothers' allowances, low interest rates on loans for young couples with children and extended maternity leave. These pro-family measures were designed not necessarily to advance women's equality, but to prevent possible manifestations of citizens' discontent and needed

3 Malgorzata Fuszara, 'Does the Law Protect Polish Women?', in Mavis Maclean and Jacek Kurczewski (eds.), *Families, Politics and the Law: Perspectives for East and West Europe* (Oxford: Clarendon Press, 1994), p. 241.

4 After February 1948 there was a tendency in Czechoslovakia for women to change their roles as a mother and a wife and to adopt a role as a worker. Women appeared in jobs completely unusual for them at that time – in blue-collar jobs, in military and police uniforms, as tractor-drivers, in miner's schools, etc. As Fuszara points out when describing the Polish situation at that time, women's unlimited access to employment was not just an attempt to implement the ideal model of equality but predominantly an economic necessity after the war. It was therefore not surprising that the birth-rate after the war, stopped rising in Czechoslovakia in 1950 and decreased continuously until 1962.

5 Alena Heitlinger, 'The Impact of the Transition from Communism on the Status of Women in the Czech and Slovak Republics', in Nanette Funk and Magda Mueller (eds.), *Gender, Politics and Post-Communism* (New York: Routledge, 1993), p. 96.

to stabilize the society, especially after the events of the so-called Prague Spring in 1968–9. In other words, the family was a good means of social control. The regime felt intuitively that the family is the basic precondition of a stable society. Certainly, the regime also supported families because they were cost-effective in providing childcare.

The family has always been a very strong and important value in the lives of people in Central Europe. The family has a special significance, even now, under the new political regime, In many public opinion polls throughout the 1990s in both Slovakia and the Czech Republic, only a very small part of the respondents (up to ten percent) believed that after 1989 it was less important than before 'to live for one's own family'.[6] Western feminists, in attacking the family as a patriarchal institution, must take into consideration the significance of the family for Central Europeans. Indeed, Nanette Funk writes :

> there are tremendous differences in culture, socialization and personality between Eastern and Western women, and in what Habermas has referred to as the 'lifeworld', that stock taken for granted of unreflected beliefs and world views... Women in state socialist countries appear to be more oriented than Western feminists toward children and the family, have different attitudes toward the individual and the collective and to authority, are more sceptical of the benefits of paid work, and have different attitudes toward men or toward collective action.[7]

In other words, as the Czech feminist Hana Havelkova suggests, a potential feminist view must be preceded by the pre-feminist reflection on the post-socialist experience.[8]

The importance of the family in the communist states was paradoxically strengthened by women's positions as full-time workers in

6 See, for example Helena Wolekova, 'Socialna politika' ['Social welfare policy'], in *Slovensko 1996* (Bratislava: Institut pre verejne otazky, 1997) pp. 185–196; *Rodina 1994* (Prague: STEM, 1994).

7 Nanette Funk, 'Feminism East and West', in Nanette Funk and Magda Mueller (eds.), *Gender, Politics and Post-Communism* (New York: Routledge, 1993), p. 320

8 Hana Havelkova, 'A Few Prefeminist Thoughts', in Nanette Funk and Magda Mueller (eds.), *Gender, Politics and Post-Communism* (New York: Routledge, 1993), p. 71.

the labour market. Proposed 'liberation through participation in production' did not lead to women's equality but a 'double burden' of domestic chores and paid employment. Hauserova stresses that even state measures of social welfare introduced in the 1970s were aimed just to enable women to bear the 'double burden' but not to alleviate it, e.g. by establishing part-time jobs and flexible working hours.[9] Moreover, for women in Central and Eastern Europe the double burden was much heavier than for their Western counterparts because of the arduous nature of daily domestic tasks

> without the aid of many consumer durable and labour saving devices, in addition to queuing and having to struggle for the means of subsistence... They had to produce many basic commodities by growing food and preserving and pickling it; almost no services are commodified.[10]

Although state measures were intended to solve women's problems connected with family and childcare, Siklova claims that 'the very nature of a centrally directed system of planning and control worked to silence women. The socialists' "pseudo-emancipation" lost any originally positive attributes and led to a new "women's fate"'.[11] The constant conflict between the demands of work and home led to women resenting equality with men as a standard of behaviour a source of their discontent. And although married women in Czechoslovakia did not have the duty to work and be employed, most worked, regarding it as their duty to contribute to the family budget.[12]

Partially as a result of dissatisfaction with paid employment (women did not achieve autonomy, freedom, self-respect, self-realization and were paid only 70 % of men's salaries for the same job), women turned to their families as a major source of meaning. In fact, both women and men escaped into the family as a place of relative freedom and privacy. According to Siklova,

9 Eva Hauserova, *Na kosteti se da i litat* ['It is also possible to fly on the broom'] (Praha: Nakladatelstvi Lidove Noviny, 1995), p. 75.

10 Claire Wallace, 'A Western Feminist Goes East', *Transit*, 9 (1995), p. 139.

11 Jirina Siklova, 'Are Women in Central and Eastern Europe Conservative?', in Nanette Funk and Magda Mueller (eds.), *Gender, Politics and Post-Communism* (New York: Routledge, 1993), p. 75.

12 Havelkova, 'A Few Prefeminist Thoughts', p. 70.

> since people did not realize themselves in their work for society and state, their private relationships were perhaps of greater importance for them than for people in the West... Moreover, work in the family had its undisputed value, whereas work for society was often senseless.[13]

This aspect of the socialist society was noticed also by Nanette Funk who sees the distinction between the family and the state as the fundamental dichotomy of state socialism:

> The family thus had a very special and powerful status as the primary institution that stood in opposition to the state. Women who wanted to be in the 'private' sphere wanted something different than what would be meant by a Western woman's orientation toward the family.[14]

Who Is the Enemy?

Now we are arriving at what is probably the central issue: the 'mysterious' attitude of Central and Eastern European women toward Western feminism and gender issues. Havelkova shows that while in Western debates the division of power corresponds with the division between the private and the public spheres, in socialism the division was drawn between the Communist Party, and its others. Women, as well as men, 'were given positions in the Party according to their loyalty, not their abilities.[15] Therefore the private sphere came to have very different connotations in socialist countries than it had for Western feminists. It was a state-free zone. *Both* women and men sought refuge from the repressive public life in the family.

Mozny also points out that the 'new' socialist regime did not fulfil a lot of promises and proclamations in helping women and lightening their responsibilities, especially in young families. The common

13 Jirina Siklova, 'Inhibited Factors of Feminism in the Czech Republic', conference paper prepared for the Crossing Borders Conference, Stockholm, 27–29 May 1994, pp. 5–6.

14 Funk, 'Feminism East and West', p. 323.

15 Havelkova, 'A Few Prefeminist Thoughts', p. 68.

worries of how to get an apartment, how to get places for children in kindergartens and in secondary and high schools, the poor performance of the service sector and other common problems meant that there was solidarity between a husband and his wife and strengthened the notion of their mutual reciprocity and dependence.[16]

It is also possible to say that a woman was oppressed much more by the society than by her husband, leading most women in Central Europe reject feminism. While the psychological perceptions of women in Central and Eastern Europe are quite similar to those of Western women, their social experiences are radically different.[17] In a sociological research study, FOCUS in Bratislava in 1994, it demonstrates that women understand their position as disadvantaged; however, the key problems for them is not the gender dimension but unambiguously social, or, to be more precise, socio-economic dimension.[18]

Furthermore, Siklova explains that in the communist states the regime's formal support of women was often misused against democracy and freedom of thought. On many occasions women had to place the fight for a democratic society, for freedom of expression, religion, and human rights above their own interests and the interests of other groups.[19]

Havelkova claims that it is necessary to differentiate between two forms of equality, positive and negative. There was a positive form of equalization enforced through law, and the negative equalization in the form of oppression of all individuals through totalitarian means. The latter meant the degradation of all persons as objects because the totalitarian regime suspended individual subjectivity, people as citizens, as thinking and acting subjects, as men and women shaping their own lives. Therefore

16 Ivo Mozny, *Moderni rodina: Myty a skutecnost* ['The Modern Family: Myths and Reality'] (Brno: Blok, 1990).

17 Jana Bodnarova, 'Makky feminizmus' ['Soft Feminism'], *Aspekt*, no. 2 (1994), p. 29.

18 Tatiana Rosová, 'Ženy na Slovensku. Vyhodnotenie výsledkov kvalitatívnej sociologickej sondy'[Women in Slovakia. An Interpretation of Qualitative Sociological Survey], *Aspekt*, no. 3 (1994), p. 113.

19 Siklova, 'Are Women in Central and Eastern Europe Conservative?', p. 80.

> the problems of subjectivity and identity are not perceived in this society as specifically female ones. In theoretical terms, identity based on sex is still approached only as a sub-problem. There are thus two reasons for making the 'generally human' superior to the 'specifically female.' First, the problem is not one concerning women more than men; and second, in its emphatic form it is an essential problem of all.[20]

Hence the situation in which both women's and men's identities were suppressed and both women and men were reduced to objects that were manipulated by the Communist system did special harm to the self-esteem of men and their masculinity. In fact 'the very ideal of a modern, self-conscious, self-evident, independently acting, powerful, in other words, 'male subject', so scorned in Western feminism, did not have a chance to develop here, or existed only as a pathetic caricature'.[21] As a result, it was difficult even to establish 'typical' male manifestations of behaviour. It will be very strange and unusual for Western women to learn that many women in socialism 'deliberately encouraged the patriarchal manners of their husbands so as to boost their husbands' self-confidence, which the latter had difficulty maintaining in the public and work spheres'.[22] Women under communism did not experience real patriarchal relations in the workplace even if their boss was a man, because the boss predominantly conformed to the political regime and obeyed the higher 'nomenclature'.[23] 'The division between the exploited and those who comfortably "settled" in the system did not precisely coincide with the relationship between men and women'.[24]

It is no surprise, therefore, to read the following definition of feminism by the Czech feminist Jana Hradilkova, which appeared in the feminist journal *Aspekt* published in Bratislava:

20 Havelkova, 'A Few Prefeminist Thoughts', p. 66.

21 Jirina Smejkalova-Strickland, 'Do Czech Women Need Feminism?', in Susanna Trnka and Laura Busheikin (eds.), *Bodies of Bread and Butter: Reconfiguring Women's Lives in the Post-Communist Czech Republic* (Prague: Gender Studies Centre 1993), p. 17.

22 Havelkova, 'A Few Prefeminist Thoughts', p. 69.

23 Siklova, 'Inhibited Factors of Feminism in the Czech Republic', pp. 7–8.

24 Havelkova, 'A Few Prefeminist Thoughts', p. 71.

> For me feminism means simply an effort to understand men and their relations to women; an effort to conceive what is male in women's mentality and what is female in men's mentality; how it is developing and how it is manifested under the ideas which are forced to us by the system.[25]

It has been already mentioned that the western dichotomy between private and public spheres did not exist in socialist countries. Another reason apart from those mentioned previously was that the family acted as a substitution for the public sphere. It was in the family and with close friends that one could safely discuss social, cultural and political issues, outside the public discourse in the media, the schools and the workplace.[26] This was reflected also in various public opinion polls. Kurczewski cites one study conducted in Poland:

> health, a happy family life and a small circle of reliable, close friends constitutes the list of goods treasured as being those that give meaning to human life... They are regarded highly for themselves, whereas the value of other objects depends on how instrumental they are in the achievement of these basic goods.[27]

With an increasing importance of the private sphere, the role of women becomes more important too. Private sphere has remained the domain of women, despite their activity also in the public sphere. Within the private sphere, the mother's role was irreplaceable. Women made use of this, for them the family represented an escape from political blackmails, for example professional advancement by joining and being loyal; to the Communist Party.[28] It was hoped that the mother's role would protect women from conforming to the communist ideals, from joining the Party, and from cooperating with the totalitarian regime, so enabling them to keep their human dignity relatively intact. On the whole, for a Central and Eastern European woman the ability to have a child represented the core of her identity.

25 Jana Hradilkova, 'Rozhovor' [Interview], *Aspekt*, no. 2 (1994), p. 64.

26 Havelkova, 'A Few Prefeminist Thoughts', p. 68.

27 Jacek Kurczewski, 'Privatizing the Polish Family after Communism', in Mavis Maclean and Jacek Kurczewski (eds.), *Families, Politics and the Law: Perspectives for East and West Europe* (Oxford: Clarendon Press, 1994), p. 27.

28 Havelkova, 'A Few Prefeminist Thoughts', p. 69.

Motherhood gave limited protection from the frustrating and anomic world of work. Although motherhood had negative social consequences for women (such as less leisure time and poor career prospects), it signified a kind of privilege and respect for them.[29] Thus, women had an important status in the family under socialism.

Going Back to the Family?

As the communist ideology broke down, many people welcomed the freedom to return to traditional practices, which were once forbidden. Often today there is a nostalgic feeling for the traditional woman's role. Hauserova claims that a Western woman is fascinated by the possibility of professional career just as much as an Eastern European woman is fascinated by her traditional role of a wife and a mother. While Western women have ambiguous attitudes toward the family, motherhood, and housework, Eastern European women have ambiguous attitudes towards their occupations and professional development. This is probably a manifestation of different cultural backgrounds: in Central and Eastern European culture motherhood represents a great natural power and not a dependency on the husband or a conformity conservative values, as most depicted by Western feminists. It is an interesting feature of post-communist societies that the humanity is connected with a turn to traditional values.[30]

We can present two examples to show how important the cultural backgrounds are for the development of feminist attitudes. The first example is that of the wife of the former Slovak President Michal Kovac, Emilia, who said in her interview for the daily *Smena*:

> In our society a woman plays two roles; she is a mother and at the same time she is a working person-breadwinner. If a couple has a good income and suf-

29 Alena Wagnerova, 'Socialismus propousti ceske zeny' [Socialism fires Czech women], *Aspekt* no. 1 (1994), p. 22.

30 Hauserova, *Na kosteti se da i litat* [It is also possible to fly on the broom], p. 59.

> ficient family allowances, I believe that it would not be necessary for women to work and they could devote their time to their primary vocation – to child-rearing. Only this can guarantee the happy future for our country and for the following generations.[31]

The second example is from an interview with the popular Slovak actress Zuzana Tluckova, who at that time was not appearing on TV and on the stage because she was taking care of her second baby and 'realizing' herself as a housewife. The journalist conducting the interview remarks that many famous actresses have babies and in a few days they work again for theatres and films. Tluckova answers:

> Don't forget that we live in Slovakia. Of course, Sophia Loren had her baby and immediately after that she worked for a film and relaxed in sauna. But I cannot do it. Cooking and child caring is my relaxation. In fact, I don't agree with emancipation of women in Eastern Europe. The woman should have a part-time job and care for the household, the family and herself.[32]

After presenting all these ideas and describing the situation of Central and Eastern European women, there seems to be an unavoidable conclusion that after the political changes in 1989 and the breakdown of communism, nothing could prevent women from leaving paid employment and staying at home. Although some women used this opportunity and became full-time housewives, the expected large-scale flow from employment did not occur. Havelkova suggests that women did not resent work during socialism in Czechoslovakia as is sometimes claimed today.[33] For most women the workplace represents a useful form of socialising: one can meet people, make friends and create new relationships (including romantic ones). There are rituals of small celebrations, birthday parties, talks, mutual compliments and little jokes at the workplace.[34]

However, the most important reason why women remain in the work force is due to economic necessity. As Heitlinger stresses, it is

31 *Smena* daily, 21 July 1994, p. 3.
32 *SME* daily, 7 June 1994, p. 4.
33 Havelkova, 'A Few Prefeminist Thoughts', p. 71.
34 Mozny, *Moderni rodina: Myty a skutecnost* ['The Modern Family: Myths and Reality'], pp. 121–122.

very unlikely that the male worker can earn enough to provide the 'family wage' to support the whole family.[35] Moreover, economic pressures on families have increased due to increases in the cost of many basic items previously subsidised by the state, such as housing, food and child care.. Therefore keeping women at home is not very practical.[36] Furthermore, Nanette Funk clearly points out that

> to have the choice not to work they [women] would have to be in stable marriages with husbands with stable jobs making a family wage. However, nothing is stable in post-communism, and none of these conditions generally hold... Many women are single mothers or are in unstable marriages, given 30 to 40 per cent divorce rates. If they have husbands, the husbands are often unemployed or inadequately compensated, and more than two jobs in a family are often necessary for survival, as in Hungary or Poland.[37]

One possible solution to integrate employment and family life, which is so important for women in Central and Eastern Europe, is to combine household chores with a part-time job. In the mid-1980s

> only 7% of women worked part-time [in Czechoslovakia], compared to 35% in Canada, 44% in the United Kingdom, 53% in Netherlands, and 30% in West Germany. However, 23–27% of all women workers and 40% of women returning to work after maternity leave stated they would prefer to work part-time.[38]

It is quite obvious that for Central and Eastern European women liberation is seen not in escaping from the family but rather in a more satisfactory integration of motherhood and work.

35 Family wage has been a suggested state measure for male workers whose wives would decide to stay at home as housewives and care for their children. It should have been high enough to support a worker's family. However, due to difficult economic circumstances of the post-communist societies the idea of family wage appears to be unrealistic.

36 Heitlinger, 'The Impact of the Transition from Communism on the Status of Women in the Czech and Slovak Republics'.

37 Funk, 'Feminism East and West', p. 326.

38 Heitlinger, 'The Impact of the Transition from Communism on the Status of Women in the Czech and Slovak Republics', p. 98.

Perspectives of Feminism in Central Europe

As noted early, traditional Western feminism does not appeal to women in Central Europe. However, it seems that the most recent developments in feminist theory correspond to some extent to the experiences and perceptions of post-socialist women. According to Tatiana Sedova, feminism as a movement with political aspirations is not relevant in Central and Eastern Europe, while feminism which articulates from different perspectives questions of female identity and self-identification, has more attractions.[39]

Zuzana Kiczkova and Etela Farkasova, two Slovak writers, who express support to the new direction in feminist theory that pays close attention to problems of identity and specificity of women, point out that

> it is relevant to distinguish between formal and real emancipation. Formal equality appeared in the form of the sexual neutrality of many social roles and in the form of universalism. Real equality must start with sexual difference as a given; it should articulate the specific nature of female subjectivity and identity. Formal equality always brings with it the possibility of real disadvantages and discrimination veiled behind data, numbers, charts and blinding statistics, thereby legitimizing and legalizing purely formal equality.[40]

This opinion reflects the writers' own experience from the socialist period. Women who underwent this formal emancipation possess a more real experience of emancipation than do Western women. As a result, Central European women do not react politically or ideologically to their own emancipation:

> The women's question here is not their independence but rather their dignity, because the great emancipation also brought disrespect and degradation with it.

39 Tatiana Sedova, 'K moznostiam a limitom feminizmu v nasich pomeroch' ['Towards opportunities and limits of feminism in our country'], in *Rodina ako predmet vedy* (Bratislava: 1994), p. 126.

40 Zuzana Kiczkova and Etela Farkasova, 'The Emancipation of Women: A Concept that Failed', in Nanette Funk and Magda Mueller (eds.), *Gender, Politics and Post-Communism* (New York: Routledge, 1993), p. 93

> [Women]...were reduced to a cheap source of labour that could be plugged in everywhere without regard to specific capabilities, prerequisites, and ambitions... Women... had no chance to become aware of and determine for themselves what it meant to be a woman and to express it in their lives, their social roles, and their personal expectations.[41]

Therefore new independent women's groups in Central Europe define their main task in terms of moral re-evaluation of women's roles, distinctive qualities and interests, such as nurturing motherhood and down-to-earth 'practical' common sense.[42] Moreover, some writers call for the advancement of those qualities into public life, into politics. For instance Jirina Siklova believes that

> our women who have had the experience of living under totalitarian regimes will not merely mimic men but will discover a new form of political participation and leadership with enough space for solidarity, one that will uphold our 'traditional' female qualities. I welcome more of such feminine traits in politics and leadership.[43]

Also some Western feminists recognize the potential value of feminism that is hidden behind the experience of post-communist women. As Canadian feminist Laura Busheikin points out, contemporary Western feminism is being challenged by Western women themselves who feel it does not sufficiently address their realities. They start to accept that 'men oppressing women' is perhaps too simple a formula, they give up celebrating sisterhood and begin celebrating differences instead. Busheikin emphasises that

> if we begin to listen to East-European voices, we are taken even further in this direction and find ourselves in entirely new territory... If we really want fem-

41 Zuzana Kiczkova and Etela Farkasova, 'The Emancipation of Women: A Concept that Failed', p. 87.

42 Heitlinger, 'The Impact of the Transition from Communism on the Status of Women in the Czech and Slovak Republics'.

43 Siklova, 'Are Women in Central and Eastern Europe Conservative?', p. 82. Similar ideas are also expressed by the Prague-based women's group New Humanity which calls attention to the fact that 'man's and woman's shares on the face of the world are precariously disharmonious, with female influence missing from society and male from the family...' (quoted in Busheikin, 'Je sesterstvo naozaj globalne?' [Is sisterhood really global?], p. 52).

> inism which would be about women and not only about some women, we must understand the women from Eastern Europe and cooperate with them.[44]

Here again one faces the issue of the existence of many different feminisms. Cavarero admits (in her article for the Slovak feminist journal)[45] that historical conditions and circumstances create for every woman a different context and a different perspective; therefore she considers harmful one universal doctrine that suppresses differences among women and their specificity as well as uniqueness. In the same vein, Busheikin writes about the impotence of words like 'equality', 'liberation from patriarchal oppression', 'emancipation', etc. in an East European context.[46] Finally, Claire Wallace also underlines that East European women find that 'many of the universalising assumptions about gender held within Western feminism apply only to those contexts in which they originated. The experience of post-communist women speaks differently'.[47]

When Busheikin looked over the literature written by East European feminists, she noticed that rather than accepting Western frameworks and terminology, the writers challenged them and used them in their own different situation. Eastern women have the power to question Western feminist theories, traditions and convictions; typical feminist practices are mostly inappropriate in Eastern Europe. This throws in doubt the Western feminists' claim of global sisterhood. Busheikin concludes that feminism imported from the West works only when it is transformed by the journey to fit the local conditions and circumstances.[48]

What is the future of feminism in Eastern and Central Europe then? What kind of feminism is likely to succeed? Many writers agree that 'maternal feminism' could develop in the region. Heitlinger de-

44 Laura Busheikin, 'Je sesterstvo naozaj globalne?' ['Is sisterhood really global?'], *Aspekt*, no. 2 (1994), p. 52.

45 A. Cavarero 'Rozhovor' ['Interview'], *Aspekt*, no. 2 (1994), p. 29.

46 Busheikin, 'Je sesterstvo naozaj globalne?' ['Is sisterhood really global?'], p. 52.

47 Claire Wallace, *A Western Feminist Goes East*, p. 131.

48 Busheikin, 'Je sesterstvo naozaj globalne?' ['Is sisterhood really global?'], pp. 50–51.

fines maternal feminism as such 'which rests on the complementarity of sex differences and the special moral qualities and needs of women'.[49] Hauserova indicates that it is quite possible that Central and Eastern European women will maintain the importance of the family and the cult of motherhood. She argues that these values may be an East European (Central European) or Slavic feature rather than a feature caused by totalitarianism.[50]

Seemingly, post-communist women convey an important message for their Western counterparts: they are probably more emancipated than their Western colleagues.[51] Most of them know that the best thing for them, for their personality and identity as well as for their families is a combination of paid work and family responsibilities. After forty years of 'full employment' it is natural for them to be employed; however, they also appreciate the value of motherhood, which is often overlooked by most Western feminists, who question 'traditional' social roles.[52]

Yet, in order to achieve a desired and balanced combination of the family and employment, it is necessary to change the organization of work in the society in such a way that would reflect the needs of *both* men and women; e.g. flexible working hours, part-time jobs and

49 Heitlinger, 'The Impact of the Transition from Communism on the Status of Women in the Czech and Slovak Republics', p. 95.

50 Hauserova, *Na kosteti se da i litat* ['It is also possible to fly on the broom'], p. 33.

51 Although they are oriented toward their families – thus from Western point of view quite traditionally and conservatively, they are aware of the value and importance of their household work. As an example one can mention that eight out of ten respondents in the Czech republic, both men and women, state that the work of women in the household and their child care should be rewarded financially (STEM, Trendy 9/1993). On the other hand, to illustrate women's activity in the workplace it may be useful to mention one piece of statistical data: 53% of doctors in medical professions in Slovakia are women.

52 Hauserova claims that the American feminists, mainly those from the period of 1960–1970, looked at career in the same way as the child looks at his/her craved for toy. In last years they became a bit disappointed: the toy is not as attractive as it seemed. Central European women are better aware of it (Hauserova *Na kosteti se da i litat* ['It is also possible to fly on the broom'], p. 54).

opportunities to work from home when possible.[53] This is summarized by Nanette Funk:

> Post-communist women's concerns should reinforce for Western feminism that work simpliciter is not the goal. Rather, a feminist demand must be for meaningful work in a rationally organized, humane society that reconciles the importance of the collective good and intersubjective needs of all persons with the instrumental needs of society.[54]

To conclude, the 'women's question' as outlined in this chapter is widely recognised in Central European societies. Signs of this development already exist as issues of 'work–family balance' and 'work–life balance' are discussed in academic and everyday circles. In the near future, we will see how expectations of women's role will shape private and public spheres in postcommunist societies.

Bibliography

Bodnarova, Jana, 'Makky feminizmus' ['Soft Feminism'], *Aspekt*, no. 2 (1994), p. 29.

Busheikin, Laura, 'Je sesterstvo naozaj globalne?' ['Is sisterhood really global?'], *Aspekt*, no. 2 (1994), pp. 49–52.

Cavarero, A. 'Rozhovor' [Interview], *Aspekt*, no. 2 (1994), p. 29.

Funk, Nanette, 'Feminism East and West', in Nanette Funk and Magda Mueller (eds.), *Gender, Politics and Post-Communism* (New York: Routledge, 1993), pp. 318–329.

Fuszara, Malgorzata, 'Does the Law Protect Polish Women?', in Mavis Maclean and Jacek Kurczewski (eds.), *Families, Politics*

53 Hauserova, *Na kosteti se da i litat* ['It is also possible to fly on the broom'], p. 80. Changes in the organization of work are also necessary in order to avoid the problem of 'feminization of poverty'. Otherwise many women who are single mothers or divorced mothers and who, therefore, have to work full-time and also care for their children could have considerable financial problems.

54 Funk, 'Feminism East and West', p. 328.

and the Law: Perspectives for East and West Europe (Oxford: Clarendon Press, 1994), pp. 239–260.

Hauserova, Eva, *Na kosteti se da i litat* ['It is also possible to fly on the broom'] (Prague: Nakladatelstvi Lidove Noviny, 1995).

Havelkova, Hana, 'A Few Prefeminist Thoughts', in Nanette Funk and Magda Mueller (eds.), *Gender, Politics and Post-Communism* (New York: Routledge, 1993), pp. 62–73.

Heitlinger, Alena, 'The Impact of the Transition from Communism on the Status of Women in the Czech and Slovak Republics', in Nanette Funk and Magda Mueller (eds.), *Gender, Politics and Post-Communism* (New York: Routledge, 1993), pp. 95–107.

Hradilkova, Jana, 'Rozhovor' [Interview], *Aspekt*, no. 2 (1994) pp. 63–64.

Kiczkova, Zuzana and Etela Farkasova, 'The Emancipation of Women: A Concept that Failed', in Nanette Funk and Magda Mueller (eds.), *Gender Politics and Post-Communism* (New York: Routledge, 1993), pp. 84–93.

Kurczewski, Jacek, 'Privatizing the Polish Family after Communism', in Mavis Maclean and Jacek Kurczewski (eds.), *Families, Politics and the Law: Perspectives for East and West Europe* (Oxford: Clarendon Press, 1994), pp. 25–52.

Mozny, Ivo, *Moderni rodina: Myty a skutecnost* [The Modern Family: Myths and Reality] (Brno: Blok, 1990).

Rosova, Tatiana, 'Ženy na Slovensku. Vyhodnotenie výsledkov kvalitatívnej sociologickej sondy' ['Women in Slovakia. An Interpretation of Qualitative Sociological Survey'], *Aspekt*, no. 3 (1994), pp. 113–116.

Sedova, Tatiana, 'K moznostiam a limitom feminizmu v nasich pomeroch' ['Towards opportunities and limits of feminism in our country'], in *Rodina ako predmet vedy* (Bratislava: 1994), p. 126.

Siklova, Jirina, 'Rozumi zapad nasim zenam?' ['Does the West understand our women?'], *Listy*, no. 5 (1991), pp. 14–17.

——'Are Women in Central and Eastern Europe Conservative?', in Nanette Funk and Magda Mueller (eds.), *Gender Politics and Post-Communism* (New York: Routledge, 1993), pp. 74–83.

——'Inhibited Factors of Feminism in the Czech Republic', conference paper prepared for the Crossing Borders Conference, Stockholm 27–29 May 1994.

Smejkalova-Strickland, Jirina, 'Do Czech Women Need Feminism?', in Susanna Trnka and Laura Busheikin (eds.), *Bodies of Bread and Butter: Reconfiguring Women's Lives in the Post-Communist Czech Republic* (Prague: Gender Studies Centre 1993).

Wagnerova, Alena, 'Socialismus propousti ceske zeny' [Socialism fires Czech women], *Aspekt*, no. 1 (1994), p. 22.

Wallace, Claire, 'A Western Feminist Goes East', *Transit*, 9 (1995), pp. 129–45

Woleková, Helena, 'Socialna politika' ['Social welfare policy'], in *Slovensko 1996* (Bratislava: Institut pre verejne otazky, 1997), pp. 185–196.

OLGA BOIKO AND ELENA CHERNYSHKOVA

Social Policy Issues through the Discourse of the Russian Press

Discourse Analysis in Researching Social Policy

In today's Russia, social policy is a rather new concept in state reconstruction. During the last decade a scope of projects has emerged on how to approach this matter. Undoubtedly, social policy is being constructed through the discourse of different social actors. Social science contributes its part, while the discourse of politicians is remarkable as they are main actors in the power scene. Other players in this field include social care professionals and practitioners in their roles as decision-makers and mediators. The following analysis introduces all the abovementioned actors, engages their opinions and considers their roles. Above all, it argues that mass media discourse is a subject for drawing upon social policy cases and meanings.

Since the appearance of the newspaper there was a core dilemma: are mass media 'moulders' or 'mirrors'? Media research has been actively conducted in the modern times when the 'media society' has become an object of analysis. Following Habermas, the model of face-to-face communication has been replaced by the concept of 'mediated communication'.[1] There have been a variety of theoretical attempts to classify the functions of media. The effects model, for example, emphasises the direct influence that mass media have on the audience. The uses and gratification model is based on the idea of function or utility for consumers, such as emotional release and school of life. The

1 Jűrgen Habermas, *The Theory of Communicative Action* (Cambridge: Polity Press, 1987), vol. 2.

cultural ratification model studies how the media perform as the actors of political control along with other social institutions.[2]

A great many names and meanings are given to the mass media. They, and particularly the press, according to J. Partanen and M. Montonen, might operate as a 'medium' or 'forum' of discussions about social problems, while serving to establish a dialogue between civil initiatives and powerful structures.[3] As the 'gate-keeper', the mass media decides which topics and opinions are allowed to come to light. Its 'agenda-setting' function determines what should be discussed on each occasion. Possibly, the media has little influence upon the construction of social problems as such, but it is important to be aware of the content it seeks to put into the minds of information consumers.

Textual analysis, particularly discourse, analysis recently became popular in Russian social studies. This was due to an overall shift towards interpretative strategy in theory and methods. The 'number game' and numerous derivatives of quantitative research such as content analysis have yielded to the 'word game'. Thus far, discourse analysis along with other sociolinguistic methods stresses the capacity of texts to convey multiple meanings and seeks to understand how contingent power relations become apparent through language.

Theoretical frameworks for discourse analysis cover a broad spectrum of dialogical, linguistic, textual, interpretative, structuralist, critical and other approaches. Their differing objectives and specific sociological postures can be exemplified through comparison. Such dialogical or conversational forms of discourse analysis are presented in contemporary social research in Russia to a lesser degree than are textual forms with an inherent political analysis of structural pressures, such as the work of Michel Foucault. Whereas Jürgen Habermas sees discourse as a cooperative search for truth, for Michel Foucault it involves exclusion. The Habermasian theory of communicative action suggests that discourse, as a dialogue without constraints, is an essential prerequisite for the ideal speech situation and for reaching mutual

2 Dennis Howitt, *The Mass Media and Social Problems* (Howitt: Pergamon Press, 1982).

3 Juha Partanen and Marjatta Montonen, *Alcohol and the Mass Media. A Thematic Review* (Copenhagen: WHO, 1987).

understanding between interlocutors.[4] The Foucauldian analysis is rather alienated from individuals and utterances; here, the focus is on statements which are blocks of a discourse in reflecting regimes of knowledge and institutional power.[5]

Postmodernist critical tradition has been proven to be especially applicable to mass media analysis. Thus far, it is not surprising that contemporary discourse studies in Russia more often than not seek to disclose structural pressures of power. Most well known work has been carried out within the framework of gender studies with the objective of disclosing language structures that reflect the manifest or latent oppression of women. Some studies of this kind uncover gender representations in mass culture and visual media; others consider gender images in printed texts such as periodicals, political leaflets and handbooks.[6] For example, Tartakovskaya stresses the transformation of gender relations in the discourse of leading Soviet (1984) and post-Soviet (1997) newspapers by showing a transition from the image of the 'Soviet women' to liberalisation and the insecurity of women's roles in contemporary Russia. In another study, Yarskaya-Smirnova demonstrates how women-politicians have been depicted in the press

4 Outhwaite, William, *Habermas: a Critical Introduction* (Cambridge: Polity Press, 1994).

5 Niels Åkerstrom Andersen, *Discursive Analytical Strategies: Understanding Foucault, Koselleck, Laclau, Luhmann* (Bristol: The Policy Press, 2003).

6 Tatiana Barchynova, 'Variatsii v zsh-minore na temu gezetu *Zavtra*: zshentshinu v simvolicheskom diskurse natsionalisticheskoi pressu' ['Variations of g-minor on the themes of newspaper *Zavtra*'], in Tatiana Barchynova (ed.), *Potolok pola* (Novosibirsk: 1998), pp. 47–90; Irina Tartakovskaya, 'Sil'naya zshentshina plachet y okna': gendernue reprezentatsii v sovetskoy i post-sovietskoi massovoi kulture' ['A Strong Woman is Crying by the Window'], in *Aspektu socialnoi teorii I sovremennogo obschestva* (Moscow: Institute of Sociology RAS, 1999), pp. 155–176; Elena Yarskaya-Smirnova, 'Sotsialnaia politika I gender v ritorike prebvubornoi bor'bu' ['Social Policy and Gender in the Election Rhetoric'], in *Sotsis*, no. 11 (2002), pp. 71–80; Elena Yarskaya-Smirnova and Galina Karpova, 'Simvolicheskie resyrsu gendernoi politiki: czshdynarodnui zshenskii den v rossiyskoi presse' ['Symbolic Resources of Gender Policy: International Women's Day in the Russian Press'], in Elena Yarskaya-Smirnova and Pavel Romanov (eds.), *Sotsialnaia politika i sotsialnaia rabota v izmeniauscheisia Rossii* (Moscow: INION RAS, 2002), pp. 145–167.

and leaflets during local election campaigns and how their professional image was undermined by sexist references. The feminist critique of patriarchy which manifests itself in men's attitudes or state policy has been justified in a great number of studies since then.

However, few works analyse how the press represents social issues and policies, very likely because of the uncertainty in finding the oppressor to blame for people's poor welfare. Among these are investigations of representations of social problems and unionist activity. One paper demonstrates how the dynamics of social problems (poverty, drugs, unemployment and child neglect) were developed in newspaper discourse throughout the 1990s.[7] While in another the mythology and reality of trade unions in one Russian region is discussed through using press images.[8]

The current analysis is based on two threads, first, the press labeling of social problems and policies, and second, theoretical considerations of what is going on in society and presented in the press. Whereas the press exercises the power of the printed word in mirroring social hardship, scientific expertise reflexively enhances the understanding of social policy. In a sense, we credit the postmodernist notion of 'intertextuality' (as for Roland Barthes) and, subsequently, 'quotation thinking'. Hence, the analysis of media images is accompanied with secondary sources and and our own interpretations.

The objective of the study is to analyse the discourse in Russian newspapers, which represented a range of social problems and policies in 2001–2002. It is guided by an ambition to outline specific episodes and topics within the broader field rather than to make claims for the generalisability to Russian social policy on a large scale. The sample consists of articles from four periodicals, two of which (*Komsomolskaya Pravda* and *Izvestiya*) are popular newspapers, and two of which are politically engaged magazines (*Profile* and *Russian Feder-*

7 Olga Boiko, 'Reprezentatsiya sotsialnuh problem v rossiiskoi press 90–h godov' ['Representation of Social Problems in the Russian Press of 90s'], *Sotsis*, no. 8 (2002), pp. 120–128.

8 Natalia Veselkova 'Prophsoyuzu i pressa: realnost i miphu' ['Trade Unions and the Press: Reality and Myths'], *Sotsis*, no. 8 (2002), pp. 128–136.

ation Today). The newspapers are published on weekdays, *Profile* is a weekly magazine and *RF Today* is a fortnightly journal.

The initial sample included 75 articles from the issues which were published during 2001–2002. In constructing our sample, we aimed to cover a wide range of topics related to social policy, such as social inequality and stratification in Russia, educational and vocational training, and the welfare system. After primary scanning we undertook an analysis of 15 articles, which were selected on our choice to focus on two predominant areas: secondary education reform and child care policy in combating homelessness. We consider the articles discussed below as the most striking illustrations of problems at stake, which accurately reflect particular social realities, rather than as examples that can be generalised across cases.

'School amidst Market'[9]

It is by no means accidental that a major social policy concern, and consequently, a major media focus, is contemporary education in Russia. Social policy determines people's well-being, which is why education has high socio-cultural value as a welfare dimension. Investment into education assumes the long-term growth of the country's social capital. Along with other areas of social policy in Russia, education is now undergoing drastic transformations.

The issues of educational reform became urgent in 2001 when debates among political decision-makers provoked a long train of government summits, special parliamentary sessions and meetings of the Presidential State Soviet. By that time the educational system, particularly compulsory secondary education, was considered as being a critically troublesome institution. Eventually it became the first and foremost problem on the state's political agenda. One deputy, a member of the Committee on Education and Science in the State Duma,

9 Vladimir Yakovlev, 'Shkola posredi rynka' ['School amidst Market'], *Rossiyskaya Federatsiya segodnya*, no. 6 (2002), pp. 29–30.

explicated the reason for these changes with the help of a maxim: 'all reforms, reconstructions and revolutions are payment for things which have not been provided, done in time, in the proper way and so forth [...] Our Russian education, unfortunately, is not an exception'.[10] This conceptualisation of the disadvantageous condition of education raises a number of points.

First of all, the message admits that a series of mistakes occurred in the transformation process; tragically, there has been little long-term vision about education in the context of other issues. However, it is a subjectless appeal, with no attempt to find someone particularly responsible for these problems. The point is rather to reduce the issue to the many other matters which have required action in the name of reform, reconstruction and revolution. Additionally, the notion of payment is introduced in order to explain that there should be shared responsibility as well as high costs. It is conventionally assumed that everyone should feel sorry about the educational system, which is subject to radical change. This may be a true premise since the country has been priding itself for having free and compulsory education for many years.

Another controversial issue is that reforms imply active, institutional changes which infringe upon the social, political and economic foundations managed by state power. According to Zaslavskaya, this was more relevant to the initial period of transformations in post-Soviet Russia.[11] Alternatively, a demand for modernization appears in political circles. In October 2001, the Government passed a bill on the 'Modernisation of Secondary Education in the Russian Federation'. The newspaper makes the situation clear to the public:

> Ask a hundred lay people: what is educational reform and what is it for? [...] Only one, if you are lucky, will correct you with a smile: modernization should

10 Alexandr Shelekhov, 'Peremeny v obrazovanii ob'ektivno neobhodimy' ['Changes in Education is Fairly Necessary'], *Rossiyskaya Federasciya segodnya*, no. 1 (2002), pp. 22–23.

11 Tatiana Zaslavskaya, 'O sotcialnom mehanisme postkommunisticheskih preobrazovanii v Rossii' ['About social mechanism of post communist transformations in Russia'], *Sotsis*, no. 8 (2002), p. 7.

> be said, rather than reform. They said our education is not that poor to claim for drastic changes. There is a need for modernization, that's right.[12]

One out of a hundred is really a lucky person, since who knows the difference between modernization and reform? Yet everybody could agree with the fact that while education is not that poor, it is deeply damaged. Modernisation, in Yukhler's view, denotes efforts undertaken with the aim to 'catch up' with a vital or at least desired adaptation. A policy of 'catching up' in the area of education is significant as long as education is a strategic component in the process of modernization: 'education ends up in economic performance by influencing labor force competence but even more in political and social impacts on democratic institutions and general life style'.[13] Therefore, educational policy has to be directed to cutting down visible gap in the liberal transition of political and economic systems in Russia.

There are a number of modernisation priorities: the prospective introduction of twelve-year secondary education, a unified State Testing System (an exam that suits both final secondary and entrance tertiary examination), State Educational Standards, computerization, rural schools development, and other policies. Apart from this the prominent objective, according to one journalist's interpretation of political speeches, is to develop teachers: 'there is no reforming without radical improvements of teachers' quality of life owing to a number of old teachers retiring and shortage of young teachers. Soon there will be none who could modernise'.[14]

Statements in relation to the gradual rise in teachers' wages, improving teachers' health care and increasing their pensions seem to be declarations and claims rather than facts. For instance, education minister Philippov might use the authoritarian vocabulary of 'should-ness' more than once even in a single interview. The minister also demonstrates true competence in delegating authority and sharing power:

12 'Golodnoe bruho uchitelya k ucheniku gluho' ['Teacher's Lean Paunch is Deaf to a Student'], *Komsomolskaya Pravda*, 10 October 2001, p. 12.

13 Yakob Yukhler, 'Dostatochno li modernizatsii?' ['Is Modernisation Sufficient?'], *Sotsis*, no. 8 (2002), p. 73.

14 'Modernizirovat obrazovanie – podnyat uchitelya' ['Do Modernise Education to Raise a Teacher'], *Rossiyskaya Federatsiya segodnya*, no. 1 (2001), p. 21.

> the question about a school week of five studying days should be solved by the school board [...] the questions of school uniform are to be discussed at the school board [...] we have to take into account children from poor families who can not afford a uniform. It might be a useful idea for teachers themselves since their salary is rather small and such a suit is cheap.[15]

The witty suggestion given about improving poor teachers' welfare suggests that the minister's recipes are probably extraordinarily convenient mainly to himself and the elite. His other point is about the credibility of school boards. Despite the fact that free education has been ensured, school boards at times play the ridiculous but honorable role of financial donor, which might be treated as an excellent example of chaotic management in educational policy. The boards are mediators, social actors that operate on the meso-level. Zaslavskaya justly stresses the difficulties which actors at that level encounter, for instance, due to the uncertainty about their power and competence. In her words, meso-level actors constitute an inwardly stratified group with indefinite functions who find themselves somewhere between the elite and ordinary people, or between rulers and the guided.[16]

The rest of items on the minister's list of concerns were successfully transferred into the sphere of regional authority. An example is granting free housing to young teachers. According to federal politicians, this question has to be discussed on the regional level. It is easy to come up with the idea that in tackling educational problems, the Russian state considers its role to be writing a concept paper and sitting sessions twice a year, namely, when the academic year begins and ends. It is hard to understand, however, how a directive of the State Soviet can be executed 'to pay a teacher's salary from the federal budget and not from the local one', taking into consideration the following method of financing modern improvements: 'for the next year

15 'Interv'yu s ministrom obrazovaniya V.Philippovym' ['Interview with V. Philip-pov, the Minister of Education'], *Komsomolskaya Pravda*, 1 September, 2001, pp. 8–9.

16 Tatiana Zaslavskaya, 'O sub'ektno-deyatelnostnom aspekte transformatsionno-go protsessa' ['About the Aspect of Human Activity in Transformation Process'], in Tatiana Zaslavskaya (ed.), *Kto i kuda stremitsya vecti Rossiu? Aktory makro-, mezo- i mikro-urovnya sovremennogo transformatcionnogo protsessa* (Moscow: MHSSSE, 2001), p. 8.

[2002] the consolidated fund is capable of issuing 380 billion roubles to education: of this, 80 billion comes out of the federal budget and 300 is the responsibility of regional budgets'.[17]

Micro-level actors in educational policy describe the situation from the opposite angle in terms of impoverishment, hopelessness, and marginality. As first-hand servants in education, teachers are among the most vulnerable. Their assessments are full of bitterness:

> A teacher is a figure of tremendous but underestimated value in society. Namely he (actually, she) moulds knowledge, attitudes and ethics upon the young generation […] At the moment this profession has no prestige.[18]

Teachers' way of thinking and, consequently, their lifestyle can hardly attract today's students and parents. That is why the main aim is to increase the significance of teachers' work, the value of which has to be considered in many respects. Otherwise, the unrealised demand for pedagogical professionals will become far more threatening, particularly in light of the current trend, with only 15–20% of graduates from pedagogical universities returning to work in schools. Pokrovskiy traces a parallel with difficulties faced by high school teachers:

> there are good lecturers and good courses, and in the universities there are a considerable number. But this situation is possible thanks only to social sacrifice rather than ordinary work in satisfactory conditions. How can life be based on the principle of sacrifice?[19]

Social sacrifice and selflessness are notions of patriotisms and deeply rooted collective responsibility. However, they are more like

17 Alexei Chernyak, 'Gosudarstvo vozvratshaetsya v sferu obrazovabiya' ['The State Turns Back to Education Sphere'], *Rossiyskaya Federatsiya segodnya*, no. 18 (2001), pp. 10–11.

18 Vasiliy Vashkov, 'Samootverzhennost uchitelya ne mozhet but bespredelnoi' ['Selflessness of Teacher Might not be Unlimited'], *Rossiyskaya Federatsiya segodnya*, no. 6 (2002), pp. 27–28.

19 Nikita Pokrovskiy, 'Universitet: hram nauki ili optovui runok znanii? Obyknovenneishaya istoriya (otkroveniya professora)' ['University: the Temple of Science or Warehouse of Information? A Commonplace Story (Revelations of Professor)'], at: http://www.auditorium.ru/Guest/pokrovsky.html

supreme categories, which determine human, social and national interests on a larger scale than in the daily work of teachers. One school principal paints a picture of the true teachers' status:

> Who is working at school today? Who holds it? Those who can be nourished by a husband? No, they are minority. Who is interested in a wife who stays at school from sunrise to sunset? Most teachers are single mothers, women who maintain family on their own [...] [20]

The image presented by the press is extremely harsh and stigmatising: 'is a menopausal schoolmistress who is persecuted by poverty and who vents her spite upon children really not a problem?'[21] Obviously, the sentence is taken out of context, but female pedagogues come from the journalistic pen in the image of maladaptive individuals on the margins of society, worthy of pity and scorn. Here we may recall a metaphor frequently found in press articles – 'education is a mirror of the country'– and from this point ask whether a holographic picture of the whole society peeps out from the picture of one professional group?

It seems likely to find a way out on the meso-level of transformations, namely, among educational institutes and structures, whose contemporary ambition is to promote the manifest and latent privatisation of educational services. Commercial relations within the system of public education have been developing in post-socialist Russia for more than a decade, that is, long before the official legitimisation of private schools. One newspaper reveals the eligibility of social practices which are a sort of financial compensation for unfulfilled social guarantees in a headline stating, 'Our education is free, that's why extortion in schools is free-will'. Those with claims in the schools have their own interpretations: 'without getting finance, a school is forced to draw money from parents. What else is left?' Romantic gratitude has already been replaced with materialised profit, as one school prin-

20 Irina Davydkina, 'Po kom zvenit zvonok' ['Whom Rings the Bell About'], *Rossiyskaya Federatsiya segodnya*, no. 6 (2002), pp. 1–2.

21 Alexei Chernyak, 'Gosudarstvo vozvratshaetsya v sferu obrazovabiya' ['The State Turns Back to Education Sphere'], *Rossiyskaya Federatsiya segodnya*, no. 18 (2002), pp. 10–11.

cipal puts cynically: 'teachers do not eat flowers; you'd better waste money for something useful'.[22]

Theoretically, it is assumed that social institutions function through certain practices, while illegal social practices are used to compensate for the inadequacy of acting 'good'.[23] School extortion is a striking example of illegitimate practices, along with other kinds of corrupt conduct such as tax evasion, bribery and blackmail. Being aggravated by the culturally mediated and fruitful soil of payments in kind, the surrogates of official and normative guarantees flourish, although they are insufficient.

Despite the declarations of free education and basic welfare provisions which had been legislated earlier, the state approved a shift to the privatisation of educational services. Whenever there is a higher demand for education than supply of it, private schools emerge. As the press reports, 'there are 45,000 children studying in 640 private schools. The average tuition is $200–400 per month. Yet this kind of education is unpopular'.[24] It is then explained that the 'limited contingent' studies at private schools and their education is considered to be the 'piece production, special design, exclusiveness of the self-actualisation of both trainers and trainees'. Apparently, it would be easy to admit that educational organisations are part of the market. The market is liberalised along the way since a desperate social gap exists, with most children being deprived of good quality services. More than a few are drop-outs from education.

We would agree with Shkaratan that social stability and anti-recessionary policies serve the interests of the political and economic elite, exceptionally and for the purpose of preserving power.[25] Most

22 'Obrazovanie u nas besplatnoe, poetomu poboru v shkolah – «dobrovolnye»' ['Our Education is Free so Extortion in Schools is Free-Will'], *Komsomolskaya Pravda*, 21 August 2001, p. 7.

23 Tatiana Zaslavskaya, *Societalnaya transformatsiya rossiyskogo obtshestva* ['Societal Transformation of the Russian Society'] (Moscow: Delo, 2002), p. 130.

24 'Litcei mestnogo razliva' ['Liceum of Local Bottling'], *Izvestiya*, 25 April 2001, p. 7.

25 Ovsey Shkaratan, 'Deklariruemaya i realnaya sotcialnaya politika' ['Declared and Real Social Policy'], *Mir Rossii*, no. 2 (2001), p. 22.

political appeals about conserving educational guarantees seem to be remarkably dubious due to the wide range of elitist opportunities enjoyed by the children of elites, while access to high-quality education remains restricted for the majority. Therefore, social inequality is spreading and eroding the educational system, and as a result the pole of the poor becomes more and more detached from the pole of the elite.

'Children in Trouble'[26]

Special programs directed towards childcare are another battlefield of social policy in Russia. Childcare policies have attracted a huge amount of public, political and professional attention in recent years. Similarly to school education problems, the press passionately highlights many troublesome issues in the social protection of children. Accidentally or not, the changes in educational and childcare policy happened simultaneously. We have chosen also to analyse media representations of the programs and institutional support for homeless children. It is crucial to bear in mind that the number of homeless children in Russia had been booming until it reached a critical peak at the end of 2002. At this point, the president announced his anxiety and issued decisive decrees for helping to combat child neglect. While the problem has long been in existence, it was quickly discharged in a period of half a year.

The press debates on the topic and calls for public concern speak to the scale of child neglect:

> It seems that nobody knows how many gutter children run in the streets in Russia at the moment. According to the data of General Office of Public Prosecutor there are 120,000. The Interior Ministry reports about 330,000 gutter children were captured during the first 10 months of 2001. Deputy Prime Minister

26 'Deti v bede' ['Children in Trouble'], *Rossiyskaya Federatsiya segodnya*, no. 7 (2001), p. 19.

> Valentina Matvienko, responsible for social affairs, estimates the number of 'Gavroshes' at no less than a million.[27]

In other words, the number of homeless children resembles an iceberg and suggests a vast quantity of unreported cases. The figures might also be easily counted by the addition of numbers from different sources as any authorised organisation registers only those whom it deals with – criminals, delinquents or orphans. The Institute of Social and Economic Problems of Population (Russian Academy of Sciences) has probably followed this rule:

> in counting three times as many homeless children as in the official statistics (that is, 3 million) – there are almost the same number as there were right after the Revolution and Civil War, when thechair of the Supreme Extraordinary Committee, Felix Dzerszhinskiy, was designated to combat the crisis.[28]

According to social constructionist theories about the life history of a social problem, by agitating and making claims, actors put a social problem forward on the agenda of legitimisation and official acknowledgement.[29] Public concern about homeless children in Russia shows itself in labeling the social problem; the press both serves this mission and reflects authorities' decision-making. The number of publications is increasing with the official approval to release an 'SOS' signal. Meanwhile, some statesmen refuse to consider the problem a disaster; for example, the Minister of Labor and Social Development, Pochinok, who is in charge of governmental social policies, pushes his expertise to protect himself:

> a buzz about 2 million gutter children has no ground [...] Yes, it is a pity that children beg on the streets of Moscow. But they are part of professional, arranged groups made of generally displaced children from Central Asia [...] It is hard to tackle it whatsoever.[30]

27 Irina Vorob'eva and Maria Mikeli, 'Bezdomnaya propast' ['Homeless Abyss'], *Profile*, no. 47 (2001), p. 34.

28 Irina Vorob'eva and Maria Mikeli, p. 35.

29 George Ritzer, *Social Problems*, 6th edition (New York: Hardcover, 1986), p. 57.

30 Vitalyi Eremin, 'Armiya besprizornuh' ['Army of Waifs'], *Rossiyskaya Federatsiya segodnya*, no. 7 (2001), p. 23.

While authorities get stuck, others naturally start to long for the appearance of someone like the 'powerful Felix'. Conventional wisdom regards the reason for the mess of tackling the problem of homeless children as a lack of the mighty macro-actor: a 'coordinating body or key figure, an Ombudsman on children rights, who would be directly subordinate to the President [...] I [a journalist] support Likhanov in his call for a Dzerszhinskiy of our times'.[31] Obviously, Dzerszhinskiy emerges as a forceful feature in the public discourse about homeless children. The press restores the words and deeds of the Red Commissar with the help of a chronicle about combating child delinquency in the 1920s, immediately after the Civil War had died down. It argues for the need of a totalitarian military discourse that has been supported by the entire history of Soviet and post-Soviet Russia.

Analogies with past policies and measures on the ground are often cited as reminiscences. At the time of the 'powerful Felix', for example, authorities established local branches of law-enforcement children's commissions, drop-in/out centers and orphanages. Similarly, now there are commissions on children's affairs, centers for the temporary isolation of underage delinquents, and shelters. Yet homeless children remain without homes, and such a situation has to be explained.

One of the reasons is related to 'the norm according to which regional and local budgets are obliged to finance combating the problem of child neglect. However, their budgets are empty'.[32] Remember, an analysis of school education found an analogous vertical delegation of authority accompanied by low efficiency of resource utilisation in local regions. This time, the poor financing of children's maintenance in shelters and social rehabilitation centres was being depicted, so that according to journalists' calculations 'there was a plan to spend 285.6 million roubles in 2001–2002. This year 205.7 million have been already expended, it means that only 79.3 million remained for 2002'.[33]

31 Vitalyi Eremin, p. 24.

32 Irina Vorob'eva and Maria Mikeli, 'Bezdomnaya propast' ['Homeless Abyss'], *Profile*, no. 47 (2001), p. 35.

33 Irina Vorob'eva and Maria Mikeli, p. 35.

Moreover, structural tensions influence the system of child care and delinquency prevention. For instance, the Federal legislation of 1999, 'About the System of Prevention of Children's Homelessness and Delinquency', results into a disadvantageous power redistribution. The norm

> puts restrictions on sheltering children under 16 in the Centers for Temporary Isolation of Juvenile Delinquents. Now they have to be kept in social shelters. But in spite of the fact that the legislation had come into power, shelters have not been established. They number just 14 in Moscow. A shelter can host 30 children, so in total – 420 children [...] The others stay in the streets, stations, cellars, and dens.[34]

Meanwhile, the comfortable Centers for the Temporary Isolation of Juvenile Delinquents stay vacant. With such legislation, lawmakers intended to treat homeless children in a more humane way. Unfortunately, there are not funds available to maintain a noble mission. Ultimately, juvenile homeless children are exposed neither to the jurisdiction of law-enforcement bodies under legislation or to social bodies, because of their shortage.

Normally, this occurs when a social problem was protractedly subjected to bureaucratic control with out-of-date official decisions. The career of the problem might also depend on the structural constraints which the authorities produce. Bureaucratic responses serve to dissociate groups who are taking part in solving the problem. In our context, meso-actors become dissociated since the Centers for Temporary Isolation of Juvenile Delinquents and shelters are administered by different bodies that are, respectively, law-enforcement organs and the Ministry of Social Development. The resolving of problems, in the words of Lenoir, sinks in the discourses of institutions.[35] At this stage the need for decisive action becomes apparent. So at the beginning of 2002, the president of the Russian Federation called for urgent action in marking a new circle in tackling the troubles of homeless children.

34 Vitaliy Eremin, 'Armiya besprizornuh' ['Army of Waifs'], *Rossiyskaya Federatsiya segodnya*, no. 7 (2001), p. 24.

35 Patrick Champagne *et al.*, *'Nachala prakticheskoi sotciologii'* ['The Foundations of Sociological Practice'] (St. Petersburg: Aleteiya, 2001), p. 131.

Another focus of the press is improving rehabilitation services for homeless children and orphans. It is shown that across the Russian regions, the actors of meso- and microlevel contribute actively in childcare management.

> following an order of the Governor of Chelyabinsk region, the local Centers of Social Rehabilitation establish foster families [founding-family groups]. Now a family, if agreeable to a number of standards such as income, housing and health, can apply for upbringing from one to three inmates of the centers. For doing this foster parents would be paid [...] If a child has obstacles with adjustment he or she has a right to leave foster parents at any time [...] Control over settling down of inmates into new families is entrusted to social specialists of the centres.[36]

Thanks to the permission issued by the local authority, fostering comes to life and at first glance the method seems to be effective for all parties.

The press as such is an actor of in the system of childcare because of its charitable role and day-to-day intervention into problematic situations that children come across. It diligently challenges the manifestations of inequality which can influence life span of maladjusted children. For instance, a newspaper from our sample reports on its own philanthropy in helping children: 'all funds raised during the action, *Komsomolskaya Pravda* spent for the welfare of inmates of the orphanage in Vladimir',[37] 'the journalists of KP presented a gift from Santa Clause to a kiddy from the Ivanovo region'.[38] In highlighting donor practices, charity aid and social partnership, the press shows social sensitivity towards marginalised children and their needs. As our previous study of the press suggests,

> multidimensional context and hardship of the situation in which many children live requires profound [and] competent protectionism. And the press could

36 'Teplo roditelskogo doma' ['The Warmth of Parental Home'], *Profile*, no. 8 (2002), p. 74.

37 '"Komsomolka" vlozshila kapitalu v detei' ['"Komsomolka" Put up Money into Children'], *Komsomolskaya Pravda*, 27 December 2001, p. 14.

38 'Tu zagovorish, Zshenechka' ['You will Begin to Speak, Janya'], *Komsomolskaya Pravda*, 29 December 2001, p. 9.

> contribute by informing and calling for public attention as well as exercising its actionist potential.[39]

Overall, discourse about the problems of homeless children consists of various perspectives that represent both the expertise of politicians and actions on the ground. The example of gutter children shows how the problem develops, and how it becomes a target for decision making and executive policies. Urgency, danger and sensitivity of the problem (such as 'Children in trouble)' are beyond the question. Both the abandonment of children and the erosion of the educational system diminish prospects for social development in Russia. On the whole, these problems go in unison with others which have a critical impact on post-Soviet society, allowing us to put these concerns into the wording of a Russian saying that 'troubles never come singly'.[40]

Conclusion

Throughout this analysis, the problematic area of social policy appears in contradictory interpretations of the state authorities, professional groups and the public. A discourse analysis of the press demonstrates how social actors at different levels suggest, influence and manage resource redistribution in tackling social problems. Intertextuality as an analytical strategy benefited us in intersecting discourses of journalists, politicians, social scientists and those who deal with problems on the front line. The discursive approach allowed for the uncovering of structural pressures which otherwise stay beyond the vista. Among those located 'between the lines' are awkwardness of the political

39 Olga Boiko, 'Reprezentatciya sotcialnuh problem v rossiiskoi presse 1990–h go-dov' [Representation of Social Problems in the Russian Press of 1990s], *Sotsis*, no. 8 (2002), p. 127.

40 Nick Manning, Ovsey Shkaratan and Natalia Tikhonova, *Work and Welfare in the New Russia* (Alderhot: Ashgate, 2000), p. 11.

system, institutional distortions, poor finance, and everyday compensatory strategies.

The newspapers' representations mediate the shortcomings of the decision-making process as well as the urgent character of social problems. By highlighting media representations of education and child care policy, our analysis demonstrates different functions of the press. While at times it serves the reporter's mission of conspicuous campaigning, at other times it gives the reader a professional, socially sensitive analysis either by presenting the official point of view or in questioning the inertia of political will. However, as a claim-maker the press tends to avoid radical critique of the authorities, possibly because it might aggravate social crisis. Indeed, we can ask, is there a single actor who can be fairly and definitely blamed for the severity of the problems? Revolutionary calls would not help either. On the contrary, newspapers deliver a message of actions coming from the political elite, and discuss possible solutions.

To sum up our analysis, we may infer the following points. The reform of school education and the troubles of homeless children were shown to be problems of high priority on the Russian political with an increase in illegitimate social practices in providing educational services. Modernisation is claimed to solve many problems, however, at this stage it is impossible to assess long-term prospects until such practices actually exist. The press discourse on the services for homeless children regards the state response to the growing number of troublesome areas as being poorly effective. The meso-level of executive policies seems to be the most vulnerable. The state predominantly initiates changes; this also confirms the reactive, responsive character of social policy.

While these conclusions were derived from the analysis of media content, they are inevitably coloured with criticism of the overall discursive strategy. We were able to show how institutional distortions are inherent to the way governmental structures, schools, and welfare institutions work, and how the language of oppression and trouble permeate into social practices of everyday life. In its turn, the press captures discourses of exclusion by fastening power regimes through the printed words. To discourse researchers, this offers a unique opportunity to reappraise social problems in connection with their own observations. There could then be no dispute that if the problematic issues of education and social care for children are underestimated, the future of the country's human capital and of the Russian welfare state will be in doubt.

Bibliography

Andersen, Niels Åkerstrom, *Discursive Analytical Strategies: Understanding Foucault, Koselleck, Laclau, Luhmann* (Bristol: The Policy Press, 2003).

Barchynova, Tatiana, 'Variatsii v zsh-minore na temu gezetu *Zavtra*: zshentshinu v simvolicheskom diskurse natsionalisticheskoi pressu' ['Variations of g-minor on the themes of newspaper *Zavtra*'], in Tatiana Barchynova (ed.), *Potolok pola* (Novosibirsk: 1998), pp. 47–90.

Boiko, Olga, 'Reprezentatsiya sotcialnuh problem v rossiiskoi presse 1990–h godov' ['Representation of Social Problems in the Russian Press of 1990s'], *Sotsis*, no. 8 (2002), p. 120–128.

Champagne Patrick, *et al.*, *'Nachala prakticheskoi sotciologii'* [The Foundations of Sociological Practice] (St. Petersburg: Aleteiya, 2001).

Chernyak, Alexei, 'Gosudarstvo vozvratshactsya v sferu obrazovaniya' ['The State Turns Back to Education Sphere'], *Rossiyskaya Federatsiya segodnya*, no. 18 (2001), pp. 10–11.

Davydkina, Irina. 'Po kom zvenit zvonok' ['Whom Ring the Bell About'], *Rossiyskaya Federatsiya segodnya*, no. 6 (2002), pp. 1–2.

'Deti v bede' ['Children in Trouble'], *Rossiyskaya Federatsiya segodnya*, no. 7 (2001), p. 19.

Eremin, Vitalyi, 'Armiya besprizornuh' ['Army of Waifs'], *Rossiyskaya Federatsiya segodnya*, no. 7 (2001), p. 24.

'Golodnoe bruho uchitelya k ucheniku gluho' [Teacher's Lean Paunch is Deaf to a Student], *Komsomolskaya Pravda*, 10 October 2001, p. 12.

Habermas, Jűrgen, *The Theory of Communicative Action* (Cambridge: Polity Press, 1987), vol. 2.

Howitt, Dennis, *The Mass Media and Social Problems* (Oxford: Pergamon Press, 1982).

'Interv'yu s ministrom obrazovaniya V.Philippovym' ['Interview with V.Philippov, the Minister of Education'], *Komsomolskaya Pravda*, 1 September, 2001, pp. 8–9.

''Komsomolka'' vlozshila kapitalu v detei' ['''Komsomolka'' Put up Money into Children'], *Komsomolskaya Pravda*, 27 December 2001, p. 14.

'Litcei mestnogo razliva' ['Liceum of Local Bottling'], *Izvestiya*, 25 April 2001, p. 7.

Manning, Nick, Shkaratan Ovsey and Tikhonova, Natalia' *Work and Welfare in the New Russia* (Alderhot: Ashgate, 2000).

'Modernizirovat obrazovanie – podnyat uchitelya' ['Do Modernise Education to Raise a Teacher'], *Rossiyskaya Federatsiya segodnya*, no. 1 (2001), p. 21.

'Obrazovanie u nas besplatnoe, poetomu poboru v shkolah – "dobrovolnye"'' ['Our Education is Free so Extortion in Schools is Free-Will'], *Komsomolskaya Pravda*, 21 August 2001, p. 7.

Outhwaite, William, *Habermas: a Critical Introduction* (Cambridge: Polity Press, 1994).

Partanen, Juha and Montonen, Marjatta, *Alcohol and the Mass Media. A Thematic Review* (Copenhagen: WHO, 1987).

Pokrovskyi, Nikita, 'Universitet: hram nauki ili optovui runok znanii? Obuknovenneishaya istoriya (otkroveniya professora)' ['University: the Temple of Science or Warehouse of Information? A Commonplace Story (Revelations of Professor)'], at: http://www.auditorium.ru/Guest/pokrovsky.html

Ritzer, George, *Social Problems*, 6th edition (New York: Hardcover, 1986).

Shelekhov, Alexandr, 'Peremeny v obrazovanii ob'ektivno neobhodimy' ['Changes in Education is Fairly Necessary'], *Rossiyskaya Federasciya segodnya*, no. 1 (2002), pp. 22–23.

Shkaratan, Ovsey, 'Deklariruemaya i realnaya sotcialnaya politika' ['Declared and Real Social Policy'], *Mir Rossii*, no. 2 (2001), pp. 3–24.

Tartakovskaya, Irina, 'Sil'naya zshentshina plachet y okna': gendernue reprezentatsii v sovetskoy i postsovietskoi massovoi kulture' ['A Strong Woman is Crying by the Window'], in *Aspektu socialnoi teorii I sovremennogo obschestva* (Moscow: Institute of sociology RAS, 1999), pp. 155–176.

'Teplo roditelskogo doma' ['The Warmth of Parental Home'], *Profile*, no. 8 (2002), p. 74.

'Tu zagovorish, Zshenechka' ['You will Begin to Speak, Janya'] *Komsomolskaya Pravda*, 29 December 2001, p. 9.

Vashkov, Vasiliy, 'Samootverzhennost uchitelya ne mozhet byt bespredelnoi' ['Selflessness of Teacher Might not be Unlimited'], *Rossiyskaya Federatsiya segodnya*, no. 6 (2002), pp. 27–28.

Vorob'eva Irina, and Maria Mikeli, 'Bezdomnaya propast' ['Homeless Abyss'], *Profile*, no. 47 (2001), pp. 34–35.

Yakovlev, Vladimir, 'Shkola posredi rynka' ['School Amidst Market'], *Rossiyskaya Federatsiya segodnya*, no. 6 (2002), pp. 29–30.

Yarskaya-Smirnova, Elena 'Sotsialnaia politika I gender v ritorike prebvubornoi bor'bu' ['Social Policy and Gender in the Election Rhetoric'], *Sotsis*, no. 11 (2002), pp. 71–80.

Yarskaya-Smirnova, Elena and Karpova Galina, 'Simvolicheskie resyrsu gendernoi politiki: ezshdynarodnui zshenskii den v rossiyskoi presse' ['Symbolic Resources of Gender Policy: International Women's Day in the Russian Press'], in Elena Yarskaya-Smirnova and Pavel Romanov (eds.), *Sotsialnaia politika i sotsialnaia rabota v izmeniauscheisia Rossii* (Moscow: INION RAS, 2002), pp. 145–167.

Yukhler, Yakob, 'Dostatochno li modernizatsii?' ['Is Modernisation Sufficient?'], *Sotsis*, no. 8 (2002), pp. 72–75.

Zaslavskaya, Tatiana, 'O sub'ektno-deyatelnostnom aspekte transformatcionnogo protcessa' [About the Aspect of Human Activity in Transformation Process], in Tatiana Zaslavskaya (ed.), *Kto i kuda stremitsya vecti Rossiu? Aktory makro-, mezo- i mikrour-*

ovnya sovremennogo transformatcionnogo protsessa (Moscow: MHSSSE, 2001), pp. 3–15.

—— 'O sotcialnom mehanisme postkommunisticheskih preobrazovanii v Rossii' [About social mechanism of post communist transformations in Russia], *Sotsis*, no. 8 (2002), pp. 3–16.

—— *Societalnaya transformatsiya rossiyskogo obtshestva* [Societal Transformation of the Russian Society] (Moscow: Delo, 2002).

Economy

JULIA DROEBER

Social Embedding of a Local Economy: Agricultural Transition and the Dungan Minority in Kyrgyzstan[1]

Introduction

In early 2003[2], the Institute of Social Anthropology at the University of Tuebingen, Germany, and the Swiss development aid organisation *helvetas* agreed to cooperate in what seemed to be a tricky case. In Petrovsk,[3] a village in Kyrgyzstan, where *helvetas* wanted to implement an agricultural advisory service, the organisation was facing an

1 This article is based on a research report, which I have submitted in a quite different format to *helvetas*, a Swiss development aid organization working in Kyrgyzstan. The ten weeks' anthropological fieldwork, on which this paper is based, was financially supported by the VolkswagenStiftung and *helvetas*, logistical support came from RAS Chui and the East-West Research Centre at the American University – Central Asia in Bishkek. The research team included anthropology students from the University of Tuebingen, Germany: Winnie Oehrlich, Anja Salzer, Anna Kohlhepp, Patric Schlager, and Sheila Brendle. They were supervised by Dr. Monika Lanik, Professor Irmtraud Stellrecht, and myself.

2 The research took thus place about eighteen month before the regime change in Kyrgyzstan (often referred to as the 'Tulip Revolution'); which kind of repercussions this political change will have for the Dungan communities (and indeed the rest of the Kyrgyzstani population) remains to be seen.

3 Pseudonyms are used throughout for individuals and locations to ensure anonymity of the research participants. Petrovsk is a village of some 11,000 inhabitants (i.e. about 2300 households) not far from the capital Bishkek. It was first settled in 1882 by about 70 wealthy families coming from Suiduna in China. The settlement stretches along the main road, with two parallel streets and 26 streets branching off this main road.

unprecedented reluctance to cooperate by the local population. These locals were members of an ethnic minority in Kyrgyzstan – Dungans or Hui, often referred to as Chinese Muslims.[4] Since anthropologists seem to have a reputation for being able to 'deal' with ethnic minorities and tricky cases, a research project was born to find out 'what went wrong'. Thus, five anthropology students and two supervisors spent ten weeks in the village and gained deep insights into the daily lives of its inhabitants, insights that went far beyond the initial aim of 'solving the problems with the Dungans'. In this paper I will tell parts of the narrative of an ethnic minority in a post-Soviet country that has been going through tremendous transformations during the past dozen of years. Their story provides an illustrative example of the important ways in which local economies are socially embedded and thus opening up or indeed closing particular economic opportunities. I will furthermore explore whether the Dungans are indeed 'difficult folk' to deal with or whether Western organisations like *helvetas* might subscribe to approaches that are eurocentric and inflexible – or whether there is a different answer to the misunderstandings in Petrovsk. Approaches commonly used by Western aid organizations in the region have previously been severely criticised. Verdery has described them poignantly:

> A number of the stories of post-socialism have the knights of Western know-how rushing in to rescue the distressed of Eastern Europe [and the former Soviet Union] [...] The rescue scenario has two common variants: 'shock therapy' and 'big bang'. The first compares the former socialist bloc with a person suffering from mental illness – that is, socialism drove them crazy, and our job is to restore their sanity. The second implies that (*pace* Fukuyama) history is only now beginning, that prior to 1989 the area was without form and void. While the image of 'shock therapy' represents Western advisers as doctors, the 'big bang' figures them as God.[5]

I will argue in this paper that despite the fact that the Dungans are experiencing the same social, political, and economic difficulties as any other group of agriculturalists in post-Soviet Kyrgyzstan, their being

4 For further historical and cultural details on this minority group see pages 10ff.

5 Verdery, Katherine, *What Was Socialism and What Comes Next?* (Princeton: Princeton University Press, 1996), p. 204f.

an ethnic minority places a particular strain on them, closes some doors that are open to others, and makes some coping strategies more compelling than others. I hope to show that the Dungans of Petrovsk are not 'difficult' but *different*, that their historic-cultural background influences their coping strategies and their interaction with external organizations and individuals. It will become clear that the social networks and kinship ties between members of this ethnic minority have become vital elements in their economic survival strategies after the collapse of the administered economy of the Soviet Union and in the face of the failure of a viable market system to emerge. Even though such networks existed and fulfilled vital functions also during communist times, they tended to be less economically crucial.

When we embarked on this research project, our knowledge base with regard to the Dungans was fairly limited. There is relatively little information available about the Dungan minority in Kyrgyzstan; the Dungans themselves have only recently begun to re-discover their roots and to record their so far largely orally transmitted history. I will return to their specific historical experience in a moment. Given this restricted availability of background information, we, a group of altogether seven researchers, were very open-minded about what we would be able to find out. We stayed in different families in the village of Petrovsk for ten weeks from July to September 2003. We used two main ways of gathering data: participant observation and structured interviews with over 240 questions that aimed at various aspects of change in social and economic life after independence.[6] For the interviews, we chose 21 adults from three categories: members of the former *kolkhoz*, independent farmers, and those who did not fit into either of these categories. We further conducted informal interviews with ordinary people as well as with experts.[7]

6 The questionnaire covered aspects such as genealogy, economic, social, and political relationships, conflict resolution and interest groups, agriculture and landownership, markets, and future strategies and planning. Interviews were generally conducted in Russian and sometimes supported by an interpreter.

7 These experts included representatives from the village administration, teachers, entrepreneurs etc.

The following discussion is mainly based on these interviews and our fieldnotes. I will briefly outline some of the issues and arguments regarding post-communist transformations as they are described in the growing body of literature in the area, and to which this study is considered to be a contribution. Having established this framework, I will then move on to provide some historical and social background information on the Dungan community with whom we worked. Finally, the two aspects – economy and ethnicity – are brought together in a discussion of the embeddedness of the local economy in the social and kinship networks of this particular ethnic minority, in order to highlight the opportunities and constraints for economic welfare posed by social obligations and interaction.

Framing Transformations

The period after independence has been marked by uncertainties, dynamics, conflicts, perennial changes, and fuzzy boundaries. Thus, people tend to calculate and develop strategies for much shorter periods of time rather than long-term. Ambiguities of a seemingly endless road to capitalism have crucial influence on distribution and consumption, on marketing techniques and production, on the definitions of property, on rural economies, and on welfare institutions, as examples from numerous post-communist/post-socialist countries show.[8] The vacuum that was left after the collapse of state-administered economies is filled in various ways, depending as much on individual actors as it does on socio-political circumstances. An ap-

8 See the collection of studies in Michael Burawoy and Katherine Verdery (eds.), *Uncertain Transition. Ethnographies of Change in the Postsocialist World* (Rowman and Littlefield: Lanham, 1999); another such anthology is Sue Bridger and Frances Pine (eds.), *Surviving Post-Socialism. Local Strategies and Regional Responses in Eastern Europe and the Former Soviet Union* (London: Routledge, 1998); a thorough study of a Russian case can be found in Caroline Humphrey, *The Unmaking of Soviet Life. Everyday Economies After Socialism.* (Cornell University Press: Ithaca, 2002).

proach that takes not only state policies, but also everyday practices into account has proven that creativity and resistance are going hand-in-glove with each other.[9]

As it has been shown in other cases, such as Russia[10] or Romania,[11] the collapse of the old order sets forth new entrepreneurs and traders, who are often perceived as a threat to local production communities as they benefit from the production imbalance between regions. Viewed as parasitic, such traders provoke political reactions – old elites rally parts of the local population around them in protest. Such dynamics seem to lie at the basis of some of the unrest in the southern parts of Kyrgyzstan. In the case of Petrovsk, it seems that very few local traders have emerged so far, and that this has vital impact on redistribution patterns and access to markets.

Shock therapy in Kyrgyzstan has often also led to unanticipated reactions and resistance, most notably the regime change in March 2005. Resorting to barter relations, for instance, nowadays takes place for very different reasons now than it did during Soviet times. Whereas under the previous order barter was characterised by surplus products,[12] it now tends to be a sign of bankruptcy.[13] The shock therapy

9 Michael Burawoy and Katherine Verdery (eds.), *Uncertain Transition. Ethnographies of Change in the Postsocialist World* (Rowman and Littlefield: Lanham, 1999); another such anthology is Sue Bridger and Frances Pine (eds.), *Surviving Post-Socialism. Local Strategies and Regional Responses in Eastern Europe and the Former Soviet Union* (London: Routledge, 1998).

10 Caroline Humphrey, 'Traders, "Disorder", and Citizenship Regimes in Provincial Russia', in: Michael Burawoy and Katherine Verdery (eds.) *Uncertain Transition. Ethnographies of Change in the Postsocialist World* (Rowman and Littlefield: Lanham, 1999), pp. 19–52.

11 Katherine Verdery, 'Fuzzy Property: Rights, Power, and Identity in Transylvania's Decollectivization', in: Michael Burawoy and Katherine Verdery (eds.), *Uncertain Transition. Ethnographies of Change in the Postsocialist World* (Rowman and Littlefield: Lanham, 1999), pp. 53–82.

12 Boris Rumer, *Soviet Central Asia. A Tragic Experiment* (Boston: Unwin Hyman, 1989), p. 45.

13 David Woodruff, 'Barter of the Bankrupt: The Politics of Demonetization in Russia's Federal State', in: Michael Burawoy and Katherine Verdery (eds.), *Uncertain Transition. Ethnographies of Change in the Postsocialist World* (Rowman and Littlefield: Lanham, 1999), pp. 83–124.

first encouraged farmers to take risks and expand production into new areas. When, however, government incentives ceased – bringing with it an end to subsidies, increasing prices for agricultural input and low consumer prices on agricultural produce – farmers got caught in a price dilemma and retreated from the market. They became very unenthusiastic about taking risks and making long-term investments, and instead turned to subsistence production that at least secured short-term survival. This situation is comparable to that in many villages in Kyrgyzstan in general, and in Petrovsk in particular, yet there is one essential difference. Most of our interview partners, by contrast, not only claimed that there are no political parties or groups to be found in Petrovsk, but they were consequently also not politically active.

There are several reasons for this disinterest, which shall only be briefly touched upon here. For one, it can be assumed that people have become increasingly disillusioned with and cynical about Kyrgyzstani politics that marked the time after independence, as the regime was not able to deliver on its promises concerning the country's 'transition' towards a free market economy and liberal democracy.[14] Our respondents also mentioned that what happened in the political sphere at the time was boring or dominated by either a 'mafia'or economic interests. Furthermore, we were told that Dungans in general and those in Petrovsk in particular worked all the time and, therefore, had no time to spare for political activism. Political activism was seen as useless, if not actually dangerous – we were pointed to the case of the former local RAS[15] advisor, who (together with others) had begun taking legal action against the former *kolkhoz* and was subsequently sacked; therefore, activism can be punished.

What can be learned from the study of other post-communist societies with regard to the transformation of the economic spheres, and what should be kept in mind when considering the case of Petrovsk, is the following:

14 For similar developments in Bulgaria see Creed, Gerald W. "Deconstructing Socialism in Bulgaria", in: Michael Burawoy and Katherine Verdery (eds.). *Uncertain Transition. Ethnographies of Change in the Postsocialist World.* Rowman and Littlefield:Lanham, 1999, pp. 223–244.

15 Rural Advisory Service, a sub-organisation of *helvetas.*

a) the economic sphere cannot possibly be separated from the socio-cultural and the political – they mutually influence and explain each other;

b) 'transition' cannot be simply explained by being rooted in a socialist past, nor by being only directed towards a future marked by (probably) a free market economy – the present transformations are suspended between the two and develop dynamics of their own;

c) development is not necessarily progressive or evolutionary – it can at the same time combine in itself regressive and progressive dynamics that are inextricably linked with each other and lend themselves to mutual explanations; and

d) it might not be helpful to see 'transition' only in terms of ideal Western models of free market and liberal democracy and compare the situation of post-communist to western countries; this merely yields an analysis in terms of deficits, lacks, and shortcomings without sufficiently taking into account particularities and specific dynamics.

Against this background, I would like to have a closer look at the situation we found in Petrovsk, which in various aspects proved not to be much different from what other studies have found in other regions of the post-communist world, as I have just pointed out. And yet, as Pine and Bridger remind us, 'diversity has been a significant factor [in the process of socio-economic change in the former communist world] not only between individual countries, but between communities and regions within each country'.[16] And, in the case of Petrovsk, being part of an ethnic minority group with a very specific history that in many regards differs from the historical experiences of other groups in the country,[17] makes some decisions that are taken by Dungans slightly different from those of other people. These historical experiences need to be taken into account when dealing with a Dungan community in Kyrgyzstan, as they inform the present situation, and the present

16 Frances Pine and Sue Bridger. 'Introduction', in Sue Bridger and Frances Pine (eds.), *Surviving Post-Socialism. Local Strategies and Regional Responses in Eastern Europe and the Former Soviet Union.* (London: Routledge, 1998), p. 6.

17 Kyrgyzstan is said to house more than eighty 'nationalities', i.e. ethnic groups in the constructed Soviet sense of the term.

shapes the ways in which the past is being re-presented.[18] At this point, I would therefore like to shed some light on the socio-cultural and historical background of the Dungan communities of Kyrgyzstan.

The Dungans of Petrovsk

As I have outlined above, the disintegration of the Soviet Union brought hardships to the majority of its population, especially in economic terms. In many respects, the Dungans of Petrovsk are no different from the inhabitants of other villages in Kyrgyzstan, especially in the Chui Valley, the fertile and agriculturally used valley of the river Chu in the north of the country. And yet, it seemed that the specific historical and cultural background of this community did and continues to have an impact on the everyday lives of individuals and the community as a whole, on how the current situation is perceived, and on the ways in which future planning is done.

To better understand this background, we have to go back at least some 130 years, before the Dungans came to Kyrgyzstan from the north-western Gansu and Shensi provinces of what is today the People's Republic of China.[19] Poyarkov's [20] historical account of the manners and

18 For comparable statements see Creed, Gerald W. 'Deconstructing Socialism in Bulgaria, in: Michael Burawoy and Katherine Verdery (eds.). *Uncertain Transition. Ethnographies of Change in the Postsocialist World.* Rowman and Littlefield: Lanham, 1999, p. 224. Humphrey, Caroline. 'Traders, 'Disorder', and Citizenship Regimes in Provincial Russia', in: Michael Burawoy and Katherine Verdery (eds.). *Uncertain Transition. Ethnographies of Change in the Postsocialist World.* Rowman and Littlefield:Lanham, 1999, p. 22.

19 For a first, albeit extremely brief overview over some aspects of Dungan history, culture, traditions, language etc. see the brochure that had been published by the Aslan Alliance and the Dungan Cultural and Education Fund, and that is available in the village upon request *The Dungan of Central Asia. Profile of the People* (Bishkek, 2002).

20 F. Poyarkov, *Pocledniy Episod Dunganskogo Vocctaniya* [The last episode of the Dungan uprising] (Vernyi, 1901); reprinted in *Dungane*, no. 1 (May 2001: 100–14), no. 2 (October 2001, pp. 111–19), no. 3 (December 2002, pp. 107–15).

customs of the Dungans at the end of the nineteenth century sheds some light on their daily lives in the past. Two developments can be discerned: the Dungans have managed to preserve many aspects of their ethno-cultural specificity, while at the same time adapting to the changing socio-political environment.

Poyarkov frames his description of the Dungans in a comparison with their Chinese and Kyrgyz neighbours, trying – in a manner typical for the early 20th century – to draw clear boundaries between these ethnic groups. He set out by describing the Dungans as 'highly appreciating their work, even the most futile kind of work'.[21] On the other hand, he suspected them to value their own lives rather little. He explained all this by 'being Chinese', by the 'blood relationship' that the Dungans shared with the Chinese population of their original environment. What differentiated them from the Chinese was their religion. Apart from this, he offered a whole shopping list of commonalities between Dungans and Chinese – language, customs, cultivating skills, food, construction of houses, physical appearance.

The peaceful lives of those 'Chinese Muslims' were unsettled, when in the winter of 1877/8, after a failed rebellion, the first three groups of about 6,000 Dungans fled across the border into what was then the Russian Empire. Thousands died of hunger and frost. After a rather reluctant welcome by the Russians, they settled in various places.[22] One group turned south towards the Ferghana valley, where they have become assimilated with the surrounding Kyrgyz and Uzbek communities in later years. In Kazakhstan and the north of Kyrgyzstan, most of them continue to live in what has been termed compact settlements – villages with an overwhelming majority of Dungan inhabitants. During the first flight waves a total of about 11,000 Dungans migrated to the Russian Empire. Many of them returned to China due to a rebellion against the Russian Tsar in the winter of 1916

21 F. Poyarkov. *Pocledniy Episod Dunganskogo Vocctaniya* (Vernyi, 1901); reprinted in *Dungane*, no. 2, October 2001, p. 117.

22 For more details see Lyu, V.G. *Pereceleniye Dungan v Kyrgyzstan v 70–80e Gody XIX Veka.* [The last Dungans in Kyrgyzstan in the 70s–80s] Bishkek: Ilim, 2002; Poyarkov, F. *Pocledniy Episod Dunganskogo Vocctaniya.* Vernyi, 1901; Yusurov, Kh. *Pereseleniye Dungan v Semirech'e.* [The last Dunguns in Semirechye], Frunze, 1961.

(together with tens of thousands of Kyrgyz who perished on the way). Most came back in 1924, when the Soviet government asked them to return. Another wave of refugees returned to China during the years of collectivisation of 1929 to 1933, which dispossessed numerous wealthy Dungans. The revolution in China in 1949, and the ensuing economic crises in the 1950s finally sent another wave of Dungan refugees back into the Soviet Union.

The historical events and experiences mentioned above are engraved into the collective memory of the Dungan communities of Central Asia and are, especially after the disintegration of the Soviet Union, being turned into a more or less unified discourse of repression and prosecution by various Dungan organisations, writers, and intellectuals.

Today, about 52,000 Dungans are living in Kyrgyzstan, forming the fourth strongest ethnic group in the country (after Kyrgyz, Uzbeks, and Russians). Around 37,000 Dungans are in Kazakhstan, and not more than 25,000 in Uzbekistan. Most of the Dungans living in Kyrgyzstan are settled in the Chui Valley (44,000), Bishkek (3,500), and Issyk-Kul (3,000).[23]

Dungans are said to be good farmers, which had resulted in considerable economic success of Dungans as communities and as individuals. Furthermore, our respondents claimed that Dungans always work, are never unemployed, are always busy, and therefore never really economically bad off; and never have been, even during Soviet times. However, to publicly show this wealth is a different matter altogether. During Soviet times, it could, of course, become dangerous to make it publicly known (or seen) that one is better off than others, so that wealth seems to have been a taboo in daily discourse. This might have been reinforced by socio-cultural norms about the equality among people, keeping conflict and jealousy in check, especially if one belongs to an ethnic minority.[24] In order to survive as a

23 R Yusupov, 'Chislennost' I razmeshcheniye Dungan v Kyrgyzstane', [Numbers and Distrbituion of Dungans in Kyrgyzstan], *Dungane*, no. 1 (May 2001), p. 40ff.

24 Cf. Myriam Hivon, 'The Bullied Farmer: Social Pressure as Survival Strategy?', in: Sue Bridger and Frances Pine (eds.), *Surviving Post-Socialism. Local*

distinct ethnic group, one would assume that there is a need to demonstrate unity and strength, glossing over internal conflicts as much as possible.[25] This has become even truer after Kyrgyzstan's independence, after the overarching communist ideology had fallen away and ethnic ideologies appeared reinvigorated.

Ethnic and Kinship Embedding of Economic Practices

Anthropologists have for a long time emphasized that classical economic theories are not or only to a limited extent applicable to non-capitalist societies, and that the economy cannot be analysed outside a holistic system of social and cultural relations. This view that every economy is embedded and enmeshed in socio-cultural institutions has been most succinctly put forward by Karl Polanyi.[26] The formalist position about the general applicability of (market) economic theory has since been severely criticized and substantivist views[27] that ask for alternative economic models, which take into account different ways of production and exchange, have found supporters outside anthropology. As the example of the Dungans lucidly shows, an analysis of rational maximizing strategies alone cannot explain their situation, and different ways of production and exchange for the maintenance of

Strategies and Regional Responses in Eastern Europe and the Former Soviet Union (London: Routledge, 1998), pp. 33–51.

25 There seems to be evidence that there are significant divisions within the village: inhabitants distinguish between three different historically developed quarters, each having a mosque and a school, and being associated with a different level of wealth and outlook.

26 Cf. Karl Polanyi, *The Great Transformation* (Boston Beacon Press, 1957); Karl Polanyi, 'Anthropology and Economic Theory', in Morton H.Fried (ed.), *Readings in Anthropology*, vol. 2 (New York: Thomas Y. Crowell, 1959), pp. 161–84.

27 One of the most influential (albeit also controversial) anthropologist contributions to the debate was Marshal Sahlins, *Stone Age Economics* (London: Tavistock, 1974).

their existence and their lifestyle have to be taken on board. Not only are goods assigned value according to diverging criteria, but they also play particular roles in what can be labeled a 'prestige economy'. Here, but particularly in the absence of a functioning free market economy, two interrelated processes are of specific interest: reciprocity and redistribution patterns. It seems that the case of the Dungans can serve almost as a textbook example of how local economies are socially embedded: economic practices, including the sharing of information, lending money, and giving favours, are largely governed by local norms, values, obligations, and customs. Reciprocity and redistribution takes place to a considerable extent along the lines of kinship and ethnic ties, so that network boundaries become not only socially and culturally, but also economically marked. As I will show shortly, the economic relationships between Dungans and 'outsiders' were severely constrained.

Yet speaking of the social and cultural embeddedness of economies in the case of the Dungans of Petrovsk also entails examining the ways in which certain economic skills are being described as ethnically specific. Dungans have the reputation of being very knowledgeable when it comes to gardening. Thus, the majority of our respondents stated that they got most of their agricultural knowledge from their parents, and would then pass it on to their children. Some of the experience that our respondents gained, they shared with their friends and colleagues at the end of a season. This, however, only seemed to relate to information that could not be directly used to obtain economic benefits and to outmaneuver oneself on the market. As one of the fulltime farmers among our respondents put it laughingly: 'Why should I tell others about my secrets?' Some explained that they obtained knowledge by observing others, but they rarely *ask* for information. Generally it seemed that people were quite confident about their skills, but they confessed a lack of knowledge when it came to 'commercial' agriculture. As I have mentioned above, during Soviet times, knowledge was mostly regulated from above and did not have to be actively sought. One of our respondents thus explained: 'There used to be academics and specialists in the various departments of the *kolkhoz*, who were well informed. However, all the information we got came from only one place and you had to work with it, like it or not. Today, I still use the knowledge I obtained during Soviet times, but we also get information from Russia, from the Academy of Agriculture.' Others maintained that they had not had any new information since independence.[28] It is also clear that such information is becoming increasingly outdated.

If information exchange even *within* the village of Petrovsk was comparatively limited, contacts to outsiders were even more restricted. Although most of the people we interviewed claimed that they were in contact with inhabitants of other villages around Petrovsk, these links were often based on either kinship or commercial ties. Little and usually rather general information was exchanged between the villagers. Many of our respondents further explained that it was actually mainly the others, who came to *them* to buy their produce and seek information rather than people from Petrovsk searching for procurers. The lack of adequate transportation rendered large-scale sales of the harvest almost impossible, so that they had to rely on transporters, who would come and collect their produce to further sell it elsewhere, for instance in Bishkek or Almaty. Hardly anyone of our respondents had links to foreign countries, be that through business contacts or acquaintances. Cross-border trade also became increasingly more difficult as controls became tighter and corruption was rampant.

Of course, the reputation of the gardeners of Petrovsk also attracted international development organizations, but they, too, had communication problems. Imprecise information and rumours seemed to dominate the discourse about and between international organisations in the village. It was striking that the absolute majority of our respondents had little or no knowledge about such organisations. Thus, people did not know who to turn to with their specific problems.

28 Comparing the analysis of the situation up to 1996 (see Mohinder Mudahar, *Kyrgyz Republic. Strategy for Rural Growth and Poverty Alleviation*, World Bank Discussion Paper No. 394 (Washington D.C.: The World Bank, 1998)) with the one of 2003, it is particularly striking that many of the problems appear to have remained the same and that little has improved since. This refers mainly to marketing and food processing, irrigation, lifestock, credits, cash crops, the land reform, and investments.

Possibly due to negative experiences with bureaucracies there was also a lack of trust in such organisations.[29]

This state of affairs seems surprising as cooperation and exchange is vital for successful cultivation and marketing of produce. In Petrovsk, many people worked together in groups, but an equally large number of people did not cooperate. Generally, such cooperation took only place on a short-term basis. Once the task was completed the group dispersed again. There appeared to be a widespread conviction that 'everyone is his {sic!} own boss', that one better worked alone, and that sharing certain tools or tasks is better on a paid basis. Having said this, one must note that there were formal and informal groups in Petrovsk. People get together informally on all sorts of occasions in varying compositions and in diverging places.

After the near-disintegration of the *kolkhoz* Druzhba and the collapse of most collectives that had dominated the world of labour during Soviet times, there appeared to be a trend towards individualism and new forms of collectivity.[30] Most workers have turned to individual survival strategies and for this purpose have fallen back on networks of family and friends rather than the former work collective. On the other hand, it was not unusual for people to search for solutions to their problems in newly formed collectives and under new strong leaders. The (positive) experiences of (symbolic) collectivism in the past were carried over into the present, albeit generally in slightly different shapes. Labour collectives and kinship groups appeared to increasingly coincide. Thus, all our respondents felt primarily re-

29 A similar situation has been reported from Russia, see Louise Perrotta, 'Divergent Responses to Land Reform and Agricultural Restructuring in the Russian Federation', in: Sue Bridger and Frances Pine (eds.), *Surviving Post-Socialism. Local Strategies and Regional Responses in Eastern Europe and the Former Soviet Union* (London: Routledge, 1998), pp. 148–169; Marta Bruno, 'Playing the Co-operation Game. Strategies around International Aid in Post-Socialist Russia', in Sue Bridger and Frances Pine (eds.), *Surviving Post-Socialism. Local Strategies and Regional Responses in Eastern Europe and the Former Soviet Union* (London: Routledge, 1998), pp. 170–187.

30 For an analysis of a similar case in Russia see Ashwin, Sarah. 'Redefining the Collective: Russian Mineworkers in Transition', in: Michael Burawoy and Katherine Verdery (eds.), *Uncertain Transition. Ethnographies of Change in the Postsocialist World* (Lanham: Rowman and Littlefield, 1999), pp. 245–272.

sponsible for the welfare of only their immediate families, followed by other relatives. The network of relatives appeared to be the most salient resource in the lives of people in Petrovsk. This referred to practical help, and bigger worries of a personal, familial, or financial nature.

One example of how kinship networks were operationalised can be seen in the use of huge refrigerators to store vegetables, mainly carrots. It seemed that the first fridges had been built about three years ago, that they had been shared by relatives, and that the idea slowly but surely spread mainly through kinship connections. Having observed that carrots yield much higher prices in winter than straight after the harvest in autumn, someone had come up with the idea of building something like big cold store, where tons of carrots (and other vegetables) can await better market prices. At the time of research there were around forty such mega-fridges in the village. People contributed their different skills to these projects and the small groups of mainly relatives then shared the profits.

Relying on individual networks not only ensures the survival of households, it also reduces the possibility of mounting a collective response to the transition. It is in this sense that the government (and other organizations) are generally not interested in supporting big businesses, cooperatives, or collective farms, but foster individualism among producers and businesses. And yet, labour collectives do have a tradition in this country and people have learned to appreciate cooperation. At times, informal groups take on formal structures and start operating in more or less systematic ways. Often a small group of relatives stands at the beginning of flourishing enterprises. Petrovsk also brought forth its fair share of successful business people.

A crucial issue mentioned to us in numerous interviews and informal conversations was the access to markets and linked to this the ability of turning agricultural produce into cash rather than relying on subsistence production alone. Whereas during Soviet times many basic services – such as education, medical care, and social welfare – were cared for by the state free of charge, these days they have to be paid for. Even though it might be quite convenient to have an allotment and be able to engage in subsistence farming, the availability of cash is vital. In this respect, one also needs to take into consideration that networking, which usually takes place along ethnic and kinship lines,[31] has crucial impact on the situation of the Dungans. Cash flows and the opening up of markets are often defined by ethnic and kinship boundaries, which significantly decreases the possibility for Dungans to expand their spheres of economic activities. This is particularly salient in Kyrgyzstan as there is no functioning financial sector and credits are not easily available,[32] even though some international organisation, amongst them *helvetas*, are offering credit schemes. Thus, kin is again the most reliable source of support, especially since the public financial sector is generally not trusted. Accordingly, the amount of money that circulated *within* Petrovsk was considerable.

In the future, people in Petrovsk would like to see more positive transformations in the agricultural and broader economic spheres. Yet, the directions of this change and how it should be brought about are heavily disputed. Possibly due to past Soviet experiences, many of our interview partners tend to expect *others* to take the initiative. They expect transformations on the highest political levels that would in a trickle-down-effect subsequently also alter their own situation. On the other hand, having grown rather disillusioned about the functioning of precisely these highest levels of politics, many were convinced that the only real help and support in the current situation will be provided by relatives and friends.

31 Traditional moral obligations force individuals to devote parts of their economic profits to the community; ignoring such obligations can lead to stigmatisation; see also Myriam Hivon, 'The Bullied Farmer: Social Pressure as a Survival Strategy?', in Sue Bridger and Frances Pine (eds.), *Surviving Post-Socialism. Local Strategies and Regional Responses in Eastern Europe and the Former Soviet Union* (London: Routledge, 1998), pp. 33–51.

32 The rather bleak situation of an availability of credits in Kyrgyzstan is described in Mohinder Mudahar, *Kyrgyz Republic. Strategy for Rural Growth and Poverty Alleviation*, World Bank Discussion Paper No. 394 (Washington D.C.: The World Bank, 1998), pp. 66–72; nothing much seems to have changed since that report was written.

Conclusions

In this chapter I have tried to capture a moment in time of the village of Petrovsk – the present of the summer 2003 as it spans between a Dungan history, a communist past, and a still uncertain, probably capitalist future. The current situation of the Dungans in Petrovsk needs to be placed in two broader frameworks – one that takes into account their experiences of a history of flight and of being an ethnic minority in a Kyrgyzstan, in which nation building processes are in full swing; and one that compares it to people's reactions in other countries to the social, economic, and political transformations of the so-called 'transition' to a free market economy and liberal democracy.

Such an approach reveals that the reactions of the Dungans bear striking similarities to those of other rural farming communities across the former Communist Bloc. Disillusionment with the 'transition' process and its projected aims, and socio-economic imbalances cause many to shorten the time-horizons of their planning, to retreat into subsistence production, and to rely more heavily on networks of relatives for support. Long-term strategies such as investment in improved production are difficult if not impossible due to a lack of available funds (through credits, for instance). They are also considered to be far too risky so long as the market situation continues to be so insecure.

The specificity of Petrovsk is played out in the perception that the unity of the community needs to be maintained at almost any cost, which results in a fairly tight system of social control. Within this order, rumour and gossip have a controlling function, and wealth is generally not openly discussed or emphasised. Individual economic success is expected to be shared by means of generous monetary presents on festive occasions. This, however, mainly concerns networks of relatives, to a far lesser degree also friends and neighbours. We therefore still find rich, middle, and poor households in Petrovsk, despite all assertions of equality.

Against this background, cooperation between inhabitants of Petrovsk and international development organisations appears somewhat hesitant. This reluctance is also due to a number of other factors, such as an insufficient self-presentation of the organisations in the village and a lack of communication and orchestration between those organisations themselves. This has led to confusion among the population as to which organisation is which, and who offers which kinds of services.

Bibliography

Ashwin, Sarah. 'Redefining the Collective: Russian Mineworkers in Transition', in: Michael Burawoy and Katherine Verdery (eds.), *Uncertain Transition. Ethnographies of Change in the Post-socialist World* (Lanham: Rowman and Littlefield, 1999), pp. 245–272.

Aslan Alliance and the Dungan Cultural and Education Fund, *The Dungan of Central Asia. Profile of the People* (Bishkek, 2002).

Bridger, Sue and Frances Pine (eds.), *Surviving Post-Socialism. Local Strategies and Regional Responses in Eastern Europe and the Former Soviet Union* (London: Routledge, 1998).

Bruno, Marta, 'Playing the Co-operation Game. Strategies around International Aid in Post-Socialist Russia', in Sue Bridger and Frances Pine (eds.), *Surviving Post-Socialism. Local Strategies and Regional Responses in Eastern Europe and the Former Soviet Union* (London: Routledge, 1998), pp. 170–187.

Burawoy, Michael and Katherine Verdery (eds.), *Uncertain Transition. Ethnographies of Change in the Postsocialist World* (Rowman and Littlefield: Lanham, 1999).

Creed, Gerald W. 'Deconstructing Socialism in Bulgaria', in: Michael Burawoy and Katherine Verdery (eds.). *Uncertain Transition. Ethnographies of Change in the Postsocialist World.* Rowman and Littlefield: Lanham, 1999:223–244.

Hivon, Myriam, 'The Bullied Farmer: Social Pressure as Survival Strategy?', in: Sue Bridger and Frances Pine (eds.), *Surviving*

Post-Socialism. Local Strategies and Regional Responses in Eastern Europe and the Former Soviet Union (London: Routledge, 1998), pp. 33–51.

Humphrey, Caroline, 'Traders, ''Disorder'', and Citizenship Regimes in Provincial Russia', in: Michael Burawoy and Katherine Verdery (eds.) *Uncertain Transition. Ethnographies of Change in the Postsocialist World* (Rowman and Littlefield: Lanham, 1999), pp. 19–52.

—— *The Unmaking of Soviet Life. Everyday Economies After Socialism.* (Cornell University Press: Ithaca, 2002).

Lyu, V.G. *Pereceleniye Dungan v Kyrgyzstan v 70–80e Gody XIX Veka.* [Movement of Dungans in Kyrgyzstan in the 70s–80s] (Bishkek: Ilim, 2002).

Mudahar, Mohinder, *Kyrgyz Republic. Strategy for Rural Growth and Poverty Alleviation,* World Bank Discussion Paper No. 394 (Washington D.C.: The World Bank, 1998).

Perrotta, Louise, 'Divergent Responses to Land Reform and Agricultural Restructuring in the Russian Federation', in: Sue Bridger and Frances Pine (eds.), *Surviving Post-Socialism. Local Strategies and Regional Responses in Eastern Europe and the Former Soviet Union* (London: Routledge, 1998), pp. 148–169.

Pine, Frances and Sue Bridger, Introduction', in Sue Bridger and Frances Pine (eds.), *Surviving Post-Socialism. Local Strategies and Regional Responses in Eastern Europe and the Former Soviet Union.* (London: Routledge, 1998), pp. 1–15.

Polanyi, Karl, *The Great Transformation.* (Boston Beacon Press, 1957).

—— 'Anthropology and Economic Theory', in Morton H. Fried (ed.), *Readings in Anthropology,* vol. 2 (New York: Thomas Y. Crowell, 1959), pp. 161–84.

Poyarkov, F. *Pocledniy Episod Dunganskogo Vocctaniya* [The Last Episode of the Dungan Uprising] (Vernyi, 1901).

Rumer, Boris, *Soviet Central Asia. A Tragic Experiment* (Boston: Unwin Hyman, 1989).

Sahlins, Marshal, *Stone Age Economics.* (London: Tavistock, 1974).

Verdery, Katherine. *What Was Socialism and What Comes Next?* (Princeton: Princeton University Press, 1996).

—— 'Fuzzy Property: Rights, Power, and Identity in Transylvania's Decollectivization', in: Michael Burawoy and Katherine Verdery (eds.), *Uncertain Transition. Ethnographies of Change in the Postsocialist World* (Rowman and Littlefield: Lanham, 1999), pp. 53–82.

Woodruff, David, 'Barter of the Bankrupt: The Politics of Demonetization in Russia's Federal State', in: Michael Burawoy and Katherine Verdery (eds.), *Uncertain Transition. Ethnographies of Change in the Postsocialist World* (Rowman and Littlefield: Lanham, 1999), pp. 83–124.

Yusupov, R, 'Chislennost' I razmeshcheniye Dungan b Kyrgyzstane', [Numbers and Distrbution of Dungans in Kyrgyzstan], *Dungane*, no. 1 (May 2001).

Yusurov, Kh. *Pereseleniye Dungan v Semirech'e.* [Settling of Dungans in Semirechye] (Frunze, 1961).

SEBASTIAN ECKARDT AND ANDREAS GOLDTHAU

Reforming into Growth or Growing into Reform? A Critical Note on the Post Washington Consensus

Introduction

Do institutions matter in economic growth? After a poor record of structural adjustment programs in developing and transition countries in the late 80s and early 90s based on the Washington Consensus,[1] its underlying concepts and policy recommendations have experienced a devastating critique. This critique mainly addressed the flaw of having underestimated the role of institutions and governance in economic development. Departing from the implicit assumption that institutions arise effortlessly and endogenously, i.e., as a 'by-product' of economic growth, the mainstream debate on development policy has shifted in subsequent years. Now, the prevalent view regards sound institutions as an essential precondition of growth.

While generally sharing the renewed emphasis on the political and institutional foundations of economic growth, we argue that the straight forward link between good governance and economic development, as assumed by the now prevalent Post Washington Consensus paradigm, is in fact not consistent with the evidence of the recent successful growth story that has occurred in Russia. If insti-

1 The notion 'Washington Consensus' 'refers to the lowest common denominator of policy advice being addressed by the Washington-based institutions to Latin American countries as of 1989' in John Williamson, 'What Should the World Bank Think About the Washington Consensus?', *World Bank Research Observer*, 15, no. 2 (2000), p. 251; see also John Williamson, 'What Washington Means by Policy Reform', in John Williamson (ed.), *Latin American Adjustment: How Much has Happened?* (Washington D.C.: Institute for International Economics, 1990).

tutions are the key to the riddle, how did Russia manage to grow over the last years despite persistently weak institutions and adverse (micro) economic policies?

'Institution' as a scientific notion is common to sociological and economic investigation. While there are differences with regards to the question how 'thick' institutions are and at which speed they may change, both disciplines are concerned with the underlying agent-structure problem.[2] In fact, sociology contributes a strong dose of structuralism to political and economic explanatory approaches to actor's behaviour. Any attempt to understand economic growth or model institutional change will fail if the insights from this 'sociological turn' are ignored. Hence, by putting the notion of institutions at the centre of analysis, this contribution is located at the interface of both disciplines. It addresses the question to what extent institutions are the causes or the effects of actors' economic behaviour in a transitional country.

The chapter is organized as follows. First, we present the change of paradigm in both development theory and policy that has taken place during the last decade. Second, we critically review some of the main conceptual underpinnings and policy conclusions of what we call the 'Post Washington Consensus'. Third, we suggest an alternative approach to 'institutions' deduced from the 'stationary bandits' – a framework established by Mancur Olson. Applied to the case of Russia, we aim to show that this framework might provide a more instrumental approach in capturing some of the dynamics of reforms and the political foundations behind Russia's current growth.

2 On the agent-structure problem see, among others, Anthony Giddens, *Central Problems in Social Theory. Action, Structure and Contradiction in Social Analysis* (Berkeley: University of California Press, 1979), Anthony, Giddens, *The Constitution of Society: Outline of the Theory of Structuration* (Berkeley: University of California Press, 1984), Alexander Wendt, 'The Agent-Structure Problem in International Relations Theory', *International Organization*, 41, no. 3 (1987), pp. 335–70; David Dessler, 'What's At Stake With the Agent-Structure Debate', *International Organization*, 43, no. 4 (1989), pp. 441–473.

The Washington Consensus and its Discontents

The Washington Consensus had focused on narrowly defined economic factors when drawing up the main pillars of political reforms in developing and transition countries. Getting prices right and freeing the invisible hand of market forces from state induced distortions were the main concerns. The ideological bias of the Washington Consensus towards free markets was spurred by an increasing suspicion about the state's role in the economic realm, which was mainly catalysed by two major developments that became evident in the late 80s: the fiscal crisis of Keynesian welfare states in most of the established industrial countries and the break-down of the state administered socialist economies.[3]

In practice, the Washington Consensus prioritized the trinity of privatisation, deregulation and macro economic stability. During the early radical phase of market reform, the priority was set on downsizing public institutions, not reforming them. The state's role in the economic realm was limited to securing property and maintaining macro-economic stability. In fact, it was argued that once basic market reforms were put into practice triggering economic growth, pressures from markets and political lobby groups would force state institutions to reorganise themselves towards higher performance.

This assumed 'Coasian' path dependency in the emergence of better institutions however turned out to be unrealistic in real world settings.[4] While it is certainly right that the state in many ways constituted a major obstacle to economic growth in the developing world, it soon became obvious that the Washington Consensus induced policy recommendations yielded results that appeared very different to the ones they were expected to deliver. A case in point is Russia during much of the 90s. Neither the Russian growth rates occurred to the extent the Washington Consensus inspired economists had pre-

3 World Bank, *World Development Report: The State in the Changing World* (New York, 1997a).

4 Ronald Coase, 'The Problem of Social Cost', *Journal of Law and Economics*, 3 (1960), pp. 1–44.

dicted, nor did there emerge functioning market institutions. In the absence of effective public control and good governance, some reforms presented enormous rent seeking possibilities for privileged economic and political elites. The shockingly high level of corruption, insider deals and asset stripping that accompanied a number of privatization deals not only undermined the legitimacy of the reform process but also – more often than not – created sub-optimal economic outcomes. The 'early winners' of reforms did not pressure for more extensive pro-market reforms; rather, they faced strong incentives to stall any further reforms in order to secure and expand their rent seeking capacities.[5] Instead of spurring efficient domestic institutions, radical market reforms resulted in a preservation of low competition on domestic markets, price distortions and soft budget constraints. State capacity was weak, the Russian tax system resembled a legal nightmare, investment rates were lower than necessary to keep the existing capital stock, and the 'oligarchs' were predominantly occupied by channelling money to Cyprus than by developing long-term strategies for sustainable business development.[6]

After Russia and some other transition countries had implemented the structural adjustment packages recommended by IMF and the World Bank, economic growth failed to generate sustainable increase. The focus of discussion shifted: economists argued that the neo-liberal prescriptions were flawed as they underestimated the role of state institutions in organising both the public and the private activities. Hence, the neoclassical bias of reform programs that had dominated the 1980s and early 1990s came under attack[7] As Daniel Kaufmann sums up:

5 Joel Hellman, 'Winners Take All. The Politics of Partial Reform in Post-Communist Transitions', *World Politics*, 50, no. 2 (1998), pp. 203–34; Joel Hellman, Geraint Jones and Daniel Kaufmann, 'Seize the State, Seize the Day: State Capture, Corruption, and Influence in Transition Economies', World Bank Policy Research Working Paper, 2444, 2000.

6 Among others, Jeremy Page, 'Russians seek new tax havens as Cyprus cleans up', Reuters, 26 June 2003; Bureau of Economic Analysis, 'Problems of Foreign Direct Investment Economic Policy', *Analytical Bulletin*, 17 (1999), p. 2.

7 Peter Murrell, 'Conservative Political Philosophy and the Strategy of Economic Transition', *Eastern European Politics and Societies*, 6, no. 1 (1992) pp. 3–16;

> Less than a decade ago, governance issues did not figure prominently in the agenda of international financial and development institutions. Then there was no road: the absence of institutional and governance reforms was arguably the most glaring omission of the 'Washington Consensus' of the past decade on the 10 tenets of sound economic policies and management. In fact, the challenges of governance and corruption were often ignored altogether.[8]

The critique of the Washington Consensus undermined the existing theoretical body of economic thought[9] New institutional economics, heavily inspired by approaches in sociology, also replaced the neo-classical rationale as the main source of inspiration for policy decisions. The new trends of economic thought argued that institutions and good governance are the prime determinants in generating economic growth.[10]

The basic discovery of this Post Washington Consensus was that the state could not simply be thrown out of the economy. Instead, reforms should aim at improving governance in order to enable public institutions to carry out their functions in reliable and efficient ways.[11] The widely used definition depicts governance as 'the manner in which power is exercised in the management of a country's economic and social resources.'[12] It comprises a whole set of 'thick' reforms

Moisés Naím, *Latin America's Journey to the Market* (San Francisco: Institute for Contemporary Studies, 1995).

8 Daniel Kaufmann, Aart Kraay and Pablo Zoido-Lobatón, *Governance Matters III: Governance Indicators for 1996–2002* (Washington, D.C.: World Bank, 2003), p. 3.

9 Phil Hanson, *Understanding Regional Patterns of Economic Change in Post-Communist Russia. Russian Regions: Economic Growth and Environment* (Slavic Research Center, Hokudai University, 2000), p. 2.

10 Among others, Douglass North, *Institutions, Institutional Change, and Economic Performance* (New York: Cambridge University Press, 1990); Thrainn Eggertson, *Economic Behaviour and Institutions* (Cambridge: Cambridge University Press, 1990); Ostrom Elinor, Larry Schroeder, and Susan Wynne, *Institutional Incentives and Sustainable Development: Infrastructure Policies in Perspective* (Boulder and Oxford: Westview Press, 1993).

11 World Bank, *World Development Report*; World Bank, *Helping Countries Combat Corruption: The Role of the World Bank* (Washington, DC: World Bank, 1997b).

12 World Bank, *Helping Countries Combat Corruption*, p. 302.

such as the capacity of the government to effectively formulate and implement sound policies, voice and accountability mechanisms that ensure the transparency of the public sector, rule of law, anti corruption provisions, and democratisation of the process by which governments are selected, monitored and replaced. The basic rationale is that if these institutions are designed properly they will shape incentives for actors – both state and private – to behave in ways that are conducive to economic efficiency and long term sustainable growth.

Posting up the Post Washington Consensus

What is wrong with the Post Washington Consensus approach? In principle, we share the view that political institutions do matter for economic performance. However, we are sceptical about the concrete concept of institutional change and development underlying the Post Washington Consensus. This is essentially for three reasons.

First, as in many cases, there can be too much even of a good thing. The broad definition of governance applied by the Post Washington Consensus implicitly emphasises that successful institutional reforms require a whole set of different, comprehensive and simultaneous changes which are seen as indispensable for a country to enter the growth path. The multiplicity of factors covered by such a broad understanding of governance renders it difficult to clearly delineate which aspects are indeed crucial at the onset of economic growth. While it is certainly hard to find arguments (and evidence) against the stance that stable property rights are a prerequisite for long term investments and thus sustainable economic growth, the same cannot be said about, for instance, corruption or democratisation.[13]

13 Daniel Kaufman and Shang–Jin Wie, 'Does "Grease Money" Speed Up the Wheels of Commerce?', *World Bank Policy Research Paper*, 2254, 1999; Mushtaq Khan, 'Corruption and Governance in Early Capitalism', in Jonathan Pincus and Jeffrey Winters (eds.), *Reinventing the World Bank* (Ithaca: Cornell University Press, 2002), pp. 164–84.

Not all institutional reforms might be equally important in initiating economic growth. Indeed, a number of recent cross country analysis of transition economies have suggested that the link between governance reforms and economic growth is more complex than many policy-makers and analysts had originally thought.[14] Although these studies detect a positive effect of reforms in the early period of transition, it tends to disappear in later stages. Furthermore, there has been a marked acceleration in growth in some of the less-reform minded countries, including Russia in the last four or five years. Others have concluded that initial macroeconomic measures aiming at stabilization and liberalization (the pillars of the Washington Consensus) have a larger impact on growth than measures to improve the institutional environment.[15] Clearly, qualitative country evidence from successful growth generators such as China, Malaysia, South Korea as well as the history of the industrialised world in the 19th and 20th centuries point in the same direction. Growth might well be spurred by partial reforms, and occur in an insufficient institutional setting. It thus seems more realistic that growth and governance evolve in a reciprocal fashion in that growth paths are initiated by certain institutional reforms. Higher income levels then are associated with progressive reforms towards good governance – a virtuous circle of growth and governance. As Rodrik argued, for a reform to kick start growth, it is most important that it has the 'ability to concentrate effort on the binding constraints'.[16]

Second, the Post Washington Consensus still seems to be biased towards market forces. Consistently, in a large empirical research pro-

14 C. Lawson and H. Wang, 'Economic Transition in Central and Eastern Europe and the Former Soviet Union: Which Policies Worked?' Department of Economics and International Development Working Paper (University of Bath), 2004; Tatiana Lysenko, *Determinants of Economic Growth in Transition economies* (Cambridge University, 2002); EBRD, *Transition Report 2004. Infrastructure* (London: European Bank for Reconstruction and Development, 2004).

15 Oleh Havrylyshyn and Ron van Rooden, 'Institutions Matter in Transition But So Do Policies', *Comparative Economic Studies*, 45 (2003), pp. 2–24.

16 Dani Rodrik, 'Getting Interventions Right: How South Korea and Taiwan Grew Rich', National Bureau of Economic Research Working Paper, 4964, 1994, p. 16.

ject conducted by the World Bank, an indicator for bad governance is the regulatory burden, which 'includes measures of the incidence of market-unfriendly policies such as price controls [...] as well as perceptions of the burdens imposed by excessive regulation in areas such as foreign trade and business development.'[17] While markets certainly provide incentives for performance, innovation and long term productivity, this market optimism again seems to run counter to the empirical evidence of some of the countries that look back at years of high rates of economic success. Again the examples of China, Korea and Malaysia come to mind, which certainly do not provide examples of perfectly deregulated regimes. In all these cases, growth occurred not only despite but precisely because of pervasive state interventions into the economy.[18]

Third, and related, the Post Washington Consensus draws empirical insights mainly from recent cross country analysis that suggest a strong correlation between the quality of governance and an economy's overall performance. As acknowledged by most researchers, these findings should however be handled with care because obtaining these quantitative data and measuring governance are fraught with difficulty.[19] But even if we share the basic observation that there is a positive correlation between the two variables, we cannot establish the causal direction underlying this observation. Kaufmann and Kray, proponents of the Post Washington Consensus, state that per capita income and the quality of governance are strongly positively correlated across countries. Regarding the reversed effect of higher incomes causing better governance they however find:

> [...] negative feedback from incomes to governance implies that without other interventions, higher incomes do not guarantee improved governance.[20]

17 Kaufmann, Kraay and Zoido–Lobatón, ibid., p. 5.
18 Rodrik, ibid.
19 Kaufmann, Kraay and Zoido–Lobatón, ibid.
20 Daniel Kaufmann and Aart Kray, 'Growth without Governance', *Economia*, 3, no. 1 (2002), pp. 169–229.

Figure 1: Competing interpretations on the governance and economic performance

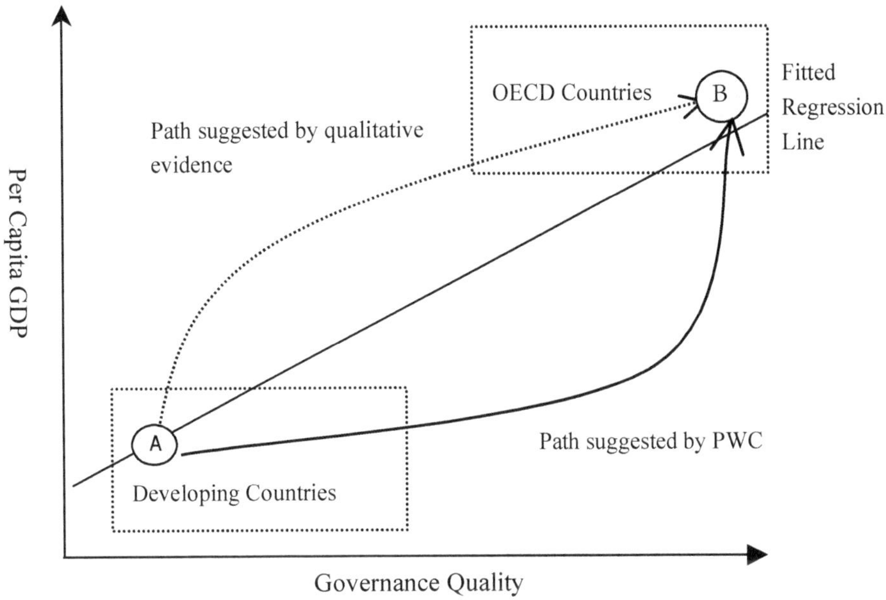

Figure 1 gives a stylised representation of the relationship between governance and growth as suggested by cross country evidence. The observed positive correlation between the quality of governance and economic growth (as found in various empirical cross country studies) is illustrated by the fitted regression line. The lower curve represents the growth path as suggested by the Post Washington Consensus. According to this approach, a country first needs to move along the horizontal axis to the right. Improved governance then leads to higher growth and income in the long run. However, the correlation might in fact be less straight forward and go both ways, with initial reforms kicking off growth which in turn leads to demand for progressive governance reforms. This is represented by the dotted curve. It suggests that countries may initiate growth with relatively small (but right) moves on the x-axis. Higher incomes then lead to a move to the right at a much higher income level.

Hence, the correlation between governance quality and economic performance needs a sound micro-foundation in order to grasp how institutional reforms and incentives work out on the ground. To illustrate this, we turn our attention to the exemplary case of Russia, where recent unpredicted growth occurred in an institutional setting, far from the ideal conditions implied by the Post Washington Consensus.

Economic Growth in Russia – Slowing and Growing without Governance

From the beginning of transition, Russia served to display reasons for economic reforms. After the initial phase of reform was carried out under the sway of the Washington Consensus, Russia for much of the 1990s presented a prime example of the flaws of the 'from plan to market' approach.[21] The subsequent 'institutions matter' paradigm and resulting Post Washington Consensus were drawn partly on the disappointing outcome of Washington Consensus informed policies in Russia.

Let's briefly recall the basic facts of Russia's transitional process. With regards to socio-economic outcomes, Russia's record is indeed rather mixed, in particular compared to Central and Eastern Europe which, after a short economic fall back, followed a continuous growth path since the early 90s. In contrast, Russia has been characterised by a pace of unpredicted and at times surprising economic and political reforms. Most of the early and mid ninetieswere characterized by the state's inability to prune public expenditure and subsidies effectively, to enforce contracts, and to collect taxes. The Russian economy possessed a poor climate for business investment, excessive market entry barriers, licenses and fees, high taxes and various types of extortion imposed by federal, regional and local governments. The weak public

21 World Bank, *World Development Report 1996: From Plan to Market* (Washington, DC.: Oxford University Press, 1996); Phil Hanson, ibid.; Peter Murrell, ibid.

financial system and sustained budget deficits in turn constantly constrained the state in paying public sector wages and pensions on time and in providing effectively poverty relief and other public goods. Perhaps not surprisingly, Russia faced a prolonged period of negative growth, stagnation and eventual collapsed in 1998.

By the late 1990s, as most analysts were writing off Russia's economic development, economic growth suddenly picked up and remained high between 6–8% annually. Between 1999 and 2001, Russia's GDP grew by 21 percent, inflation fell from 86% to 18%, the fiscal situation turned around from a deficit of 5% of GDP to a surplus of 3% of GDP. Other economic indicators such as foreign direct investment as share of GDP, capital investment rate and industrial output have taken off and continue to show positive digits.[22]

While it remains questionable whether this is a short-term blessing spurred by favourable external conditions, or a long-term growth path for the Russian economy, it still offers an interesting puzzle.[23] During 'ten years after' debates, there were heated discussions on whether Russia was finally on its way to a success story or not.[24] In fact, following the Post Washington Consensus paradigm, the academic and political mainstream for much of the late 1990s have attributed Russia's poor performance to major flaws in institutional design and adverse incentives that actors face in Russian business and the public sector. Notions, such as 'Russian ersatz (i.e. substitute) capitalism'[25] or 'virtual economy',[26] circumscribe the fact that Russia's situation is a mixture of markets, informal networking and institutional

22 World Bank, *Russian Economic Report* (Moscow: World Bank, 2003b).

23 Some authors associate recent growth in GDP with high oil prices and a post 1998 devalued rouble rather than substantial growth. However, a recent study by the World Bank attributed only about three percent of the 7.2% growth in 2003 to the direct and indirect effects of the oil price increase and 4.2% to non-oil factors. See World Bank, *Russian Economic Report.*

24 World Bank, *Transition Newsletter*, 14, no. 1–3 (2003a).

25 Joseph Stiglitz, *Globalization and its Discontent* (Washington, 2001).

26 Clifford Gaddy and Barry Ickes, 'Russia's Virtual Economy', *Foreign Affairs*, 77, no. 5 (1998), pp. 53–67; Anders Aslund, 'Russia's Virtual Economy: A Comment', *Post-Soviet Geography and Economics*, 40, no. 2 (1999), pp. 98–102.

legacies of Soviet past.[27] They point out that the Russian economy has been characterized by the pervasive existence of red tape and over-regulation, state intervention, soft budgets and delayed restructuring, combined with crony capitalism, rent seeking and asset stripping as well as partially insecure property rights and poor rule of law. Adding the high scores Russia received in the Transparency International Corruption Perceptions Index (CPI),[28] the country gets a showcase for a suboptimal institutional environment. In light of this interpretation only a few were still wondering whether growth could occur without major reforms. Some even highlighted that Russia was locked into a suboptimal but stable equilibrium, which could bring about neither reforms nor economic growth.[29] However, contrary to the Post Washington Consensus expectations, economic growth has suddenly occurred. What has gone right?

Consistent with our general critique of the Post Washington Consensus in section 3 we now propose an alternative explanation for the path taken by Russia during the last years. It is based on late Mancur Olson's metaphor of stationary bandits. Against the supposed rationale of the Post Washington Consensus, our analysis of Russia's growth story will show that growth might well be generated without thick governance reforms in place.

In his article 'Dictatorship, Democracy, and Development', Mancur Olson addresses the question of the political foundations of economic development.[30] In order to explain why some political regimes fail to spur growth while others are successful growth generators, Olson distinguishes between 'roving' and 'stationary bandits'. What happens in many regimes hostile to growth is an uncoordinated competitive redistribution of income by a predatory state of 'roving bandits' who

27 Klaus Segbers (ed.), *Explaining Post-Soviet Patchworks. Volume 2: Pathways from the past to the global* (Aldershot: Ashgate, 2002)

28 The TI Corruption Perceptions Index (CPI) ranks countries in terms of the degree to which corruption is perceived to exist among public officials and politicians. In the most recent update Russia ranks 87 out of 133. http://www.transparency.org/pressreleases_archive/2003/2003.10.07.cpi.en. html

29 Hellman, ibid.

30 Mancur Olson, 'Dictatorship, Democracy, and Development', *American Political Science Review*, 87, no. 3 (1993), pp. 567–576.

enrich themselves at the cost of exploiting the population. This leads – as Olson argued – to high formal taxation and/or pervasive and uncoordinated corruption, e.g. overgrazing of the tax base. A state led by roving bandits will provide low incentives to invest and produce, because the fruits of production and investments are redistributed to an extent that the marginal cost of increasing production are not offset by the expected private, 'tax reduced' benefit. To put it simply, in a world of roving bandits, there is little incentive for anyone to accumulate anything because it might be appropriated by the state.

On the contrary, Olson suggests that there are growth-inducing regimes that develop what he calls encompassing interests. These 'stationary bandits' have a long-term interest in their victims. They rationalise theft in the form of taxes at levels that leave the population with a sufficient incentive to produce, in order to maximize the tax benefit over time. Moreover, in the long run, it is in the interest of stationary bandits to provide growth enhancing public goods. Or, as Olson puts it, the stationary bandit '[...] is not like the wolf that preys on the elk, but more like the rancher who makes sure that his cattle are protected and given water.'[31]

In order to move from a low growth to a high growth environment, as Olson implies, one needs in fact institutional reforms. However, Olsonist types of reform are rather thin focussing on specific binding incentives and constraints instead of optimizing the overall institutional setting. While the overall institutional environment might still be suboptimal, any prolonging of planning horizons will create incentives that kick start growth. This type of reform has not much to do with thick governance reforms suggested by the Post Washington Consensus. It suggests a more reciprocal path of initial thin reforms kick starting growth, which in turn enables the state to ameliorate the institutional environment and to further invest in growth enhancing public goods, thereby continually establishing more productive incentives for the population.

What does this tell us about institutional change and economic growth in Russia? Following the financial crisis in 1998, the Russian government embarked upon an important reform package. First and

31 Ibid., p. 570.

foremost, intergovernmental accountability was restructured by re-establishing central control over fiscal regional affairs. One of the most important parts of these reforms was the gradual shift away from a tax system, in which Russia's various taxes are divided among different levels of government, towards a 'one tax one budget' system where one tax would go entirely to one level of government.[32] Second, a new Tax Code defined a clear set of tax rates and ended day-to-day bargaining between subjects and tax authorities. The tax reform, setting a flat rate of 13% income tax as well as introducing a variety of other innovative tax instruments, was even applauded by international and domestic analysts.[33]

This reform package resembles thin Olsonist reforms in that it changed the incentive structure of certain state agents. To be more precise, these reforms have three principal effects. First, the re-establishment of monopolies over various tax bases enabled federal and regional authorities to develop the necessary encompassing interests, Olsonist prerequisite for rational taxation.[34] Unlike in the previous setting of weak central control and various government levels (roving bandits) exploiting tax bases in an uncoordinated fashion, each level now has the opportunity to develop a long-term interest in the development of the tax base. In other words, state agencies now have an incentive to maximize tax revenues over time. Second, and related, tax rates are set at a level which allows enterprises to gain high enough profits (after tax) and still have an incentive to increase productivity. Third, enterprises and individuals face a clear perspective for inter-temporal allocation and consumption since they find a relatively stable set of rules of the tax game with state authorities. These reforms

32 Andrei Shleifer and Daniel Treisman, *Without a Map: Political Tactics and Economic Reform in Russia* (Cambridge, Mass: MIT Press, 2000), chapter 6; Alexei Lavrov, John Litwack and Douglas Sutherland, *Fiscal Federalist Relations in Russia. A Case for Subnational Autonomy* (Paris: OECD, 2001).

33 See Pauline Jones-Luong and Erika Weinthal, 'Contra Coercion: Russian Tax Reform, Exogenous Shocks, and Negotiated Institutional Change', *American Political Science Review*, 98, no. 1 (2004), pp. 139–152.

34 See Sebastian Eckardt, 'Russia's Market Distorting Federalism–Decentralisation, Governance, and Economic Performance in Russia in the 90s', FUB Institute for East European Studies Working Paper, 42, 2002.

are still far from enhancing the institutional environment in Russia to the optimal level required by the Post Washington Consensus. They however stimulate growth, at least in the short run. Russia has taken a path similar to the dotted line in Figure 1.

Figure 2: Governance and Growth in Russia

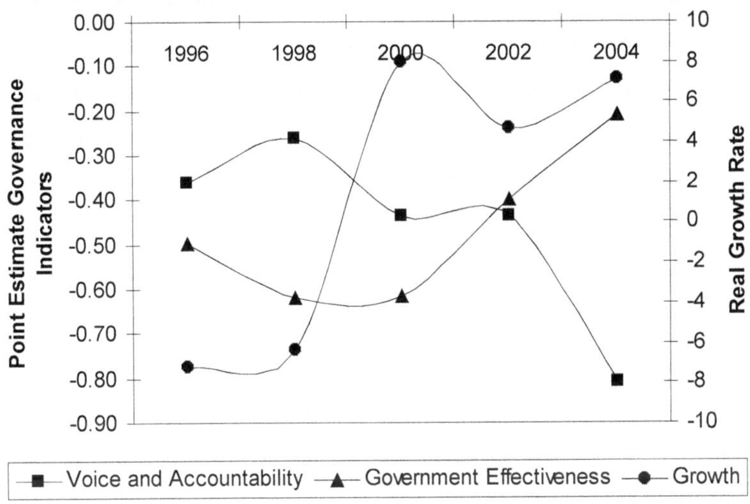

Source: World Bank Governance Matters Dataset 2004, World Bank SIMA.

As can be seen from Figure 2 these policy changes are well reflected in existing measurements of governance. As one might expect, the government effectiveness indicator for Russia has been rising since 2000, when the most crucial reforms were implemented. The growth rate picked up around the same time. Interestingly, the voice and accountability indicator, which essentially measures how democratically countries are governed, moves in the opposite direction during the same period, again a fact that should surprise nobody following political developments in Russia. Here, a short but cautious remark must be made. Initiating and sustaining growth are two different things. Olson stresses that autocratic regimes led by stationary bandits can certainly generate economic growth over a certain period of time. The nature of their regime is however liable to endanger growth in the long run. This is mainly for two reasons. First, law enforcement is restricted to the relationship between citizens, but does not apply to relations between the citizens and the state. This creates the possibility of sudden changes in the rules of the game which diminishes the citizens' planning security. As a consequence, short-term investments still pay off to the detriment of – often more productive – long term investments. This, in turn, reduces efficient allocation of productive resources over the long run. As some concerned observers remark, the economic success in Russia indeed came at the political cost of somewhat reduced press freedom, recentralization and the like. The recent Russian success should thus be seen in the light of further necessary reforms in order to sustain the present upswing.

Some Preliminary Concluding Remarks

In this contribution we aimed to critically examine some of the core recommendations of what we call the Post Washington Consensus. We have further suggested a different perspective on recent economic growth in Russia by applying an Olsonist framework.

We make three cautious conclusions. First, institutions do matter in sustainable economic growth. Second, in order to kick start growth, changing institutional settings should concentrate on binding factors rather than implementing an overcrowded agenda of reforms. It is in this sense that we attribute present Russian growth to Olsonist type reforms. The most important feature of these reforms is that they align the interests of the government and the public sector as a whole to economic growth. Third, arguably such thin reforms – while prompting short-term growth – might not generate sustainable economic success over the longer term, which requires progressive investments in improving the institutional environment. For developing and transition countries to sustain the momentum of high growth they have to conduct progressive 'thicker' governance reforms. Whether Russia will be able to turn the comparatively short-term growth levels into a long term trend will merely depend on its ability to keep pace and pursue further reforms.

Bibliography

Aslund, Anders, 'Russia's Virtual Economy: A Comment', *Post-Soviet Geography and Economics*, 40 no. 2 (1999), pp. 98–102.

Bhagwati, Jagsish, *Foreign Trade Regimes and Economic Development: Anatomy and Consequences of Exchange Control Regimes* (Cambridge, MA: Cambridge University Press, 1978).

Buchanan, James (ed.), *Towards a Theory of the Rent Seeking Society* (College Station Texas A&M University Press, 1980).

Coase, Ronald, 'The Problem of Social Cost', *Journal of Law and Economics*, 3 (1960), pp. 1–44.

Dessler, David, 'What's At Stake With the Agent-Structure Debate', *International Organization* 43, no. 4 (1989), pp. 441–473.

EBRD, *Transition Report 2004 Infrastructure* (London: European Bank for Reconstruction and Development, 2004)

Eckardt, Sebastian, 'Russia's Market Distorting Federalism-Decentralisation, Governance, and Economic Performance in Russia in the 90s', FUB Institute for East European Studies Working Paper, 42, 2002.

Eggertson, Thrainn, *Economic Behaviour and Institution* (Cambridge: Cambridge University Press, 1990).

Elinor, Ostrom, Schroeder, Larry and Wynne, Susan, *Institutional Incentives and Sustainable Development: Infrastructure Policies in Perspective* (Boulder and Oxford: Westview Press, 1993).

Gaddy, Clifford and Ickes, Barry, 'Russia's Virtual Economy', *Foreign Affairs*, 77, no. 5 (1998), pp. 53–67.

Giddens, Anthony, *Central Problems in Social Theory. Action, Structure and Contradiction in Social Analysis* (Berkeley: University of California Press, 1979).

—— *The Constitution of Society: Outline of the Theory of Structuration* (Berkeley: University of California Press, 1984).

Hanson, Phil, *Understanding Regional Patterns of Economic Change in Post-Communist Russia. Russian Regions: Economic Growth and Environment* (Slavic Research Center, Hokudai University, 2000).

Havrylyshyn Oleh and van Rooden, Ron, 'Institutions Matter in Transition but So Do Policies', *Comparative Economic Studies*, 45 (2003), pp. 2–24.

Hellman, Joel, Jones, Geraint and Kaufmann, Daniel, 'Seize the State, Seize the Day: State Capture, Corruption, and Influence in Transition Economies', *World Bank Policy Research Working Paper*, 2444, 2000.

Hellman, Joel, 'Winners Take All. The Politics of Partial Reform in Post-Communist Transitions', *World Politics*, 50, no. 2 (1998), pp. 203–34.

Jones-Luong, Pauline and Weinthal, Erika, 'Contra Coercion: Russian Tax Reform, Exogenous Shocks, and Negotiated Institutional Change', *American Political Science Review*, 98, no. 1 (2004), pp. 139–152

Kaufmann, Daniel, Kraay, Aart and Zoido–Lobatón, Pablo, *Governance Matters III: Governance Indicators for 1996–2002* (Washington, D.C.: World Bank, 2003).

Kaufmann, Daniel and Kray Aart, 'Growth without Governance', *Economia*, 3, no. 1 (2002), pp. 169–229.

Kaufmann, Daniel and Shang-Jin, Wie, 'Does "Grease Money" Speed Up the Wheels of Commerce?' World Bank Policy Research Paper, 2254, 1999.

Khan, Mushtaq, 'Corruption and Governance in Early Capitalism', in Jonathan Pincus and Jeffrey Winters (eds.), *Reinventing the World Bank* (Ithaca: Cornell University Press, 2002), pp. 164–84.

Krueger, Anne, 'The Political Economy of the Rent-Seeking Society', *American Economic Review*, 64, no. 3 (1974), pp. 291–303.

Lal, Deepak, The Political Economy of the Predatory State', World Bank Discussion Paper, 105, 1984.

Lavrov, Alexei, Litwack, John and Sutherland, Douglas, *Fiscal Federalist Relations in Russia. A Case for Subnational Autonomy* (Paris: OECD, 2001).

Lawson C., and Wang, H., 'Economic Transition in Central and Eastern Europe and the Former Soviet Union: Which Policies

Worked?', Department of Economics and International Development Working Paper (University of Bath), 2004.
Lysenko, Tatiana, *Determinants of Economic Growth in Transition Economies* (Cambridge University, 2002).
Murrell, Peter, 'Conservative Political Philosophy and the Strategy of Economic Transition', *Eastern European Politics and Societies*, 6, no. 1 (1992), pp. 3–16.
Naím, Moisés, *Latin America's Journey to the Market* (San Francisco: Institute for Contemporary Studies, 1995).
North, Douglass, *Institutions, Institutional Change, and Economic Performance* (New York: Cambridge University Press, 1990).
Olson, Mancur, 'Dictatorship, Democracy, and Development', *Amer ican Political Science Review*, 87 no. 3 (1993), pp. 567–576.
Rodrik, Dani, 'Getting Interventions Right: How South Korea and Taiwan Grew Rich', National Bureau of Economic Research Working Paper, 4964, 1994.
Segbers, Klaus (ed.), *Explaining Post-Soviet Patchworks. Volume 2: Pathways from the past to the global* (Aldershot: Ashgate, 2002).
Shleifer, Andrei and Treisman, Daniel, *Without a Map: Political Tactics and Economic Reform in Russia* (Cambridge, Mass: MIT Press, 2000).
Srinivasan, T. N., 'Neoclassical Political Economy: the State and Economic Development', *Politics and Society*, 17, no. 2 (1985)
Stiglitz, Joseph, *Globalization and its Discontent* (Washington, 2001).
Wendt, Alexander, 'The Agent-Structure Problem in International Relations Theory', *International Organization* 41, no. 3 (1987), pp. 335–70.
Williamson, John, 'What Washington Means by Policy Reform', in: John Williamson (ed.), *Latin American Adjustment: How Much has Happened?* (Washington D.C.: Institute for International Economics, 1990).
—— 'What Should the World Bank Think About the Washington Consensus?', *World Bank Research Observer*, 15, no. 2 (2000), pp. 251–264.
World Bank, *Transition Newsletter*, 14, no. 1–3 (2003a).
—— *Russian Economic Report* (Moscow: World Bank, 2003b).

—— *World Development Report: The State in the Changing World* (New York, 1997a).

—— *Helping Countries Combat Corruption: The Role of the World Bank* (Washington, DC: World Bank, 1997b).

—— *World Development Report 1996: From Plan to Market* (Washington, DC. Oxford University Press, 1996).

LUKASZ HARDT

Institutional Disequilibrium: Formal Institutions in Polish Cultural Space

> It is now becoming apparent that the transplantation of formal law does not necessarily alter behavior ... .Where formal and informal institutions evolve over time, they tend to complement each other. In the context of a political or economic regime change, however, new formal and pre-existing informal institutions compete. Formal law may be rejected, or ignored and substituted with informal institutions that operate independently of and frequently in contradiction to the formal legal system. (Katharina Pistor).[1]

Introduction

Institutions, understood as rules of the game, affect economic practices and relationships, and are responsible for social and economic order. Formal and informal institutions complement each other in sustaining economic and social stability. Douglass North states that the major role of institutions is to establish 'a stable (but not necessarily efficient) structure to human interaction.'[2] Institutions, by lowering costs of economic transactions and reducing uncertainty, make cooperation possible. Without legal rules, social sanctions and trust, economic actors would find trading goods, hiring workers and co-operating with colleagues quite difficult as there is always a temptation to cheat. By its very nature, institutions are quite stable. However, institutional

1 Katharina Pistor, 'The Evolution of Legal Institutions', paper prepared for the Annual World Bank Conference on Development Economics in Europe on Governance, Equity and Global Markets, Paris 21–23 June 1999, p. 2

2 Douglass North, *Institutions, Institutional Change and Economic Performance* (Cambridge: Cambridge University Press, 1990), p. 6.

change[3] is possible, but it should be incremental rather than discontinuous. In order to understand the dynamics of institutional change, different characteristics of formal and informal institutions should be taken into account. According to North these differences can be explained as follows: 'although formal rules may change overnight as a result of political or juridical decisions, informal constraints embodied in customs, traditions, and codes of conduct are much more impervious to deliberate policies. These cultural constraints not only connect the past with the present and future, but provide us with a key to explaining the path of historical change.'[4] Thus, the core problem is whether we can change formal rules in order to implement new institutional matrix without taking into account informal mechanisms.[5] Katharina Pistor's quotation at the beginning of the chapter addresses this point too. This is a key issue in post-communist countries, where new institutions are imported from the West and implemented in societies with little to no democratic and capitalistic traditions.

North describes this problem as an 'institutional disequilibrium'; the tension and conflict between formal and informal institutions, which produces inefficient outcomes. Balcerowicz points to this phenomenon in discussing the transformation of post-socialist countries with a communist legacy embodied in people's behavior and mentality.[6] It is certain that the communist legacy influences our decisions; however, the question is to what extent. It is worth noticing, that Balcerowicz claims that informal institutions, namely the communist legacy, can be changed by formal ones, for example shock therapy.

3 In this chapter, we will focus on the imposed institutional change, precisely a change that is introduced by government decision. We do not put emphasis on the induced institutional change, which can be understood as the voluntary response of the individuals to a change in external conditions (for an in-depth study on the difference between induced and imposed institutional change, see e.g., Justin Yifu Lin, 'An Economic Theory of Institutional Change: Induced and Imposed Change', *Cato Journal*, 9 (September 1989), pp. 1–33).

4 North, *Institutions, Institutional Change and Economic Performance*, p. 6.

5 The institutional matrix is defined as the set of institutions (rules) which form the incentive structure of the society.

6 Leszek Balcerowicz, *Socialism, Capitalism, Transformation* (Budapest: Central European University Press, 1995).

Though, many thinkers argue that an effective law system could only arise through formalization of informal and decentralized mechanisms created by the civil society, as Pistor suggests. Yet, transition economies operate the other way round. In this chapter, we highlight some institutional disequilibria in the Polish transition economy, and what analytical frameworks can be employed to make sense of the relationship between individuals, institutions and technology. We will suggest that a new socio-economic paradigm is required.

The Role of Institutions in Transition Economies

After fifteen years of transition one could notice a great economic diversity among former communist countries. Some countries, for example Hungary and Poland, succeeded on their way to free market, but some, like Ukraine, failed. Neoclassical economics cannot explain why the same reforms implemented in Poland and Russia resulted in different outcomes. Not only ordinary people were surprised, but also economists who had thought that liberalization and deregulation would work equally well everywhere. After more than a decade of transition, it is obvious that culture, religion, and tradition matter. Thus, they should be taken into consideration while analyzing market reforms. When neoclassical methods of economic analysis are insufficient for explaining such economic outcomes, we must take into account how people behave, and what, social, cultural and human assets they possess. Balcerowicz, the author of shock therapy in Poland, claims that socialism is still in our minds and in everyday interactions. Not surprisingly, he stated in his book, *Socialism, Capitalism, Transformation*, that as well as classical economic measures, psychological and sociological circumstances should be taken into account when designing reforms. In a way, Balcerowicz supports the hypothesis that transition economies can be affected by instituteional disequilibria. If institutions had played no role in creating and sustaining market order, then one could have created market economy 'artificially' by formal measures. However, the experience of post-communist countries suggests otherwise.

Cases of institutional disequilibria could be easily found in Poland. At the beginning of the economic transition, many new institutions were imported from the West. In 1990, Parliament voted a law establishing a stock exchange in Warsaw, similar to Western European stock markets. Consequently, very few people in Poland knew what the stock market was, or how it functioned. The majority of the Poles treated stock market like a casino or lottery. However, this has changed over the last decade or so. Platteau argues that 'legality is better established in countries that have developed a legal order internally or in those that have familiarity with the country or countries from which they have taken the legal order, or again in those that have transplanted the external formal legal order with significant adaptation so as to make it appropriate to prevailing conditions.'[7] Consequently, the same stock market law that is taken from western countries works more efficiently in countries that are similar in terms of civic and economic tradition to the West. After decades of communist rule, Warsaw could hardly be regarded as similar to London or New York!

Another example of institutional disequilibrium was the legal attempt of the Polish government to create large producer groups in agriculture by giving farmers strong financial incentives to integrate and merge their businesses. However, only a few dozens of producer groups have merged. Why did the farmers not establish producer groups despite strong financial motivation? One answer is that Polish farmers have low-trust of each other, so that they are afraid of being cheated by their prospective partners. The culture of distrust affects Polish rural communities, making joint ventures and co-operation problematic. Therefore, the government's attempt to establish large producers groups resulted in failure, as there was a mis-match between the intention of the formal law and farmers' social practices.[8]

7 Jean-Philippe Platteau, 'Market Order, the Rule of Law and Moral Norms', unpublished working paper, FUNDP University, 2000, p. 5.

8 For an in-depth study on the factors hampering the establishment of producer groups in Poland, see Kai Maack, 'An Analysis of Business Relations in the German and Polish Fruit Supply Chain', Paper prepared for the 15th Annual

The crucial role of trust in sustaining social and economic order in post-communist countries is stressed by Misztal.[9] Trust can be understood as an important informal institution, because it reduces the costs of transacting with each other, and uncertainty about contracts and social climate of business. Even well designed formal institutions regulating interactions among people would be inefficient without trust. One could say that 'without trust life would not be possible.'[10] The cornerstones of economic order are cooperation and exchange. Thus trust can ease that process and makes economic exchange less costly and consequently more efficient. In a society of free riders, it is hardly imaginable to implement any reform requiring without a certain level of trust. That is a case of many post-communist countries where people are used to free ride on the state due to their deeply internalized conception of the state as a totalitarian one. Therefore, the combination of social distrust and suspicion with social order being imposed from above makes the tension with western institutions and practices more problematic and harmful to the functioning of socioeconomic system. This is a case in many post-communist countries.

Territorial Reform in Poland

One of the most striking examples of institutional disequilibrium is the territorial reform, namely the introduction of county (*powiat*) and self-governed province (*wojewodztwo*). This reform introduced democratic elections at the local level, transferred the ownership of public property from the central to local communities, and decoupled local budgets from the central one. Decentralization gave a strong impulse for polit-

Food and Agribusiness Forum, Symposium and Case Conference Chicago, 25–28 June 2005.

9 Barbara Misztal, *Trust in Modern Societies* (Bristol: Policy Press, 1996). In that book, the author focuses on Western democracies, however, there is a strong comparative emphasis with reference to Eastern and Central European societies.

10 Ibid., p. 13.

ical activism, offered more responsibility to local governments, and put a share of income taxes in the hands of local authorities. Territorial reform was designed to achieve the following:

- to dismantle the administrative system originating from the communist period;
- to transfer power from the center to the locally governed territorial units hoping that they would make better use of existing information, and consequently would be more efficient (sub sidiary principle);
- to decentralize decision-making, so that risk would be diversified and operations transformed into many smaller ones; and[11]
- to stimulate civil society by creating elected local councils.

Yet, local governments act inefficiently due to incoherently designed legal system and lack of understanding of reforms by ordinary people. Counties are unable to perform their duties, e.g., local hospitals are badly resourced and funded and the local infrastructure (including roads) is in poor state. On the one hand, the new legal system promotes decentralization by transferring power from the centre to local governments; but on the other hand, it does not guarantee enough money for counties and provinces to fulfill their new duties. There is a suspicion that the central government did not really want Poland to be decentralized. Politicians at the centre simply changed the way they controlled the local affairs. Instead of direct control, they used a system of direct payments and subsidies.[12] As a result, independence of counties is questionable. The following data supports this thesis:

11 Joseph Stiglitz, 'Whither Reform? Ten Years of the Transition', Keynote Address at the World Bank Annual Bank Conference On Development Economics, Washington D.C., World Bank, 1999.

12 Political property rights are defined as the right to change private property rights. Economic actors compete for property rights, rather than for political property rights as politicians do.

Table 1. Incomes of local governments in Poland (in percent).

Sources of incomes	Municipality (*gmina*)	County (*powiat*)	Province (*wojewodztwo*)
Self-generated revenues (e.g., immovable property tax)	55.5	5.1	22.2
Subsidies (e.g., monetary assistance granted by government for financing primary and secondary schools, and local infrastructure)	35.4	46.5	42.1
Direct payments (i.e., government co-financing of various tasks within the prerogatives of local governments, e.g., police)	9.1	48.4	35.7

Source: Ministry of Finance, May 2001

From the above table we can see that the most independent of local governments is the municipality.[13] Slightly worse situation is at the provincial level. The worst income structure is the counties. The counties without their own revenues are, by definition, dependent on the central government. Consequently, the key goals of the territorial reform were not achieved. However, only in the municipalities' case were the goals and the reform partially successful.

Not only do the financial aspects matter in the case of territorial reform, but also people's attitudes towards the reform. First, the new institutions constituting the decentralized system need people's participation to work efficiently. The idea of decentralization is to give power into the people's hands. If the inhabitant are not interested in local issues and do not want to participate in local political life, then the system will fail to achieve its aims and collapse. In many cases,

13 The share of self-generated income to total revenue measures the territorial unit level of independence.

there was public apathy, resulting in the people not engaging with the new institutions.

Second, people should know how the system works. Opinion polls show that Poles do not know the functions of different levels of local governments. The Public Opinion Research Center (CBOS) asked in 2000, 'Are you well informed about the new levels of local governments (what affairs are in a county's control)?'[14] Nearly 77% of respondents answered that they have only remote ideas of local governments' prerogatives. People also see the new institutions just as the previous ones. Counties are perceived as former government's administrative units (*urzad rejonowy*), province is perceived as a superior level of local governments created in order to control counties and municipalities. Thus, people perceive the reality subjectively. Following Denzau and North, one can say that people see the outside world through their own descriptions, concepts and models, which 'are the internal representations that individual cognitive system create to interpret the environment and the institutions are the external (to the mind) mechanisms individuals create to structure and order the environment.'[15] Taking into account that each person is not a *tabula rasa*, previously internalized mental models of public administration and local governments matter. People still regard the new administrative units as similar to those of the previous regime. Consequently, people complain to the chief of the county (*starosta*) about the mayor's decisions, however, there is no direct link between them. Thus informal institutions (deeply internalized way of structuring the outside world) contradict formal institutions (mechanisms establishing vertical structure of central and self-government administration) that results in institutional disequilibrium. Different institutional disequilibria are shown using the following diagram.

14 See CBOS, 'Cztery Reformy w Opinii Społecznej: Poinformowanie i Ocena' ['The Four Reforms: Social Perception'], National Survey, 2000.

15 Arthur Denzau and Douglass North, 'Shared Mental Models: Ideologies and Institutions', Working Paper, Center for the Study of Political Economy, Washington University, 1999, p. 2.

Graphic 1. Institutional disequilibria touching the system of local governments in Poland.

FORMAL INSTITUTIONS ⇨	⇦ INFORMAL INSTITUTIONS
CONTRADICTION	
Non-hierarchical system of self-governed administrative units established by formal law. ⇨	⇦ People's tendency towards hierarchization of the reality, including system of self-governed administrative units.
Prerogatives of newly established self – governed territorial units. ⇨	⇦ Deeply internalized mental models of local governments prerogatives'. People still think that self-governments have the same functions as they had in the communist époque.
Peoples' participation, required by formal law, makes it more efficient. ⇨	⇦ Lack of the civil society. One can hardly find any spontaneous initiatives concerning functioning of the territorial governments.

Taking into account the characteristics of divergences between formal and informal institutions, one could argue that history also matters. Not only the public, but also politicians who prepared territorial reform, are 'locked-in by historical events.'[16] It means that institutions

16 North, *Institutions, Institutional Change and Economic Performance*, p. 94.

are path-dependent; once they prevail, institutions establish practices in a particular manner. Not surprisingly, this phenomenon can be noticed in the legal system constituting the institutional matrix for local governments. In 1998, Parliament created 376 counties, pretty much the same number as before 1975, when the communist government liquidated counties. An analysis made by Kiezun shows that the most appropriate number of counties is about one hundred.[17] But 376 counties were created. Why? One could answer that politicians are 'locked-in by historical events', which resulted in creation of the same structure as it had been before. Therefore, history and institutions matter.

Toward a New Socio-Economic Paradigm[18]

The above-presented discussion raises the following question: what method should be used in order to properly analyze institutional change? As it was shown, new institutional economics (NIE) offers some useful tools such as the concept of institutional disequilibrium. However, many aspect of institutional change are still poorly understood within institutional economics framework. Nor is examining institutional change through the theoretical lens of sociology of institutional change a solution.[19] The core assumption of sociology of institutional change is that societal change is characterized by inertia and hence it is difficult to change socioeconomic system quickly. However, sociology of institutional change does not offer a simple and comprehensible definition of institution as NIE does. The research program of NIE is individualistic, as individual self-interest dictates

17 Witold Kiezun, 'Powiaty – Fikcja Samorzadnosci' ['Counties – the Illusion of Self-governance'], in *Rzeczpospolita*, 258 (5 November 2001), p. A8.

18 This section is based on the discussion entitled 'Critical Forum: "Toward a New Socio Economic Paradigm"', *Socio-Economic Review*, 1, no. 1 (2003), pp. 105–134.

19 Some of the main contributors to this field are Claus Offe, Jon Elster, David Stark, Laszlo Bruszt, Piotr Sztompka, and Andrzej Rychard.

how institutions operate. However, sociology of institutional change offers group analysis, and how collective actors and norms affect practices and relationships. NIE assumes that people are poor processors of information and hence they act to save scarce cognitive resources. Sociology of institutional change neglects the cognitive dimension of socioeconomic system, but raises the question of networks, norms, social capital and their role in the dynamics of societal change.

A paradigmatic shift is necessary in order to develop a socio-economic approach, namely a research program, which will combine NIE and sociology of institutional change. The socio-economic approach should be based more on induction, less on deduction in order to avoid the idealism of neoclassical economics. The emergence of the new paradigm should be stimulated by continuing development of NIE and especially its departure from the neoclassical assumptions (e.g., perfect information and zero transaction costs). On the other hand, sociology of institutional change should broaden its research program in order to incorporate the achievements of cognitive sciences, political sciences, and psychology. As the number of inexplicable characteristics of the process of institutional change grows (e.g. different outcomes of the same market reforms in various countries), 'there comes a point when some practitioners of the discipline no longer consider the current paradigm tenable and start looking for a modified or improved one. As this sentiment spreads, the discipline enters into a crisis: practitioners are no longer convinced that their theory and associated research procedures are well-founded. An outsider may have the impression that research stagnates and that there are interminable discussions about foundations and methodology.'[20]

Prospective practitioners of the new paradigm can be found among institutional economists, critical sociologists and scientists working in cognitive sciences departments. What is needed is the will to use an interdisciplinary approach, namely vigorous methods of modern economics (including quantitative ones) combined with more sociological tools of analysis. Douglass North called the new para-

20 Ejan Mackaay, 'Schools: General', in Boudewijn Bouckaert and Gerrit De Geest (eds), *Encyclopedia of Law and Economics* (Cheltenham: Edward Elgar Publishing, 2000), pp. 404 – 405.

digm as an institutional/cognitive one.[21] According to North the emergence of the new paradigm will achieve the following:

- to explain path-dependent phenomena;
- to explicate the interplay between institutions, technology and demography in the process of institutional change; and
- to find hidden patterns of economic performance.

There are more questions than answers about the new socio-economic paradigm. But one thing is clear: new institutional economics and sociology of institutional change are insufficient research programs to explain the dynamics of societal change. What is needed is a new paradigm, which should outgrow from the tradition of these two branches of sciences.

Some Concluding Remarks

Institutions significantly define and constitute the socioeconomic order. They help us to structure and understand the environment and predict how individuals will behave. Consequently, institutions reduce the cost of transacting with each other and uncertainty of future economic activities. Nobody can neglect the role of institutions in transition economies. Transition from plan to market can be understood as an institutional change. Government can easily change formal institutions. However, informal institutions cannot be affected so easily. As Balcerowicz stated one can gradually influence informal institutions by changing formal ones. Similarly, North says, '(...) a new informal equilibrium will evolve gradually after a change in the formal rules.'[22] Thus, to escape from institutional disequilibrium, one can change formal rules and wait until an equilibrium is reached.

21 Heard by the author during North's visit to the Faculty of Economic Sciences, Warsaw University in 2002.

22 North, *Institutions, Institutional Change and Economic Performance*, p. 86.

Various forms of institutional disequilibria were found in transition economies. Not surprisingly, formal institutions imported from the Western European countries are in tension and conflict with existing informal ones. Institutional economics approach argues that by not taking into account informal institutions, one cannot explain why well-designed formal laws fail. This was the case with the territorial reform in Poland. If the tradition of self-government had existed in Poland, then implementing county and province forms of self-government would have succeeded. It was shown that informal institutions conflict with formal ones, which results in institutional disequilibrium.

Finally, institutional economics approach has proved useful while analyzing many aspects of changes in the former communist states. However, the development of a new paradigm, which combines NIE and sociology of institutional change, is needed in order to better understand the dynamics of societal change. This remains the challenge for the current generation of economists and sociologists working interdisciplinarily on understanding and explaining major institutional changes and reforms in the former communist countries.

Bibliography

Balcerowicz, Leszek, *Socialism, Capitalism, Transformation* (Budapest: Central European University Press, 1995).

CBOS, 'Cztery Reformy w Opinii Społecznej: Poinformowanie i Ocena' ['The Four Reforms: Social Perception'] (National Survey, 2000).

Denzau, Arthur and North, Douglass, 'Shared Mental Models: Ideologies and Institutions', Working Paper, Center for the Study of Political Economy Washington University, Washington D.C., 1999.

Kiczun, Witold, 'Powiaty – Fikcja Samorzadnosci' ['Counties – the Illusion of Self-governance'], in *Rzeczpospolita*, 258 (5th November 2001), p. A8.

Mackaay, Ejan, 'Schools: General', in Boudewijn Bouckaert and Gerrit De Geest (eds.), *Encyclopedia of Law and Economics* (Cheltenham: Edward Elgar Publishing, 2000), pp. 402–415.

Maack, Kai, 'An Analysis of Business Relations in the German and Polish Fruit Supply Chain', paper prepared for the 15th Annual Food and Agribusiness Forum, Symposium and Case Conference, Chicago, 25–28 June 2005.

Misztal, Barbara, *Trust in Modern Societies* (Bristol: Policy Press, 1996).

North, Douglass, *Institutions, Institutional Change and Economic Performance* (Cambridge: Cambridge University Press, 1990).

Pistor, Katharina, 'The Evolution of Legal Institutions and Economic Regime Change', paper prepared for the Annual World Bank Conference on Development Economics in Europe on Governance, Equity and Global Markets, Paris, 21–23 June 1999.

Platteau, Jean-Philippe, 'Market Order, the Rule of Law and Moral Norms', unpublished working paper, FUNDP University, 2000.

Stiglitz, Joseph, 'Whither Reform? Ten Years of the Transition', Keynote Address at the World Bank Annual Bank Conference On Development Economics, Washington D.C., World Bank, 1999.

Yifu Lin, Justin, 'An Economic Theory of Institutional Change: Induced and Imposed Change', in *Cato Journal*, 9 (September 1989), pp. 1–33.

MAKS KOBONBAEV

The Failed Transition from a Planned to a Market System in Kyrgyzstan

After the demise of the Soviet Union the radical change from a planned to a market economy was instituted through structural adjustment programmes imposed by the International Monetary Fund and the World Bank. Kyrgyzstan has become one of the champions of the free-market economy among the post-Soviet countries. For instance, it was the first country to introduce a national currency, liberalize the internal and external trade regimes, and undertake aggressive privatization reforms.

However, the radical economic reforms have failed to deliver the promised results. Kyrgyzstan has not achieved successful economic transition and development. The question arises: why the radical reforms have not brought the promised expectations. Douglass North, argues that institutions matter in a society because they provide the rules of the game and incentives that govern human and organizational behavior.[1] He contends that economic change is a complex process that cannot be achieved without necessary changes in the formal and informal institutions and their enforcement characteristics.

The radical reforms initiated in Kyrgyzstan have neglected the importance of formal and informal institutions and their enforcement mechanisms in providing the enabling environment for successful reforms. For example, the lack of credible institutions, governing market operations (e.g., credible contracts, courts, sound tax collection agency, etc) during the early stages of the reforms reinforced rent seeking, tax evasion, patronage, and other forms of unproductive activities. In the absence of sound macro institutional environment, such as the weak

1 Douglass North, *Institutions, Institutional Change and Economic Performance* (Cambridge, England: Cambridge University Press, 1990), p. 118.

state governance and rule of law, corrupt and noncompliant activities have flourished and become deeply ingrained in the political, economic and social exchange, hindering economic development.[2]

Since 1990 post-Soviet societies experienced the largest decline in production output. The economic regress affected severely the living conditions of ordinary people. The majority of the people in the Soviet Union were employed in the industrial complex and in the public sector (e.g., teachers and doctors). These segments of society suffered the most because large industries became idle and the central government had no longer the capacity to subsidize the industrial complex and support the public sector. It was staggering to witness how well-educated teachers and doctors started to sell fruits in the market to earn a living.

Kyrgyzstan had been so dependent on the integrated Soviet economy and Moscow's financial assistance that it was hard to predict how the country would develop. Policy-makers immediately faced the difficulty of formulating the path of economic and political development. After ruling out the existing command economic system, they opted for reforms like other post-socialist countries. At that time, other countries, especially Poland and Russia, adopted the 'shock therapy' doctrine – a radical transformation from a planned economy to a market economy.[3] In the next section, the major assumptions of the radical transformation in Kyrgyzstan are discussed. Then, I will discuss the institutional approach, and its implications for the economic and political future. I will end with some concluding remarks.

2 Maks Kobonbaev, 'Informal Costs of Doing Business: The Case Study of the Registration and Regulation of Firms in Kyrgyzstan,' *Central Asian Journal of Management, Economics and Social Research*, 4, no. 1 (September 2004), p. 80.

3 For shock therapy doctrine, see John Marangos, 'The Political Economy of Shock Therapy,' *Journal of Economic Surveys*, 16, no. 1 (February 2002), pp. 41–76.

Radical Economic Transformation of Kyrgyzstan

The radical approach suggests that universal laws and reforms can be applied equally across countries. Moreover, these reforms can be initiated drastically through the destruction of the old system and the introduction of the new system.[4] In addition, the radical approach seemed attractive because by dismantling drastically and quickly the command economy, the new regime realized that the opposition could forestall the economic and political reforms at that time since the regime possess general goodwill and support from the public.

Furthermore, because of the lack of natural resources (unlike in Kazakhstan, Uzbekistan and Turkmenistan), the new government pushed for market-oriented reforms to seek international financial and technical assistance. Whereas other resource-rich countries could resist international pressures for reform by drawing on their oil, gas and mineral reserves Kyrgyzstan became dependent on the international financial system to secure economic survival.

Following the assumptions of radical transformation, the government officials introduced the structural adjustment program of liberalization and deregulation. The actions were initiated in six areas: macroeconomic stabilization, price liberalization, trade liberalization, current account convertibility, enterprise and institutional reform.[5] The first phase of reforms aimed at price and trade liberalization, which turned out to be successful. These reforms were very radical and in fact Fischer argues, 'the big bang could apply only to certain aspects of the reform process – macroeconomic stabilization and price and

4 Indeed, Sachs points out, 'the communist system was a despicable and inefficient system, but it was a system nonetheless' (Jeffrey Sachs, 'Privatization in Russia: Some Lessons from Eastern Europe', *The American Economic Review*, 82, no. 2 (1992), p. 43). That is to say, some advisors and experts to the governments of the formerly communist countries were aware that the old institutions had societal functions but the command system in general was inimical to the market economy and its drastic destruction was necessary.

5 Stanley Fischer, Ratna Sahay and Vegh A. Carlos, 'Stabilization and Growth in Transition Economies: The Early Experience', *The Journal of Economic Perspective*, 10, no. 2 (1996), p. 46.

trade liberalization. Other aspects of the reform process inherently take time.'[6]

In the second phase, technocrats undertook the enterprise reforms.[7] The enterprise reforms took place before the institutional reforms; i.e., privatizing the state enterprises occurred before the establishment of rules governing the proper functioning of enterprises, effective property rights and credible contract mechanisms. There were three stages to the privatization program.

The first stage was implemented from 1992 to 1993, and involved 'small-scale' privatization of enterprises in the trade, services and consumer products. This phase of privatization was relatively successful because 'small scale' enterprises were more familiar with market operations. The second stage started in 1994 and was named 'systematic' and 'mass' privatization. The mass privatization fitted well into the concept of radical transformation and was implemented through the exchange coupons. The Privatization of the Enterprises Special Adjustment Credit project (PESAC) under the World Bank carried out the privatization of 27 major industrial enterprises during this period.

The third stage, from 1996 to 1998, was a continuation or completion of the mass privatization program and incorporated the denationalization of major state-owned enterprises, monopolies and holding entities such as energy, telecommunication, and tourism infrastructure.[8] This stage was incomplete because there were no potential local investors in these capital-intensive sectors. The government hoped to attract foreign investors who had already invested in several sectors of the economy (e.g., 'Kumtor' Gold Operating Company and Hyatt Regency-Bishkek).

The proponents of radical reforms claim that the privatization program was successful since it achieved the result of denation-

6 Fischer, Sahay and Carlos, ibid., p. 46.

7 *Kyrgyz Republic Country Brief.* World Bank Group, 2005.

8 Askar Akaev, *Kyrgyzstan: An Economy in Transition* (Australia: Asian Pacific Press at the Australian National University, 2001), p. 128; Rafis Abazov, 'Policy of Economic Transition in Kyrgyzstan' *Central Asian Survey*, 18, no. 2 (1999), pp. 197–223.

alization of the state owned enterprises into the privately owned enterprises.[9] The number of state-owned enterprises decreased by six times from 1991 to 1998, and the number of privately owned enterprises increased to 20 times. If the state-owned enterprises generated 45.6% of the GDP in 1991, by 1998 it fell to 3.4%. In contrast, the privately owned enterprises gained 28% of the GDP in 1998 (see Table 1). The World Bank Data confirm the increasing role of the private sector in the Kyrgyz Republic. While the private sector share of GDP in 1991 was 18.8%, it became 76.4% in 1997 and the private sector share of employment rose from 26.1 in 1990 to 74.2 in 1997.[10] The biggest increase in the number of privately owned enterprises was in 1994 because of the top-down initiation of the mass privatization reforms (see Table 1).

In spite of the general satisfaction of the government with the privatization reforms, ordinary people have termed privatization a *prihvatization*, which can be translated from Russian as gaining ownership drastically and illegally. Shleifer and Vishny have also used a 'grabbing hand' analogy for prihvatization, in which politicians pursue their own selfish interests instead of the interests of the public.[11] Indeed, in the absence of institutions that protect property rights and enforce contracts, new entrepreneurs and often politicians themselves grabbed the state owned enterprises through machinations and manipulations, often surpassing the formally declared privatization laws and regulations. For instance, the winners of privatization biddings were often the participants who offered the highest bribes and who had the best connections instead of those who offered the highest bid or the best investment plans. The government sold enterprises at below their real value as the government sought to increase the number of denationalized entities rather than maximize the revenue

9 Anders Aslund, 'Kyrgyzstan, the Road to Sustained Economic Growth and Welfare', Working Paper, Carnegie Endowment for International Peace, Washington, D.C., 1998.

10 Public Enterprise Reform and Privatization Database, ECSPF and DECRG, The World Bank, 2005, available at: http://www.worldbank.org/ecspf/PSD-Yearbook/kyrgyz.html

11 Andrei Shleifer and Robert Vishny, *The Grabbing Hand: Government Pathologies and Their Cure* (Harvard: Harvard University Press, 1998).

from the sales. The government argued that as there was no capitalist class willing to invest into the existing state-run enterprises, they had to be sold off cheaply to encourage investors to buy them. Only those who were able to pay bribes, were in the higher echelons of the government or had access to government officials (e.g., relatives or friends) actively participated in privatization. Unfortunately, as Shleifer and Vishny note, in the absence of capitalist class, the privatization is the only fast way to toward the market system and the hope is that the growing private sector will pressure the state to credibly enforce contractual agreements and protect property rights afterwards.[12]

Table 1: Shift from State Owned Enterprises to Privately Owned Enterprises

	Number of State-Owned Enterprises		Number of Privately-Owned Enterprises		Number of Farms	
	Enterprises	Share of GDP	Number of Enterprises	Share of GDP	Farms	Share of GDP
1991	6794	45.6	406	2.6	4567	–
1992	6756	45.4	500	3.9	8695	0.8
1993	4862	33.3	3443	9.1	15810	2.0
1994	3947	17.9	5165	14.1	21264	2.5
1995	2076	13.5	5853	21.6	23180	6.3
1996	1548	10.3	5605	21.7	31078	11.8
1997	1438	7.7	8004	27.8	38724	11.7
1998	1071	3.4	8484	28.3	49277	12.4

Source: Askar Akaev, Kyrgyzstan: An Economy in Transition (Australia: Asia Pacific Press, 2001) (for the number of state and privately owned enterprises see, pp. 108–109, and for the number of farms, see, p. 121).

To sum up, only the first stage of privatization was relatively successful because it involved the privatization of small enterprises that were more adaptable to the market environment and less capital intensive. The second stage of mass privatization meant the destruc-

12 Shleifer and Vishny, ibid.

tion of the old enterprises rather than creating new ones. It was also a highly patronage type of privatization that boosted illegal practices. The third phase of privatization remained incomplete. The new entrepreneurial class that emerged after the previous privatization processes has been unable to make large investments due to the lack of capital. Gaining ownership illegally through bribes or other means has become a well-accepted practice.

Nonetheless, the beneficial part of privatization was the creation of private property rights that facilitated the creation of small and medium size enterprises, small farms and peasant enterprises, and became a first step for the formation of the entrepreneurial class. These reforms have established a partial market environment for business conduct. Yet, problems of large government bureaucracy, of complex and ineffective laws and of numerous government restrictions have not been solved.

While radical reforms created a partial market economy, they failed to boost economic development. The country faced economic crisis and decreased living standards of the population. The leading industrial sector has become the second sector after agriculture. The industrial output in 1993 was only 55.3% of the 1989 level.[13] The decline in national income from 1990 to 1994 was 74.1% and by 1995 national income was a mere 25.9% of that in 1990.[14] From 1991 to 1995, the real GDP declined to 50% of the 1990 level.[15] As Table 2 shows, the level of poverty in 1996 was 43.5%, and by 2000 more than half of the population lived in poverty. Poverty was more chronic and devastating in the rural and mountainous areas.

13 Koichuev, ibid., p. 171.
14 Koichuev, ibid., p. 171.
15 *World Bank Report*, 'Country Brief,' at: http://www.worldbank.org.kg/

Table 2: Poverty in Kyrgyzstan

	Per cent of All-Poor			Per cent Extremely Poor		
Year	Total	Urban	Rural	Total	Urban	Rural
1996	43.5	30.3	49.6	19.1	10.3	23.3
1997	42.9	22.2	55.3	14.8	4.9	20.7
1998	54.9	42.2	62.4	23.0	18.3	25.8
1999	55.3	42.4	60.0	22.3	17.1	25.6
2000	52.0	43.9	56.4	17.8	12.7	20.5

Source: *Comprehensive Development Framework*, 'The Comprehensive Development Framework of Kyrgyzstan to 2010: National Strategy.'

The decline in the economic output was largely a result of the economic disintegration. Garland states that Kyrgyzstan was overly dependent on trade with the former Soviet countries and the sudden disruption of this relationship resulted in a loss of output. Soviet Kyrgyzstani economy was an integrated economic system, and the loss of imported raw materials, intermediate goods and access to output markets resulted in the output decline.[16]

Institutional Approach to the Economic Transition

> In almost all societies, the socioeconomic framework has been built up in a gradual process of accumulating small changes. As each new institution arises, it is fitted into a larger pre-existing structure.[17]
>
> While the rules may be changed overnight, the informal norms usually change gradually. Since it is the norms that provide 'legitimacy' to a set of

16 John Garland, 'Evolution and Emergence of Markets in a Developing Post-Socialist Economy: The Case of Kyrgyzstan', in Horst Brezinski and Michael Fritsch (eds), *The Emergence and Evolution of Markets* (US: Edward Elgar, 1997), p. 181.

17 Peter Murrell, 'Conservative Political Philosophy and the Strategy of Economic Transition', *East European Politics and Societies*, 6, no. 1 (1992), p. 4.

> rules, revolutionary [radical] change is never as revolutionary as its supporters desire, and performance will be different than anticipated.[18]

Institutions matter because they include constraints that shape human interaction. Institutions in a society provide the rules of the game that shape the incentives for individuals to engage in productive or destructive activities. Institutions can be formal and informal. Formal institutions are written or codified rules and informal constraints are unwritten norms of conduct. In other words, formal institutions are rules that human agents devise to provide a framework within which human interactions take place. Informal constraints are norms and codes of behavior that humans naturally follow. [19] There are two major assumptions of the institutional change that need be considered in understanding the failure of transition in Kyrgyzstan. First, institutions change and adjust gradually overtime, in particular informal institutions. Second, informal institutions matter as much as formal institutions, especially in developing countries.

Gradual Change of Institutions

The radical approach to economic transformation suggests that the economic knowledge that was a product of evolutionary development in the West could be applied without modification to Kyrgyzstan, and makes it prosperous in a short period of time. It was rather idealistic to imagine such a positive scenario. In reality, the consequences of radical reforms have turned out to be lamentable as we illustrated in the previous section.

In contrast, the advocates of incremental reforms (e.g., Polanyi, Popper, Lindblom, etc)[20] contend that society's social constructs are

18 Douglass North, 'Economic Performance Through Time', *The American Economic Review*, 84, no. 3 (1994), p. 366.

19 For formal and informal institutions, see North, *Institutions, Institutional Change and Economic Performance*, pp. 36–54.

20 Michael, Polanyi, *The Tacit Dimension* (New York: Anchor Books, 1967), Karl Popper, *All Life is Problem Solving* (London: Routledge, 1999); Charles Lind-

based on two types of knowledge: the explicit technical knowledge as well as the implicit practical type. The nature of implicit practical knowledge suggests that people in emerging societies cannot quickly acquire the knowledge required to implement radical policy, and that a gradual and incremental policy approach is more relevant.[21] This is in contrast with the radical approach of immediate change of ownership rights and mass privatization implementation that technocrats suggested for Kyrgyzstan.

Murrel, one of the major proponents of gradual change, argues that the radical approach focuses on the outcome to replace existing institutional structures urgently, without concern about the immediate economic costs to society. [22] The existing state enterprises will need changes in specialization, production technology and market orientation, and a swift changeover to the market system endangers the output of existing enterprises.

Small innovations that foster growth can be more suitable based on incremental changes. The implication is that perhaps too much damage is done by the radical privatization of the state sector. A gradual transformation approach rests on a more systemic understanding of personal and organizational behavior and the role of institutions, and accounts for path dependence, existing institutions and norms.

blom, 'The Science of Muddling Through', in Stella Theodoulou and Matthew Cahn (eds.), *Public Policy* (New Jersey: Prentice Hall, 1995).

21 For instance, Lindblom argues that there are limits in human capacity to approach policy problems comprehensively and rationally. Policy makers approach policies within a framework given by their 'view of a chain of successive policy choices made up to the present' using trials and errors to eliminate irrelevant alternatives and solutions (see Charles Lindblom, p. 126).

22 Peter Murrell, 'Evolution in Economics and in the Economic Reform of the Centrally Planned Economies', in Christopher Clague and Gordon Rausser (eds.), *The Emergence of Market Economies in Eastern Europe* (Blackwell: Cambridge: Massachusetts, 1992), pp. 35–55.

Informal Institutions: Problems of Corruption and Noncompliance

It is important to note that the same formal rules imposed on different societies produces different patterns of development depending on societal values, habits, routines, cultural heritage, historical experience and past polities. While the formal institutions and rules can be changed quickly, the informal norms can be changed or are changed gradually.[23] It means that the drastic introduction of new formal institutions and rules consistent with the market economy in Kyrgyzstan has not necessarily made these institutions and rules workable and effecttive.

The assumption of policy-makers that the radical model would bring the development of formal institutions consistent with the market economy has not materialized. Polishchuk points out that opportunistic politicians and misleading policies have resulted in a weak economic transition.[24] Instead, market institutions emerge in an incremental manner that become fully functioning if members of the society respect them.

The absence of formal institutions that could support effective functioning of input markets has generated an institutional vacuum. The institutional vacuum during the early stages of the reforms created 'socially counterproductive surrogates for missing institutions.'[25] In the absence of appropriate institutions and rules supporting the new market system, social actors have constructed alternatives, such as 'networks of closed relationships'. Unfortunately, these new informal norms of interaction have become antithetical to the functioning of the market economy, creating an underground economy characterized by noncompliance and tax evasion. Let me illustrate one simple example from the real-life situation that describes the systemic nature of noncompliance in Kyrgyzstan:

23 North, *Institutions, Institutional Change and Economic Performance*, pp. 83–118.

24 Leonid Polishchuk, 'Missed Markets: Implications for Economic Behavior and Institutional Change', in Joan Nelson, Charles Tilly and Lee Walker (eds.), *Transforming Post-Communist Political Economies* (Washington D.C: National Academy Press, 1997), p. 99.

25 Polishchuk, ibid., p. 98.

Imagine that a law-abiding person, whom I call a 'good guy,' wakes up in the morning and decides to drive to work. The good guy stops on the red traffic light while others continue to drive. When he starts to drive on the green light, drivers do not yield the right of way. While he continues to drive, the state traffic inspector stops him. The good guy makes sure that all the documents are proper and gives them to the inspector. The inspector tacitly wants the good guy to give the bribe but the good guy does not do so. As a result, the inspector checks the technical safety of the car, asks for the first-aid box and other numerous things to keep the good guy nervous. The inspector finally gives up and lets the good guy go. Although the good guy does not pay anything, he is nervous and late for his work. Imagine that the good guy faces this problem at least twice a week and at least twice a week he apologizes for being late to his boss.

The good guy's colleagues at work are noncompliant citizens – 'smart guys.' Smart guys seldom stop on the red light. When a traffic inspector stops them, they give bribes instead of giving documents for timely and unpleasant scrutiny. A happy inspector wishes good luck to smart guys and sometimes they establish good relations so that when they meet next time, the inspector does not stop them. Thus, smart guys are never late at work. They never regret the bribes they pay to inspectors because they take bribes from their clients as well (especially if they work for one of the state agencies). Most bosses of the state agencies appreciate smart guys because they share revenues gained from bribes together. Smart guys are very loyal and have prospects for career advancement. With regard to the bosses, inspectors never stop them because they drive cars with government plates. The bosses benefit from the noncompliant system, and possess many 'evasion privileges' such as traffic rule evasions. The conclusion from this simple illustration is revealing. The law-abiding person experiences many problems in a system riddled with corruption. It seems that one day the low-abiding person will join the smart guys, as the social cost of being a good guy is too high.

Leff has argued that corruption is functional because it promotes private investment and competition. Leff claims that corruption allows businesses to get around a maze of government regulations.[26] In other words, corruption allows firms to avoid burdensome regulations or confiscatory tax rates and thus decreases the economic costs of transactions.

Likewise Nye (1968) has outlined both benefits and costs of corruption on development. In his view, corruption can benefit development in several ways: (i) it can be an important source of capital formation; (ii) it can allow businesses to get around red tape; and (iii) it can foster entrepreneurship and allow entrepreneurs to get access to political decisions. At the same time, there is no guarantee that capital may be invested and investments may be channeled into productive activities.[27]

However, during the last decade, innovative research in understanding corruption, governance and institutions has been conducted. Murphy, Shleifer and Vishny assert that rent-seeking activities distort investment climate and hinder entrepreneurship.[28] In 1995, the publication of Mauro's article on corruption and Keefer and Knack's article on institutions challenged the myth of positive effect of corruption on development.[29]

The lack of rule of law and the prevalence of predatory non-compliant behaviors by political, economic and social actors are the main obstacles for economic development and political stability in Kyrgyzstan. When people constantly engage in non-compliant behav-

26 Nathaniel Leff, 'Economic Development through Bureaucratic Corruption', *American Behavioral Scientist*, 8, no. 2 (1964), pp. 8–14.

27 Joseph Nye, 'Corruption and Political Development: A Cost Benefit Analysis', *American Political Science Review*, 61, no. 2 (1967), pp. 419–422.

28 Kevin Murphy, Andrei Shleifer, and Robert Vishny. 'Why is Rent-Seeking so Costly to Growth', *American Economic Review*, 83, no. 2 (1993), pp. 409–414.

29 Mauro, using the indices of bureaucratic efficiency, provides empirical evidence on the negative effect of corruption on investment and growth. Based on indices such as bureaucratic quality, corruption in government and rule of law, Keefer and Knack provide empirical evidence for the positive effect of institutional quality on investment and growth (see Paolo Mauro, 'Corruption and Growth', *Quarterly Journal of Economics*, 110, no. 3 (1995), pp. 681–712, and Philip Keefer and Stephen Knack, 'Institutions and Economic Performance: Cross-Country Tests Using Alternative Institutional Measures', *Economics and Politics*, 7, no. 3 (1995), pp. 207–227.

iors, the system becomes chaotic. The main custodians of law such as the government officials and lawyers benefit from the noncompliant system and participate in the creation of new institutions of non-compliance.[30]

Some Implications of the Institutional Approach

Montesquieu, in *The Spirit of the Laws in 1748*, wrote that the institutions of one nation were not suitable to another. Evidently, political institutions should respond to the needs of local conditions and have the likelihood of becoming legitimate. The country ownership of its political institutions is essential for successful development. Only when politicians have stakes in the future of their country can they design institutions that can balance stability and development.[31] There are no universal institutional designs that can be equally applied to all countries.[32] Even though the design of political institutions is a unique process and there is uncertainty on what would work in Kyrgyzstan, several general recommendations to address corruption and non-compliance can be offered.

30 Kobonbaev, ibid., p. 90.

31 The process of institutional design in the United States and United Kingdom are cases in point. Besides, China has created its own unique institutional setting of strong national government balanced by the degree of freedom to conduct market activities by provincial governments to balance Marxism with capitalism. Even overly centralized system in the U.S.S.R had worked relatively well up until 1980s because the political institutions were more or less capable, and credible.

32 For the uniqueness of institutional design in the UK, see Barry Weingast, 'The Political Foundations of Limited Government: Parliament and Sovereign Debt in 17th- and 18th-Century England', in John Drobak and John Nye (eds.), *The Frontiers of New Institutional Economics* (San Diego: Academic Press, 1997).

Promote Secure Property Rights and Rule of Law

Coase emphasizes the impact of proper definition of property rights on transaction costs.[33] Alston, Eggertson and North argue that the link between institutions and wealth is curtailed when property rights to valuable assets are undefined because vague property rights tend to give rise to wasteful behavior and stay with individuals who do not put the assets to their most valuable uses.[34] The rule of law and secure property rights are essential to reduce corruption and provide favorable business investment climate. The formation of the private sector requires well-defined property rights that ensure security from government expropriation, and in place independent courts that provide arbitrage and rule of law.

These are essential market institutions that provide incentives for entrepreneurs to commence and expand their businesses. Firms and entrepreneurs make investments if they have a certain degree of predictability of future events. In other words, they calculate within their capacity the costs and risks of investing in certain types of business opportunities. Corruption and insecure property rights increase the uncertainty and costs of doing business.[35] To ensure secure property rights, the government should strengthen the independence and capacity of the judicial system while forming a highly competitive system of recruitment of lawyers.

Simplify Regulatory Business Environment

The role of regulation of business entry and conduct can enable and constrain firms operating in a market economy. For example, de Soto argues that cumbersome regulatory regimes are the root causes of the formation of the shadow economy. de Soto's famous experiment to set

33 Ronald Coase, *The Firm, the Market and the Law* (Chicago: University of Chicago Press, 1988).

34 Lee Alston, Thrainn Eggertsson, and Douglass North (eds.), *Empirical Studies in Institutional Change* (Cambridge University Press, 1996).

35 Kobonbaev, ibid.

up a small garment firm on the outskirts of Lima is a case in point. It took de Soto's team 289 days to fulfill 11 requirements and cost US$194 including two bribes they were obliged to pay to fulfill the task.[36] Djankov *et al.*, show that in order to start a business in Mozambique, an entrepreneur completes 19 procedures and spends 149 days. In Canada it takes only two procedures and two days. Moreover, countries with onerous regulations have higher corruption, larger informal economy and lesser economic development.[37]

Regulatory regimes essentially consist of two parts: registration and regulation of businesses. With regards to the registration, the government could publicize the simplicity of registration process and sanction mid-level bureaucrats for engaging in bribery. While it is not very difficult to improve the registration process, it is challenging to improve the regulation of existing businesses. From 1999 to 2000, the size of the informal economy in Kyrgyzstan constituted 39 per cent of the entire GNP. According to Schneider's data, the natural level of informal economy should be below 20 percent. For example, the average share of the informal economy in the OECD countries is below 18 percent of GNP. [38]

The government should make efforts to formalize the informal economy by providing economic incentives such as tax breaks and government subsidies. Moreover, the provision of secure property rights can provide incentives for firms to abandon the shadow economy. It is suggested that firms earn higher profits by minimizing formal payments (e.g., taxes, registration fees, inspection fees, etc). By reducing formal payments, the government can attract business in the formal economy.

36 Andrew Stone, Brian Levy and Ricardo Paredes, 'Public Institutions and Private Transactions: A Comparative Analysis of the Legal and Regulatory Environment for Business Transactions in Brazil and Chile', in Lee Alston, Thrainn Eggertsson, and Douglass North (eds.), ibid., p. 105

37 Simeon Djankov, Rafael La Porta, Florencio Lopez-de-Silanes, and Andrei Shleifer, 'Regulation of Entry', *Quarterly Journal of Economics*, 117, no. 1 (2002) pp. 1–37.

38 Friedrich Schneider, 'Size and Measurement of the Informal Economy in 110 Countries around the World', paper presented at the Australian National Tax Center Workshop, Canberra, Australia, 2002.

Ensure Transparency in the State Administration

The state plays a crucial role in providing predictable taxation policy, secure property rights and rule of law. While the government should be exempt from corruption, political elites benefit from corruption and the challenge is to make these beneficiaries commit themselves credibly to put an end to the main source of their wealth and power. The first step in fighting corruption is to reform the executive branch to make it more capable, legitimate and transparent. In this respect, bureaucracies must be coordinated and simplified. Existing government bureaucracies are characterized by non-transparent expenditures, the lack of clear division of authorities and functions between politically elected and appointed officials.

The tradition of appointments on the basis of loyalty, region and tribes should be changed to a merit-based system of recruitment. Salaries of bureaucrats need to be increased. Of course, low salaries encourage corruption but high salaries are not panacea to corruption when it penetrates deeply into the political culture. Yet, performance based salaries and other incentives are essential for an accountable and professional state administration. A merit-based system and higher salaries can recruit a more accountable generation of younger managers to the state service, who are employed currently in the private sector and international development projects.

The reforms in state bureaucracies can increase the credibility and capacity of the state to provide public goods. Indeed, a strong and capable state is essential until an independent judiciary emerges to ensure the rule of law. The checks and balances should be exerted by an independent judiciary, the parliament, the private sector and political parties. In addition, civil society needs to be nourished. NGOs can play a role in fostering democracy and combating corruption, making people aware of their rights, counterbalancing the power of the government.

Conclusion

After the collapse of the Soviet Union, Kyrgyzstan had implemented radical economic reforms. Unfortunately, the radical reforms have failed to work in Kyrgyzstan. One of the alternatives to the radical approach is an institutional transformation that rests on a better understanding of the role of institutions and values. North shows that institutions form an incentive structure made of formal and informal constraints, and thus are the underlying determinants of economic performance.[39] Thus, the difference in some countries' success and failure in promoting growth depends on how these economies nurture institutions such as the legal system, property and contract rights, governance and compliance structures, and technical and social infrastructure to support economic output. North stresses the role of the state at the initial stages of economic transition to enforce formal rule. However, 'the long-term economic growth entails change in informal norms and the development of the rule of law.'[40]

Bibliography

Abazov, Rafis, 'Policy of Economic Transition in Kyrgyzstan' *Central Asian Survey*, 18, no. 2 (1999), pp. 197–223.

Alston, Lee, Eggertsson, Thrainn and North, Douglass (eds), *Empirical Studies in Institutional Change* (Cambridge: Cambridge University Press, 1996).

Akaev, Askar, *Kyrgyzstan: An Economy in Transition* (Australia: Asian Pacific Press at the Australian National University, 2001)

Aslund, Anders 'Kyrgyzstan, the Road to Sustained Economic Growth and Welfare' (Carnegie Endowment for International Peace, Washington, DC: 1998).

39 North, *Institutions, Institutional Change and Economic Performance*, p. 107.
40 Douglass North, 'Economic Performance Through Time,' p. 367.

Comprehensive Development Framework, 'The Comprehensive Development Framework of the Kyrgyz Republic to 2010: National Strategy,' at http://www.cdf.gov.kg/

Coase, Ronald, *The Firm, the Market and the Law* (Chicago: University of Chicago Press, 1988).

Djankov, Simeon, La Porta, Rafael, Lopez-de-Silanes, Florencio and Shleifer, Andrei, 'Regulation of Entry', *Quarterly Journal of Economics*, 117, no. 1 (2002) pp. 1–37.

Fischer, Stanley, Sahay, Ratna and Carlos, Vegh, 'Stabilization and Growth in Transition Economies: The Early Experience', *The Journal of Economic Perspective*, 10, no. 2 (1996), pp. 45–66

Garland, John, 'Evolution and Emergence of Markets in a Developing Post-Socialist Economy: The Case of Kyrgyzstan', in Horst Brezinski and Michael Fritsch (eds.) *The Emergence and Evolution of Markets* (US: Edward Elgar, 1997).

Leff, Nathaniel, 'Economic Development through Bureaucratic Corruption', *American Behavioral Scientist*, 8, no. 2 (1964), pp. 8–14.

Lindblom, Charles, 'The Science of Muddling Through', in Stella Theodoulou and Matthew Cahn (eds.), *Public Policy* (New Jersey: Prentice Hall, 1995).

Keefer, Philip and Knack, Stephen, 'Institutions and Economic Performance: Cross-Country Tests Using Alternative Institutional Measures', *Economics and Politics*, 7, no. 3 (1995), pp. 207–227.

Kyrgyz Republic Country Brief. World Bank Group, 2005.

Koichuev, Turar, 'Kyrgyzstan Economic Crisis and Transition Strategy', in Boris Rumer (ed), *Central Asia in Transition* (London: M.E. Sharpe, 1996)

Kobonbaev, Maks, 'Informal Costs of Doing Business: The Case Study of the Registration and Regulation of Firms in the Kyrgyz Republic', *Central Asian Journal of Management, Economics and Social Research*, 4, no. 1 (September 2004), pp. 77–102

Marangos, John, 'The Political Economy of Shock Therapy', *Journal of Economic Surveys*, 16, no. 1 (February 2002), pp. 41–76.

Mauro, Paolo, 'Corruption and Growth,' *Quarterly Journal of Economics*, 110, no. 3 (1995), pp. 681–712.

Montesquieu, Charles de Secondat, *The Spirit of the Laws* (1748), edited and translated by Anne Cohler, Basia Miller and Harold Stone (Cambridge University Press, 1989)

Murrell, Peter, 'Evolution in Economics and in the Economic Reform of the Centrally Planned Economies', in Christopher Clague and Gordon Rausser (eds.), *The Emergence of Market Economies in Eastern Europe* (Blackwell: Cambridge: Massachusetts, 1992).

—— 'Conservative Political Philosophy and the Strategy of Economic Transition', *East European Politics and Societies*, 6, no. 1 (1992), pp. 3–6.

Murphy, Kevin, Shleifer, Andrei and Vishny. Robert, 'Why is Rent-Seeking so Costly to Growth', American Economic Review, 83, no. 2 (1993), pp. 409–414.

North, Douglass, *Institutions, Institutional Change and Economic Performance* (Cambridge, England: Cambridge University Press, 1990)

—— 'Economic Performance through Time', *The American Economic Review*, 84, no. 3 (1994), pp. 359–368

Nye, Joseph, 'Corruption and Political Development: A Cost Benefit Analysis', *American Political Science Review*, 61, no. 2 (1967), pp. 419–422.

Polanyi, Michael, *The Tacit Dimension* (New York: Anchor Books, 1967).

Polishchuk, Leonid, 'Missed Markets: Implications for Economic Behavior and Institutional Change', in Joan Nelson, Charles Tilly and Lee Walker (eds.), *Transforming Post-Communist Political Economies* (Washington D.C: National Academy Press, 1997).

Popper, Karl, *All Life is Problem Solving* (London: Routledge, 1999).

Public Enterprise Reform and Privatization Database, ECSPF and DECRG, The World Bank, 2005, available at: http://www.worldbank.org/ecspf/PSD-Yearbook/kyrgyz.html

Sachs, Jeffrey, 'Privatization in Russia: Some Lessons from Eastern Europe', *The American Economic Review*, 82, no. 2 (1992), pp. 43–48.

Shleifer, Andrei and Vishny, Robert, *The Grabbing Hand: Government Pathologies and Their Cures* (Harvard University Press, 1998).

Schneider, Friedrich, 'Size and Measurement of the Informal Economy in 110 Countries around the World', paper presented at the Australian National Tax Center Workshop, Canberra, Australia, 2002.

Stone, Andrew, Levy, Brian and Paredes, Ricardo, 'Public Institutions and Private Transactions: A Comparative Analysis of the Legal and Regulatory Environment for Business Transactions in Brazil and Chile', in Lee Alston, Thrainn Eggertsson, and Douglass North (eds.), *Empirical Studies in Institutional Change* (Cambridge: Cambridge University Press, 1996).

Weingast, Barry, 'The Political Foundations of Limited Government: Parliament and Sovereign Debt in 17th- and 18th-Century England', in John Drobak and John Nye (eds.), *The Frontiers of New Institutional Economics* (San Diego: Academic Press, 1997).

World Bank Report, 'Country Brief', at: http://www.worldbank.org.kg

BALIHAR SANGHERA AND AIBEK ILYASOV

Theorising Morality and Economic Behaviour in Kyrgyzstan: Some Issues of Professional Practices

The 'transition' to a market economy has raised important questions about what activities ought to be governed by market principles, norms and customs, and values and sentiments, and what practices are corrupt.[1] This paper examines how the Kyrgyzstani economic strategy of 'shock therapy'[2] brings together the new liberal ethos and the legacy of communism to impact on post-soviet professionalism.[3] The paper addresses the nature of ethical dilemmas facing professionals as they undertake their practices in institutional and social context. Ethical concerns have become stark and vivid for professionals and the public since the collapse of the Soviet Union left its overarching communist ideology in ruins. There is widespread public distrust at the

1 See Murat Cokgezen, 'Corruption in Kyrgyzstan: the facts, causes and consequences', *Central Asian Survey*, 23, no. 1, 2004, pp. 79–94; Balihar Sanghera and Elmira Satybaldieva, 'Kyrgyzstani Political Economy: moral reflections on the transformations of the society', *Research Paper*, American University – Central Asia, Bishkek, 2004.

2 See Kathryn Anderson and Richard Pomfret, 'Living Standards during Transition to a Market Economy: the Kyrgyz Republic in 1993 and 1996', *Journal of Comparative Economics*, 28 (2000), pp. 502–523.

3 Sarah Amsler, 'From Truth to Strength to Strength in Truth: Sociology, Knowledge and Power in Kyrgyzstan, 1996–2003', PhD Thesis, London School of Economics, London, UK, 2005; Madeleine Reeves, 'Of Credits, Kontrakty and Critical Thinking: encountering "market reforms" in Kyrgyzstani higher education', *European Educational Research Journal*, 4, no. 1 (2005), pp. 5–21; Anna Smolentseva, 'Challenges to the Russian academic profession', *Higher Education*, 45 (2003), pp. 391–424; Svetlana Pasti, 'Two Generations of Contemporary Russian Journalists', *European Journal of Communication*, 20, no. 1 (2005), pp. 89–115; Pavel Osinsky and Charles Mueller, 'Professional Commitment of Russian Provincial Specialists', *Work and Occupations*, 31, no. 2 (2004), pp. 193–224.

huge level of official corruption, and many individuals are cynical of how public employees and professionals behave.

We will argue that in spite of the widespread corruption and distrust professionals are *actually* moral actors. Archer[4] suggests that individuals are evaluative beings who deliberate and pursue goals, concerns, life projects and commitments. They are reflexive of their practices, and, through self-reflection, consider appropriate actions subject to structural and cultural constraints and enablements. Individuals have reason to value particular activities (such as education, friendship and health) because they contribute to human well-being. Were they not important to human development, we would not be upset when we lack them. As Sayer[5] notes, moral reflections of what is appropriate behaviour occur in our everyday life, moral reflexivity is what individuals do, and we need to conceptualise and analyse such behaviour. In this respect, the positive/normative split is inappropriate, since any account of human action involves explanatory, interpretative and normative dimensions. This paper aims to show how we can conceive individuals as moral agents, and how different theoretical approaches try to capture the normative quality of human action.

This pilot study on post-soviet professions draws on 15 semi-structured interviews and 10 open-ended questionnaires with professional practitioners (e.g., doctors, lawyers, lecturers and journalists) and leaders of professional associations and trade unions. Furthermore, one of the authors has lived and worked in universities in Novosibirsk in Russia and Bishkek in Kyrgyzstan for four years, and collectively the authors have collected participant observations on academic and other professional practices in the region.

The chapter is divided into five sections. In the first section, we will discuss three theoretical approaches to morality and economic behaviour: the economic market, the socially embedded and the internal

4 Margaret Archer *Structure, Agency and the Internal Conversation* (Cambridge: Cambridge University Press, 2003), pp. 19–32.

5 Andrew Sayer, 'Restoring the Moral Dimension: Acknowledging Lay Normativity', published by the Department of Sociology, Lancaster University, Lancaster LA1 4YL, UK (2004), at http://www.comp.lancs.ac.uk/sociology/papers/sayer-restoring-moral-dimension.pdf

embedding approaches. The next section examines the history of professions and the process of 'de-professionalisation' during the Soviet Union. The third section discusses how higher education has fared in Kyrgyzstan after the collapse of communism, suggesting a possibility of 're-professionalisation'. The fourth section evaluates the different theoretical approaches in light of our understanding of professionalism in Kyrgyzstan. And finally, we will make some concluding remarks.

Conceptualising Morality in the Economy

Broadly speaking, there are three key approaches to understanding how ethical relationships and economic practices have developed in transition societies:

a) the economic market approach stresses the private and civilised aspects of economic exchanges;
b) the socially embedded approach emphasises collective values, rights and entitlements; and
c) the internal embedding approach focuses on moral sentiments, character and recognition.

We will discuss the key features of each approach in turn.

a) The Economic Market Approach: Market Exchanges and Civility

Early classical writers on political economy recognised the moral ambiguity of capitalism as societies came to develop complex social division of labour in a highly competitive environment.[6] On the one hand,

6 See Albert O. Hirschman, 'Rival Interpretations of the Market Society: Civilising, Destructive, or Feeble?', *Journal of Economic Literature*, 20, no. 4 (1982) pp. 1463–1484; John O'Neill, *The Market: Ethics, Knowledge and Politics* (London: Routledge, 1998).

individuals are free from feudal-like bondage and hierarchical societal relationships. In the marketplace, individuals are all formally equal and free, and they develop a capacity for making personal judgements and for being responsible for their own actions.[7] Indeed, liberals argue that trade and commerce can strengthen moral attitudes of a society as competitive market forces tame individuals' passions and individuals learn to honour contracts, respect natural justice, and obey the common law for fear of losing their reputation as trustworthy economic actors. Moreover, society benefits from cooperation, reciprocity and self-responsibility, otherwise the social division of labour breaks down and the generation of economic wealth comes to a halt. As Simmel notes, in competitive markets, the loss of income and sales to rivals can civilise unsocial and dishonest behaviour.[8]

On the other hand, Adam Smith[9] and Veblen[10] recognise that wealth can undermine integrity, worthiness, judgements and duties; for example, consumption can become conspicuous to demonstrate economic affluence rather than enjoyed for internal pleasures. Moreover, in a fiercely competitive environment, individuals may act opportunistically and break promises for immediate profit.[11] And as Adam Smith[12] notes, professions can conspire together to act against the public interest.

The economic market approach to moral changes in transition economies focuses on how individual actions are mediated through the market system, acknowledging the latter's liberating and civilising

7 William Booth, 'On the idea of the moral economy', *American Political Science Review*, 88, no. 3 (1994), pp. 653–667.

8 Georg Simmel, *Conflict and the Web of Group-Affiliation* (New York: The Free Press, 1955), pp. 61–64.

9 Adam Smith, *The Theory of Moral Sentiments* (Indianapolis: Liberty Fund, 1976), pp. 61–66.

10 Thorstein Veblen, *The Theory of the Leisure Class: an economic study of institutions* (New York: Book-of-the-Month Club, 1918), Ch. 4.

11 Oliver E. Williamson, *Markets and Hierarchies: Analysis and Anti-Trust Implications: a study of in the economics of internal organisations* (New York: The Free Press, 1975).

12 Adam Smith, *The Wealth of Nations Books I–III* (Harmondsworth: Penguin Classics, 1974), p. 232.

effects as well as its corrosive and destructive effects.[13] Moral actions can be regarded as rational decisions to weigh up the personal utility of costs and benefits.

b) The Socially Embedded Approach: Economic Rights and Rules

Various writers, such as Polanyi[14] and Thompson,[15] argue that non-contractual elements such as tacit knowledge, institutions, rules and customs shape economic rationality and constrain self-interest. As Polanyi[16] notes, contrary to formal economics, economic practices are socially embedded and the economy is an instituted process, involving market and non-market relationships. In contrast to the individualistic framework of the first perspective, this approach argues that interest groups, professions and the state negotiate to construct codes of practice, guidelines and agreements.

There is a tension in how the economy is socially embedded. On the one hand, the economy must be adequately embedded to ensure effective communication, trust and coordination.[17] For instance, a market economy can experience a crisis if there is insufficient stability and inadequate time for capital to realise its surplus value. Non-market institutions (such as the welfare state and professional associations)

13 Deema Kaneff, 'The Shame and Pride of Market Activity', in Ruth Mandel and Caroline Humphrey (eds.), *Markets and Moralities: ethnographies of post-socialism* (Oxford: Berg, 2002); Kazimierz Poznanski, 'The Morals of Transition: Decline of Public Interest and Runaway reforms in Eastern Europe', in Sorin Antohi and Valdimir Tismaneanu (eds.), *Between Past and Future: the revolutions of 1989 and their aftermath* (Budapest: Central European University Press, 2000); Marie Lavigne, *The Economics of Transition: from socialist economy to market economy* (Basingstoke: Palgrave, 1999).

14 Karl Polanyi, 'The Economy as Instituted Process', in Mark Granovetter and Richard Swedberg (eds.), *The Sociology of Economics Life*, 2nd edition (Boulder: Westview Press, 2001).

15 Edward P. Thompson, 'The Moral Economy of the English Crowd in the Eighteenth Century', Past and Present, 50 (1971), pp. 76–136.

16 Ibid.

17 Mark Granovetter, 'Economic Action and Social Structure: The Problem of Embeddedness', *American Journal of Sociology*, 91, no. 3 (1985), pp. 481–510.

and networks of trust relationships provide necessary conditions for successful reproduction and transformation of capital.[18] Without proper formal and informal safeguards, excessive labour exploitation, consumer deception and poor networks can endanger the viability of commerce in the long run.

On the other hand, 'the market' must disembed social relationships, liberate economic commitments from ossified obligations and social habits, and forges new relationships.[19] 'The market' spurs creativity, innovation, and enterprise, as it undermines traditional rights, historical entitlements and collective norms. Cries of progress and injustice can be heard at moments of economic disembedding, such as factory closures and organisational reforms. The capitalist state, civic institutions, professional associations and social groups have to carefully regulate the causes and consequences of market forces without threatening the circuit of capital.[20]

The socially embedded approach to a post-soviet moral economy examines how social and political changes to civil rights, welfare entitlements, and social conventions have re-organised the economy through privatisation programmes and de-regulation of economic rights and labour laws. It also points to how new structures, rules and rights enable and constrain the development of human needs.[21]

18 See Claus Offe, *Contradictions of the Welfare State* (London: Hutchinson, 1984); Karl Polanyi, *The Great Transformation* (Boston: Beacon Press, 1957) on 'double movement' and 'deep-seated institutional strain'.

19 Andrew Sayer, *Radical Political Economy: A Critique* (Oxford: Blackwell, 1995), pp. 88–90.

20 Claus Offe, *Contradictions of the Welfare State*, 1984.

21 For example, Chris Hann, 'Introduction: Decollectivisation and the Moral Economy', in Chris Hann and the 'Property Relations' Group (eds.), *The Post-socialist Agrarian Question: property relations and the rural condition* (New Brunswick: Transaction Publishers, 2003); Claus Offe 'The Morality of Restitution: Reflections on Some Normative Questions Raised by the Transition to a Private Economy' (with Frank Bonker), in *Varieties of Transition: The East European and East German Experience* (Cambridge: Polity Press, 1996); Jeffrey Kopstein, 'Globalisation in One Country: East Germany between Moral Economy and Political Economy', in Christopher Candland and Rudra Sil (eds.), *The Politics of Labour in a Global Age: Continuity and Change in Late-Industrialising and Post-socialist Economies* (Oxford Scholarship Online:

Largely, moral decisions can be seen as following rules, norms and duties.

c) The Internal Embedding Approach: Character and Recognition

As Adam Smith[22] argues, proper character and moral sentiments often secure good and worthy acts that are recognised by others as deserving praise and recognition. In contrast to the external embedding of the economy in the second perspective, this third approach emphasises the internal values and reflexive attitudes of economic actors. Furthermore, social practices and relationships possess their own internal standards that enable individuals to identify good actions from bad,[23] irrespective of economic rewards and external recognition. These internal standards are important for identifying and achieving human well-being. For instance, a medical operation performed by a good doctor has the following internal qualities: attention to care and well being of the patient, satisfaction with medical diagnosis supported by colleagues, outstanding surgical skills sharpened through much practice and training, and a successful outcome.

The internal embedding approach to a moral economy highlights two critical pairs of opposing forces that affect our well-being.[24] In the first pair of forces, an economic activity consists of internal worth and external recognition, and both are required for a successful outcome.[25] However, social practices risk losing their integrity and worthiness if individuals excessively pursue external goals, such as money, power

Oxford University Press, 2001); Amitai Etzioni, 'Eastern Europe: The Wealth of Lessons', *Challenge* (July-August, 1991), pp. 4–11.

22 Adam Smith, The *Theory of Moral Sentiments*, pp. 113–134.

23 For instance, Alasdair MacIntyre, *After Virtue: a study in moral theory* (London: Duckworth, 1985); Michael Walzer, *Spheres of Justice* (New York: Basic Books, 1983).

24 Alasdair MacIntyre, ibid., pp. 187–195; Russell Keat, *Cultural Goods and the Limits of the Market* (Basingstoke: Macmillan, 2000), pp. 22–25.

25 William Booth, *Households: on the moral architecture of the economy*, pp. 55–66; 'On the idea of the moral economy', 1994; Andrew Sayer, *The Moral Significance of Class*, pp. 111–117.

and status. For instance, if lecturers are only mindful of income, promotion and reputation, then scholarly knowledge, deep learning and critical reflection may suffer. Nonetheless, good academics require a certain level of praise and income; claiming otherwise would be deceitful.

In the second pair of forces, for social practices to endure and develop, professionals require an adequate level of economic and political resources and support, such as well-heated buildings, state of the art technology and social honour. Economic institutions, such as markets, organisations, and the state, enable successful outcomes of professional practices.[26] For instance, medical operations take place in a hospital, usually in competition with other hospitals. Markets, organisations and the state are resource-hungry and need capital, money, power and prestige to fund and develop hospital wards, surgical tools and medical staff. However, the need of institutions for economic resources can override and compromise internal values and worth, as professionals strive and accumulate external and economic rewards to the point of sacrificing ethical commitments and quality of work.[27] Indeed, Adam Smith[28] and Bourdieu[29] note how wealth and status can distort judgements of taste and propriety.

The internal embedding approach highlights how personal character, emotions and integrity (such as sympathy for others, compassion, corporate identity and professionalism) connect with performance. Glover[30] and Oakley and Cocking[31] describe how moral dispositions and virtues, such as beneficence, truthfulness and humility, are human responses to social encounters; though, all too often self-

26 Russell Keat, ibid., pp. 22–28; 111–115; Andrew Mason, 'MacIntyre on Modernity and How It Has Marginalised the Virtues', in Roger Crisp (ed), *How Should One Live? Essays on the Virtues* (Oxford: Oxford University Press, 1996), pp. 201–206.

27 Russell Keat, ibid., pp. 81–85; 86–91.

28 Adam Smith, The *Theory of Moral Sentiments*, pp. 61–66.

29 Pierre Bourdieu, *Distinction: A Social Critique of the Judgement of Taste* (London: Routledge, 1984).

30 Jonathan Glover, ibid., pp 22–30.

31 Justin Oakley and Dean Cocking, *Virtue Ethics and Professional Roles* (Cambridge: Cambridge University Press, 2001), pp. 80–94.

interest, greed, terror and insecurity can force individuals to acts inhumanely. Decisions to act draw on moral resources, critical reflection and social approval of significant others, such that good practices are acts of propriety with (self-)approbation.[32] Moreover, 'practical reasoning' is employed to balance praiseworthiness with praise, and excellence with efficiency, so that judgements are neither arbitrary nor obligatory.[33]

As well as proper sentiments and emotions, moral order requires a community of respected fellows, friends and family, whose good opinions and approval are essential for individuals. For instance, combining the internal worth of professional identity and ethical commitment with an independent professional association can produce good practices in higher education, journalism, policing and so on. Conversely, 'corrupt' professional practices can arise from fragile commitments, a weak professional identity and a poor sense of social belonging (e.g., soviet professionalism).[34] Strong administrative and political pressures, pervasive distrust and cynicism of the public sector and poor household finances can also weaken professional relationships.

The Soviet Union and Professions

Under the Soviet regime, professions were transformed from semi-independent organisations to become part of the Communist State; in the process, professionals lost their distinct social identity, and were obliged to embrace the 'new soviet man'. This process has been characterised in several ways: from individual professionalism to bureau-

32 Adam Smith, The *Theory of Moral Sentiments*, pp. 109–113.

33 Andrew Sayer, 'Restoring the Moral Dimension: Acknowledging Lay Normativity', 2004.

34 See Anthony Jones (ed), *Professions and the State: Expertise and Autonomy in the Soviet Union and Eastern Europe* (Philadelphia: Temple University Press, 1991).

cratic professionalism;[35] technicalisation and instrumentalisation of professions;[36] de-professionalisation and proletarianisation of professions;[37] and, in some cases (such as medicine), feminisation of professions.[38] We will discuss several ways in which professions became 'de-professionalised' as professional practices came to be shaped by institutions, such as the local Communist Party and the state ministries, and by external recognition, such as career promotion, welfare entitlements and Party status. In the next section, we will explore how the soviet legacy continues to affect professional practices and ethics in Kyrgyzstan.

Several features of soviet professionalism can be highlighted:[39]

1. professions became increasingly managed by the state bureaucracy as private markets for professional services disappeared;
2. professional ethics and mission statements conformed to communist ideas;
3. pre-soviet professional associations were disbanded forcing professionals to join all workers' unions – though some (e.g., lawyers and academicians) retained quasi-professional status;
4. professions were no longer self-regulating and relinquished their autonomy;

35 Andrew Abbott, 'Professional Ethics', *American Journal of Sociology*, 88 (5), 1983, pp. 855–885.

36 Peter Solomon Jr., *Soviet Criminal Justice Under Stalin* (Cambridge: Cambridge University Press, 1996).

37 Anthony Jones, ibid.; N.S. Timasheff,, 'Business and the Professions in Liberal, Fascist and Community Society' *American Journal of Sociology*, 45 (6), 1940, pp. 863–869.

38 Jeni Harden, '"Mother Russia" at Work: Gender Divisions in the Medical Profession', *European Journal of Women's Studies*, 8, no. 2 (2001), pp. 181–199; Kate Schecter, 'Soviet Socialised Medicine and the Right to Health Care in a Changing Soviet Union', *Human Rights Quarterly*, 14 (1992), pp. 206–215.

39 Anthony Jones, ibid.; Sheila Fitzpatrick, *The Cultural Front: Power and Culture in Revolutionary Russia* (Ithaca: Cornell University Press, 1992); Harley Balzer (ed), *Russia's Missing Middle Class: The Professions in Russian History* (New York: M.E. Sharpe, 1996).

5. professional practices (e.g., in higher education curriculum content and research) became restrictive and disciplined by local Communist Party officials; and
6. in effect, soviet professionalism was an ideological construction enabling the authoritarian state to control 'at a distance'.

Two points can be further developed. First, with professional associations disbanded, professionals were compelled to join all workers' unions. Typically, all employees of a factory or an institution belonged to the same union, so that, say, in a hospital the union consisted of doctors, nurses, engineers, cleaners, drivers and others; the doctors' sense of shared values, commitments and professional identity with other doctors were weakened. Moreover, as welfare and other entitlements were administrated through local unions, rather than through state ministries, union membership was important to access valuable resources.[40] Seemingly, union membership was more significant to gain social provisions (e.g., child care and vacation trips) than for professional training and development.

Second, some professions (such as lawyers and judges) were deeply embedded in the local state administration resulting in distorted practices and ethics, especially when career promotion and basic amenities depended on the support of the local Communist Party.[41] For instance, the local Party cooperated with the district attorney and court judges to ensure that central state targets for legal convictions and court appeals were met. Judges and attorneys would twist legal judgements, otherwise the local Party would delay repairs to court-houses or withhold support for attorneys' promotion.

For soviet professionals external recognition (promotion and status) and institutions (e.g., the local Communist Party) were dominant in shaping their practices, and their internal values were distorted by the communist ideology. The collapse of communism did not necessarily result in better practices as we shall now see.

40 Anthony Jones, ibid.

41 Peter Solomon Jr. ibid.; Gregory Massell, 'Revolutionary Law in Soviet Central Asia', in Donald Black and Maureen Mileski (eds.), *The Social Organisation of Law* (New York: Seminar Press, 1973).

Post-Soviet Kyrgyzstan and Higher Education

The legacy of communism continues to shape post-socialist countries, and despite being hailed as the most liberal society in Central Asia, Kyrgyzstan has inherited some key aspects of soviet professionalism. By drawing on our interviews, questionnaires and observations, we will discuss the nature of post-soviet professionalism in higher education, and its implications for professional character and practices. External factors and a lack of enabling associations affect how lecturers can behave, testing the limits of their professional concerns, commitments and goals.

a) The Soviet Legacy

Notwithstanding greater openness in higher education, cultivating proper sentiments and appropriate character remains problematic as institutional and external factors continue to exert much influence on professional practices. The following three points can help to demonstrate this point.

First, there are no independent university associations organising social gatherings to facilitate lecturers to interact with each other, share their understandings, and create their own distinct identity. Often, conferences and workshops are arranged by university administrations for self-promotion and corporate identity – speakers from other universities are not unusually invited. For instance, at a well-known university, conferences were organised to discuss critical thinking and teaching methods in higher education. Conference speakers and participants from the university were obliged to attend by the university administration. Many participants resented this control and imposition 'from above', though they were careful not to voice it. They mimicked the rhetoric of critical thinking, progressive teaching and interactive learning, though were cynical and dismissive in private. Older participants remarked how soviet-like the university and the administration were.

Second, and related, discipline associations are either non-existent or fragmented, so that academic sensibilities acquired through practical training and peer approval are not fostered. For most Kyrgyzstani lecturers in social sciences, there is no effective association or professional organisation that can nurture their sentiments, judgements and practices *qua academicians*. An association of sociologists was formed in 1999, though it has only met several times; university rivalry, personal animosity and a lack of funds prevented its members from organising national seminars and conferences.[42] One interviewee described that the sociological association as a 'phantom' organisation, and cynically remarked that committee members often attended trips abroad to represent Kyrgyzstani sociology though doing very little for it at home. Another interviewee felt that in part the feeling of personal isolation and a lack of professional togetherness contributed to sociologists and other social scientists making 'compromises' with their students and the university administration.

There are several political science associations, but they regard each other as rivals and fail to cooperate. Several conferences were held, but members of other associations were not invited. One respondent said that major universities formed their own political science association with the aim of controlling lecturers' activities and ensuring that their teaching and research did not upset the Ministry of Education.

Third, the Ministry of Education approves all teaching programmes, and any changes to an existing curriculum require its agreement. University administrations are careful not to antagonise the Ministry for fear of losing their university charter and teaching license. Invariably, departments are obliged to follow the Ministry's guidelines in designing academic programmes and courses. Any aspiration for curriculum reform is held in check. A couple of years ago, the Ministry of Education required all university students to learn the history of Kyrgyzstan, so as to promote its ideology of statehood. It also aimed to examine the course. Though many lecturers resented this blatant state intervention, they were resigned to it.

42 Sarah Amsler, ibid.

b) Re-professionalisation?

Despite the enduring weakness of the academic profession, there are some grounds for optimism for greater professionalism. We suggest that the internationalisation of professions offers to create, revive and nurture appropriate sensibilities, judgements and practices through, say, exchange trips to western countries.[43] For instance, at a well-known university, many lecturers have been educated in the US and Europe, and their level of professionalism (such as commitment to research, anti-corruption and fulfillment in teaching) compares favourably to other universities in the region. These younger academics have started to reform their departments' teaching and research practices. In addition, western faculty members teach at the university aiming to foster good practices, as well as to mentor local faculty, for some of whom teaching is a new experience.[44]

In addition, international organisations (such as the Organisation for Security and Cooperation in Europe, the Open Society Institute (OSI) and the Aga Khan Humanitarian Project) are funding huge educational programmes in the region to develop critical teaching and learning practices.[45] For instance, OSI supports three-year long programmes in sociology, anthropology and political science in Central Asia to train and develop a small core of primarily young active academics. These academics develop their own culture different from some of their more traditional inactive colleagues, and participate in seminars, summer schools and other professional projects. However, at the moment, this core group is not yet a 'critical mass' to start affectting professional culture at large.

43 Our thanks to Tanya Yarkova for impressing upon us this point.

44 See Sarah Amsler, ibid.

45 See Madeleine Reeves, 'Of Credits, Kontrakty and Critical Thinking: encountering ''market reforms'' in Kyrgyzstani higher education', 2005.

Assessing the Theoretical Approaches

After having discussed the nature of professionalism and higher education in Kyrgyzstan, we can assess the three approaches to morality and economic practices, and suggest which is better in explaining the Kyrgyzstani 'moral economy'. For each approach, we will discuss a) how it would answer the question, 'what is a good professional?'; b) how well it relates to the Kyrgyzstani professional context; and c) what are its theoretical problems and strengths.

a) The Economic Market Approach: Subjectivism and Relativism

To the question of 'what is a good professional?', the proponents of the economic market approach would suggest that individuals pursue their own self-interests, and calculate the social worth of acting in a particular way. Perverse consequences may occur as a result of well meaning but misguided interventions of the state and/or professional groups. In the market approach, individual moral desires and preferences define worthwhile projects and goals, and moral actions are shaped by private utility calculations. There are opportunity costs to acting ethically, and individuals have to balance the costs with the benefits.

Using the economic market approach, we can understand how professionals in Kyrgyzstan operate in 'imperfect markets', where information is asymmetric and detection of misbehaviour is weak, so that dishonesty pays. Corruption can be depicted as an economic exchange between consenting individuals, and bribes and payments as part of 'transaction costs'. Public officials, lecturers, police officers and doctors are corrupt, in part, because of low salaries, a lack of transparency and insufficient fines and penalties.[46] While corruption is

46 Murat Cokgezen, 'Corruption in Kyrgyzstan: the facts, causes and consequences', 2004; William Miller, Ase Grodeland and Tatyana Koshechkina, *A Culture of Corruption? Coping with Government in Post-communist Europe* (Budapest: Central European University Press, 2001), pp. 289–298.

widespread, the public judges it as inappropriate, though understandable.

However, there are two key weaknesses of the economic market approach. First, as it predominately sees moral behaviour as a private exchange in the marketplace, it does not adequately conceptualise social relationships in professional, family and community settings, where integrity, honesty, generosity and respect are not easily quantifiable and negotiable,[47] and where social encounters emit 'natural' moral sentiments and emotions (such as sympathy, dignity, anger and shame) affecting social conduct.[48] Often, moral behaviour involves making deep commitments and doing worthwhile acts, and is a matter of proper recognition from significant others rather than simply wanting public attention.[49] Professionals are distinct by their commitment to key values and principles, and seek proper recognition from their respected peers.

Second, there is no real discussion on how individuals come to possess their moral desires and preferences; they are assumed to be given and unchangeable. As the economic market approach regards moral behaviour as a private matter, it has an individualistic 'asocial' conception of morality, where each individual possesses a set of moral preferences without much discussion with others. But, professionals come to agree on shared values and commonly adhere to ethical codes of conduct.

This approach is morally subjective as only private costs and benefits, and not commitments to principles, determine how individuals act. The approach lapses into moral relativism as individuals are indifferent to each other, and unable and unwilling to pass moral judgements on others' actions. But, in reality, professionals debate and discuss about the appropriateness of their own and others' behaviour; they are reflexive of their own action; they employ arguments on why others should behave in a particular way, largely because they care about their own and others' well being.

47 William Booth, *Households: on the moral architecture of the economy* (Ithaca: Cornell University Press), pp. 41–42; 47–55.

48 Adam Smith, The *Theory of Moral Sentiments*, pp. 9–13.

49 John O'Neill, *The Market: Ethics, Knowledge and Politics*, pp. 102–106.

b) The Socially Embedded Approach: Cynicism and Alienation

The embedded approach would respond to 'what is a good professional?', by examining social rules, codes of practices, historical duties and evolved habits, and obliging individuals to follow them. As Etzioni[50] notes, to live well is to know one's duty and to respect social conventions. Journalists, doctors and teachers must perform according to their professional code of ethics. This does not mean that individuals become 'over-socialised' to norms, but nevertheless their behaviour must remain rule-bound. Professional groups seek to negotiate social rights, entitlements and agreements with the state and employers. Moral disorder occurs when individuals fail to adhere to the rules of the game.

Seemingly, the socially embedded approach has some plausibility in post-communist countries. During the Soviet Union, professions were guided by communist ideals, rules and norms, and were directed by the Communist Party; professional associations and unions lacked any critical autonomy from the state to negotiate alternative professional ideals. In the earlier stages of communism, there was a social agreement between radical professionals and the Bolsheviks as professional expertise and technical knowledge were exchanged for special privileges to build a communist state; however, this quickly turned into an imposition 'from above'. Professionals increasingly found themselves unable to negotiate the terms of their employment, as state coercion replaced state-society partnership. In post-soviet Kyrgyzstan, the situation did not change significantly despite formal democracy and freedom.

However, the socially embedded approach has two major problems. First, individuals are not so much as ethical but dutiful, obliged to follow rules without making their own judgements. Glover[51] recounting the atrocities in gulags and acts of inhumanity in Stalinist Soviet Union, argues that moral decisions must involve deliberation

50 Amitai Etzioni, *The Moral Dimension: Toward a New Economics* (New York: The Free Press, 1988), pp. 11–13.

51 Jonathan Glover, *Humanity: A Moral History of the Twentieth Century* (London: Pimlico, 1999), pp. 257–261; 274–282.

and discretion, so that a person is called *good* who uses appropriate judgement and not just obeys orders. Following Adam Smith,[52] we can distinguish between 'just acts' and 'virtuous acts': the former are governed by laws and conventions, and the latter are generated from moral sentiments, sympathy and beneficence, where individuals have reason to value worthwhile actions because they contribute to well being. Professionals, during the last stages of communism, opposed the rules and values of soviet professionalism. By the end, there was a collective sense of moral decay of communism together with widespread cynicism and a longing for 'living in truth'.[53] Clearly, it was not enough to have a particular set of rights and rules; the professions aspired to work and live in conditions that contributed to their own well being and development of others.

Second, while rules, customs and traditions can instruct individual action in general circumstances, they lack appropriate sensitivity for cases which are complex or vague. In deciding how to behave, individuals must use their own judgement and discretion. For instance, how should a doctor care for a frail and poor patient who cannot pay for her medical treatment? How should a journalist report an opposition rally calling for democracy when there is a government censorship on reporting opposition activities? To make such judgements, professionals must develop proper sensibilities and emotions, rather than rely on external rules and conventions.

In effect, morality seen as rules, norms and customs becomes 'alienating' in everyday life since traditions and laws become an unfeeling exterior shell to the self.[54] Havel[55] comments how during communism the masses were forced to demonstrate their communist faith especially during parade days, but they quickly became cynical as they resented the patronising moralism of the Communist Party.

52 Adam Smith, The *Theory of Moral Sentiments*, pp. 78–82.

53 Havel, Vaclav, *Living in truth* (London: Faber, 1987).

54 Andrew Sayer, *The Moral Significance of Class* (Cambridge: Cambridge University Press, 2005), pp. 8–9.

55 Ibid.

c) The Internal Embedding Approach: Reflexivity and Sentiments

To the question 'what is a good professional?', the proponents of the internal embedding approach would suggest individuals act to balance between internal and economic values in social and institutionalised settings. Blackburn[56] argues that a good lecturer making appropriate judgements would possess the following internal values:

1. honesty in giving accurate academic assessments to students;
2. courage in taking difficult decisions and dealing with confrontations with the university administration and students;
3. justice in being fair to all students and opposing prejudice or bias;
4. beneficence in having compassion for students' academic needs; and
5. patience in allowing students space to reflect and improve.

The internal embedding approach to morality in transition economies has two major advantages. First, although integrity, character and social recognition are deeply ingrained into our human psyche, they are influenced by social practices and economic relationships. Consequently, internal values are not fixed but path-dependent, context-dependent and historically specific. This grants the importance of the legacy of communism in shaping post-soviet professionalism in Kyrgyzstan.

Second, individuals are fallible, and can mistakenly identify appropriate behaviour despite receiving public approval and acting within the law. Good actions possess internal qualities that permit individuals to judge whether their behaviour has contributed to human well-being. For instance, in identifying corrupt teaching practices in post-soviet societies, individuals usually agree that some internal properties (i.e., honesty and truthfulness) of teaching have been violated, and this can lead to unintended consequences, such as grade inflation and distrust of academic qualifications. By being aware of

56 Margaret Blackburn, 'Talking Virtue: professionalism and virtue ethics' (2003), at http://www.iipe.org/conference2002/papers/Blackburn.pdf , pp. 7–8.

appropriate internal qualities, professionals develop a critically reflexive attitude, which is important for rectifying past mistakes to forge better practices.

We suggest that the internal embedding approach can better explain some aspects of professionalism in Kyrgyzstan. Under communism, professional associations and trade unions lacked autonomy and critical reflexivity, and the present situation is no better. Combined with severe cutbacks in the public sector so depriving most professionals of a decent income, many Kyrgyzstani professionals lack the capability, power and freedom to successfully pursue internal values, professional identity and ethical commitments.[57] Not surprisingly, many professionals compromise the integrity of their practice by accepting bribes, though often to ensure household survival and to make ends meet.

In our study, most professionals faced an acute trade-off between internal and economic values, and many experienced considerable economic hardship and self-sacrifice to live on a low salary and to spurn bribes and administrative pressures. Professionals most able to cope and resist external rewards and pressures had acquired their training and professionalism abroad, had participated in local training and development programmes, and/or belonged to local professional networks. Moreover, professionals who had a good source of income or worked for a prestigious employer (such as the World Bank, the United Nations or the Open Society Institute) were less willing to compromise their integrity. Furthermore, local universities, hospitals and media centres with partnerships with western organisations were careful to generate an image of honesty and integrity for fear of losing their reputation and possible funding.

57 Madeleine Reeves, 'Academic Integrity and Its Limits in Kyrgyzstan', *International Higher Education*, 37 (Fall), 2004, pp. 22–24; 'Of Credits, Kontrakty and Critical Thinking: encountering "market reforms" in Kyrgyzstani higher education', 2005; Balihar Sanghera and Elmira Satybaldieva, ibid.; Svetlana Kulikova and Gulnara Ibraeva, *The Historical Development and Current Situation of the Mass Media in Kyrgyzstan*, Occasional Paper 1 (Bishkek; Cimera Publications, 2002); for Russia, see Anna Smolentseva, ibid.; Irina Butenko, 'The Russian Sociological Association: Actors and Scenery in a Revolving Stage', *International Sociology*, 17, no. 2 (2002), pp. 233–251.

Concluding Remarks

The article discussed three competing approaches to moral economy in post-communist transition societies. We suggest that the internal embedding approach offers a better understanding and explanation of ethical decisions and practices, focusing on professionals as evaluative beings who deliberate the internal worth and external recognition of their professional practices. Furthermore, professionals operate within institutions which possess their own logic of practice. Internal values and moral sentiments are necessary to balance the competing demands made on professionals; and the lack leads to compromises and corruption.

In discussing higher education in post-soviet Kyrgyzstan, we suggest that lecturers, to be motivated to act ethically, require cultivating proper sentiments and creating sympathetic communities and networks of fellow professionals. In the Kyrgyzstani case, where the national state is hostile and/or indifferent to good practices, lecturers look to agents and sites overseas to foster such feelings and ties.

While it is acknowledged in the literature on social embeddedness that economic behaviour involves external forms of embedding such as norms, rules, rights, entitlements, customs and conventions, we have shown how internal forms (moral sentiments, emotions and feelings) are also significant. Individuals are reflexive of their actions, and deliberate on ways to pursue ultimate concerns, commitments and life projects. Being psychologically dependent upon others, we cannot avoid caring and having sympathy and responsibilities for others. While social practices and institutions cannot be indifferent to external values, such as income, power and status, individuals must evaluate and judge their own behaviour and others' in terms of internal values, such as integrity, justice, worthiness and goodness. Accordingly, moral economies are in part shaped by moral sentiments, ethical valuation, concerns and commitments.

Acknowledgements

The research project was funded by the American University – Central Asia Research Grant Committee and Kent University Social Science Faculty Grant Committee. We are grateful to Chris Pickvance, Sarah Amsler, Vanessa Ruget, Tanya Yarkova, Judith Shapiro and Russell Kleinbach for their constructive comments and advice. Our thanks to Emil Juraev, Mehrigiul Ablezova and Elmira Satybaldieva for their contribution to the study. Finally, we would like to express our gratitude to the interviewees for their time, guidance and patience. The usual disclaimers apply.

Bibliography

Abbott, Andrew, 'Professional Ethics', *American Journal of Sociology*, 88, no. 5 (1983), pp. 855–885.

Amsler, Sarah, 'From Truth to Strength to Strength in Truth: Sociology, Knowledge and Power in Kyrgyzstan, 1996–2003', PhD Thesis, London School of Economics, London, UK, 2005.

Anderson, Kathryn and Pomfret, Richard, 'Living Standards during Transition to a Market Economy: the Kyrgyz Republic in 1993 and 1996', *Journal of Comparative Economics*, 28 (2000), pp. 502–523.

Archer, Margaret, *Structure, Agency and the Internal Conversation* (Cambridge: Cambridge University Press, 2003).

Balzer, Harley (ed), *Russia's Missing Middle Class: The Professions in Russian History*. New York: M.E. Sharpe, 1996).

Blackburn, Margaret, 'Talking Virtue: professionalism and virtue ethics' (2003).at http://www.iipe.org/conference2002/papers/Blackburn.pdf

Booth, William, *Households: on the moral architecture of the economy* (Ithaca: Cornell University Press, 1993).

—— 'On the idea of the moral economy', *American Political Science Review*, 88, no. 3 (1994), pp. 653–667.

Bourdieu, Pierre, *Distinction: A Social Critique of the Judgement of Taste* (London: Routledge, 1984).

Butenko, Irina,, 'The Russian Sociological Association: Actors and Scenery in a Revolving Stage', *International Sociology*, 17, no. 2 (2002), pp. 233–251.

Cokgezen, Murat, 'Corruption in Kyrgyzstan: the facts, causes and consequences', *Central Asian Survey*, 23, no. 1 (2004), pp. 79–94.

Etzioni, Amitai, *The Moral Dimension: Toward a New Economics* (New York: The Free Press, 1988).

—— 'Eastern Europe: The Wealth of Lessons', *Challenge* (July–August 1991), pp. 4–11.

Fitzpatrick, Sheila, *The Cultural Front: Power and Culture in Revolutionary Russia* (Ithaca: Cornell University Press, 1992).

Glover, Jonathan, *Humanity: A Moral History of the Twentieth Century* (London: Pimlico, 1999).

Granovetter, Mark, 'Economic Action and Social Structure: The Problem of Embeddedness', *American Journal of Sociology*, 91, no. 3 (1985), pp. 481–510.

Hann, Chris, 'Introduction: Decollectivisation and the Moral Economy', in Chris Hann and the 'Property Relations' Group (eds.), *The Postsocialist Agrarian Question: property relations and the rural condition* (New Brunswick: Transaction Publishers, 2003).

Harden, Jeni, '"Mother Russia" at Work: Gender Divisions in the Medical Profession', *European Journal of Women's Studies*, 8, no. 2 (2001), pp. 181–199.

Havel, Vaclav, *Living in truth* (London: Faber, 1987).

Hayek, Friedrich von, *The Road to Serfdom* (London: Routledge & Sons, 1944).

Hirschman, Albert O., 'Rival Interpretations of the Market Society: Civilising, Destructive, or Feeble?', *Journal of Economic Literature*, 20, no. 4 (1982), pp. 1463–1484.

Kaneff, Deema, 'The Shame and Pride of Market Activity', in Ruth Mandel and Caroline Humphrey (eds.), *Markets and Moralities: ethnographies of postsocialism* (Oxford: Berg, 2002).

Keat, Russell, *Cultural Goods and the Limits of the Market* (Basingstoke: Macmillan, 2000).

Kopstein, Jeffrey, 'Globalisation in One Country: East Germany between Moral Economy and Political Economy', in Christopher Candland and Rudra Sil (eds.), *The Politics of Labour in a Global Age: Continuity and Change in Late-Industrialising and Post-socialist Economies* (Oxford Scholarship Online: Oxford University Press, 2001).

Kuehnast, Kathleen and Dudwick, Nora, 'Better a Hundred Friends Than a Hundred Rubles? Social Networks in Transition – The Kyrgyz Republic', *World Bank Economists' Forum*, 2 (2002), pp. 51–88.

Kulikova, Svetlana and Ibraeva, Gulnara, *The Historical Development and Current Situation of the Mass Media in Kyrgyzstan*, Occasional Paper 1 (Bishkek: Cimera Publications, 2002)

Lavigne, Marie, *The Economics of Transition: from socialist economy to market economy* (Basingstoke: Palgrave, 1999).

MacIntyre, Alasdair, *After Virtue: a study in moral theory* (London: Duckworth, 1985).

Mason, Andrew, 'MacIntyre on Modernity and How It Has Marginalised the Virtues', in Roger Crisp (ed), *How Should One Live? Essays on the Virtues* (Oxford: Oxford University Press, 1996).

Massell, Gregory, 'Revolutionary Law in Soviet Central Asia', in Donald Black and Maureen Mileski (eds.), *The Social Organisation of Law* (New York: Seminar Press, 1973).

Miller, William, Grodeland, Ase and Koshechkina, Tatyana, *A Culture of Corruption? Coping with Government in Post-communist Europe* (Budapest: Central European University Press, 2001).

O'Neill, John, *The Market: Ethics, Knowledge and Politics* (London: Routledge, 1998).

Oakley, Justin and Cocking, Dean, *Virtue Ethics and Professional Roles* (Cambridge: Cambridge University Press, 2001).

Offe, Claus, *Contradictions of the Welfare State* (London: Hutchinson, 1984).

—— 'The Morality of Restitution: Reflections on Some Normative Questions Raised by the Transition to a Private Economy' (with

Frank Bonker), in *Varieties of Transition: The East European and East German Experience* (Cambridge: Polity Press, 1996).
Osinsky, Pavel and Mueller, Charles, 'Professional Commitment of Russian Provincial Specialists', *Work and Occupations*, 31, no. 2 (2004), pp. 193–224.
Jones, Anthony (ed), *Professions and the State: Expertise and Autonomy in the Soviet Union and Eastern Europe* (Philadelphia: Temple University Press, 1991).
Pasti, Svetlana, 'Two Generations of Contemporary Russian Journalists', *European Journal of Communication*, 20, no. 1 (2005), pp. 89–115.
Polanyi, Karl, *The Great Transformation* (Boston: Beacon Press, 1957).
—— 'The Economy as Instituted Process', in Mark Granovetter and Richard Swedberg (eds.), *The Sociology of Economics Life*, 2nd edition (Boulder: Westview Press, 2001).
Poznanski, Kazimierz, 'The Morals of Transition: Decline of Public Interest and Runaway reforms in Eastern Europe', in Sorin Antohi and Valdimir Tismaneanu (eds.), *Between Past and Future: the revolutions of 1989 and their aftermath* (Budapest: Central European University Press, 2000).
Reeves, Madeleine, 'Academic Integrity and Its Limits in Kyrgyzstan', *International Higher Education*, 37 (Fall 2004), pp. 22–24.
—— 'Of Credits, Kontrakty and Critical Thinking: encountering "market reforms" in Kyrgyzstani higher education', *European Educational Research Journal*, 4, no. 1 (2005), pp. 5–21.
Sanghera, Balihar and Satybaldieva, Elmira, 'Kyrgyzstani Political Economy: moral reflections on the transformations of the society', *Research Paper*, American University – Central Asia, Bishkek, 2004.
Sayer, Andrew, *Radical Political Economy: A Critique* (Oxford: Blackwell, 1995).
—— '(De-)Commodification, consumer culture and moral economy', *Environment and Planning D: Society and Space*, 21 (2003), pp. 341–357.

—— 'Restoring the Moral Dimension: Acknowledging Lay Normativity' (2004), published by the Department of Sociology, Lancaster University, Lancaster LA1 4YL, UK at http://www.comp.lancs.ac.uk/sociology/papers/sayer-restoring-moral-dimension.pdf

—— *The Moral Significance of Class* (Cambridge: Cambridge University Press, 2005).

Schecter, Kate, 'Soviet Socialised Medicine and the Right to Health Care in a Changing Soviet Union', *Human Rights Quarterly*, 14 (1992), pp. 206–215.

Simmel, Georg, *Conflict and the Web of Group-Affiliation* (New York: The Free Press, 1955).

Smith, Adam, *The Wealth of Nations Books I–III* (Harmondsworth Penguin Classics, 1974).

—— *The Theory of Moral Sentiments* (Indianapolis: Liberty Fund, 1976).

Smolentseva, Anna, 'Challenges to the Russian academic profession', *Higher Education*, 45 (2003), pp. 391–424.

Solomon, Peter Jr., *Soviet Criminal Justice Under Stalin* (Cambridge: Cambridge University Press, 1996).

Thompson, Edward P., 'The Moral Economy of the English Crowd in the Eighteen Century', *Past and Present*, 50 (1971), pp. 76–136.

Timasheff, N.S., 'Business and the Professions in Liberal, Fascist and Community Society' *American Journal of Sociology*, 45, no. 6 (1940), pp. 863–869.

Veblen, Thorstein, *The Theory of the Leisure Class: an economic study of institutions* (New York: Book-of-the-Month Club, 1918).

Walzer, Michael, *Spheres of Justice* (New York: Basic Books, 1983)

Williamson, Oliver E., *Markets and Hierarchies: Analysis and Anti-Trust Implications: a study of in the economics of internal organisations* (New York: The Free Press, 1975).

World Bank, *Making Transition Work for Everyone: poverty and inequality in Europe and Central Asia* (Washington, D.C.: World Bank, 2000).

Notes on the Contributors

SARAH AMSLER is a lecturer in sociology at Kingston University, UK. Her fields of expertise are the sociology of knowledge and science in cultural institutions (the university, the museum, the school) and the politics of science, particularly in post-colonial and post-Soviet societies. She recently completed a doctoral dissertation in the history and sociology of sociology in Kyrgyzstan. She is currently pursuing a critical theoretical inquiry into the 'sociology of hope' as it relates to problems of utopia and social change in late capitalist societies.

ZOLTÁN BERÉNYI is a lecturer at the Institute of Political Science and Sociology, University of Debrecen, Hungary. His academic interests are political science and European Integration studies. During the past few years his research has focused on the interrelation between the development of civil society and political institutions as well as on the effect of European integration on Hungarian policy-making. He is the author of *Constitutional Democracy and Civil Society in Post-Communist Hungary* (1999) and *Democratic Values and Civic Culture in Hungary* (2001). Currently he is working in a transnational research project aiming to reduce gender gaps and segregation in the European Union.

OLGA BOIKO is a doctoral student at the University of Sheffield, UK. Over the past five years she has conducted research on social problems, social policy and other social-work-related issues in Russia. She has published several journal articles, including 'Representations of Social Problems in the Russian Press in the 1990s', *Sotsis* (2002). She has authored a textbook for social work students, *Mental Health Protection* (Moscow: Academia, 2004). Her current research project is related to the sociology of medicine and the problem of contingent relations in clinical encounters.

ADRIAN BRISKU is a doctoral student, researching on discourses of the idea of Europe in Albania and Georgia at the Department of History at European University Institute, Florence, Italy. He holds two Masters Degrees at the University of Sussex, UK (2000) and the Central European University, Hungary (2001).

ELENA CHERNYSHKOVA is the Chair of Foreign Languages at Saratov Medical University in Russia, and holds a candidate of sociology degree. Her key publications include 'The Social Setting of Language in Newspapers Articles', *Problemy Normy i Patologii: Sovremennyie Disccursivnyie Praktiki* (Saratov, 2002). At present, her research interest is focused on the medical aspects of social policy and discursive technologies.

IVAN CHORVAT is a research fellow and lecturer in sociology at the University of Matej Bel, Banska Bystrica, Slovakia. His main areas of research include the sociology of family, the sociology of tourism, practical theories of consumption, the history of sociological thought and contemporary sociological theories. He is the author of *Man–Father in Contemporary Family* (1999), and the editor of *Changes of Family in the Urban Environment* (2002) – both published in Slovakia.

JULIA DROEBER is a social anthropologist and teaches Islamic Studies at Al-Maktoum Institute for Arabic and Islamic Studies/University of Aberdeen, Scotland, UK. Her research has focused on issues of gender, religion, social transformation, migration, and ethnic minorities, mainly in Central Asia and the Middle East. Recently, she has also turned her attention to questions of multiculturalism, gender, and religion in a UK context. She has published widely in these areas; her latest book is *Dreaming of Change – Young Middle-Class Women and Social Transformation in Jordan.*

SEBASTIAN ECKARDT is a doctoral student in public management at the Faculty of Economics and Social Sciences at the University of Potsdam, and a doctoral fellow of the German Business Foundation (Stiftung der Deutschen Wirtschaft). His current research blends quantitative and qualitative forms of evidence in an attempt to understand the dynamics of institutional and policy change, and to discover links between public service outcomes, growth and poverty reduction. He also works as a consultant on governance reforms with various donor agencies, including GTZ, The World Bank and USAID.

ANDREAS GOLDTHAU is a doctoral student in political science at Free University Berlin, and a doctoral fellow of the Konrad Adenauer Foundation. His current research and teaching focus lies on economic reforms in post-soviet and developing countries. Among other, he has been affiliated with IERES (Washington, DC) and the Institute for Research on Eastern Europe, Berlin.

LUKASZ HARDT is a doctoral student in economics at the Faculty of Economic Sciences Warsaw University, Poland. His research themes are new institutional economics, transaction cost economics, economics of transition, territorial reforms in Poland and European integration.

ANNA HOROLETS is a lecturer in political sociology, communication and marketing at Warsaw School of Social Psychology, Poland. Her academic interests concentrate on methods and theoretical models underlying discourse analysis, the anthropology of media and the symbolic politics and cultural dimensions of European integration. She is the editor of the volume 'Europa w polskich dyskursach' on the representations of Europe in various discourses (forthcoming in Adam Marszalek Publishing House, Torun). She has several articles on European integration and press discourse, including a recent paper in Polish Sociological Review (2003).

AIBEK ILYASOV currently works as a researcher at the SIAR research company, Bishkek, Kyrgyzstan. His research interests include applied quantitative social research, critical theory, network analysis, political sociology, international political economy and social movements. He has published many reports including *National capacity self-assessment for implementation of the 3 UN global ecological conventions in Kyrgyzstan* and *Exit Poll in Parliamentary elections 2005.*

BORIS KAPUSTIN is a senior research fellow of the Institute of Philosophy, Russian Academy of Sciences, a professor of political science at the Moscow School of Social and Economic Sciences, and a recurrent visiting professor of political science at Yale University. His major recent publications include *Moral Choices in Politics* (Moscow: The Moscow State University Press, 2004, in Russian) and 'Modernity's Failure / Post-modernity's Predicament', *Critical Horizons* (2003). Currently, he is working on a book entitled *Violence: an Elusive Category of Political Philosophy*.

MAKS KOBONBAEV is a doctoral student in political science and public policy at the University of Missouri–St. Louis. He is currently employed at the World Bank's Public Sector Governance Unit. His current research focuses on corruption, public sector governance, aid-effectiveness and development. His previous publications include 'Informal Costs of Doing Business: The Case Study of the Registration and Regulation of Firms in the Kyrgyz Republic', *Central Asian Journal of Management, Economics and Social Research* (2004).

STEPHAN E. NIKOLOV is a senior research fellow at the Department of Sociology of Politics and Organizations and the Institute of Sociology, Bulgarian Academy of Science. He is also the editor-in-chief of the Bulgarian Sociological Review Journal since 1991. He used to teach at several universities: St. Kliment Okhridski Sofia University, Neophyte Rilski Soutwestern University, Blagoevgrad, both in Bulgaria, and at Southeastern European University, Macedonia, and was visiting professor at George Mason University, USA, and King's College, London.

DONNACHA Ó BEACHÁIN is an associate professor and the director of Undergraduate Studies at the Department of Political Science, Kazakhstan Institute of Management, Economics and Strategic Research (KIMEP) in Almaty. He has published a number of scholarly articles on topics ranging from Irish politics, western European political parties, teaching methodology, and on contemporary politics in the Caucasus and Central Asia.

VANESSA RUGET currently teaches comparative politics at Bentley College, Massachusetts, USA. Her research focuses on citizenship and democracy in Kyrgyzstan. Her recent publications and presentations include (with Emil Juraev) 'Looking at Political Culture in Kyrgyzstan: The Evaluative Dimension', *Eurasian Political Studies Network*, 2nd International Conference, Yekaterinburg, Russia (2004).

BALIHAR SANGHERA is a lecturer in sociology at Kent University, UK. His research interests include political economy and ethics and morality in postcommunist societies. Balihar Sanghera and Aibek Ilyasov are currently conducting a research project on ethical values and professionalism in the public sector in Kyrgyzstan.

GEORGE WELTON is currently the director of a Cross Caucasus Masters program at the Centre for Social Sciences in Tbilisi, Georgia. His current research focuses on the connection between national identity and the political decision-making in the former Soviet Union.

TATIANA YARKOVA is a doctoral student in sociology at the Center for Social Studies, Institute of Philosophy and Sociology of the Polish Academy of Sciences in Warsaw, Poland. Her research interests include political sociology, Eastern European and Central Asian studies. She currently works as an academic leader in sociology at the Central Asian Resource Center in Almaty, Kazakhstan.

www.ingramcontent.com/pod-product-compliance
Ingram Content Group UK Ltd.
Pitfield, Milton Keynes, MK11 3LW, UK
UKHW021845100926
8556IPUK00019B/1070

9 783039 103294